Dewey and Elvis

Music in American Life

A list of books in the series appears at the end of this book.

Dewey and Elvis

The Life and Times
of a Rock 'n' Roll
Deejay

Louis Cantor

University of Illinois Press
Urbana, Chicago, and Springfield

Frontispiece: Dewey Phillips, mid-1950s.
(Dorothy Phillips Collection)

∞ This book is printed on acid-free paper.

1 2 3 4 5 C P 6 5 4 3 2
The Library of Congress cataloged the cloth edition as follows:
Cantor, Louis.
Dewey and Elvis: the life and times of a rock 'n' roll deejay /
Louis Cantor.
p. cm. — (Music in American life)
Includes bibliographical references (p.) and index.
ISBN 0-252-02981-X (cloth: alk. paper)
1. Phillips, Dewey—Biography. 2. Presley, Elvis, 1935–1977.
3. Disc jockeys—Biography. 4. Rock music—Tennessee—
Memphis—History and criticism. 5. Popular culture—United States.
I. Title. II. Series.
ML429.P52C36   2005
782.42166'092—dc22   2004022008

Paperback ISBN 978-0-252-07732-6

For Laura Jane

Contents

Illustrations follow pages 86 and 158.

Acknowledgments

One of the pleasurable tasks in writing a book is giving thanks to the special people who provided invaluable assistance. I owe a unique debt to several folks in particular. Because Dewey left little important printed material, I had to rely primarily on oral accounts, especially from those closest to him. Beyond the interviews conducted with family and friends, I was fortunate enough to obtain a treasure trove of data from Charles Raiteri, a former WHBQ employee who conducted extensive interviews back in 1977 while putting together a documentary film video on Dewey's life (*Daddy-O-Dewey: A Natural Star*). Raiteri was gracious enough to allow me to use these interviews. Given the fragile nature of memory, they provide what is presumably an even better source of information than my own interviews because Charles was talking to people who were much closer to the events being described. Some of the quotations that follow reflect the attitudes of earlier times rather than ours.

I owe another special thanks to my longtime acquaintance George Klein, whose friendship goes back to our early days together at L. C. Humes High School. George patiently sat through numerous hour-long interviews, allowing me to pick his brain about the unique perspective that only he had from both working with Dewey and from his close association with Elvis Presley.

This book did require at least some traditional hard-nosed research, and for the assistance I received while conducting it I can do no better than gather up the usual Memphis suspects to thank. Judy Peiser, at the Center for Southern Folklore, allowed me to use the material she has collected over the years, especially the center's extensive interviews with so many of the critical players in the early Memphis music scene. And then there are Jim, Patricia, Wayne, and the whole gang at the Memphis–Shelby County Room, who seemed always to be able to respond to my requests or else spin me around in the right direction to find what I was looking for. Finally, Ed Frank and Jim Cole in the Special Collections Room at the University of Memphis Library were always helpful and considerate.

Robert Dye needs to be singled out for his help, which went far beyond what I asked of him. Robert's father was responsible for taking the now-famous photographs of the early Elvis on the brink of stardom. The younger Robert has continued in this tradition. He provided me with several pictures—especially the wonderful one taken by his father that graces the cover of this book—and also offered helpful assistance in gathering and codifying all the other photographs.

A very special thanks, of course, has to go out to Dewey's wonderful family—to Dot, Randy, Jerry, Marjorie, Bill and Betty, and Billy Mills. All willingly gave unselfishly of their time and energy, never tiring of my seemingly never-ending questions.

Last of all, it is a pleasure to express my appreciation for everything my editor, Judith McCulloh, has done. Judy is one of those wonderful, user-friendly people who not only provided the expert guidance needed but also encouraged me through those inevitable tough times that seem to come with the territory of writing a book.

I might have been able to do it without all these people, but their help certainly made my job much easier and—I am certain—helped me produce a better book.

Introduction

Dewey Phillips's name is best associated with a single moment in the history of American popular culture. He is the disc jockey who introduced Elvis Presley to Memphis and the Mid-South by playing his first record and then conducting his first live on-the-air interview.[1] More important, however, if less well known is the contribution Dewey made to the rock 'n' roll revolution of the 1950s by both turning on a huge southern white audience to the previously forbidden "race" music and by providing indispensable assistance to Elvis's early career at a time when Elvis and his local record label, Sun, were still virtually unknown.

Years before the famous Presley interview, Dewey Phillips's famous late-night radio program *Red, Hot and Blue* was already changing the musical landscape of the South if not the nation. Dewey's inspired lunacy made rock 'n' roll much more palatable for a generation whose parents were still outraged by the music itself. *Red, Hot and Blue,* which took Memphis by storm in the early 1950s, not only prepared the Mid-South for Elvis's rise to stardom but also became the launchpad for Jerry Lee Lewis, Johnny Cash, B.B. King, Carl Perkins, and dozens of other top recording artists.

Although Dewey's uniqueness seems to defy almost any categorization, he nonetheless belongs to that singular group of white radio personnel who were put on the air in the immediate post–World War II period (before stations in the South were willing to try black disc jockeys) in an attempt to capture a rapidly growing and potentially lucrative black audience.[2]

It all started in Memphis back in 1949, in what local veteran entertainer and film-score producer Jim Dickinson calls the "it" year. Two gigantic events occurred: Memphis's own WDIA became the first radio station in the country to switch to all-black programming, and WHBQ's Dewey Phillips became one of the first southern white radio announcers to legitimize the new black rhythm and blues sound by making it acceptable and respectable to a white teenage audience. Within a decade, race music would become part of the white mainstream, Memphis would become home to some of the biggest names in the music industry, and Elvis Presley would detonate a cultural explosion that would do no less than rearrange the entertainment map of much of the world.

The Dewey Phillips story is the stuff that movie scripts are made of. As we fade in, Memphis in the early 1950s already looks like a scene from *American Graffiti,* the only departure being that the ubiquitous voice blaring from the radio of every teenage drive-in in town is not Wolfman Jack but that of Daddy-O-Dewey, the hottest deejay in the Mid-South.

Now flesh out the script with Dewey himself, a character right out of central casting. If ever there was a diamond in the rough it was Daddy-O-Dewey. He was to totally dominate the ratings on late-night radio in Memphis and the Mid-South throughout the 1950s, but he had absolutely no formal training and knew next to nothing (and could have cared less) about proper radio protocol. More important, he quickly acquired the reputation of being an absolutely wild man whose behavior both on and off the air would, by today's standards, make grist for the scandal-hungry media mill. With a motor-mouth delivery, a "violate all the rules" attitude, and an absolute devotion to the music he played, Dewey was a Hollywood persona waiting to be discovered.

Moreover, the events surrounding Dewey's surge to stardom are themselves dramatic enough that they require none of the usual flourishes that Hollywood likes to add in the name of artistic license. Indeed, if presented accurately, the historic recreation of Phillips's meteoric rise has all the characteristic traits needed to qualify for Best Original Screenplay Based on a True Story. That story goes like this.

WHBQ, the radio station that provided the vehicle for Dewey's ballistic ascent, was floundering badly in the late 1940s, due primarily to the sudden appearance in Memphis of all-black WDIA, which had gobbled up a huge share of the listening audience. Memphis was already 40 percent black, so WHBQ decided that if it couldn't beat them it had better join them—and quickly. WDIA was just a small, 250–watt, dawn-to-dusk station. It signed off when the sun went down, which was as early as five o'clock in the winter months. In 1949 Gordon Lawhead, WHBQ's desperate program director, decided he would try to capture some of the newly discovered black audience in the evening after WDIA left the air by putting Dewey Phillips on for fifteen minutes at night in a new show called *Red, Hot and Blue.*

The Hollywood punch line is that in the process of trying to capture the exclusive black audience, Dewey ended up instead capturing the heart and soul of practically every teenager—black and white—within listening range of his voice. The rest, as they say, is history. Unfortunately, however, not only has history *not* recorded this but it has also not noted that he did it all *two full years before* Alan Freed "discovered" rock 'n' roll. Indeed, Dewey was blasting Howlin' Wolf (Chester A. Burnett), B.B. King, and Muddy Waters (McKinley Morganfield) throughout the Mid-South airwaves while Freed was still playing classical music in Cleveland.[3]

The experimental fifteen minutes quickly expanded to three full hours as Dewey became the coolest thing in town and the hottest thing on the dial for miles around. *Red, Hot and Blue* became a household phrase, and late-night WHBQ became the unofficial capital of the entertainment industry in Memphis and throughout the Mid-South. Dewey owned not only the airwaves but also the devotion of nearly every white youth around.

During the 1950s it is estimated that as many as a hundred thousand fans were tuned in and turned on to the Dewey Phillips spectacle from nine until midnight. At the peak of his popularity he was getting three thousand pieces of mail a week, receiving up to fifty telegrams nightly and more than a hundred on Saturday nights. He made Falstaff the number-one best-selling beer in the Mid-South while other sponsors clamored to get on his show, which sometimes had an advertisers' waiting list backed up for six months.[4]

But if Dewey was the man, Memphis was the place. Inevitably, this book is more than just a biography of Dewey Phillips. It also examines Beale Street and the Memphis music scene on the eve of both Dewey's and Elvis Presley's rise to fame. In essence, it is the story of the big bang of rock 'n' roll—how that music was born, and how one of the most important musical upheavals of the last century evolved out of Memphis during the late 1940s and early 1950s.

Many contemporary Memphis musicians whose lives were significantly changed by the musical explosion that became rock 'n' roll are convinced that it only could have happened in their particular city and at that particular time. "Memphis in the 1950s. Where else on earth?" asks Jim Dickinson. "Memphis was the place to be at that moment."[5]

Sid Selvidge, another veteran Memphis performer, speculates that we will never see anything like it again because the circumstances were so peculiar to Memphis at that time. Today it is another world. Now, Selvidge notes, "The kid in Cleveland is listening to the same stuff and watching the same stuff on MTV that the kid in Memphis is watching." He maintains that because cultural segregation was still so rigid among the races in the late 1940s and early 1950s "when they got together musically, something unique happened."[6] That uniqueness gave birth to rock 'n' roll. Dewey Phillips was not only present at that birth but he was also in many ways its indisputable midwife.

Elvis's discoverer Sam Phillips's now-famous comment about finding a white man who could sing like a black man in order to make a kajillion dollars speaks volumes about the musical seismic shift taking place in Memphis on the eve of Elvis's emergence. "That was the time and that was the place," exclaims Marion Keisker, the woman who encouraged Sam to recall Elvis Presley to his Sun studios in 1954, adding her voice to the notion that it had to happen right then in Memphis. "It stands to me as absolutely the point at which our society was ready to change."[7]

Keisker's take on the moment is as perceptive as her precocious recognition of Elvis's importance. The early 1950s was the last moment of a pretelevision era, when radio, with all its magical, other-worldly qualities, still fascinated and obsessed the country. In particular, it was Dewey Phillips's early-1950s' radio show that set the stage for the big change. Dewey's early introduction of rhythm and blues music to the Mid-South was a crucial prerequisite for Elvis Presley's initial acceptance. Turning the white audience on to black artists in the early 1950s was just as much a necessity for Elvis's early success as the musical collaboration of Sam and Dewey was for the King's later rocket ride to stardom.

The *Sam* Phillips saga has now become a familiar one, but very little has been written about his namesake, Dewey, and the personal and professional relationship between the two men. Nonetheless, Dewey was just as instrumental in shaping Sam's early professional life as he was in assisting Elvis's budding career. Just as it is almost impossible to imagine a time when Elvis Presley's name was still foreign to most listeners, so it is difficult—given Sam Phillips's national media attention—to recall a time when Memphis's most famous record producer was still completely unknown outside the city limits of his hometown. But such was the case when Presley made his first recording on the Sun label. At that time both he and Sam were practically unheard of, while Dewey was already the most popular deejay in the Mid-South. It was just as advantageous for the relatively unknown Sam Phillips (at the beginning of his career in the record business) as it was for the underexposed Elvis to have his name linked with the star power of Dewey Phillips while being promoted on the most-listened-to record show in the Mid-South.

Dewey and Sam were not kin, but they quickly became soul brothers for life. As a twosome they not only exposed the Mid-South to Elvis and the other Sun Records stars but also they turned the Memphis music scene upside down and helped changed the face of American popular culture.

I have a unique perspective. I grew up in Memphis during this era and went to school with Elvis Presley. I later worked in radio in the city and was a close friend of George Klein, who worked at WHBQ as a gofer for Dewey Phillips during the mid-1950s. George was the first of what many would later jokingly refer to as Dewey's "babysitters"—folks who were supposed to keep a close eye on the totally unpredictable star while he was on the air. George himself later became a famous radio and television personality in Memphis. He is an important player in this story. He was not only at Dewey's side while he did his show but he was also Elvis Presley's closest friend, having served as president of the senior class at Humes High School the year Elvis graduated.

Nonetheless, it is Dewey who is the key to it all. By introducing Memphis and the Mid-South to black rhythm and blues, he, as much as any white man in the Mid-South, helped narrow the gap between the two races by almost single-handedly making black music part of white mainstream culture. His captivating style disrupted the white-bread, button-down mindset of the early 1950s, shattered the color barrier, and ultimately succeeded in bringing about a cross-cultural miscegenation unparalleled in musical history.

David Halberstam, in his best-seller on the 1950s, wrote, "[Memphis] political boss Ed Crump might keep the streets and schools and public buildings segregated, but at night Dewey Phillips integrated the airwaves."[8] That musical integration helped forge the path for Elvis Presley's legendary walk into history. Sam Phillips may have discovered Elvis, but it was Dewey Phillips who literally introduced him to the Mid-South and, ultimately, the world. Elvis could not have occurred any other way at any other time in any other setting. Dewey's part in making it all happen is still the untold story in the history of rock 'n' roll. This is that story.

1

Programmed Chaos:
Dewey Phillips on the Air

> Oh, yessuh, good people, this is ol' Daddy-O-Dewey comin' atcha
> for the next three hours with the hottest cotton-picking records
> in town—(*aside:* Ain't that right, Diz? "That's right, pahd'ner.").
> Yessir, we got the hottest show in the whole country—*Red, Hot
> and Blue* coming atcha from W H Bar B Q right here in Memphis,
> Tennessee, located in the Chisca Hotel, right on the magazine
> floor—I mean mezzanine floor (*aside to himself:* Aw' Phillips, there
> you go again, you're always messin' up!).

On the air, the real Dewey Phillips was always a bit stranger than any
fictional radio character ever invented. The style was without precedent.
He made no effort to imitate anyone on the airwaves or in the entertainment business. Most fans agree that they had never heard anything quite
like him and no doubt ever will again. In essence, he did nothing less
than deconstruct Memphis radio entertainment during the 1950s, and
in the process he proclaimed a kind of Declaration of Radio Indepen-
dence for all future programming. Like Elvis, his style not only violated
a staid and conventional past but also marked a quantum leap into an
irreversible future.

Above all, there was no one around for comparison. One writer, noting
that Dewey was a one-of-a-kinder, quickly added, "One was enough."
Elvis's famous response to Marion Keisker's question, "Who do you sound
like?" ("Why, I don't sound like nobody, m'am") could also apply perfectly to Elvis's close friend and unofficial mentor, Dewey. Dewey didn't
sound like anybody but Dewey.

On his show, he was a combination of a kid in a candy store and a bull
in a china shop. A master of unpredictability, his anything-goes-and-to-
hell-with-the-rules-and-the-regular-format-approach-cause-I'll-do-any-

damned-thing-I-want-to attitude on the air made his nightly *Red, Hot and Blue* program synonymous with radio entertainment in Memphis and the Mid-South during the 1950s. His WHBQ studio was the broadcasting epicenter of the rock 'n' roll revolution.

"He was completely without a governor," exclaims Charles Raiteri, a professor of journalism at the University of Mississippi, Dewey Phillips expert, and a longtime observer of the Memphis music scene. "There was no way you could control him. When he was in that broadcasting booth he was going to do and say what he wanted to and that was it." Sun Records legend and Dewey's consummate lifelong friend Sam Phillips, who with every utterance on the topic normally exuded respect and admiration for Dewey, was no apologist for his behavior on the air, beginning with his celebrated manner of operating the control board: "Dewey was not too mechanical," he recalled. "When Dewey Phillips was in a little control room, I mean things were flying off the wall. I mean it was a three-ring or a four-ring circus." Pointing out that it was absolutely necessary for WHBQ to always have someone else in the studio with Dewey to make sure things were reasonably under control, Sam said diplomatically, "Dewey was not into production. Dewey had a little problem with his mouth [laughter]. Whatever came in his mind, he would say it."[1]

His performance between records could best be described as one endless stream-of-consciousness monologue. So rapid-fire was his machine-gun delivery that there was never time for him to think out what he was going to say, let alone carefully plan a structured program. Above all, there was never a hint of order or sanity. The foot-to-the-floorboard personality and the revved-up rhetoric spewed forth in a constant fusillade of senseless non sequiturs. Most of the time, listeners felt they were being bombarded by what one writer termed a "verbal assault."[2]

The immediate audience reaction was one of unalloyed fascination—albeit not always positive, especially among those accustomed to "normal" radio programming. Robert Johnson, the *Memphis Press-Scimitar* entertainment writer, was closely acquainted with Dewey and observed that the Memphis listening audience of the 1950s was divided into two groups: Those taken by everything Dewey did, and "those who, when they accidentally tune in, jump as tho stung by a wasp and hurriedly switch to something nice and cultural, like Guy Lombardo."[3]

Dewey's on-the-air escapades are now the stuff that help manufacture legends. In order to savor them completely, however, you must begin by recalling what Memphis radio was like in 1949, when he first began to attack the Mid-South airwaves. Music was monotonously pedestrian ("I'm Looking over a Four-leaf Clover" and "How Much Is That Doggy in the Window?"), and most Memphis stations spent the better part of their broadcast day carrying soap operas and variety shows from the network. Local programming was definitely a bit livelier with country and western bands or an occasional black gospel group, but staff announcer Fred Cook remembers that when he joined WREC in 1950 there was a pipe organ built into the side of the studio, and owner Hoyt Wooten's secretary played it for live shows.[4]

Most important, Memphis radio was still characterized by radio announcers who were supposed to sound like, well, like radio announcers. They were, that is, supposed to convey their message in impeccable English, slowly articulate each phrase in perfect cadence, speak in carefully modulated tones, and always enunciate each syllable.

Come again! Dewey Phillips had a hard time making simple sentences let alone trying to enunciate them slowly. Proper grammar? Forget that one, too. Maybe even forget the entire English language. He not only slaughtered it, but there was also no such thing as actually "reading" a commercial. Copywriters knew better. He was usually supplied with a "fact sheet" from which he could ad lib commercial spot announcements. Whenever he attempted the impossible and actually tried to read a commercial all the way through—a practice sponsors strongly discouraged—he usually botched things so badly that he'd say, "Aw, Phillips, you're always messin' things up."

But who cared? His highly stylized, streetwise argot might not have had correct syntax, but when it came to selling a sponsor's product he left grammarians standing in the dust. "He seldom spoke the King's English in the grammatical sense," Sam Phillips said, "but he knew he could communicate." Indeed, it was Dewey's remarkable ability to ad lib spot announcements that brought some of his greatest fame. He made Falstaff Beer the favorite of Mid-South listeners not because he read coherent commercials about it but because everyone remembered his ad-lib catch phrases. "If you can't drink it, freeze it and eat it," he'd scream. "If you can't do that, just open up a rib and pour it in." Not a single sponsor—certainly not Herb Saddler, the owner and distributor of Falstaff—bothered to complain for a single Memphis radio minute.

That Dewey would do the unexpected was always anxiously expected. In fact, the inability to predict what he was going to do was the only thing listeners to *Red, Hot and Blue* could rightfully predict. That was what made him so fascinating. You didn't know what you were going to hear when you tuned in, but you knew it wouldn't be said the same way on any two occasions.[5]

Despite the unpredictability there was nonetheless a certain method to the madness. You could be pretty certain, for example, that at some point in the evening Dewey would do one of the following: cue up a record right on the air; play two of the same records simultaneously—one slightly ahead of the other—in order to get an echo effect; put his hand on a record and stop it in midplay; or talk continuously the entire time the record was spinning.

Most people who observed Dewey's programmed chaos on the air say they never saw him actually cue up a record except when he played two at once. Most of the time he'd put a record on the turntable, slap the needle down, start talking, and turn up the volume. You could hear the crackling static as the needle ran around several grooves before it started, and maybe—if you were lucky—he'd quit talking when the first part of the record came in. As often as not, however, he'd talk some more. Sometimes, in instances when he would talk through the entire vocal, or if he wanted to hear a favorite part of the vocal again, he'd just pick up the needle and set it back down.[6] His favorite practice was to stop a record he didn't like by screeching the needle across it while it played. The writer Stanley Booth, who spent a considerable period of time hanging out with Dewey, says, "Every time I start to cue a record and the arm falls off the turntable I tell people I went to the Dewey Phillips school of broadcasting."[7]

Bob Lewis's 75-cents-an-hour job as Dewey's first gofer required him to do a great many things around the studio, but running the control board was not one of them. After being sufficiently broken in, Dewey was allowed to run his own board. According to Bob, however, "The whole thing was foreign to him. Things like proper [volume] levels just didn't bother him. Sometimes the level would just 'peg in the red' for long periods of time." (In radio jargon that meant the sound was loudly over-modulated, causing the needle to cross into the forbidden red area.) Lewis laughs when he recalls how he would cringe whenever Dewey wanted to play a record that was badly warped. "The needle would be skipping, so Dewey would get a heavy object, like a book or something— and actually put it on the [turntable] arm to force it down so the record would play." Lewis admits not being able to "even imagine what the engineers would have done if they could have seen that one."[8]

Part of Dewey's spontaneity encompassed chatting over the air with people who dropped by the studio. Never a traditional interviewer (no such rigid formality for Daddy-O-Dewey), most conversations with guests were carried on without disruption from whatever else he happened to be doing at the time. Sam Phillips recalled that Dewey's legendary first interview with Elvis was a rare event for *Red, Hot and Blue.* Except for Elvis, he seldom sat interviewees down in front of the microphone and talked directly to them. Most of the time he would chat with them while records were playing, scream at them from the other side of the studio, or use noisemakers to interrupt what they were saying.

This is rather remarkable considering those who, at one time or another, dropped by a typical Dewey Phillips show. It was common to see big-name people in the control room with him. Over the years, most had come to be close friends who would stop by for a quick visit whenever they were in town.[9] The list Dewey's widow Dorothy (or Dot, as she likes to be called) kept of everyone he interviewed during just one year reads like a who's who of American entertainment for 1954. Besides Elvis, of course, there was "Roy Hamilton, B.B. King, Joe Hill Lewis, Ivory Joe Hunter, Kay Star, Jimmy Witherspoon, Fats Domino, Hank Williams, Hank Snow, Les Paul and Mary Ford, Faron Young, . . . Dizzy Dean, Jane Russell, Patti Page, Lionel Hampton, Joe Liggins, Kim Novak, Natalie Wood, Nick Adams, . . . Carl Perkins, [and] Johnny Cash."[10]

It was quite common for Dewey to talk to guests on the air, but the process bore little resemblance to a typical and orthodox radio interview. Whenever a studio guest appeared, Dewey would begin talking, usually with the mike open and ignoring the fact that the guest was all the way across the room. Sometimes Dewey would repeat whatever was said, but more often than not he'd try to pick up the guest's voice from wherever they happened to be standing by turning his own control board mike up full volume and letting the guest holler.[11]

While he worked the board, Dewey's sleight of hand with his microphone's volume level makes for some of the best on-air stories about him. Stanley Booth remembers one night when the studio was full of the big boys—Jerry Wexler and Ahmet Ertegun from Atlantic Records and the flamboyant Leonard Chess from the rival Chess label. Dewey was always at his craziest when they were around, and this night was no exception. These people were pros, Stanley says, and they knew proper procedure during a live show. You keep absolutely quiet when the microphone is open and the on-air sign lights up. At the end of the record, Dewey opened the mike but secretly slipped the volume level down so he could not be heard. Then, Booth recalled, he "pretends as if he were talking on the air. This means that the 'on-air' switch is on but the level is down to zero, and Dewey is saying 'motherfucker this and motherfucker that' and they're thinking he's on the air."[12]

Unprogrammed programming was the characteristic trait of a typical Dewey Phillips show. At first, station personnel tried to suggest a little organization, maybe even drawing up a list of the records he might play prior to his show, but that, like all other efforts at superimposing order, quickly fell by the wayside. Just trying to keep track of the records Dewey actually played on a given night was not easy says Louis Harris, who should know. Harris worked with George Klein inside the studio, helping him help Dewey. "I was kind of the 'gofer's gofer,'" he says with a chuckle. Sometimes, Harris remembers, Dewey would have a general idea of what he was going to play, and Louis and George would help him pull records before the show. Once the show started, however, the usual pandemonium followed. "He'd have records scattered everywhere, and he'd holler, 'Gimme that record over there,'" Harris says, but because of the total disarray by that time "I wouldn't even know which one he was talking about."[13]

What seemed like total chaos was actually Dewey's strongest suit. Given conventional radio at the time, much of the audience's attraction to him was this very distinct lack of on-air formality. Gut-level spontaneity and the way he would generally botch up everything on the air are the very things that endeared him to the audience. "Dewey was just Dewey," observes Charles Raiteri. "He'd make a mistake and he'd say, 'Oh, yeah, Phillips, you're doing it again. Messin' up.'" That, Raiteri says, made Dewey much more human, and fans ate it up. "It was like there was a 'real' person on the air instead of a 'radio announcer.' And that was a big part of his charm."[14]

Contemporary columnist Robert Johnson, commenting on Dewey's unrestrained spontaneity, remarked, "Sometimes I wonder if there is a real Dewey, or if he's just something that happens as he goes along. He says whatever happens to come into his head, and there have been times when it was the wrong thing." Johnson noted that a newcomer to the city, hearing Dewey for the first time, might be shocked. But once past that initial impression, which sometimes seemed "crude and low-brow," Dewey "came over the air as the voice of a rather strange friend, whom they knew and understood."[15]

Some of Dewey's fans, of course, found him irresistibly captivating. His ardent listeners, especially the young, impressionable ones, were so caught up in the craziness that they ignored most everything else they were doing. Memphis musician Jim Dickinson remembers going to dances at White Station High School in Memphis at the time *Red, Hot and Blue* was on the air: "There'd be as many people in the parking lot listening to Dewey as there were inside at the dance." One particular night, he recalls, Dewey had just gotten his hands on Little Richard's "Long Tall Sally." "He played it about ten times in a row, and nobody did things like that except Dewey. So everybody went out in the parking lot at the dance to find out how many times Dewey would end up playing it."[16]

More than anything else, Dewey enjoyed himself on the air and loved every minute of being there. He frequently sang over the records he was playing, to either the delight or consternation of listeners, and even made a record on the Fernwood label, both sides of which—"I Beg Your Pardon" and "White Silver Sands"—he played repeatedly without identifying himself as the singer.

He was doing exactly what he wanted to do. So married was he to his job that he was reluctant to go on vacation because he knew he would miss his show if he did. Sam Phillips once attempted to get him to travel with him on the "dust bowl" circuit, promoting the various Sun Records artists, but to no avail. The show was, to a great extent, his entire life. "No matter how bad he felt, he just came to life when he'd open that microphone," Sam told Elvis Presley biographer Peter Guralnick. "[He] wasn't just playing records and cutting the monitor down. He was enjoying everything he said, every record that he played, every response that he got from his listeners."[17]

Above all, Dewey's over-the-top enthusiasm while doing *Red, Hot and Blue* was contagious. His on-air persona was but an extension of his actual personality. What you heard was what he was. Friends say his endless off-the-air practical jokes were merely attempts to win the affection of those around him, just as his clowning on the air was a constant effort to make everyone in his audience like him. It worked wonderfully. It was extremely difficult for the average listener not to be both affected and infected by a typical evening of *Red, Hot and Blue*. It was impossible to listen to Dewey casually. No one would have him on the radio just for background music. Most fans could tell you everything he did or said on a given evening, recalling the famous unplanned mistakes as well as usual gimmicks and wisecracks. "Get off the turntable Mable," he'd shout. "You're too old to be goin' round with a musician." Or he'd interrupt a record with a hot news item: "Somebody just reported there's a grasshopper out on the freeway with his hopper busted."[18]

Temporary suspension of disbelief was also a prerequisite for listening to any Dewey Phillips show. It was sometimes difficult to tell if the "news" he reported was fact or fiction. He would occasionally try to give the national news—getting about as straight as he ever did. Billy Lee Riley, who, like most Sun Record artists was a hard-core Dewey fan, says whenever Dewey read the news he would invariably add his own personal flourishes. He might say something like "There's a whole lot of fightin' goin' on over there in Iran—I mean a whole lot goin' on. So, you better stay out of that area for a while."

Moreover, he would frequently make up his own local news stories and then pass them along as if they were true. At the peak of Elvis's popularity in the 1950s, Dewey had a field day. Whenever Presley dated a new starlet or leading lady from his newest movie for any length of time, for example, rumors would fly in Memphis that he was about to get married. Because everyone knew that Dewey and Elvis were very close, one of his favorite pastimes was to pretend that Elvis had personally confided in him about the long-awaited announcement. On at least several occasions he informed listeners that Elvis and Ann Margaret were either already married or would be married very soon. The announcement would be made right on the air and without the slightest hint of facetiousness. Dewey would even add flourishes like, "They're gon' live right here in Memphis. They've already picked out a house over by me."[19]

Of all the wild stories associated with his name (and almost every close friend has some bizarre tale), the most interesting by far are those connected with a phrase that became synonymous with *Red, Hot and Blue* in Memphis during the 1950s: "Tell 'em Phillips sencha." The phrase, Dewey-ese for "tell them Phillips sent you," started out innocently enough when he began using it as the tagline for commercials. Dewey's mentor and WHBQ program director Gordon Lawhead, whose humility prevents him from taking undue credit for anything, modestly admits that, yes, he had probably—and inadvertently—started it himself when Dewey asked how to end a commercial announcement when Gordon was breaking him in at the control board. "Dewey said, 'What do I do when I finish reading this commercial?' I said, 'Just say, "When you go in the store, tell 'em Phillips sent you."'"[20]

That was, of course, a very normal procedure in radio at the time, urging listeners to let a particular store know where they had heard about a particular product. By the time Dewey got through with it, however, the phrase was hardly standard. "I don't care who you go with or how you get down there!" he'd shout, whatever the store and whatever the product. "But when you do" (his voice raising for the peroration) "tell 'em that Phillips sencha from *Red, Hot and Blue,* the hottest thing in the country!" The *Memphis Commercial Appeal* reported that the phrase was "to the 1950 lexicon what 'twenty-three skiddoo' was to the 1920s."[21]

No less than the governor of Tennessee was quite familiar with the expression. When Gov. Gordon Browning paid a visit to Memphis in the 1950s, he said that his appearance onstage at Lowe's State Theater, along with Patti Page, resulted from the fact that "Phillips [had] sent him." The phrase became so popular that Lionel Hampton and Joe Liggins and the Honey Drippers, on at least one occasion, threatened to write and record a song that would be titled "Phillips Sent Me."[22]

Stories abounded during the 1950s concerning the phrase—most of them no doubt apocryphal but revealing nonetheless a great deal about Dewey's popularity and power. So many customers reportedly were nonchalantly announcing that Phillips had sent them that salespeople began demanding to know just who this Phillips person was. The *Commercial Appeal* once reported that he erroneously announced the start of a sale of women's dresses at a local store on a Tuesday that was supposed to begin on a Wednesday. So many people showed up chanting "Phillips sent me" that "bedlam threatened, [and] the store had to change its whole operation and hold the sale on Tuesday."[23] According to Memphis musician Randy Haspel, "The high school kids even developed a variation of an obscene hand gesture, so that by holding up just the little finger of the right hand, that meant, 'Go to hell and tell 'em Phillips sencha!'"[24]

Perhaps the most famous story of all, however, concerned a case of domestic violence. According to local lore, one woman did enough serious damage to her husband with a knife to require sending him to the hospital. The way this version of the story goes is that when the ambulance arrived, the woman casually announced, "Take him to a doctor at the hospital and tell 'em Phillips sent 'im."[25]

The phrase achieved such widespread acceptance in Memphis that Dewey began to develop variations on the theme: "You getcha a wheelbarrow full of monkeys [or goober dust, or bald-headed nanny-goats or lizard gizzards, or fur-lined mousetraps or whatever] and run it through the front door and tell 'em Phillips sencha!"[26] Most regular listeners can still remember a variety of the infinite variations.

Though he occasionally threw out nationally popular radio and TV phrases—Red Skelton's "Boy, a flock of 'em flew over that time!" or Joe Penner's "Wanna buy a duck?"—the best-remembered are those he repeated like a personal mantra: "That'll git it—that'll flat git it," "You'd better bleve' it," "Call Sam," "Cotton-picking bird-brain," and

"De-gaaaw." The latter expression meant absolutely nothing, but that did little to discourage fans from yelping it every chance they had.

Sound effects were also part of the regular three-hour nightly ritual. Here again, Dewey was not averse to borrowing ideas and gimmicks freely from others, especially his predecessors. Bill Gordon—WHBQ's hottest deejay before *Red, Hot and Blue*—had a fondness for noisemakers, one of which was a duck called Quacky, perhaps the inspiration for Dewey's Myrtle the Cow. He especially liked to use Myrtle on the show. "Ain't that right, Myrtle?" she was always asked. The obedient, and predictable, response was a long, sonorous, low-pitched "mooooo."

Perhaps equally well known to Memphis audiences were the many voices Dewey created for the show. Undoubtedly, the best known was that of the former baseball great and popular TV commentator Jay Hanna "Dizzy" Dean. "Ol' Diz" was in fact Dewey's good friend, who would drop by to see him whenever he was in Memphis.

It was not so much Diz himself, though, but rather Dizzy's voice (and Dewey did a remarkably good impersonation of it) that was heard on *Red, Hot and Blue,* practically every night. Even though most fans knew the voice from Dean's regular TV broadcasts of major league baseball, so good was Dewey's characterization that listeners, whenever the celebrity did appear in person, were unable to distinguish the real Diz from Dewey's imitation. The impression was a natural one for a man whose hominy grits accent matched Diz's drowsy drawl. Dewey would usually finish a spiel with "Ain't that right, Diz?" "That's right, pahd'nah!" was the quick response. "Did I tell 'em right, Diz?" "You shore did, pahd'nah!"

So real was the impersonation that it sometimes got Dewey into trouble. Dot Phillips recalls that once, while pretending to be Dizzy, her husband said, "Hey, Dewey, you got anymore of them marijuana cigarettes?" And Dewey replied, "No Diz, I gave my last one to Inspector Gagliano, down at the police department." Dot says he had a call from Gagliano on that one. "He used to run the police department crazy." Dot also had trouble distinguishing the real Diz from her husband's flawless imitation. Her inability to discern which voice was which may have, on occasion, distorted her perception of reality. Given Dewey's later ill-famed reputation for philandering, one is uncertain whether Dot is being honest, cynical, or naive when she casually reports—without apparent irony—that "Dizzy would come in town, and he'd call me on the phone and say: 'Mrs. Phillips, don't worry about your husband, he's up here in a hotel room with me and my wife.'"[27]

Dizzy Dean was not the only famous fabricated voice to be heard on

Dewey's show but certainly the one he impersonated best. Regular listeners, for instance, recall that frequently, during the course of an evening's broadcast, Dizzy Dean's sudden appearance would be quickly followed by ones from "Marilyn Monroe" and "Kim Novak," both of whom, for some unexplained reason, sounded just like Dean. (No one ever expected a logical explanation for anything Dewey ever did). "Well, here comes Marilyn Monroe," Dewey would shout (always the emphasis was on the first syllable of the second name: Marilyn *Mon*-roe). Then he would make an awkwardly unsuccessful effort at sounding sexy and use the same phrases he used for Diz ("Whata' ya' say, pahd-nah?"). Novak also made regular appearances. Dewey, of course, always pretended to lust after both women, making remarks that were invariably double entendres. Kim, also indistinguishable from Diz—except that Dewey, for yet another undetermined reason, would add a slightly deeper bass inflection—would then chant the same mantra: "Whata' ya' say, pahd-nah?"

If his recreations of the voices of the famous sometimes faltered, Dewey more than compensated with his ability to invent a cast of imaginary characters who appeared regularly on his nightly show. So much happened on a typical show that sometimes it was difficult to appreciate what this multifaceted talent accomplished. Some who remember listening to Dewey when they were young thought all the ingenious mythical characters he made up were actually there, in the studio with him. Even a WHBQ audio engineer says that before coming to work at the radio station he had heard Dewey's show and thought Dewey was an actor who impersonated various voices. Once on the job, the engineer was surprised to find a different kind of reality—"just Dewey, doing his thing."[28]

Dewey loved to shift into a falsetto voice whenever he had soliloquized conversations with an ever-present mother-in-law, who was usually checking up on him or dumping a truckload of grief on his head. Dot says at first her neighbors were shocked by "Dewey's 'carrying-on,'—they'd come 'round and say, 'Did you hear what he said about your mother?' But they soon got used to it and laughed with everybody else."[29]

Better still was when he encountered "Grandma," who usually hung out at People's Furniture Store, one of his most enduring sponsors. His voice impressions, especially that of Grandma—who was always trying to "find Elvis"—rivaled the best of Jonathan Winters or Rich Little. ("'When do you reckon Elvis is comin' down to the store to see me?'" *Aside:* "Oh, don't worry, Grandma, sit tight, he'll be down there right soon.")

In addition, Dewey had "Lucy Mae," a black woman whose voice sounded for all the world like an early version of Flip Wilson's character Geraldine. Lucy Mae, too, was always looking for Elvis or making inane comments. Given the status of race relations in Memphis during the 1950s, one needs no better example of Dewey Phillips's amazing rapport with a black audience than the fact that he, a white man, was somehow able to get away with a perfect impression of a screeching, scatterbrained black female and yet not alienate the black community.

His vocal creations would often grow out of a single incident or a radio show he had heard. *Red, Hot and Blue,* for example, occasionally came on the air right after a show from the Mutual Network that one evening had something of a French overtone. That entire night Dewey Phillips was Du-*wee* Phil*leep,* a combination of mutilated French and country twang.[30]

One of his most frequent voice impressions was that of Brother Dave Gardner, who attracted a lot of attention in the 1950s with several comedy records in which he did a country preacher bit. Andy Griffith had become popular originally on radio with a "Deacon Andy Griffith" routine, and Gardner followed in the same genre. Dewey loved to fade the music in the middle of a serious romantic ballad and insert brief excerpts from one of these routines—Griffith, for example, doing his Romeo and Juliet bit in a deep southern drawl ("And then Romeo, why he took the poison and he expired").

Dave Gardner was from Jackson, Tennessee, near Dewey's hometown, so the two became close friends. Dewey played Gardner's records, talked about him, and could do a perfect impression of Brother Dave's voice—a blend of country preacher, black jive-talker, and raunchy joke teller.

Some who were riveted to *Red, Hot and Blue* as youngsters remember that Dewey was not only constantly doing other characters on his show but also, if you listened closely, you could tell that he "positioned" their voices.[31] "Diz" usually stood directly behind him (an effect Dewey created by turning his head away from the microphone), and other voices might seem to be coming from under the control board or behind the studio's glass window.

Selecting mike positions for voices on his nightly parade of mythical characters was only part of Dewey's constant movement while on the air. "He was a very visual performer, even on radio at that time," George Klein recalls. "He would stand up and holler and scream, he'd hit the microphone and slap the tables and, [pause for effect] consequently, he tore up the control room."[32]

George (more popularly known by his initials, G.K.) worked closely

18

with Dewey, and his observation underscores an important aspect of Dewey's performance: His failure to follow customary on-air procedures paralleled closely his failure to respect the station's equipment. Jerking needles across records, spilling coffee on the turntable, writing on the control room wall, screaming into mikes, and "messing up" in general on the air were all part of an evening's activity and gave WHBQ's studio engineers palpitations.

As a result, Dewey was always confined to his own area and never allowed to use the "regular" control board the other announcers used. WHBQ had a special studio built just for him at the Gayoso Hotel, the station's original location, and then made it part of the plans for the station's new home in the Chisca Hotel. When asked why it was essential to give Dewey his own special space, G.K. made doing so sound like a practical necessity. "He would destroy a control room within six months," George announced with a straight face. "And they would have to rebuild it."[33]

Besides Dewey's specially constructed space, the Gayoso Hotel studios had three control rooms: a large studio for broadcasts before live audiences, a smaller one for newscasts and record shows, and a medium-sized facility equipped to make transcriptions. When WHBQ moved to the Chisca Hotel in 1953, it had essentially the same arrangement. Each room containing state-of-the-art sound-proofing that rested, the *Press-Scimitar* proudly reported, on "three inches of felt."[34]

At both hotels the chief engineer added Dewey's studio behind the primary control room. Catty-cornered from the main console, and much smaller than the other studios, Dewey's facility was for his use almost exclusively. On rare occasions, and if the station got in a bind and it was necessary that a regular announcer do a commercial, Dewey's control room would be used. "The quality was good," remembers co-worker Jack Parnell, "but it was an old console, old turntables, and that was Dewey's place."[35]

In building the special studio, WHBQ's primary concern seems to have been to keep Dewey from wrecking the regular control board. It might appear that station personnel were trying to hide Dewey as much as possible from public display, but that was not their intention. Quite the contrary. He still had a lot of exposure to both fans and hotel guests while on the air because the radio station's facilities were built on the mezzanine floors of each hotel. WHBQ obviously liked that arrangement, because its previous studio, before the move to the Gayoso in 1942, had been on the mezzanine floor of the old Claridge Hotel.

At both the Gayoso and Chisca hotels the outside doors were locked at night during Dewey's show, but hotel guests could wander by at any time and check him out through the studios' large, open, glass windows that faced the mezzanines. More important, at the Chisca, teenagers soon learned that they could sneak in through the back door of the hotel to see him. Regular fans would telephone George Klein first and request permission to come up. If he gave the word, they proceeded on an outside stair, where he would meet them at the second-floor back door and let them in. Even if they didn't telephone, G.K. says Dewey always left the control room door open so that he could hear loud knocking and let people in. It helped if you knew someone or pleaded a special case, especially on weekends when the place was crowded. Bob Lewis says that Dewey would sometimes parade female groupies in front of the glass window and "give a thumbs up if he wanted those women to stay."[36]

Though Dewey's specially built structure at the Chisca may have given the appearance of inferior construction, those who have spent time studying the arrangement say that it was the most technologically advanced creation of its day. Local Memphis radio announcer, record collector, and music history buff Alex Ward says that once Dewey's fame spread, studio people from all over the country would come to town to study the way the studio was built. "It was up a ramp—actually built up off the floor—so they could get the wiring underneath it," Ward points out. "That gave the room an unusual sound because of the 'boominess,' the aura of that hollow floor under it because it was concrete. The resonance in the room was unbelievable."[37]

A special control room pleased everybody, even Dewey, who definitely liked to have his own space; that way he could appear to be running his own show. Lawhead says he would spit so much because of his natural "exuberance of talking that the saliva would go into the microphone," and the engineer was convinced "that it was rusting it out."[38] It was mostly the engineer who insisted that Dewey be carefully "quarantined" in a special studio, away from the other regular equipment. He had already had to put a special limiter on the console because Dewey's volume would peg in the red so frequently. Essentially, Dewey's studios at both hotels consisted of just two turntables and a mike. There was also a reel-to-reel tape machine in each room, but most are convinced that he didn't know how to work it.[39]

The engineer may have been concerned only with the equipment, but the isolation in a special control room was, in part, a metaphor for Dewey's alienation from the other regular announcers. They were perfectly content to keep their distance from this "character" who seemed to be the complete antithesis of everything they had all aspired to become. If Dewey had been broadcasting from a small independent station, perhaps he might not have been such an anomaly. WHBQ, however, was a network affiliate (Mutual) and had studios in one of Memphis's best hotels. The entire WHBQ staff—always nattily attired and socially correct—had been trained to be perfectly straight in their on-air delivery and in their general deportment. Around them, Dewey stood out like a used jalopy in a showroom of new cars. He was an island of insanity in an ocean of decorum and restraint. "Other announcers didn't associate with Dewey," says WHBQ-TV Director Durrell Durham. "He was not really part of the 'staff,' as far as they were concerned."[40]

The one exception to this "no contact" approach was when WHBQ would have a staff party, and Dewey and Dot Phillips would socialize with the other personnel. Dot remembers attending several dances put on by the station and emphasizes that before Dewey injured his leg "he was quite a dancer" who always seemed to have "quite a bit of fun."[41]

Apart from these few socials, however, there was essentially no camaraderie between Dewey and other deejays. Durham thinks the main reason for this was that to almost everyone who first met Dewey—and who came to know him only superficially—(as most of the other staff announcers did) "he appeared not to be very intelligent." Durham quickly adds, however, that this was certainly not the case. Dewey was no country bumpkin, an inaccurate impression undoubtedly created because of his poor, working-class background, thick country accent, and general "hang-loose" style. George Klein also emphasizes that Dewey was often misjudged because of his speech. "Dewey was not an idiot," G.K. maintains. "He may not have been educated, but he was a real sharp white guy who was like a streetwise black."[42]

More important, and perhaps inevitably, there was also more than a faint resentment from the paid professional staff announcers as they watched the totally untrained and unprofessional Dewey Phillips leave them standing at the gate with his record-shattering ratings and devoted fans. Envy sometimes turned to bitterness as *Red, Hot and Blue* grew in popularity. "He did more by accident than a lot of those guys did on purpose," Dewey's friend Milton Pond told Robert Gordon. "That's what really bothered them."[43]

Some regular announcers' subtle enmity can be gleaned from comments they made while conducting tours of the WHBQ studios during the 1950s. John Fry, founder and owner of Ardent Recording Studio in

Memphis, listened to Dewey religiously as a boy. He remembers—while still very young—taking one of the tours just to get a look at the studio that broadcast Dewey's show. Fry says that the announcer at the time, Lance Russell, "pointed to his control room and acted as though it was kinda like, 'This is the cage that we keep this guy in, separated from the rest of the equipment.'"[44]

Others have childhood recollections of the same Lance Russell tour. "Everything else in the studio was just immaculate, shiny, all the latest little lights that blinked," says John King. Then "you passed this room, where there was just a mike, and two turntables. The mike was one of the old-timey ones—about eight feet [sic] round—taped together." King says that Russell pointed out a long footlocker across the room, and he told visitors that when Dewey finished playing a 45 he'd toss it into his footlocker. Russell would add, "That's how he kept up with who he played for that night."[45]

Though Russell's remarks were obviously designed to entertain tourists, he may have given at least a partially accurate description of Dewey's method of handling the records he played. Because he didn't like to screen them, quite often while on the air he'd dispose of those he didn't like either by tossing them into the wastebasket or dropping them loudly on the floor. Sometimes he'd sail a record across the room, especially if he was listening to it for the first time and didn't like it. Frequently, he didn't wait for the record to finish. He would "just jerk it off right then, and then say something like, 'You ain't never gonna make it, so just forgit it.'"[46]

Louis Harris had the job of cleaning up the studio after Dewey got off the air. "He was not neat," says Harris, generously choosing his words. "George Klein would go in early sometimes and clean it up," but that usually didn't last long once Dewey arrived. After he got into the studio you could forget neatness and order. "He would send me and G.K. down on Beale Street to Culpepper's for barbecue. I'd go get it and bring it up to the station." Apparently it didn't take long after the barbecue arrived before the place would be in shambles. "He just had a good time on the air and didn't particularly care what the studio looked like."[47]

Harv Stegman, who announced the Memphis Chicks baseball games just before Dewey came on the air, remembers feeling comfortable with the fact that he was in a separate control room. Stegman, who would still be broadcasting the ball games when Dewey arrived early to do his show, speaks positively of Dewey as a person and performer. "He was one of a kind," Stegman observes. "You'd have to love the guy with all his craziness." But he makes no effort to deny his approval of the arrangement by which Dewey was isolated from the other announcers. "He had a good mind. He was an original," Stegman says but then adds, "I was separated by the large studio glass window, and that's just the way I liked it."[48]

Wink Martindale, a WHBQ deejay before he moved on to national television, got along with Dewey better than any of the other announcers, in part because he liked him a great deal and also because he worked the early-morning shift and seldom crossed paths professionally with late-night Dewey. Martindale could joke, however, about being relieved when Dewey left the station in 1958. Dewey's cousin Billy Mills remembers talking to Wink on an airplane in 1961. "I asked him how the world was treating him, and he laughed and said, 'It's a lot better since I don't have to fool with that durn Dewey all the time.'"[49]

Even broadcast personnel at other Memphis stations, conventional members of the radio community whose traditional formats he did most to upset, envied Dewey's off-the-charts ratings. Almost all were quick to recognize his importance. "Dewey was a genuine personality," says WREC's Fred Cook, who perhaps personifies the best of the announcers who followed a fairly traditional format. Cook gives Dewey credit, even though he makes no pretense of caring for his unprofessional style or for the music he did so much to promote. "Whatever it was he had, he was able to communicate to people," Cook acknowledges. Moreover, almost all other Memphis radio announcers, including himself, were always designated as "air personalities." Neither he nor any other Memphis disc jockey, Cook recognizes, had the "kind of readily identifiable whatever it is" that Dewey possessed.[50]

That is not to say there were no other well-known deejays in Memphis. Sleepy-Eyed John Lepley, for instance, had a huge following, most of which was among older (nonteenaged) country and western fans. Dewey, however, whose listeners included country and western followers, also captured fans from a broader audience. Unlike specialty country disc jockeys such as John, his off-the-wall on-air presence, in fact, seems to have attracted all types—country and urban, black and white, and rich and poor. Not only did his listeners transcend race, class, and gender, but he often appealed to those whose listening habits did not normally identify with a particular announcer.

Sam Phillips, who always kept a close watch on the demographics of Dewey's audience, was so impressed that he studied the topic closely to make certain he was correct. He claimed that Dewey's audience, "economic-wise, education-wise, anyway you name it, was the broadest of any single disc jockey I've known, even when he was playing strictly nothing but R&B and gospel." Phillips also recognized that Dewey's strongest appeal was among the rock 'n' roll generation, but he quickly added, "He appealed to the white collar, the blue collar and the no collar. He was just one of those totally natural-born, totally unexplained personalities that made contact [with everybody] in the first degree."[51]

Ron Meroney, who joined WHBQ when Martindale left for the West Coast, knew Dewey well and seems to have a good read on him. Meroney, who describes himself as someone who can get along with almost anyone, says his recollections of Dewey are all fond ones. He also recognizes, however, that Dewey "was not somebody you would be a tight friend with, because I don't think he had tight relationships—maybe among his family he did—but among the jocks, he didn't." Most deejays, Meroney says, accepted Dewey but kept their distance. Recognizing that he was "in your face" long before that expression came to identify all too many of today's shock jocks, Meroney adds, "He wasn't abrasive, but in your face all the time. Unless you sat in the fifth row," he laughs, "be careful—the first four rows got showered." When asked if most of the WHBQ personnel just "tolerated" Dewey, Meroney smiled and responded, "It wasn't a matter of tolerating Dewey. It was a matter of coexisting with him on the same planet because he was such a whirlwind."[52]

Other staff personnel may have learned to coexist with Dewey, but the station management at WHBQ was barely able to endure him. Certainly, executives at the top were never totally comfortable with Dewey and seldom relaxed the entire time he was on the air. They always feared that something he might do or say would cause embarrassment to the station. Very little was ever said to him, however, until the end. That was for one reason only: They could not afford to do otherwise. George Klein says that Dewey always worried them, but then he adds, almost parenthetically, "But I think it was worth it to the station because they made a lot of money on advertising on his show."[53]

To say the station put up with Dewey because he made it a lot of money is one of the rare instances when G.K. engages in understatement. A more accurate way of putting it is to say that Dewey Phillips held WHBQ hostage. *Red, Hot and Blue* pulled the station from the brink of economic collapse, and no matter how wild or uncontrollable he became studio executives were not about to get rid of their cash cow. Gordon Lawhead says that Dewey and the radio station were always locked in a marriage of convenience at best, dictated largely by hardnosed economic reality. During the mid-1950s, Lawhead points out, the first half of *Red, Hot and*

Blue—from 9:15 to 10:45—was "completely sold out for five straight years. All together, his nightly three-hour show generated more revenue for the station than most of the other shows *combined.*"[54]

Nothing better demonstrates WHBQ's financial dependence on Dewey than its dramatic rags-to-riches comeback from 1949 to 1951. When Dewey first came on the air in October 1949 the station was taking a beating in the ratings and was also nearly broke, but by the spring of 1951 it was making so much money that a "profit-sharing plan" for all employees was announced. Station manager John Cleghorn and George S. Benson, president of Harding College in Searcy, Arkansas, which owned WHBQ, said that the station "had reached the point where we will have profits to share."[55]

It is true that Benson had a reputation for promoting "the American free enterprise system," and he also ran a series of "Freedom Forums" on stations around the country that "warned that Communist Russia seeks to wreck that system by sabotaging employer-employee relations." So perhaps some of Benson's enthusiasm to divide his gain could be attributed to anticommunist fervor. Nonetheless, so close had the station been to financial disaster—until Dewey came to its rescue—that at the time the profit-sharing scheme was announced Benson felt he had to brag publicly that "Harding College wants you to know how much WHBQ is making."[56] Other station personnel who appreciated Dewey's importance to WHBQ's financial health scoff at the idea that management could have entertained the notion of firing him. "He put WHBQ back on the map," says their television director. "He saved them. It's that simple."[57]

Indeed, these observations are borne out by WHBQ's intense efforts to keep Dewey at all cost, best exemplified by its determination to have him continue to broadcast while convalescing from two major car wrecks. WHBQ set up remote equipment while he was recovering so he could broadcast first from Kennedy Veterans Hospital and, later, directly from the bedroom of his house. All of this so that he would never lose any on-air time—or more specifically, any on-air *commercial* time.

Jim Dickinson thinks that a marriage of convenience is far too polite a description for the way the station viewed his childhood hero. "You know what they thought of him?" he asks rhetorically. "WHBQ talks differently now, but they *hated Dewey.*" Dickinson, who has strong feelings on the subject, goes further. "And they resented Dewey. They resented every penny he made and he made plenty."[58]

Dickinson, with characteristic enthusiasm, might be using strong language, but his point is no less valid. That the station was in a state of continuous apprehension about Dewey's behavior—never knowing what new prank might prove to be calamitous—is evidenced by the fact that Gordon Lawhead, Bob Lewis, George Klein, Louis Harris, and a host of others all served as Dewey's gofers—or what they unanimously refer to as his babysitters. The jokes about always needing someone in the studio with him when he was on the air were but a subtext to a larger problem of the adverse publicity that he did indeed occasionally generate.[59]

Even so, the station learned to live with almost anything he said on the air. And he said plenty. Just what he said during a typical nightly broadcast, however, should be kept in proper perspective. Some, for example, have described Dewey's oral barrage on *Red, Hot and Blue* as "verbal masturbation"; Elvis Presley's guitarist Scotty Moore even referred to him as a "sort of southern-fried Howard Stern." In fact, Dewey, if judged by today's standard of shock jocks, seemed like a mild-mannered Boy Scout.[60]

It is true that he delighted in taking his show to the edge of what was then considered to be acceptable broadcast norms. But he always carefully avoided the traditional four-letter words, choosing instead to get most points across by ambiguity, innuendo, and suggestion. His famous "that'll flat git it," for example, many understood to mean "that'll flat-ass git it." George Klein remembers that he frequently used the term *mother* (as in, "Boy, did you see that mother?"). Listeners knew, G.K. says, that the word stood for a more popular expression.[61]

Dewey was also extremely fond of double entendres, which may have allowed his audience to share a feeling of subversive camaraderie, one of the many bonuses for tuning in to the show. In addition, Dewey liked to play songs that had obviously risqué lyrics, sending them out especially for the benefit of Lloyd T. Binford, Memphis's notorious censor, who, for more than a quarter of a century from 1928 to 1954, determined exactly what Memphians did or did not see on stage and screen.[62] During his iron reign as chair of the Memphis Board of Censors, Binford banned any movie that disagreed with his personal political and moral philosophy. He had a particularly censorial eye for films featuring Americans of African descent. Perhaps reflecting racial views all too typical of southerners at the time, he was especially on guard against any form of "race mixing" in movies and once banned a Hal Roach film, *Curley,* because many of the "little Negroes in it" were seen playing right alongside white children. Binford justified his action by pointing out that "the South does not recognize racial fraternization even in children."[63]

Binford soon made Memphis the butt of national jokes, and Dewey Phillips took personal delight in giving him as much grief as he could—and as often as possible. Whenever he played a scatalogically scandalous song on *Red, Hot and Blue,* for example, Dewey loved nothing better than adding, "This one's especially for you, Lloyd!"[64]

All this might seem harmless now, but put in the context of the socially conservative 1950s many were scandalized by some of Dewey's language. This was an era when words such as "pissant" (one Dewey somehow managed to say over the air) still outraged the general populace. That he was able to get away with it is a testament to Dewey's unrivaled popularity. Sales manager Bill Grumbles had him on the carpet several times for "pissant," but the warning, as usual, did little to deter him from using the word frequently on the air. Contemporary WHBQ deejay Jack Parnell remembers, "When he was called in and they said, 'Dewey, what is this I hear about pissants?' He'd say, 'Hell, Bill, don't you know what pissants are?'"[65]

On other occasions, however, Dewey could be downright raunchy. Then he stepped over the line and not only upset the station's sensibilities but also gave listeners choice moments to remember. Stories abound of his off-color remarks on the air, some of which are no doubt embroidered versions of what was actually said. One thing, however, is certain. His on-the-air raunchiness seems to have been almost directly proportional to his later substance abuse, which means that most of the really far-out material likely occurred later and on the other stations where Dewey worked after being dismissed from WHBQ.

According to one story, Dewey was doing a commercial for a meat company and—in typical Dewey fashion—began a long digression about how he had been in the store, "talking to ol' Billy Bob or somebody down there about what good meat they had in the place." Then, Alex Ward recounts, "Dewey says, 'All of a sudden somebody yells 'fire,' so I grabbed my meat and beat it.'" He followed that with, "We are going to send this one out for all the pregnant women in Memphis, titled 'Sorry, I didn't know the gun was loaded.'"[66]

Even more shocking were the alleged comments that left little to the imagination. Dewey apparently never had a second thought about anything he said on the air, perhaps because he never thought anything he said was bad. Dot Phillips says that whenever she'd ask about something wild he'd said while broadcasting he'd reply, "Oh, come on, I didn't say that."[67] The radio station endured Dewey's reckless pranks and brazen behavior for as long as it could, no matter how embarrassing. That he managed to stay on at WHBQ until scandals, pills, booze, and—most important—a radical change in station format finally did him in is perhaps the greatest compliment to Dewey Phillips's indispensability.

Occasionally, the embarrassment he caused the station bordered on the unlawful. Perhaps nearly everyone's all-time favorite Dewey story—if one is to judge by listeners' recollections—concerns the night he decided to use his personal Dewey Phillips "scientific method" to determine just how many people were actually listening to *Red, Hot and Blue.* All traditional ratings methods for determining precise audience numbers indicated that the show had gone through the roof. Dewey, however, decided to conduct his own popularity test by having everyone listening in their automobiles blow their horns at a designated time.

Even though Memphis antinoise ordinances specifically forbade idle horn-blowing, he announced repeatedly that when he gave the command at 10 o'clock sharp he wanted everyone to cut loose for thirty seconds. He knew that the biggest segment of his audience was composed of teenagers cruising in their automobiles on dates or parked at local drive-ins, having something to eat and listening to his show. As the fateful hour approached, people began to cue their cars around the Chisca Hotel studio, blocking traffic on Main Street and giving police apoplexy. [68]

If you were almost anywhere in the city of Memphis—whether indoors or out, whether engaged in activity or mindlessly strolling down the street—when the actual moment came it was hard to escape the spontaneous cacophony of automobile horns. Even people inside large buildings reported the noise pouring through. Sun recording artist Dickie Lee, who was inside the WHBQ studio with Dewey, remembers that "you could hear it filtering back into the studio inside the station, which remember, was itself inside the hotel." Many Memphians knew that excessive horn-blowing was illegal, and perhaps people recalled celebrating the end of World War II by blowing horns loud and long. More than a few were frightened. "A lot of people thought somebody had bombed the city or something, you know," Lee remembers. Dewey's sister Betty Kirby, commenting on the most famous of her brother's shenanigans, apologetically observes, "I'm surprised that they didn't put him in jail for that one."[69]

As was almost always the case with Dewey, however, the best part of the story was yet to come. When the irritated chief of police reminded him that blowing a horn too loud and too long was against the law in Memphis and that he could be arrested for telling people to do so, Dewey responded by carefully instructing listeners the following week that they were not to blow their horns at a new predesignated time. "Now, Police Chief McDonald has called me up and said that we ain't supposed to do this," he admonished. "I was gon' tell ya'll to do it again at 10 o'clock, but I can't 'cause there is some kinda ordinance that says you're not supposed to." Then came the lethal punch line: "So, if you got a mind to blow your horn at 10 o'clock, I can't tell you to do that cause its against the law!" Dickie Lee's description of what happened next sums it up best: "Oh boy, at 10 o'clock sharp. . . . gaaaaa!"

2

Before the Storm:
Dewey Arrives at the Five-and-Dime

Dewey Phillips was the Wolfman Jack of Memphis. He frequently had more listeners than all other Memphis stations put together.[1] Whether or not a new record got Dewey's approval and subsequent promotion on his show would often determine the success or failure of that record. Under Dewey's reign, Memphis had the reputation of being the predictor of whether a tune would hit nationally or not. "A record will hit No. 1 position here," Robert Johnson of the *Press-Scimitar* wrote, "in most instances long before it catches on nationally."[2] Frank Berretta, who worked at Memphis's legendary Poplar (Pop) Tunes Record Shop where Dewey and Elvis loved to hang out at the peak of their fame, dealt daily with national record distributors. Once Dewey broke the hits, he says, "then the distributors would start to work Detroit, or wherever. If it was gonna hit in Memphis, it was gonna hit everywhere."[3] Such was Dewey's power and fame in the 1950s.

But it wasn't always that way. Though he rose to stardom rapidly, success did not come easily to this working-class country boy with a hominy grits accent and an unrefined upbringing—especially at first. Indeed, during the early years it was necessary for him to do battle with the Powers That Be just to get noticed. At the start there was a lot of scuffling and numerous refusals. If both Dewey and Elvis's lives shared a similar tragic ending they also had common origins; Dewey Phillips's beginnings were as genuinely humble as Elvis's.

Just as the dirt-poor Vernon Presley had come to Memphis from Mississippi in 1948, seeking a better way of life for his wife and son, Dewey had come, a decade earlier during the Great Depression, leaving his hometown of Adamsville, Tennessee, to find work in Memphis because his father had a stroke. The remainder of the family—his mother and two sisters—were counting on him to help out.[4]

Dewey was one of six children, three of whom died at birth. Though he spent most of his youth in Adamsville, a town of only several thousand, he was born on May 13, 1926, in Crump, Tennessee, about four miles away. Crump, even smaller than Adamsville, has a post office, a few stores, and the cemetery that holds most of Dewey's clan. He is buried there in the family plot.

His mother, Odessa, taught school until she quit after marrying. As she said, "That's just the way it was done back then."[5] The father, Jesse, farmed and ran a small store for awhile but had to sell it during the depression.

Dewey's two sisters, Marjorie Barba and Betty Kirby, say that their mother, called Odie or Od (with a long *o*), was a saint who had the trials of Job. Jesse had difficulty earning a living after his stroke, so Od became the family's breadwinner. When Dewey went to Memphis, she followed the next year and began work at Fisher Aircraft. She worked hard all her life to help provide for her family, even doing a long stint building tires at Firestone in Memphis, one of the few good-paying jobs for white women in those days. "Between Dewey and mother, we weren't poor," Betty, the younger sister, proudly recalls. "We were not as poor as we would have been had we stayed back in Adamsville."[6]

Both sisters say that Dewey loved his mother and was closer to her than to his father or to them. Betty recalls her brother's unusual devotion: "To Dewey, my mother was like a God. My mother comes first. My mother was number one in Dewey's book." When her brother started working in Memphis, he would bring his paycheck home each week and give it to her.[7]

Jesse Phillips, who was reclusive, never provided a strong role model for Dewey, especially after his stroke. Billy Mills, Dewey's cousin and lifelong close friend, thinks it was natural for Dewey to draw closer to his mother and seek out other strong males with whom he could identify. In the early years he became quite fond of his Uncle Marvin—Billy's father—who apparently became a convenient father surrogate. Later in life Dewey enjoyed playing the same surrogate role himself to Elvis Presley, George Klein, Sun artist Dickie Lee, and a host of other up-and-coming young stars.[8]

Both of Dewey's sisters say that their father was distant even while at home and never showed much interest in his children. Dewey did, apparently, pick up his proclivity for music from Jesse, who would occasionally spend an evening entertaining his family by playing both guitar and harmonica in a fashion that anticipated Bob Dylan by half a century. He played both instruments at the same time, according to Dewey's elder sister, Marjorie, by "wiring the harmonica into place before his mouth with a coat hanger." He used to play "Old Joe Clark" a lot, but usually it was "country and religious songs."[9]

As might be expected from his outrageous radio behavior, Dewey quickly acquired a reputation as being class clown and an endless cutup during his early years. Those close to him at this time say that he was constantly drawing attention to himself and getting into mischief. Cousin Billy, who remembers playing with Dewey as a child, says that he was already a bit of a hustler when he was young. "He would go out to the Fairgrounds and talk people into going on a ride," Billy laughs, "then he would talk them into buying his ticket." Most kin in Adamsville, who became some of Dewey's biggest fans, believe that his large following was due to his honest sincerity and lack of pretense while on the air. "Dewey was just as 'ordinary' as he could be," proclaims Aunt Jewell, Dewey's centenarian aunt, who uses plain, unaffected language. "He just talked like he pleased. He was so countrified, and he would say things that just kinda tickled everybody."[10]

Indeed, Dewey's folksy, "plain-as-pig-tracks" way of talking was without question another key to his enormous success. His style not only warmed the hearts of his rural, working-class Mid-South audience who lived deep in the Delta but it also connected with urban Memphis listeners, many of whom had rural roots or at least friends or family who did. Like Dewey, many country folk had headed for the urban life in Memphis immediately following World War II, and by the early 1950s "rural migrants" made up 60 percent of the city's population.[11] Dewey's radio show was obviously an irresistible attraction to those people, who saw him as the "good ol'" working-class country boy who had come to the vast metropolis and made it big-time on the radio.

Dewey's down-home rural upbringing was paramount in shaping his persona. He may have been perceived as outlandish because of the music he played or totally off the wall because of his on-air performance, but in many other ways he was, like a great many other rural, working-class people, the epitome of traditional and conventional values. He was, for example, an intensely nationalistic American whose loyal allegiance and grass-roots patriotism were frequently exercised over news items detrimental to the country. Close friends report that he was often upset when stories came over the wire about anti-American activity abroad.

He was also conventional about keeping listeners posted on such mundane matters as local basketball scores. Dewey was unquestionably a basketball fanatic of the first order. The only thing he might have enjoyed more than being a disc jockey would have been to serve as basketball coach at Memphis State University (now the University of Memphis). He had played basketball in Adamsville and was frustrated by the fact that he never had a chance to coach. "All my friends went on to be coaches," he told his friend Robert Johnson.[12] Indeed, when an MSU coach left once, Dewey repeatedly telephoned the athletic office "to offer his services." On the air, he regaled his audience with constant updates on MSU scores; he also drove back home every chance he had to see basketball games, especially those involving teams from the tiny hamlets of West Tennessee.

Dewey maintained a lifelong affection for those tiny country hamlets. Even after becoming a famous radio star in the big city he maintained constant contact with friends and family back home. His frenetic energy while still a young man, not surprisingly, was too much for the miniature community of Adamsville, however. With one movie theater there and very little else for entertainment, Dewey had to get out. In 1942, shortly after his father's stroke, the rambunctious sixteen-year-old and two friends decided to make their way to the bustling municipality of Memphis, where bright lights and a growing economy promised not only fun and adventure but also the steady job he needed to supplement the family income. The three loaded up their worldly possessions; jumped on a Greyhound at the local drugstore, which also served as the bus station; and headed for new adventures.

When the group arrived in Memphis, the only obtainable jobs were at a service station, which worked out nicely for their transition because they were able to live in the station owner's home. After attending Tech High School for only a brief period Dewey, sixteen, dropped out in the tenth grade. He had never been much of a student in Adamsville and saw no need to make an effort in Memphis.[13]

Dewey was employed for a very short time at the William R. Moore Clothing Store, but when his mother got to Memphis she helped him get a job at Taystee Bread, where he worked the ovens on the night shift, a task Betty Phillips says he thoroughly enjoyed. It appeared as if Dewey had finally found a niche. Betty remembers him coming home from the bakery, singing loudly. He didn't get off until midnight, and he'd bring home hot raisin bread. "He'd always wake me up to give me some. It was delicious. I can still remember the taste," she recalls. One unauthenticated story has Dewey persuading others on the assembly line to join him in making gingerbread men from the passing lumps of dough instead of loaves of Taystee Bread. It is a story in character if not in fact.[14]

Dewey stayed on at Taystee for a while, relishing the regular income the bakery provided. He had money for the first time in his life, making about 50 cents an hour, which, says Cousin Billy, "was a good bit of change for a kid that never had anything." It was during this time that Dewey started buying clothes with his newly acquired wealth, attaining a reputation—at least among his immediate family—as an immaculate dresser and rakish man about town. He seemed drawn immediately to Lansky Brothers' Clothing Store, the Beale Street establishment that would become the favorite haunt of the young Elvis. Indeed, Dewey was probably a customer at Lanskys' long before Presley was. It is likely that Elvis didn't get to Lanskys' until he started chumming around with Dewey, who introduced him to most of Beale Street.

Dewey's love of Lanskys' wild clothes stayed with him. Later in life his favorite attire was a chartreuse sport shirt, preferably one with a lot of palm trees. The shirt was never tucked in, always hanging out over seersucker or sharkskin pants—themselves neatly draped over wing-tip, lace-up shoes. Even at this early stage Dewey leaned toward the flashy. "He was always snazzy, a real 'sporty cat,'" says Billy, no doubt the result of having purchased a great many of the Lanskys' Beale Street specials. Dewey would give Billy his old clothes. "I was the best-dressed kid in Germantown [a Memphis suburb]," Billy recalls. "I went from one Sunday-go-to-meeting shirt and pants to about four sport coats, pants with the belt in the back, and shirts one color in front and sleeves another color."[15]

Dewey's good-hearted tendency to give away possessions was not limited to immediate family. In the early days, George Klein says, his mentor would bring him home with him, feed him, and often give him clothes. Indeed, the compulsion to hand over garments to close friends would become one of Dewey's most distinct personal characteristic traits. When the young Elvis was still scuffling in the very early days, for example, Dewey frequently brought him to the house and gave him his own sport coats and shirts to wear.[16]

A preoccupation with personal appearance meant that Dewey seldom left the house unless he looked sharp. Alas, however, his stunning appearance in new civilian duds didn't last long. He was drafted into the army when he turned eighteen and went to Germany with the Fourth Infantry Division. Coming into the war in 1944, Dewey was late in arriving, but he did manage to win the Bronze Star, although how much combat he saw remains uncertain. Dewey seldom talked about his military experiences but did recall for Robert Johnson that he got shrapnel in his leg while "being pinned down in a foxhole for several days" during the Battle of Hurtgen Forest. He had "a couple of tales about the service," says Cousin Billy with a skeptical snicker, "but I didn't know what to believe." He brought back clothes from a dead German, so it is quite likely that he saw combat. One thing is certain. He continued to send a check home to his beloved mother all the while he was in the army.[17]

Discharged at the end of the war, Dewey returned to Memphis permanently but continued to flounder for a time as he tried various jobs for very short periods. His real calling, of course, was as an entertainer, but it took him a while to find his precise role. Using the GI bill, he started in that direction when he attended the Memphis College of Music, a private school, with what seems to have been the sole intention of becoming a professional singer. In public school Dewey may have been the class clown, but after enrolling in the College of Music he took his education seriously, if only for a short while. "Two distinguished Memphis teachers trained him," *Radio-TV Mirror* later reported, "and thought he showed real possibilities in the popular music vein."[18]

Dewey desperately wanted to be a successful singer, practicing every free moment he had and often late into the night. His determination undoubtedly sprang from what would become a lifelong love for music. Both sisters remember that Dewey constantly listened to the radio as a child, fascinated by the country music that would always remain close to his heart.

Like the many rural fans who would later tune into his radio show, Dewey grew up listening to the *Grand Ol' Opry*. "Country music was about all that was available to us back in Adamsville," Marjorie remembers. They listened to the *Opry* coming out of WSM in Nashville. "Dewey especially used to like Minnie Pearl." As a youngster, he and his parents traveled to Nashville, where his mother had a good friend. It was quite a trip from their hometown. They had to go thirteen miles to Selmer in the old Model A and catch a train from there to Nashville.[19]

Although Dewey's musical taste can best be described as eclectic, his attraction toward country and western led him to persuade WHBQ program director Gordon Lawhead to put him on an early morning country music show shortly after joining the station. The show, however, which ran simultaneously with *Red, Hot and Blue,* didn't last long. It, along with everything else, had to be dropped so Dewey could concentrate on the kind of music that was to give his late-night program the unique quality that locked in devoted listeners and ensconced his name in the annals of popular culture.[20]

It was his persistence in playing the new African American artists on *Red, Hot and Blue* that would help launch the Mid-South's rock 'n' roll ship of state. It was a brand new sound, and it would come to be synonymous with both Dewey Phillips's name and the title of his show. The new sound, which some black people were already calling rhythm and blues (R&B) and white people would soon call rock 'n' roll, was, in the late 1940s, still referred to in the popular press and trade publications as "race music."

Almost as soon as he became a young adult Dewey was taken with the sound of the music that stemmed from the throbbing heart of Beale Street—the musical center of Memphis's black community. The attraction might have been part forbidden fruit and part over-compensation; Dewey had never been exposed to such music as a child. Even though many black people inhabited rural west Tennessee, few lived in the small towns where Dewey grew up. It is certain that he had little opportunity to be exposed to anything like an authentic African American culture. Both sisters remember no black people living in Crump; only two black women, both of them maids, lived in Adamsville, where he spent his youth. "They would come down and help my mother do washing," Betty Kirby remembers. "The people in Adamsville treated them well and Dewey knew them."[21]

A casual association with two black women, neither of whom apparently had musical ability—such was the extent of Dewey Phillips's childhood exposure to African Americans and their music. That was it. That was it, that is, until he got to Memphis. Once the young teenager arrived in the home of the blues, however, he wasted little time gaining exposure to black people and to what he found an irresistibly attractive black culture. Specifically, he seems to have instantly acquired a love for rhythm and blues music, which was beginning to explode in the African American community. That love would last for life.

By the time Dewey arrived in Memphis shortly after the war, about 40 percent of the city's population was black. In spite of rigid segregation he was in contact with Memphis's black community almost immediately. He worked closely with black people on the job at Taystee Bread, for example, and made many visits to his Cousin Billy, who lived in the Germantown section of Memphis, whose rural population included many black citizens. "Dewey would come out to our little ol' country store in

Germantown, and most of our clientele was black, and so he was around a lot of black people when he was still a teenager," Billy recalls.[22]

Dewey was later to maintain that he became interested in the music of African Americans during this period. "While he was attending the Memphis College of Music," the *Memphis World,* a black newspaper, reported after interviewing him early in his career, "he became keenly interested in . . . 'race music.'"[23] Dewey also told the *World* that he became equally interested in religion at this same time. Even though he did not elaborate on the connection between the two, Dewey Phillips, from the beginning of his career in Memphis, had an almost evangelical zeal to spread the new music to all who would listen.

The "pulpit" he chose to conduct this crusade, of course, would be his famous radio show *Red, Hot and Blue.* He didn't have to wait for that show, however, to begin to proselytize. Nearly two full years before he spoke into a WHBQ microphone—two years before he skyrocketed to fame and fortune as the wildest deejay on southern airwaves—Dewey Phillips was already practicing the formula that would link his name in perpetuity with late-night entertainment in Memphis and the Mid-South. In 1947 he began "broadcasting" a kind of dress-rehearsal of *Red, Hot and Blue* in, of all places, the middle of the record department of the W. T. Grant five-and-dime at 113 South Main Street in downtown Memphis.

He began to work for Grant's in 1947, shortly after dropping out of the Memphis College of Music.[24] Dewey started out as a stock boy but soon took over the failing record department. Once he assumed control, Grant's was never the same.[25] Dewey began to sell records like Microsoft sells computer-operating systems. He was a natural-born salesman with a rapid-fire spiel as long as his gangly frame. Not only was he a made-for-the-movies character who attracted a huge audience immediately but his explosive presentation also made him the kind of pitchman every sponsor dreams of.

Grant's management didn't know how people would take Dewey at first because he was so different from anyone they had ever seen. Once over the initial shock, however, they quickly sensed Dewey's extraordinary appeal. His sales pitch was part cornpone hard-sell and part Dewey Phillips's showmanship. In almost no time at all he acquired a reputation, and crowds began to congregate in his tiny little corner of the store to hear him peddle his wares.[26]

Most customers were drawn to the blaring pitch as soon as they walked into the store, even though, at this stage, Dewey had no microphone.

Those who heard his spiel at the five-and-dime say he didn't need one; he would walk up and down the aisle, screaming at the top of his voice like he was selling the records at auction. "What did he need a mike for?" asks Frank Berretta. "Hell, you could hear him for four blocks!"[27]

He didn't need a mike but soon decided to get one. In fact, he confiscated Grant's public address system, which had been used previously only to make announcements inside the store, and converted it into a broadcast mechanism to peddle records. Initially, he would do commercials for other departments at Grant's, but it wasn't long before the record department was the focus of the store's activity and Dewey was its superstar.

He knew every traditional record the store handled, but more important, he had keen appreciation for music that was soon to be labeled "rhythm and blues," the new sound beginning to be gobbled up in ever-larger quantities by Memphis's rapidly expanding black clientele. In no time at all a great many black people began to walk the several blocks over from Beale Street to the five-and-dime on Main to observe Dewey Phillips and hear his elaborate spiel about records he was hawking.

Abe Schwab, proprietor of the most famous dry-goods emporium on Beale Street, remembers that Dewey proved to be stiff competition for his store because he was close enough to Beale to pull Schwab's black customers up to Main Street. For a great many African Americans, records were a main form of entertainment, and they purchased them in increasingly large numbers.[28]

Dewey's newly discovered black audience at Grant's record department attracted instant attention in highly segregated Memphis, and no one was more pleased than his boss, store manager H. E. Van Meter. The department had been losing money, and Van Meter seems to have immediately recognized that Grant's, like every other Memphis store after the war, would be wise to take advantage of the increased purchasing power of the city's rapidly growing, more affluent black population. Little wonder that sales began to accelerate rapidly when Dewey began pushing race records.[29]

In no time at all Grant's became one of the first Memphis businesses not located right on Beale Street to see that black was never greener. Until that time, virtually no one on Main Street had been overly concerned with the black dollar. Before 1949, for instance, when Memphis's WDIA became the first all-black radio station in the country (and began accumulating data on the surrounding area's black population), white merchants on Main Street had assembled only an occasional dollop of statistical information on the new purchasing power of the local African American community. Nonetheless, by the time Dewey started stirring things up at the five-and-dime almost any casual observer could see the changes. Following World War II a more urbane, affluent black community began to appear on the streets and in the shops of Memphis and the Mid-South. Nowhere was that more dramatically evidenced than among the increasingly large numbers of African Americans who began to gather in Dewey's department at Grant's.[30]

Starting out at only $30 a week, Dewey's one-man show quickly converted the record department into one of the top five most profitable departments in Grant's chain—quite a feat considering the nearly five hundred stores in the chain. According to Van Meter, it wasn't long before he found it necessary to put Dewey on a percentage basis "to keep from losing him."[31] Grant's manager quickly sensed that the explosive Dewey Phillips was the best enticement he had to lure black customers into his establishment.

Vassar Slate, the black bartender at the Variety Club of Memphis, a spot Dewey frequented often after he joined the radio station, remembers the lure Dewey used to attract African Americans to Grant's. Slate, a veteran observer of the Memphis entertainment scene, dates his long-time friendship with Dewey to the days he first encountered him at Grant's. "He knew what records the customers liked to hear," Slate observes. "If you liked the blues, as I did, he'd put on a blues record when you walked in the store; if you liked another type—say country—he'd grab that one and have it on the record player when he saw you coming through the door."[32]

Dewey's large black following did not automatically mean a total exclusion of white fans; both black and white clientele quickly became part of his large discipleship. No matter what color, though, it was mostly teenagers who seemed to be as fascinated with him as he was with them. Friends and relatives who visited Dewey at Grant's report a predominance of girls among the teenagers, both black and white.[33]

Later, when he was on the air, Dewey's audience would include every age group, but from the beginning it was young people in particular who were at the core of his most ardent fans. He was still in his early twenties when he worked at Grant's and had little difficulty relating to the teenaged after-school crowd who came as much to catch his antics as to hear the race music he played. Visitors were surprised at the crowds. "My lord," Billy Mills says, "half the store was back in that corner where he was."[34]

Grant's PA system had outside speakers that blared onto the sidewalk and street in front of the store, so Dewey's audience was not confined to those who entered the building. When potential customers strolled by, he would spot them through the front window and shout over the mike as they passed to "git on in here, good people, and listen to these here good records we got for ya'." Dewey wasted little time expanding his solo operation. Once he took over the PA system it was only a matter of time before he set up a raised platform in the record department, making it as impossible to avoid seeing him as to avoid hearing him.

It doesn't require much to imagine Dewey doing his thing at work. Perched high atop an elevated counter in the middle of Grant's record department, he was a commanding presence, complete with microphone and turntables, and at eye level with every shopper who walked through the front door. He would yelp at each customer as they entered, besieging them with nothing short of a vocal barrage. He would also spin records and read various commercials for other departments. If for some reason a customer failed to see his striking sandy-red hair and gangly frame there was no way of missing the raunchy sounds reverberating off the walls. "How could you miss him?" asks Billy Mills. "First of all the music was playing at about three thousand decibels!"[35] Dewey, his voice unmistakable over the intercom, would scream and shout like a sideshow carny enticing followers to do his bidding.

His outrageous escapades with records made him known in the city long before he got on the air at WHBQ. His famous spiels, for example, were not confined to the lulls before and after a record played. A favorite practice was to begin hollering in the middle of a record, either jerking the arm off the turntable (with the inevitable excruciating scratch) or, more often than not, grabbing a disc while it was playing and bringing it to a screeching halt, right in the middle of a song.

Thus, Dewey Phillips, while still in the Grant's record department, was in essence a disc jockey without a radio station—a personality without a program. For the fortunate number who happened to enter the five-and-dime during the late 1940s, it was a brief preview of the coming attraction that would later mesmerize much of the city. All who saw him were mesmerized. "He would yell and scream and just carry on," Gordon Lawhead said after observing Dewey at Grant's. "Do almost anything to get people to buy records." George Klein becomes animated as he describes Dewey's style in the record department. "He was like those guys on Beale Street trying to pull you inside the store. You know how they'd do—they'd practically grab you by the neck to get you in there."[36]

While at Grant's (and later on the air), Dewey was in the habit of saying whatever was on his mind. Even if it was occasionally shocking, many who heard him were delighted by the novelty. "He might be crude, but he was always funny," Van Meter says. "You couldn't help but like him."[37] The only difference between Dewey at Grant's and Dewey on *Red, Hot and Blue* was that the pitch at the five-and-dime was always designed to sell a record rather than a particular sponsor's product. Even that difference blurs, however, when you recognize that Dewey's over-the-top performance at both venues was always fired with a missionary zeal to spread the sound of the music. His sister Marjorie, who watched him operate in both places, detects no difference. While at the five-and-dime, she says, "He would just be standing there, yellin' and carryin' on, sellin' those records, just acting silly, just like he was later on the radio." When asked what he was like his first night on WHBQ with *Red, Hot and Blue,* Marjorie responded without missing a beat: "Just like he was at Grant's. Just Dewey acting crazy."[38]

But just acting crazy, playing records, and spreading the new rhythm and blues sound was not all Dewey had in mind. It was while he was at Grant's that he met the woman who would share his life, bear his children, and serve as the perfect antidote to his otherwise turbulent personality. The soft-spoken Dorothy Phillips is, by every conceivable measure, a stark dramatic contrast to her late husband, whose reputation was justly earned by a notorious volcanic delivery on the air and a disorderly life-style when off-duty. Almost all who knew both Dewey and Dot agree that her quiet, mild manner provided a perfect counterbalance for her untamed spouse. She was the mellow yin for his hyperactive yang.

"I was working for my uncle at Barham Credit Clothing Store at 108 South Main, near the corner of Main and Gayoso, directly across the street from W. T. Grant's," Dot Phillips recalls with a friendly smile. She had wandered into Grant's one day not because she heard a raucous blare from the record department but because she wanted to purchase a record for a friend who had just moved to Memphis, and she knew the five-and-dime had a record department. It was 1948, and even though WHBQ and Dewey Phillips wouldn't team up for another year Dot was instantly smitten. "After we met at Grant's, we'd have coffee everyday because I'd go over there on breaks," she remembers. "Our favorite song was 'That's My Desire,' which we'd listen to in the restaurant downstairs on the corner. When I went on vacation, Dewey called, sang 'That's My Desire,' and then proposed to me over the phone."[39]

Dot Phillips manifests most of the positive attributes of the southern rural tradition. A calm, kind-hearted gentlewoman, she laughs quietly as she recalls the early, happy days of her association with the wildest of the wild men, Daddy-O-Dewey. Even though at the time everyone at home told Dot that she was "marrying a maniac," it becomes immediately apparent that she has no reservations about her marriage. She would eventually have to leave Dewey, mostly for their children's sake, but never considered divorce and resents the assumption that they were officially separated. She speaks of Dewey in almost exclusively positive terms, although even when he was at the top of his form he was still too much for some of Dot's friends. "People would say to me, 'How can you stand him at home?'" she says. "And I would usually say, well most of the time he is asleep [laughter]." Dewey's now-famous on-the-air antics—ones that had dress rehearsal from that high platform in the middle of the Grant's store—were not what attracted her initially. Rather, what impressed her the most on their first encounters was his singing ability. He would almost always sing along with the record he was playing, and, "He really did have a nice voice."[40]

A nice voice is perhaps something his enormously faithful and devoted fans might have missed while he was on the air, even though, later on, he would occasionally croon along with the record he was playing on *Red, Hot and Blue.* Later still, when he would bring a live entertainment "package show" to town, he liked to get out of his role as emcee at the Handy Theater and vocalize with some of the top black rhythm and blues artists on stage. Marjorie and Betty Phillips remember going with Dot and Dewey to the Handy Theater on several occasions. It was a big event when Dewey brought a package show to town. "That was about the best thing we had here in Memphis," Betty says. "Mainly it would be just bands, but there would also be singing and comedians, and every now and then Dewey would actually break out into song." Both remember seeing a fantastic performance there by Lionel Hampton. Betty's husband, Bill Kirby, and Cousin Billy Mills were also there and recall that Dewey would excite the crowd with raucous carryings-on. By the time the evening was over he would have "that place jumping. People were dancing in the aisles," remembers Kirby. Then, at the height of the frenzy, "when he got real worked up, he might cut loose with just a few bars and the crowd loved it."[41]

Despite these later and rare displays of vocal dexterity Dewey apparently realized early on that although his true calling might have been in front of the microphone, he would not achieve fame or fortune exclusively as a crooner. His real forte, of course, was as a deejay, playing (and evangelizing about) other singers' records. But all that would be a while coming. For the time being he was in his element, drawing large crowds of the curious to Grant's, people who came not to hear him sing but to catch a glimpse of the star attraction pushing red-hot records.

More important, he was beginning to receive media attention—even at this very early stage of his career. Not insignificantly, the first media he attracted was printed rather than electronic. Robert Johnson took a liking to him immediately; started writing about him in his regular entertainment column, even before Dewey got on the air; and established a friendship that would last for life. Johnson did an early story on Frankie Laine's "Mule Train" after Dewey telephoned him and insisted that he come down to Grant's record department the next day to hear it. Dewey was already in the business of promoting himself—a practice he would cultivate and fine-tune throughout his career.[42]

Dewey was also already in the business of predicting which records would hit. Long before Sam Phillips and Sun Records, Robert Johnson came to appreciate his uncanny sense of knowing what records would make it. Johnson was quite impressed, and reported to readers that during his visit to the five-and-dime Dewey told him, "'Mule Train is going to be,' [Dewey] paused for emphasis, 'the greatest all-time hit since "White Christmas."'" The song didn't achieve quite that kind of notoriety, although Johnson later noted that Dewey had sensed that the record would go to the top of the charts before others realized it. He was convinced that Dewey was able to pick hits because he had a love for the records themselves. Later, after Dewey went on the air, Johnson reported, "It's not just a job, it's his life. When he gets a new [record] he likes, he'll play it by the hour, call friends and have them listen over the phone."[43]

The "Mule Train" newspaper story brought Dewey his first local renown and no doubt attracted additional curious customers to Grant's, making him more popular than ever. Besides becoming a minor celebrity, his department was selling records in unprecedented numbers, mostly because black Memphians kept dropping in from Beale Street to check out his act. But it wasn't just the ordinary who were coming around. In no time at all the most famous of Beale Street's entertainment cadre was stopping by to see this unusual white man who was so enthusiastically promoting black artists' records. Beale Street musicians, who needed only to walk a few blocks to Grant's in order to make Dewey's acquaintance, soon appeared and struck up close friendships.

And Dewey, being Dewey, wasted no time at all in returning those friendships. He not only sought out Beale Street's best musicians but also began to saturate himself in the black culture partly responsible for their music. If black people on Beale were beginning to come up to Main Street, Dewey believed, then total reciprocity was in order. He started dropping in on Beale.

3

The White Brother on Beale Street

"In 1948 and '49, Dewey Phillips would have been one of the rare white faces you'd see hanging out on Beale Street," says longtime observer Charles Raiteri, who worked at WHBQ. "Dewey was already well known in the black community before he ever began *Red, Hot and Blue.*"[1] Of course, other white faces were familiar on Beale Street in the late 1940s and early 1950s, but apart from a few musicians, most of the others, like Abe Schwab, Jake Salky, or the famous Lansky brothers, were merchants who ran stores there. They were there, that is, strictly for business, and thus they related to blacks in a totally different way than Dewey did. He was neither a merchant looking for business nor a musician. Dewey just hung out.

Bernard Lansky, who, like Dewey, hit Beale Street fresh out of the army following the war, remembers that Dewey liked to walk up and down the street. "He loved being on Beale. He'd slap you on the back, wrap his arm around you, call you pahd'nah. You had to like him."[2] By the time Dewey arrived at Grant's, Beale Street—with its jug bands, juke joints, and wildly uninhibited night life—had acquired the status of a landmark institution. It was a kind of unofficial capital of black America. That reputation would continue to spread, especially among musical devotees, no matter what their style or background. Beale was known not just to funky, down-home musicians but to jazz lovers and the musically elite as well. When New York Philharmonic conductor Leonard Bernstein made his first appearance in Memphis in 1959, the *Commercial Appeal* reported that "the one sight he asked to see was Beale Street."[3]

Running due east, straight from the bank of the Mississippi, the famous one-mile stretch of Beale had been a magnet for Memphis's African American community since the first half of the nineteenth century.[4] Already attracting a small collection of free blacks before the Civil War, Memphis was the big city at the top of the Mississippi Delta—the only major metropolis for several hundred miles around. For the large surrounding rural black population, Beale Street was where all the action was. During and especially after the war, newly freed former slaves flocked to the city in such numbers that by the first half of the twentieth century Beale had become what the postcards of the era described as "the social and economic capital for Negroes of Mississippi, Arkansas and West Tennessee."[5]

Blacks always made up a very large percentage of Memphis's population, but it surprises many (Memphians included) to learn that by the early 1900s that population was almost evenly divided—black and white. By 1900 Memphis's nearly 50 percent black population made it the city with the largest percentage of African Americans in the country, ahead of New York and Chicago.[6] No doubt when Dewey Phillips arrived in Memphis in the 1940s the plentiful numbers of black people came as something of a shock for the young white man from rural west Tennessee whose hometown harbored not a single black family.

Although a large segment of the black population had originally come to Memphis from surrounding rural areas, demographics shifted rapidly following World War II. Just about the time H. E. Van Meter hired Dewey Phillips to work in the record department at Grant's, new, urban blacks were beginning to appear in Memphis. Driven off farms by mechanization and lured to the city by the prospect of postwar industrial prosperity, this ever-expanding African American community—what may have been the last sharecropper generation—was a huge potential market waiting to be entertained by both live and recorded music.[7]

Although Grant's, like most other stores on Main Street, may have been mystified by the large numbers of urban blacks who flocked to Dewey's record department, what was happening in Memphis was part of a much larger pattern that was occurring throughout the nation. The Great Migration moved African Americans from south to north, but an equally important migration shifted half of America's rural blacks into urban settings by the time of the war. Because of the availability of jobs in Memphis during World War II, the city acquired a large, relatively prosperous black population.[8] By the time blacks began dropping into Grant's on Main Street to see Dewey, Beale Street had become a black Main Street for the entire Mid-South. African Americans who poured into the city for jobs sought out Beale as a haven and sanctuary; for those who sought its comfort and camaraderie, the street was a friendly oasis in a desert of discrimination.

Early on, Beale was also a cultural headquarters for southern blacks. There was precious little to do for entertainment in the huge rural area surrounding Memphis. Music was an inseparable part of Beale Street—"the glue," one writer suggested, "which binds it to history"—and few whites appreciated that music more than Dewey Phillips.[9] Fascinated by the country music of the rural folk he grew up with in west Tennessee, Dewey was drawn to the same earthy quality of African American blues.

The origins of the blues are, of course, embedded close to the banks of the Mississippi River, which rides along under the high bluffs of Memphis. The river marks the western boundary of the city, separating it from its sister state of Arkansas. Today, Memphis prides itself on being the birthplace of this peculiarly American music, having been officially proclaimed the "Home of the Blues" by an act of Congress in 1977. "The roots of the blues," it has been said, "are deep in the Memphis mud."[10]

Because Grant's five-and-dime was located on Main Street, right off Beale, Dewey had only to walk two short blocks from the store to stand on the bluffs and look out over the mighty Mississippi. Most of the more important music came not from the river itself but from the rich delta that extended alongside it. Running south from Memphis for approximately two hundred miles, the Delta spreads out on both sides of the Mississippi, producing not only some of the richest farmland on earth but also the great mother lode of black artists who would drastically alter the face of American popular music.[11]

Whenever Dewey Phillips started looking for music (and that seems to have been most of the time), he found it at every turn on Beale Street. The music that attracted him the most was being generated by then-unknown black musicians whose reputations he would help spread once he went on the air. By the time Dewey hit town, the haunting melodies of deep Delta blues could be heard as clearly on street corners and park benches as any other variety of music heard in the juke joints and night clubs that lined the avenue.[12]

But even though Beale Street acquired a national reputation and had long become a mecca for black music and entertainment, most of Memphis's white population, even as late as World War II, never saw the famous avenue nor heard its even more famous music. Apart from a rare oddball maverick personality like Dewey Phillips or a few curious music aficionados, most of whom were color blind, white Memphians had no occasion to frequent Beale Street. Moreover, because of the city's rigid racial division, white citizens had neither opportunity nor inclination to listen to black music.

The avoidance was due as much to politics as to culture. Race relations, like everything else in the city from 1909 to 1948, were tightly controlled by one of the most powerful political machines that Memphis (or any other American city) had ever witnessed. E. H. "Boss" Crump, who totally dominated the municipal and state government during these years, regulated racial matters as he did all other aspects of city life. Crump personally orchestrated segregation through the discreet selection of black "accommodationist" leaders. By delicately manipulating them, his machine was able to control the black vote, maintain total separation of the races, and provide the stabilizing racial influence he sought.[13] After Dewey got on the air with *Red, Hot and Blue* he liked to evoke Boss Crump's name frequently. The comments were not always complimentary, but he usually provided a fairly accurate account of a man who not only controlled the city but had also been responsible for "cleaning it up."

By this time, Beale Street was reputed to be the meanest, most dangerous street in America. The wild life and general debauchery there were legendary. Nat D. Williams, who knew the street better than anyone, said that many black church people considered it "almost a sin" to be seen walking there.[14] Stories of its wickedness—many no doubt wildly exaggerated—abounded. Supposedly, Beale at one time had more than five hundred saloons and a score of whorehouses frequented by blacks as well as whites. One popularly circulated fabrication had it that a meat wagon was stationed at the end of the street on Saturday nights to pick up dead bodies. It was W. C. Handy who immortalized the avenue by writing in his "Beale Street Blues" that "business never ceases 'til somebody gets killed."

Just before Dewey arrived in Memphis, Crump had managed to change a lot of that reputation. He had come into power as mayor in 1909 by running on a reform ticket promising to rid Memphis of vices and calling for the elimination of saloons and dives. In his most widely publicized effort in 1940, Crump—assisted by Police Commissioner Patrick "Holy Joe" Boyle—not only cleaned up the saloons, gambling houses, and bordellos of Beale Street but also imposed racial restrictions and curfews on the city's entertainers. The police commissioner was the perfect foil for Crump's machinations. Boyle minced no words in his blatant, white-racist rhetoric: "This is a white man's country and always will be," he once publicly proclaimed, "and any Negro who doesn't agree to this had better move on." Crump was equally blunt. "You have a bunch of niggers teaching social equality, teaching social hatred," he scolded the editor of the *Memphis World* in 1940. "I am not going to stand for it. I've dealt with niggers all my life, and I know how to treat them."[15]

Crump's action, of course, greatly displeased Memphis's black community and left a damaging legacy for race relations in general. Practically all that the majority of Memphis's white middle class knew about Beale came from the highly publicized crackdown. The stereotypical view of Beale as Sodom and Gomorrah was strongly reinforced by the publicity Crump's clean-up generated. By the time it was over, many whites saw Beale Street not as the birthplace of the blues but as the murder capital of the world.[16]

Dewey, fascinated with Beale Street almost as soon as he arrived in Memphis, could have cared less about the restrictions Crump placed on the street. Indeed, given his generally dissident personality he was probably attracted to the street as much because of its bawdy reputation as its ubiquitous music.

Whatever the attraction, as a white man who was welcomed with open arms on Beale Street, Dewey's confident and comfortable presence there is as difficult to explain as it is hard to find precedent for. Most blacks felt that because whites controlled every other facet of life in the city during this pre–civil rights era Beale Street was the one retreat that black people enjoyed exclusively. B.B. King, for example, had gravitated there from Mississippi not only because of the music but also because "we believed Beale Street was ours." The sense that the street belonged to the African American community of Memphis, according to King, meant that "you could get justice on Beale Street, you could get whatever was available for people on Beale Street. We didn't feel like that if we walked downtown [on Main Street]."[17] The white community was essentially all of Memphis, but Beale Street was considered African American turf—what one writer termed "a universe unto itself." In short, white folks didn't hang out down there.

All white folks, that is, except Dewey. How, then, did he pull that off? How did a white man invade an area traditionally reserved for blacks and in the process manage to ingratiate himself with most of the avenue's most prominent black citizens? And all before he became famous on the radio? "They all loved Daddy-O-Dewey," says Jim Dickinson. "It was just that he was cool when cool mattered. He was the coolest person there was. Dewey could hang out on Beale Street and get away with it. [Except for the musicians], nobody else who was white could do that."[18] Dewey's Cousin Billy offers further explanation, pointing out that Dewey felt at home on Beale because of the black acquaintances he made at Grant's five-and-dime. "Dewey knew people down there because those people had been coming in to the record department." Moreover, he had established his reputation "as the guy who was playing the black artists. When he got on Beale, he just melded right in."[19]

Elvis biographer Peter Guralnick has pointed out that "Dewey Phillips was something like a roving ambassador from another galaxy." It was an observation made after Guralnick noted how well Beale Street's black community received Dewey, especially in the early days when he introduced the young Elvis to hot spots along the avenue.[20] Dewey was acquainted with almost all of them, having frequented most shortly after arriving at Grant's. Everyone on the street liked him, but it was black entertainers in particular—already drawn to Beale like pilgrims to a crusade—who made his acquaintance.

By the time Dewey arrived there after World War II the black entertainment venues on Beale were among the comparatively few businesses in Memphis owned and operated by blacks. It is true that a cadre of black professionals (doctors, dentists, and lawyers, many of whom started their own professional schools) practiced along the street during the late 1940s, but the great majority of its stores, shops, and businesses were owned by white merchants yet frequented mostly by a black clientele. Beale historian George W. Lee seems to have coined the phrase about the street being "owned largely by the Jews, policed by the whites and enjoyed by the Negroes."[21] That axiom, however, has since had a number of variations, including mention of the important roles played by the Italians, who owned theaters, and Chinese, who ran restaurants.

Following Crump's segregation customs, Main Street was strictly forbidden to most black businesses, but because Crump's peculiar version of racial apartheid made no pretense of fairness, exclusion was not reciprocal. White businesses were always perfectly free to locate on Beale. And locate they did, most of them along the top part of the mile-long stretch. Abe Schwab recalls the racial practice of the time. He should know it well. As the long-time (white) owner of Schwab's Dry Goods Store, he is the third generation of his family to run the business his grandfather founded in 1876. He has worked at the store, one of Beale Street's oldest establishments and the only one on the street now owned by the city, since he was ten. He estimates that by the 1940s, whites owned 90 percent of the stores on his block of Beale. "That means white merchants downstairs in the storefront. [In] upstairs [living quarters] there was like 100 percent black occupancy."[22]

Another unique segregation practice drastically affected the racial distribution of Beale Street's customers. Almost all of its merchants maintain that the closer a shop was to the top of the street, where it intersected with predominantly white Main Street, the greater the likelihood that store would have at least some white customers. Jake Salky's popular pawnshop was located in the second block off Main Street. He was among a number of Jewish merchants who ran pawnshops on Beale in the 1940s (for some reason almost all were on the north side of the street). "Those stores that were down closer to Third or Fourth street [three or four blocks away from Main] were over 90 percent black customers," Salky says. His store, however, had "about 75 percent black customers; the rest white."[23]

Lansky Brothers' Clothing Store, located at the end of the first block, had a considerable white clientele and catered especially to show people. There is no accurate or scientific method for determining racial balance exactly, but one might infer from Schwab's and Salky's observations that the first block off Main, containing not only Lanskys' but also the famous Home of the Blues Record Shop (only two doors down from Main Street and a favorite hangout of Dewey's and Elvis's) likely had something close to a 50–50 mix.[24]

One might also assume that even if a young Elvis were buying clothes from Lanskys' in the early days he probably never made it much further down Beale Street until after he met Dewey, which, according to all well-informed sources, was not until later. Stories persist of the young Elvis, newly arrived from Mississippi in 1948, hanging out in clubs and juke joints further down Beale Street, but there is little evidence to support them.

The argument over when Elvis first appeared on Beale will undoubtedly never be completely settled, but many locals, including B.B. King, Rufus Thomas, and Robert Henry and his wife, confirm that Dewey, with or without Presley, was visible on the street during his earliest days in Memphis. Stories abound of Dewey, like Elvis, hanging out with Howlin' Wolf or playing poker with Johnny Ace, even before he became the Mid-South's most famous deejay.[25]

Unlike the Elvis stories, however, at least some supporting evidence exists for Dewey's presence early on. Although substantiation depends on little more than the recall of people interviewed years later, some memories can be verified. Even without actual recorded proof, several important Beale Street personnel are able to be fairly accurate about when Daddy-O-Dewey was a definite presence on the street. B.B. King, for example, was still trying to make a name for himself on Beale at the time and well remembers meeting Dewey before 1949, the year *Red, Hot and Blue* began to air. King, whose recall is remarkable, remembers playing Beale Street in the late 1940s and also is clear about his first encounters with Dewey. The bluesman, who had not yet achieved the stardom he would later enjoy, told Charles Raiteri in a 1982 interview that he played Beale Street in 1948 and 1949. "Late 48, early 49—right?" Raiteri asks. "And Dewey was hanging out on Beale Street?" "Yeah," B.B. answers. "That's when I met him. I met him before I was popular."[26]

King did not achieve even local popularity until after he became a regular disc jockey on WDIA, which was not until 1949. Before that, when he arrived in Memphis from Indianola, Mississippi, he, like a lot of other local musicians, attempted to make a name for himself by performing as much as possible on Beale Street, generally playing Amateur Nights at the Palace Theater. I have checked his recollections of specific dates on a number of occasions, and they are always reliable. King says, for example, that he arrived at WDIA in December 1948 and began to appear regularly on the station in March 1949. Those dates are confirmed by the *Memphis Commercial Appeal,* which began to list King's name in its radio time schedule at precisely that time.[27]

Sam Phillips also confirms B.B.'s observation. Sam, who confesses hardly ever venturing down on Beale until Dewey took him there during the late 1940s, remembers that it would have been usual to find Dewey hanging out with musical stars Sam later recorded—B.B. King, Little Junior Parker, or Howlin' Wolf.[28] Significantly, however, B.B. says, "I don't think he [Dewey] actually put me in touch with him [Sam], but I knew him before I did Sam." Although Sam did not record King until 1950, Dewey was checking him out on Beale Street, probably when King appeared on Amateur Night at the Palace Theater.[29]

Amateur Night at the Palace, the hottest entertainment venue on Beale Street in the 1930s and 1940s, was a favorite haunt of Dewey's. The Palace, built by Anselmo Barrasso, acquired its much-deserved reputation because it not only played movies during the week but also provided a stage for big-name road shows that came through Memphis. Most important, however, it also served as home base for Amateur Night, a premier drawing card for Memphis's black community.[30]

Begun in the late 1920s, Amateur Night had achieved enough notoriety by the 1930s that it was carried live on Memphis's all-white radio station WNBR (later WHBQ). Starting in 1933, the show was emceed by the ubiquitous Nat D. Williams, a Booker T. Washington High School history teacher, nationally syndicated newspaper columnist, popular entertainer, and, later, the first publicly recognized black disc jockey in the South.[31]

Featuring a variety of entertainment, Amateur Night was just that. Taking its cue from New York's Apollo Theater, the Palace would put anyone onstage who had enough courage to walk out and give it a try. The $5 first prize was big money then, and performances ranged from singers and dancers to fire-eating acts and cool cats playing the dozens (a forerunner of dissing).

Williams emceed the show until 1940, when Rufus Thomas—comic, tap-dancer, songwriter, WDIA disc jockey, recording star, talent show director, and Williams's former student—took over as master of ceremonies. Amateur Night introduced Beale Street audiences to the likes of B.B. King, Bobby "Blue" Bland, Roscoe Gordon, Al Hibbler, and Johnny Ace to name but a few. It is quite likely that Dewey first encountered B.B. at Amateur Night because King was a regular participant in the early days and Dewey attended regularly. Struggling to make a name for himself, B.B. would appear as often as possible, not only to try to win the $5 first prize but also for the $1 paid for just entering the contest. "That dollar kept me going," he recalls.[32]

Both B.B. King and Rufus Thomas attribute Dewey Phillips's remarkable ability to blend in on Beale Street—and transcend the color line—to his closeness to music, especially the blues. "That was unusual for most people, especially a white guy," says King. Because of his affinity with the music of Beale, B.B. maintains that by the time Dewey did get on the air with *Red, Hot and Blue* in 1949, "he had as many black listeners as any other black disk jockey [on WDIA] had at the time and in a lot of cases more."[33]

Virtually every black entertainer close to Dewey in those early years agrees that he was color-blind; he was, in the words of Peter Guralnick, "transracial."[34] "When Phillips talked to me, I never thought about race," is how Beale Street bluesman Edward "Prince Gabe" Kirby put it. Gabe remembers Dewey dropping in on clubs where his band played. He'd usually come into the backroom or kitchen and have a drink "right out of the bottle with us" and "then hang around for the last set."[35]

"I didn't think of him as black or white," says B.B., who some say was the first to label Phillips "Daddy-O-Dewey." Later on, after Dewey hit the air with *Red, Hot and Blue,* King "thought of him as a great disk jockey and a person who knew what he was doin'." Rufus Thomas repeats the same sentiment. "He was the only white person who could go anywhere in the black neighborhood anytime he wanted to go and be accepted." Rufus, who maintains that it was "the unwritten law that whites didn't come to Beale Street," says that when it came to Dewey, most black people "didn't care. They didn't even think about Dewey Phillips as being white."[36] And how did he manage to break through the color barrier? "Dewey was not white," Rufus says with streetwise perception. "He had no color."[37]

Both B.B. and Rufus recall Dewey establishing rapport right away with many black musicians on Beale. In a city where blacks and whites were still separated as much in spirit as in flesh, he is remembered as that rare white soul brother who was not only accepted but also warmly embraced, eliciting nothing but superlatives from all who came in contact with him. "I always think of him as the buddy next door," B.B. fondly recalls. "That's the type of guy I thought he was. He was always a lot of fun, always a lot of fun."[38]

Dewey's remarkable capacity to win the hearts and minds of the black community still baffles white Memphians who remember what race relations were like then. One plausible explanation is that Dewey dealt with racial matters as he dealt with the other issues in his life—as unseriously as possible. Discussions, whether of race or music, were never grim or solemn, and neither were they grave or severe. His comedy always undercut adversity. Dewey seldom, if ever, approached a serious level. He could disengage the overly serious and deal with a potentially grave subject with the same inexhaustible, absurd buffoonery that had been responsible for his widespread popularity in the first place.

His constant sense of nonsense was severely tested during Memphis's racially difficult period but always seemed to work. Dewey was that rare white person who could entertain black people without being paternalistic—a cool cat who could be funny yet not condescending. No doubt the strong ties he established early on in the black community, especially his frequent forays into the musical culture of Beale Street at a time when other whites carefully stayed away, were critical to this success. For many blacks on the street, that early connection was the true litmus test for being a cool white brother. That alone was a sufficient enough credential to allow a large number of African Americans to enjoy the presence of Dewey's company and, later, the lighthearted humor of his radio show, even through the tough days of the civil rights movement when there was often little to laugh about. It helped sustain his credibility and maintain his popularity throughout his career.

Moreover, his early ties with the black community served Dewey's personal interests after he got on the air. It could be argued that his visibility on Beale—even during his early days at Grant's—was somewhat self-serving. In making regular appearances on the street he was perhaps concerned less with racial camaraderie than with drumming up black customers for his cherished record department at the five-and-dime. After all, Dewey told the *Commercial Appeal* in his first in-depth interview, his initial effort to get on the radio was "to increase his record sales and percentage" at Grant's.[39] That certainly seems to have been the case, especially after Van Meter put him on commission.

Even so, it seems obvious that Dewey's presence on Beale Street amounted to much more than hustling for business. He was there as much to hear music and immerse himself in black culture as to stir up potential customers. Charles Raiteri concedes that his presence on Beale might have been motivated in part by a desire to sell records yet argues that Dewey's evangelical passion for music was equally important. "He just loved the music so much, he's like a religious fanatic who wants to share their religion with you," Raiteri says. "He just wanted to spread this particular gospel."[40]

It is probably closer to the truth to say that Dewey's early appearances in the black community were a mixture of both business and pleasure, perhaps best illustrated by the regular drop-in calls he made on Robert Henry's place of business. Henry's establishment on Beale was a combination record store and pool hall—a perfect dual attraction for Memphis's most famous renegade radio star. On the one hand, Dewey popped in frequently because he loved to shoot pool almost as much as he liked to go to MSU basketball games. On the other hand, he came around because he wanted to know what records black people were listening to.[41] There was still no official tabulation kept of which "race" records were selling in Memphis. A regular visit to Henry's was the quickest, easiest, and most accurate way to find out what was hot in the newly emerging field of rhythm and blues.

Robert Henry was Dewey's key black connection. He was one of a handful of black entrepreneurs who owned several places of business on Beale, and his name was already synonymous with African American entertainment in Memphis. Early on it was Henry who came to be the major booking agent for black entertainers in the city, working closely with the William Morris Agency out of New York. He was responsible for booking many Memphis greats into the big cities of the East and bringing stars such as Count Basie, Ella Fitzgerald, Duke Ellington, Dizzy Gillespie, Nat "King" Cole, Fats Waller, and many others to Memphis.[42]

By the time Dewey met him, Robert Henry had a monopoly on handling black entertainment in the city. He booked not only the biggest of the big names but also those individuals still struggling night after night in juke joints and small clubs around town. "Dewey loved to come down there to Robert's record shop on Beale Street," Mrs. Henry remembers, recalling that she and her husband looked forward to the regular visits. It was, she points out, peculiar for a white man to appear on Beale Street at the time. What was unusual about Dewey, she emphasizes, was that "people didn't bother" about him being white. It "didn't make no difference about the color. He just loved people. And everybody had got to know him." No matter how often he came, he would always "just have a lot of fun while he was down there."[43]

Once Dewey teamed with Elvis, he also liked nothing better than for the two of them to stop at Henry's as they set out for a long evening's adventure on Beale. They would shoot a few games of pool before hitting other hot spots further up the street. Mrs. Henry points out that Dewey would see white merchants as well as black friends whenever he was on Beale. He might stop in at Lanskys' to talk with several of the now-famous Lansky brothers. She says that Dewey loved to absorb the entire Beale Street scene, including its stores and the people who frequented them. His ritual—after getting off work at Grant's—was to walk the few short blocks over to Beale, drop by Henry's record shop, and then get barbecue at Culpepper's, one of the best-known eating establishments on the street.[44]

Dewey favored Culpepper's place to Johnny Mills' Barbecue, just off Beale, the more preferred eating establishment for famous white entertainers such as Bing Crosby and other Hollywood stars who would frequently drop by during their stays in Memphis. Perhaps Johnny Mills', which had a convenient counter in the middle of the store (one side, of course, for whites and one for blacks) was too segregated for Dewey's taste.[45]

Dewey cultivated many close friends on Beale, but the relationship he struck up with Robert Henry would be lifelong. Whether dropping by his record shop or eating barbecue with him at Culpepper's, Dewey saw Robert on a regular basis. The two became so close that Henry frequently came by the WHBQ studios while Dewey was broadcasting. Indeed, it was not unusual for Henry to go to the Phillips's home after Dewey got off work. Dot Phillips remembers him being there frequently and says, "They would usually bring the barbecue home from Culpepper's." Robert Henry, she recalls, had the same frenetic energy that drove Dewey. "They could spend hours entertaining each other. You know he had to be a kind of a cut-up to put up with Dewey."[46]

Once Dewey joined forces with Robert Henry he began to connect with most of the major black entertainment that came to Memphis. After he went on the air he persuaded visiting stars to come up to the WHBQ studios and appear on *Red, Hot and Blue.* He would also emcee the high-powered shows Henry brought to town. Henry not only booked all the big-name dance bands into the Beale Street Auditorium but he also helped the entrepreneur Nate Evans bring those same bands to the Orpheum Theater on the corner of Beale and Main for predominantly white audiences. Blacks could attend but were required to sit in the balcony.[47]

Those close to Dewey say that he preferred to attend the shows on Beale rather than those on Main Street. For most Memphis blacks, kept systematically away from all-white theaters, these were the only places where professional black talent could entertain a black audience. Before WDIA went on the air, the primary source of entertainment and the vehicle for showcasing talent for Memphis's black community were theaters on Beale Street and nightclubs around town. Local talent and the big-name black artists Robert Henry brought in during these early days meant that not only Memphis's black population but also curious whites like Dewey could be treated to live black entertainers on Beale.[48]

Dewey didn't drop in on just theaters and night spots. If an all-black package show were in town—one with a lot of big-name entertainers—a favorite Beale hangout in the early days was Andrew "Sunbeam" Mitchell's hotel. Although it is true that whites came to dominate most mercantile activity on Beale Street, a number of special commercial enterprises there were owned and operated by African Americans exclusively. Some places served as home turf for the black performers who played Memphis; undoubtedly, the most popular of such establishments was Sunbeam's.[49]

Mitchell's was one of only three Memphis lodging establishments that allowed out-of-town black entertainers. Larger cities such as Memphis and New Orleans had all-black hotels—Memphis even enjoyed unofficial first- and second-class ones—but black entertainers were not so lucky in other southern venues. Most of the time they stayed with local families, a kind of "underground" living accommodation. "Hotel's out of the question," Rufus Thomas recalls from his days with the Rabbit Foot Minstrels. "No such thing as hotels, you know, expressly for blacks." There were families in every city on the circuit, Rufus says, usually for "50¢ a day, 75¢, that was the extent of it. If you got a meal it was a dollar." Even those who stayed in hotels had no guarantee of entry into restaurants. Most entertainers carried hotplates and cooked in their rooms.[50]

After a stop at the hotel, Dewey's frequent practice was to drop in on Sunbeam's other, equally well-known establishment, Mitchell's Grill. Located on the corner of Third and Beale across the street from Paul's Tailor Shop, the little cafe served classic soul food that ranged from ham hocks to pigs' tails. Regular dinners were served, too. Mitchell's chili was legendary. Ernestine Mitchell cooked it and also served as part-time manager and bookkeeper. She "had a big old army of pots," her husband recalled. "She cooked that thing full of chili every day and she just set it out overnight. Thirty-five cents a bowl."[51]

Later, after Sunbeam opened the Club Handy in the second-floor lounge of his hotel, local and out-of-town musicians would go there to jam after everything else had closed at 1 A.M., but first they'd go up the street for some of that glorious chili. Club Handy soon became the favorite Memphis venue of most big-name entertainment, which made the club a favorite of Dewey's. He was that rare regular white customer at Club Handy and would, on occasion, emcee shows there for an all-black audience.[52]

Some of the most famous in the business performed at the club over the years. B.B. King and Bobby "Blue" Bland played there on many occasions "for five dollars a night and all the chili they could eat." The chili ritual came to be de rigueur for every entertainer who made the Memphis scene. "Ray Charles come to town," Sunbeam remembers. "Every time he hit Memphis, that's the first place he wanted to get to. 'Where is Ernestine with that chili?'"[53]

Dewey liked to drop by Sunbeam's because it was one of the few places in town where both black and white musicians felt comfortable jamming together. B.B. King, who still refers to Sunbeam as the "godfather for the musicians in Memphis," remembers that when blacks and whites played together on the street the city's all-white police force would frequently hassle them. At Sunbeam's, however, musicians could cut loose. "Even the police knew Sunbeam," B.B. recalls, "and usually we had no problem, as long as we were up there. If it was out in the park you would always have some flack from the police."[54] The sessions at Sunbeam's would usually last into the wee hours of the morning if well-known artists happened to be in town. Dewey slept late, however, so no matter.

Even while he was working at Grant's he had plenty of free time, and when he wasn't on Beale Street he often tried to absorb its music through the medium which provided the vehicle for his own success—good, old-fashioned AM radio. Dewey had been an avid radio fan since childhood, and he continued listening after arriving in Memphis. Every time he and Dot got into their car, the first thing he did was turn the radio up "good and loud."[55]

Surprisingly enough, most music that fascinated Dewey when he arrived on Beale Street had yet to reach Memphis's airwaves. Later on, of course, when WDIA came on, it afforded an opportunity to hear Nat D. Williams and Rufus Thomas. Most music Dewey picked up when he arrived was an amalgamation of traditional formats, even by Memphis standards. Although there were some important exceptions, most of what he heard was conventional programming fare—the very type of conventional programming he would later help turn upside down with *Red, Hot and Blue.*

Memphis's broadcast media immediately after the war still bore a striking resemblance to radio's very early days. Most stations, apart from some important exceptions, were mirror images of the conventional music they played. Tied closely to the programming of their network affiliates, they engaged in very little, if any, experimentation at the local level. When Fred Cook joined the CBS affiliate WREC in 1950 as a staff announcer, for example, "probably 95 percent of air time was network programming."[56] Like announcers at the other network affiliates in Memphis at the time—WMC (NBC), WMPS (ABC), and WHBQ (Mutual)—those at WREC did little more than station breaks and local news.

On the eve of the Memphis music explosion the city officially had five radio stations. A sixth, KWEM, had its transmitter in West Memphis, Arkansas, across the Mississippi River and was thus technically outside city limits although it was a Memphis station. Other stations played mostly standard music when they left the network feed. The unaffiliated KWEM, however, one of the area's most experimental stations, had an unconventional format: abundant amounts of country and western music mixed with the newly emerging field of gospel as performed by both black and white artists.

There were other exceptions to the traditional format. Even though no one had attempted anything that defied social convention the way

Dewey Phillips would, several Memphis stations were experimenting with what would subsequently be called "black programming." During the 1930s one station in particular, WHBQ, featured short segments of "race music" that was directed at black listeners but used white staff announcers. Without actually labeling it as "black programming" (a phrase that did not come into being until later), Robert Alburty began the practice in 1931 when he took over as general manager of WHBQ, which would later carry Dewey's show. WHBQ did not pick up the Mutual Network until 1944, so Alburty had considerable freedom to experiment with local broadcasts.

Even without the name, the format has to be defined as black programming because Alburty was clearly trying to attract a black audience. He moved initially in that direction by broadcasting several black choral groups. The Le Moyne College chorus was given a thirty-minute weekly segment, and the Booker T. Washington High School glee club aired three mornings a week.[57] Next, Alburty carried the midnight convocation of the all-black Church of God in Christ, which was headquartered in Memphis. He then advanced far beyond the standard black music being played on the air by broadcasting—live from Beale Street (via remote control)—Amateur Night and the Midnight Rambles, both directly from the stage of the Palace Theater.

Finally, in what would be the closest forerunner of the Dewey Phillips experiment, Alburty put on a late-afternoon record show called *Jitterbug Johnny* that featured a white deejay who played black artists. Without mentioning race music, a man named Johnny Poor played what was euphemistically labeled "jitterbug music." Most of what he played was jazz, especially that performed by African American artists. His preference was for what was still officially designated as swing music, often featuring Memphis's most famous black orchestra leader Jimmie Lunceford or people like Fats Waller and Chick Webb.[58]

So it could be said that WHBQ had a musical continuum of sorts that ran from Jitterbug Johnny to Dewey Phillips. Whatever resemblance Johnny Poor's show had to Dewey's, however, ended as soon as the turntables stopped. Poor's on-air disposition and temperament made his radio persona the polar opposite of the always-manic Daddy-O-Dewey. For a man who was already a favorite with Memphis audiences as a bass soloist with St. Mary's Episcopal Cathedral Choir and the Memphis Open Air Theater (MOAT), which featured light opera, Jitterbug Johnny bore more resemblance to Luciano Pavarotti than to Dewey Phillips.[59]

Another Memphis station, WMC, also tried programming exceptions to traditional music. In 1941, WMC, the city's first radio station, apparently had an early precursor of rock 'n' roll with a fifteen-minute segment called *In the Groove* with Aubrey Guy. Reporting on the show in his entertainment column, Robert Johnson, said that it featured "what was then called 'race' music, . . . directed to negro listeners." Its format varied, but the show managed to stay on the air for six years.[60]

That particular show had been dropped by the time Dewey arrived in Memphis, but a few other anomalies were still around. KWEM, for example, during the postwar period had begun to carry both Howlin' Wolf and Sonny Boy Williamson, both doing live shows on the air. Sam Phillips made the historic decision to record Howlin' Wolf in his Sun Studio only after hearing him on the air in a regular fifteen-minute segment on that station. Each show featured the individual artist performing, but white staff announcers read all commercials on both and served as hosts. Each show was sponsored by the same product, King Biscuit Flour.

It was WHBQ, however, which quickly caught Dewey's ear when he arrived in Memphis shortly after the war.[61] Johnny Poor had gone into the army during the war and never came back. Alburty decided not to revive the show with another announcer, which meant that its black programming effort—never carried out on more than a crude and somewhat ad hoc basis—never became part of the regular format. Still, Alburty told me that he had "a solid black audience from the mid-thirties to the mid-forties."[62]

Jitterbug Johnny never returned to the air, but by the time Dewey arrived the station still retained a version of its quasi-black programming, if only quite by accident. This was a show that started solely as a practical expedient because of the war. Devoted almost exclusively to Dewey's favorite musical genre, black rhythm and blues, the program—a first for Memphis—came about because of a rather strange set of circumstances.

World War II brought economic hardship to a great many people, but the demand for race records was still sufficient enough during the conflict to cause Beale Street's Schwab's Department Store to begin one of Memphis's first full-time "regular" radio shows pitched to a black audience. Beale Street also changed considerably during the war years. According to Abe Schwab, it was declared off-limits to all white military personnel, an order that was rigidly enforced. Schwab remembers coming home on furlough during the war and being stopped by military police when he pulled up in front of his own store in uniform. "I showed them my ID, and they let me stay, but there were thousands of [white] servicemen who were not allowed on Beale, and that hurt our business."[63]

The store, whose motto was "if you can't find it at Schwab's, you're better off without it," catered to a predominantly black Beale Street clientele. Nonetheless, because it was in the first block off Main Street it also had a considerable number of white customers. Therefore, it tried to make up for lost white business during the war by increasing advertising aimed at black customers. As fate would have it, however, Schwab's traditional newspaper advertising was unavailable during the war because paper was rationed. The solution, therefore, was to turn to the radio and advertise by sponsoring a fifteen-minute show on WHBQ. *Blues Time* began in 1943 and ran from 4:15 until 4:30 each afternoon.

Designed for black Beale Street listeners, *Blues Time* featured almost all African American artists. The program's announcers were white, and the records they played came from Schwab's, having been delivered there directly from the record distributor. In addition to running regular commercials advertising Schwab's latest bargain-basement prices, the store received the added advantage of promoting its own records. Once aired, those records became one of the hottest-selling items in the store.

Radio sales personnel from WHBQ would visit the store weekly and take about twenty-five records to play on the air. Both blues and spiritual music was played on *Blues Time,* but Schwab was always careful to adopt the practice (later followed closely by station manager Bert Ferguson at WDIA) of not playing a spiritual record immediately after a blues record. On any given Saturday Schwab's would be packed with people scrambling for the selections played the previous week. When large crowds tried to get to the single record player and hear their favorite blues song, the only recourse was to put on a religious record. "It was like waving a cross in front of the devil," Abe Schwab recalls, his pink, cherub cheeks turning red as he breaks into laughter. "And that would clear the crowd out real quick."[64]

WHBQ continued to run *Blues Time* after the war ended, extending its life until 1948, so Dewey had ample opportunity to hear it. The program ended about the time he started worrying Lawhead to get on the air. There is no evidence to suggest that either Dewey or WHBQ wanted to replace Schwab's show, but it is certain that Dewey began thinking about broadcasting at about the time *Blues Time* was discontinued.[65]

And why shouldn't Dewey broadcast? After all, he already had all the necessary accouterments at Grant's—records, turntables, and, most important, a microphone that carried the sound of his voice to a public on the sidewalk and beyond through large speakers in front of the store.

Once he began operating on a percentage basis at Grant's, Dewey seems to have decided that even the range of the outdoor public address system was totally inadequate. Why restrict the sound of his voice to those in the immediate vicinity of the five-and-dime? According to Dewey's way of thinking, the public address setup imposed a major limitation on his ability to be heard. The entire city of Memphis, not just Main Street or Beale Street, needed to know about his record department.

It was only a matter of time, therefore, before the inevitable. Dorothy Phillips vividly remembers the night not long after their marriage in July 1948 that Dewey decided he wanted to become a disc jockey. He had worked at Grant's for a little less than a year. They were in bed one night, listening to the radio, when they heard Gordon Lawhead playing rhythm and blues on WHBQ. "As soon as he heard Lawhead on the air," Dot remembers, "why Dewey just sat up in bed and said that he'd like to have that show." He cried out, she says, as if announcing to the world, "I could play that music, and do just as good as he's doing." Dot laughs as she recalls that Dewey then proceeded to "go up to the station and just worry Gordon to death until he finally gave it to him."[66]

Luckily for Dewey (and also for Gordon Lawhead as it turned out), the WHBQ studio was located on Main Street, only a half block from Grant's. In no time at all he began popping out of the five-and-dime and darting across Gayoso—the little side street that separated Grant's from Goldsmith's, Memphis's oldest and best-known department store. Just on the other side of Goldsmith's was the Gayoso Hotel, whose mezzanine floor housed the WHBQ studios. It was not long after he discovered that extraordinary convenience that Dewey made it part of his ritual. His almost daily appearance at the studio began the practice of what seemed to Gordon Lawhead like a seemingly never-ending, frantic plea to get himself on the radio.[67]

Early requests for air time were flatly rejected. The simplest way to explain these early rebuffs is to say that WHBQ radio was not yet ready for Dewey Phillips. Perhaps it is more accurate to say that the Memphis and Mid-South listening audience was not yet ready for him. Indeed, before he could broadcast his first show that audience would have to experience a momentous shift in programming format. The shift occurred in 1949 when WDIA went all-black and turned the Memphis radio market completely on its head.

4

The New Memphis Sound:
The Birth of Black Programming

Before Dewey Phillips could become the Pied Piper of the new rhythm and blues hit parade, Mid-South radio fans would have to be shaken out of their traditional listening habits. That is precisely what happened only months before *Red, Hot and Blue* first aired. The breakthrough occurred late in 1948 when WDIA put the South's first publicly recognized black disc jockey—Nat D. Williams—on the air. His immediate success was so overwhelming that it caused a shift in the station's programming to an all-black format, something completed by the summer of 1949. By breaking the color barrier in the South, this Memphis radio station started nothing less than a national entertainment media upheaval. After 1949 stations not only in the South but also throughout the entire country began to follow WDIA's lead and adopt some form of black programming, often by adding black deejays to their staffs.[1]

Bert Ferguson, WDIA's congenial white manager and co-owner, may have quietly started a musical revolution with his all-black format, but he certainly never intended one as such. He began the experiment only because the station was going broke—and fast. He was, to put it quite simply, completely and utterly desperate.[2]

WDIA had come on the air in 1947 as a conventional station with conventional programming. Ferguson had tried classical music first, then country, and a finally a little bit of everything, but he was still unable to make even the slightest dent in the Hooper radio ratings. It seemed that Memphis lacked the market for yet another radio station. Going under financially and sensing the hopelessness of employing a traditional format, Ferguson decided to experiment with what was then still an unusual notion: black programming.

The concept had been around a short while, albeit in a scattershot form. WHBQ's fledgling attempt to appeal to an all-black audience in Memphis during World War II was only a temporary expedient and used a white announcer. Likewise, Schwab's *Blues Time* was established only because there was a war on. The program was run by regular WHBQ staff personnel—white announcers only.

WDIA's real breakthrough was the use of all-black on-air personalities. Before that there was still no such thing as a publicized black disc jockey south of the Mason-Dixon line.[3] The only other radio station in the South that had attempted anything approximating a black format was Nashville's powerful fifty thousand–watt, clear-channel WLAC, but here again the experiment had been conducted with all-white personnel. Although some commercials were aimed at a black audience, WLAC's entire format was not. Its experiment was nonetheless an innovative breakthrough, even though, like WDIA's, it came about inadvertently.

It began innocently enough when legendary white deejays Bill "Hoss" Allen, Gene Nobles, and John Richbourg ("John R.") began playing race music exclusively on late-night radio in Nashville. Though Nobles, Allen, and John R. were incalculable innovators, the real "grand old papas" of the rock 'n' roll revolution (the "Holy Trinity of rocking white deejays" as Brian Ward has labeled them), the task they accomplished was simplicity itself.[4] All they did was successfully persuade station management, which insisted on sticking to its traditional format during the day, to allow them to experiment late in the evening hours with shows featuring up-and-coming black artists. Until that time WLAC, like all the other radio stations in the South, had mistakenly assumed that its audience consisted almost exclusively of white people who would be offended by the boogie and blues sounds of black artists.[5]

Nothing could have been further from the truth, as was quickly evident from stacks of mail that began to pour into the radio station instantly. "People started writing in from El Paso to Richmond," remembers Hoss Allen, "and from Detroit to New Orleans and from the Bahamas and all over."[6] In no time at all, WLAC began devoting its entire evening programming to the new black sound. With its powerful signal booming throughout the South—sound traveled even further during evening hours—the station quickly accumulated an audience of blacks and whites far beyond its wildest expectations.

Thus, almost effortlessly, WLAC had invented black programming, which in the South in the days before WDIA meant having the white deejays at the station play black artists and, between records, read commercials for products geared for what white sponsors assumed black people would want to purchase—skin-lighteners and hair-straighteners, for example. Commercials for Royal Crown hairdressing, a favorite John R. sponsor, suddenly saturated the late-night southern airwaves.

Given WLAC's start, it was only a relatively short step for WDIA to become the first radio station in the country to go to full-time black programming. Not only were all of its on-air personalities black, but the station also adopted a format aimed solely at a black audience by playing nothing but African American recording artists.[7]

The nation's first all-black station cast a long shadow and would ultimately alter the listening habits of a great many fans, black and white, throughout the country.[8] Its immediate audience, however, was the Mid-South African American community, whose loyal listeners rejoiced in the fact that they at last had a station to call their own. Before the music could cross over to the white audience, radio stations in Memphis and the Mid-South would have to change—and they did so very quickly. Indeed, WDIA's most easily measured initial impact was the effect it had on every other Memphis radio station.

Those local stations saw what was quickly apparent to nearly everyone around the country. WDIA's record-shattering format made it the biggest commercial success in radio. Only months after Bert Ferguson made his switch, the figures were in. By instantly capturing virtually all of the 40 percent of Memphis's audience that was black, a gigantic slice of the market pie, WDIA's ratings after 1949 went through the ceiling. The other five white Memphis stations had jockeyed for a mere 10 or 12 on the Hooper scale (15 or 20 percent was almost unheard of), but it was not unusual for the city's newest station to draw as much as 30 to 40 percent of the entire local listening audience during the broadcast day.[9] Ferguson had discovered a proverbial goldmine—an almost totally untapped radio market—and he hastened to take advantage of it. With little or no accessible data, Ferguson was savvy enough to realize how important the new urban black audience was for Memphis radio. It was about time.

The large numbers of rural African Americans who had poured into Memphis following World War II found steady jobs that quickly translated into much higher incomes. By the late 1940s the city's black community was a microcosm of the nation's. A huge income gap still existed between the races, but the black median income across the country rose 192 percent between 1940 and 1953.[10] In Memphis, the increase is evident in the data WDIA furiously began to compile after its switch-over.

According to one of its first economic surveys done in 1950, half of the five hundred black families interviewed earned what at the time were considered middle-class incomes, between $2,000 and $5,000 annually.[11]

Black was never greener. Given that Memphis had a huge black populace and was located at the very top of the Mississippi Delta, the city was ideally positioned to take advantage of that wealth. Not only was there an untapped urban black audience in Memphis itself but also, and even more significant, three million African Americans were estimated to live in the surrounding rural area.[12]

After WDIA went to fifty thousand watts in 1954, booming its signal directly South into the heart of the Delta, it estimated that it reached an incredible 10 percent of the total black population of the United States. Nat D. Williams, with his usual facility for turning a phrase, wrote in his nationally syndicated column, that Memphis had become "the Harlem of the South."[13] Given those figures, it is mystifying that the electronic media had made no previous attempt to commercially exploit the potentially huge black listening audience. Why, before WDIA, had no other mainstream radio stations in the Delta attempted to capitalize on the market? Why were others not doing the same thing?[14] Such questions, of course, were suddenly the primary focus of all other station managers in Memphis and the Mid-South. Once WDIA pulled the plug the deluge began, and—as in most periods of rapid commercial transformation—once things began nothing changed quite as quickly as change itself.

Because this was a zero-sum game, WDIA's jump in ratings could not occur unless all other stations' ratings went down. (Although the black audience had never been accurately measured, the new ratings strongly suggest that many African Americans, before WDIA, had been listening all along to other Memphis stations.) The audience was composed of only a finite number of people; with WDIA now grabbing the lion's share of them, every other station took a ratings hit. Caught in a much more competitive market, stations had either to pay attention to the previously neglected black audience or radically alter their programming.

Among all Memphis's stations it was WHBQ that had to make the biggest change immediately. With its ratings already perilously low even before WDIA, it needed a quick fix to survive.[15] Minor shake-ups had occurred in WHBQ's managerial staff, but after WDIA appeared it decided to make a complete overhaul. In September of 1949 it hired John Cleghorn as its new manager and kicked Gordon Lawhead, a staff announcer, upstairs as program director. As manager, Cleghorn was in charge of the station's entire operation and so could not focus exclusively on program content. That burden fell on Lawhead, who had the unenviable task of devising some sorcery with which to pull WHBQ's sagging ratings out of the cellar. It is Lawhead who must be credited for working magic by putting Dewey Phillips on the air with *Red, Hot and Blue.* It was also Lawhead who provided the formula that not only resurrected the station's ratings but also took them to heights not even he could have imagined.

A transplanted New Yorker who had been a classmate of Bert Ferguson's at what was then called State Teachers College (later Memphis State University and now the University of Memphis), Lawhead had no master plan when he assumed his new duties as program director. He did know, however, that the station was frantic and a major overhaul had to be made in WHBQ's format. What he finally came up with was a stroke of genius. The station's only salvation, as Lawhead saw it, was to try to beat the competition at its own game. WDIA was still a small, 250-watt, dawn-to-dusk station in 1949 and would remain so until 1954, when it went fifty thousand watts and expanded its hours of broadcast. It signed off when the sun went down.

Lawhead decided to try and capture some of the newly discovered black audience with black programming in the evening after WDIA shut down.[16] By the time he took over as program director at WHBQ, WDIA had already done its damage, gobbling up the black audience and cutting deeply into the ratings of every other Memphis station. The aura of despair at work is still vivid for Lawhead. "I couldn't afford an automobile," he says, "and [deejay] Bill Gordon used to drive me home. We'd listen to 'DIA on the way home. We heard all those commercials on 'DIA. We knew that they were making big money."[17] He remembers that what now appears to have been a momentous decision seemed at the time to be a simple and logical one. "They [WDIA] had to sign off at 5 o'clock in the wintertime, or at 4:45 or something. I figured I'd go for that black audience after they left the air." To Lawhead's way of thinking, WDIA's audience was already listening—all he had to do was switch them over to WHBQ's end of the dial.[18]

That switch, however, was not to be as easy as it sounds. Don Kern, WDIA's production manager, maintains that his station's listeners were so loyal (because black people finally had a radio station that gave them a voice) that they would set their dials to the station's frequency and not move them again.[19] When Lawhead began to experiment with black programming he had the same problem Bert Ferguson had originally. He didn't know whether his effort to win a black audience would work.

More particularly, during the transition he didn't want to alienate the loyal, albeit small, white audience he already had.

Lawhead was convinced that WHBQ's listeners were not yet ready for an African American announcer. The solution, as he saw it, was to follow the example of Nashville's WLAC and make the switch to black programming less drastic by using a white announcer who would play black music. It would be the best of all possible worlds. He could introduce the new rhythm and blues sounds without hiring a black disc jockey; the music would serve as a hook for the black audience; and, best of all, Lawhead could still (he hoped) maintain white listeners. The announcer Lawhead initially chose to begin the experiment was not Dewey Phillips. He would do the job himself.

Dewey, of course, had been around the station for some time, bugging Lawhead for air time. At this point, however, the program director gave no serious consideration to putting a local yokel with a gutter mouth in front of a live microphone. "He would literally bring his records up to 'HBQ," Lawhead recalled, remembering Dewey's early station appearances while working at Grant's. "At first, he was trying to get Bill Gordon to play them." Gordon was at the time Memphis's number-one deejay. He had the after-school crowd sewed up but was, like his competitors, still playing conventional popular music. Dewey thought that if he could get Gordon to plug R&B records the result would be a bonanza of sales at Grant's. Bill Gordon, however, like almost every conventional radio announcer in those days, would also have nothing to do with Dewey.[20]

Although being program director precluded Lawhead from running regular record shows, he decided that doing this one himself was infinitely preferable to experimenting with the totally unknown, highly unpredictable Dewey Phillips. When Dewey first approached him, Lawhead remembers, he thought Phillips's idea was ludicrous and carefully explained to the pest that radio announcers were supposed to talk like radio announcers—something Dewey Phillips definitely did not do.

So Gordon Lawhead began his trial run alone. In the fall of 1949 he started a late-evening (10:15 to 11 P.M.) show, *Red, Hot and Blue.* The program's name was borrowed from the title of a show that had been on WHBQ since 1947 but on an irregular basis—alternating with shows like *Fashions in Rhythm* and *Dance Orchestration.*[21] More important, until Lawhead started running it in 1949, the show always featured conventional popular music, meaning absolutely no R&B.

Even after taking over, Lawhead gave listeners very little of the new, predominantly black, sound. Proceeding cautiously and following a fairly standard format, he introduced the new music slowly, using already familiar black artists at first. Louis Jordan, for example, was played frequently before Lawhead began to sneak in funky new material. "I think I tried to play about four rhythm and blues songs per hour," he recalled. Even then, he did so with great trepidation.[22]

Totally lacking confidence in the music selections he made—he knew next to nothing about R&B—Lawhead sensed from the beginning that he would never be comfortable doing the show himself. "The job was always a chore," observes Charles Raiteri, who later worked with him at WHBQ-TV. "He didn't like doing it at all." Raiteri, a former announcer, does a wonderful impression of a very conventional Gordon Lawhead, trying desperately to get loose and be hip while on the air. In his best deep "radio announcer" voice, carefully enunciating each syllable, Raiteri says, "Lawhead would go, 'And now, ladies and gentlemen, for your late-night listening pleasure, on this wonderful evening here we have one from Big Mama Thornton, entitled 'You ain't nothing but a hound dog.'" Raiteri laughs and quickly adds, "Poor Gordon, he was such a nice, quiet man; he was just as embarrassed as he could be by the whole thing."[23]

Lawhead's awkward discomfort came through loud and clear with every record he played, but he continued to plod along for about a month, allowing himself to anchor *Red, Hot and Blue* solo. He seemed determined to conduct the experiment unaccompanied, despite considerable uneasiness and not a little embarrassment. "I'd work all day and have to come back at night at 10:15," he says, indicating his dread of the show. "That was before audio-tape." The implication is that Lawhead might have lasted longer had he the convenience of being able to record the show earlier.[24]

Despite perseverance it soon became abundantly clear that *Red, Hot and Blue* with Lawhead at its helm was just one step short of a monumental disaster. The station's clumsy efforts at "getting groovy" made no discernible dent in ratings. Even after several months Lawhead was without a single sponsor. "I had to be feeling that I had no audience at all," he later confessed, and then added in a major understatement, "I didn't understand the black-oriented music of the late 1940s and early 1950s."[25]

In fact, it was Lawhead's unfamiliarity with the music that provided the impetus he needed to make the memorable decision to put Dewey on the air. It was a decision that came only after a long period of arduous soul-searching. What seems to have made Lawhead turn the corner was not embarrassing displeasure at running the show but insecurity about selecting records. Given the abysmal ratings, it was obvious that his choices were not drawing hoped-for audiences. What was needed was an expert in this new field of music—and that master was close at hand. Dewey, despite the station's repeated efforts to get rid of him, had not quietly disappeared.

Most people would have given up long before. Ordinary people, in a similar situation, would have quickly appreciated the futility of trying to get on the radio without any preparation to do so. It is still mind-boggling to recall that Dewey Phillips was put on the air—and in a choice night spot at a major metropolitan radio station—despite having absolutely no radio training or experience. The thought of an uneducated neophyte, his backwoods accent as thick as pea soup, walking in off the street and taking a job that would carry his voice throughout the Mid-South still seems as implausible as Elvis Presley becoming an iconic superstar just by walking into a small recording studio to make a personal record.

When Lawhead finally threw in the towel and hired Dewey, it was still with strong mixed feelings. He would later admit that the last thing he expected was for Dewey Phillips to become, somehow, someday, the Mid-South's most famous disc jockey. It is not an exaggeration to say that what started as a relatively modest effort on Lawhead's part to improve his station's ratings ended by influencing the musical taste of much of the South.

After Dewey catapulted to fame, others would say that they had anticipated his stardom. They would also at least try to claim responsibility for getting him before the microphone. According to WHBQ salesperson Alex Bonner, he was the one who had strongly encouraged Lawhead to put Dewey on the air. Bonner first encountered Dewey at Grant's while selling radio time there. According to Bonner's version of the story, he began trying almost immediately to persuade Lawhead to give Dewey a shot. "I suggested in the sales meeting that we go to rhythm and blues at night," he says. "WDIA was a very dominant station in the market, but they signed off at dark, so everyone thought it was a good idea." General Sales Manager Bill Grumbles, Bonner adds, also thought it was an excellent idea, "but we just didn't have anyone who knew that kind of music. And I said 'I know this fellow down at Grant's who just knows this stuff like a book.'" Grumbles, Bonner maintains, suggested that "I bring Dewey up to talk with him, and they got together." Emphasizing that familiarity with the music was Dewey's strongest source of appeal, Bonner suggests that the original thinking was for him "to work in the control booth—pick out the records and so forth and Gordon Lawhead was going to be the disc jockey."[26]

Bonner's story does have a ring of truth. He was, after all, selling radio time in the community and meeting clients at stores such as Grant's. Too, it would have been difficult to be anywhere near the five-and-dime—let alone actually inside the store and near its record department—and not be captivated by Dewey Phillips's outlandish antics. Still, it was Gordon Lawhead who made the decision to put Dewey on the air. Realizing full well when he hired him that Dewey was a wild man, Lawhead assumed that any shortcomings as a professional radio announcer would be more than compensated for by Dewey's familiarity with (and love for) the music he constantly hyped. Lawhead's final capitulation might also have been in part due to Dewey's inimitable gift for gab. "Dewey had that way of making you laugh that could disarm even the most sophisticated," Gordon would remember without consciously recognizing that he was probably one of the most sophisticated of those people.[27]

Once the decision was made, Lawhead still had the job of selling Dewey to John Cleghorn, who, as general manager, still had to give the final say-so. Even for an experienced radio announcer like Lawhead, it was not an easy sell. Cleghorn already knew better than most, however, that something radical had to be tried if his station were to survive. After all, he had personally given Lawhead the green light to begin *Red, Hot and Blue.* Still, he was understandably leery about Dewey Phillips and all too familiar with his famous peddle-to-the-floor-board personality. Experimenting with *Red, Hot and Blue* with Gordon Lawhead as deejay was one thing. Actually putting a human cyclone on the air was something else indeed.

Cleghorn, of course, had justification for his fears, if for no other reason than the fact that WHBQ was at the time owned by Harding College, a Church of Christ School in Searcy, Arkansas. According to Dewey's gofer Bob Lewis, once Dewey was hired Cleghorn was always somewhat uncomfortable "with the relationship of Harding College and Dewey Phillips." Lewis laughs as he points out the obvious anomaly: "Here we are owned by a school affiliated with the Church of Christ, and Dewey is doing his thing at night."[28]

Despite his apprehension, Cleghorn knew that WDIA's switch had pressured every other station in town, and he had no other choice but to hire Dewey. In the final analysis WHBQ executives realized that—like Bert Ferguson's experiment with all-black programming—they had very little to lose by giving Phillips a trial run.

On October 10, 1949, almost a year to the day after Nat D. Williams had broken the color barrier on WDIA, Lawhead put Dewey Phillips on the air from 10:45 to 11 P.M.—strictly on an experimental basis.[29] The Mid-South's airwaves immediately became a very different space. Little did Lawhead know that the quarter hour would quickly blossom into three full hours and in the process totally alter the Memphis audience's listening habits. Life would never be the same for a great many teenagers in the Mid-South.

Given his many reservations about Dewey, Lawhead was quick to lay down the rules in no uncertain terms before letting him actually open a microphone. Not only was Dewey unable to run a control board or read commercials the way announcers were supposed to, but his totally unpredictable behavior also strongly suggested that he would require constant supervision. Gordon Lawhead became the first of what would be many Dewey babysitters.

Dewey's major job, as Lawhead saw it, was music selection, which meant he was allowed to make all decisions concerning which record would be played on the air. As far as the program director was concerned, that was about it. Apart from determining the music, Dewey's role would be minimal. Every other aspect of the radio show Lawhead expected to control himself. He minced no words in making it clear that he was the boss inside the studio. Before they started, for example, Lawhead made a serious attempt to teach Dewey how to run the control board and then how to read a commercial. Once on the air he constantly stayed right by Dewey's side to make certain he followed proper station procedure. Dewey was to mind his manners, speak as clearly as possible, and generally conduct himself in a personal and gentlemanly manner. Under no circumstances was he ever to violate proper radio decorum. In short, Lawhead thoroughly expected that he would be able to carefully police and control the actions, if not the thoughts, of Dewey Phillips during the entire time he was on the air.[30] Boy, was he in for a surprise.

5

"What in the World Is That?"
Is This Guy Black or White?

When Gordon Lawhead finally got around to hiring Dewey Phillips to work for WHBQ he got one of the planet's greatest bargains. The man who would totally dominate Memphis radio entertainment in the early 1950s and whose commercial-laden show would almost single-handedly pull the station out of its ratings doldrums started work for the munificent sum of absolutely nothing. Strange as it now seems, Dewey received no actual salary when he began his radio career at WHBQ.

The bargain was struck only because both sides were happy with the arrangement. Indeed, it was Dewey who helped orchestrate it.[1] After worrying Lawhead for months for a chance to go on the air, Dewey was delighted at last to have his own show, even if compensated only by the privilege of plugging his precious records during the broadcasts. The plugs were no small remuneration because he continued to work at Grant's from 11 to 5:30 daily, even after joining the station. Peddling his records on the air rather than hawking them in the store made for a quantum jump in sales at the five-and-dime. And because Dewey worked there on a percentage basis, increased sales meant a lot more take-home pay.

For its part, WHBQ was content to allow Dewey to throw in a word for Grant's record department in lieu of giving him a paycheck.[2] The radio station had to be pleased with its end of the deal. It not only picked up a free announcer but also received an endless supply of music from Grant's, compliments of Dewey Phillips. The latter was a larger bonus than it might seem because in those days not all record companies sent stations complimentary copies of new releases. More important, WHBQ now had access to the hot new R&B material that Dewey began peddling on his show. "We probably broke every law there was," Lawhead says when recalling the story. "Nobody talked about payola or anything like that in those early days."[3]

Unfortunately for WHBQ, its super-bargain deal didn't last long. Once on the air Dewey took off—as Rufus Thomas liked to say—"like a late freight." It's hard to resist superlatives when describing the way fans immediately tuned in and turned on to Dewey Phillips's broadcast. On his initial show he asked listeners to write him a letter if they wanted to request a song. ("Write Me a Letter" by the Ravens soon became the show's theme song.) So much fan mail poured into the station that Gordon Lawhead would still become uncharacteristically enthusiastic years later when recalling his protégé's instant success; nothing in Lawhead's radio career was comparable to how quickly it all happened—especially the initial volume of letters Dewey received. "Perhaps about seven letters came in from his first night on the air," he says, emphasizing that these were only ballpark figures, "but then it was more like seventy the next night, and by the end of the first week, it was closer to seven hundred! It was a monsoon of mail." Lawhead could have added that he soon received thousands of letters a week and the show was sold out commercially—and that was just in the first six weeks.[4]

Dewey almost immediately assumed the status of a rock star, especially among teenagers. Once Elvis began to drop in on *Red, Hot and Blue* there would, of course, be mass confusion at the station, but even during the very early, pre-Elvis days, Bob Lewis remembers the necessity of sneaking Dewey out the back door after work at midnight in order to avoid the frenetic teenagers waiting outside.

So rapid and steep was Dewey's initial rise in popularity that after only about six months a radio station in Birmingham, Alabama, tried to lure him further south by offering $125 a week. WHBQ quickly had to make what is politely known as an agonizing reappraisal of its previous position. In other words, there was no more no-pay policy for Daddy-O-Dewey. The station realized it would be wise to double the Birmingham offer to be certain of keeping him around, even though most think Dewey would never have left Memphis and would have stayed on without being paid much. "We didn't dare lose him," Lawhead recalls of the quick adjustments the station had to make. "We had to create a one-hour country music show at noontime for him" to justify the unprecedented pay.[5]

A salary of $250 a week was huge money for Memphis radio personnel in 1950. Lawhead, for example, says that Dewey's weekly salary brought him about $12,000 a year, whereas "I was making, as the program director of the station, only $5,200." Other Memphis radio personnel fared even worse. Fred Cook started at WREC, the CBS affiliate in Memphis in 1950, at $50 a week. Durrell Durham, who was to direct Dewey's television show in the late 1950s, can't recall the exact figure but remembers making "little more than minimum wage."[6]

By the time Dewey left the station nearly a decade later he had more than doubled the $250 a week. Moreover, he received additional money beyond his base salary. As was customary with almost all big-name radio personalities, once *Red, Hot and Blue* totally dominated late-night ratings sponsors had to pay Dewey a "talent fee" if they wanted him to read their commercials. Dorothy Phillips can't recall the exact amount of talent money he received but remembers it being beyond his regular base pay.[7]

Immediate audience reaction once Dewey hit the air could perhaps best be described as a mixture of intrigue, exhilaration, and total confusion. Most first-time listeners remained glued to the dial just to find out what he was all about. Robert Johnson said that the most frequently heard comment was, "What in the world is that?" Once past the initial shock, however, the most significant aspect of the response—judging from a brief sampling of those who heard him on his earliest broadcasts—was that a great many listeners thought Dewey was either black himself or attempting to mimic a black person. At the very least, most assumed that his early allure was based primarily on his appeal to an almost exclusively African American audience.

A completely random sample of listeners indicates a variety of reasons for people thinking that Dewey was black. First, his unorthodox on-air style contrasted with the way "regular" radio announcers behaved. Before Dewey arrived in Memphis, announcers sounded like radio announcers were supposed to sound. Given the prevailing prejudices of all too many white southerners, most seem to have assumed that Dewey, who could barely speak discernible—let along proper—English, was black. Second, the race music he was so fond of playing was virtually never heard on other Memphis radio stations of the era, so it was natural to suppose that a black man had to be playing it. Finally, the explanation most people like to offer—and the one that makes the least sense—was that Dewey had a "black accent."[8]

The first two interpretations might have had some validity given the racially biased climate of Memphis, but the third was ludicrous. Dewey's accent was little more than old-fashioned, home-grown, white country.

He spoke with the thickest hillbilly twang south of the Mason-Dixon line. "His Southern drawl," the *Commercial Appeal* reported, "is as thick as a stack of Aunt Jemima's pancakes."[9] Apparently, only a small leap in imagination was required to falsely assume that Dewey's "southern sound" and the "black sound" were one in the same.

His country delivery fit so perfectly with that genre of music that Lawhead made Dewey's noon-hour show entirely country and western. *Phillips Country Style*, however, didn't last long; *Red, Hot and Blue* became so popular that the midday show had to be dropped. Nonetheless, while he was still doing the country and western show his accent and poor grammar were so outlandish that Lawhead briefly had another announcer read Dewey's commercials.

Despite his country accent (or perhaps because of it) many listeners believed Dewey was black until the following summer of 1950, when the *Commercial Appeal*, Memphis's largest daily, and the *Memphis World*, the city's leading black publication, ran their first in-depth stories on Dewey. The pictures of him that accompanied both features clarified, once and for all, that the man readers found so fascinating on the radio was indeed white. The *Commercial Appeal* ran a large picture of Dewey at the station's console and minced no words about what were presumed to be his intentions. He was "beaming his radio program over WHBQ at Memphis Negro listeners." The article added that he played "blues and spirituals, too, whatever Negro listeners like."[10]

The *Memphis World* indicated that it had learned from its predominantly African American subscribers that they were indeed excited about the new voice on the air. In addition, Dewey's show had "caught the fancy of Negro listeners through Phillips's zestful expressions [and] his 'punchy jives' between and during the playing of numbers." In case there was any question about Dewey's immediate popularity among African American fans, the black press reported that he had "gained record breaking popularity among Colored listeners."[11]

Once the pictures appeared and fans learned Dewey was, in fact, white, the next question concerned whether he intentionally tried to "sound black" in order to pitch his show exclusively for African Americans. Most who were curious were unaware that a number of radio stations around the country, just before and after WDIA's initial success, were beginning to consider the black audience's commercial promise and were already using white announcers to try and attract African Americans.[12]

The broader effort of whites to mimic stereotypical black speech patterns goes back to nineteenth-century blackface minstrel shows. In an excellent account of the African American experience on the radio, William Barlow has used the term *racial ventriloquy,* and he points out that it worked both ways.[13] Some of the earliest black deejays, for example, would try to "sound white" long before whites tried to sound black. Because prejudiced ears expected all African Americans to sound alike, some blacks had to "work at fake accents" and "learn to talk as white people believed Negroes talked."[14]

Even when whites were successful at sounding black, however, their intentions were not always certain. Without trying to do so, white announcers who first played black R&B on WLAC in Nashville, for example, confused many in their audiences. John R. always insisted that even though he had never attempted to sound black on the air, many listeners thought he was. "I had people come into the radio station . . . They'd say: 'I'm looking for John R.' and I'd say, 'You found him, man.' Their mouth would fly open. 'You?'"[15]

Dewey's case is especially puzzling because he never gave the slightest indication of what he would do once he got on the air. Given the subtle and slippery nature of measuring an individual's intentions, about all one can do is turn to those who knew the person best. For Dewey, however, this is a dead-end street; there is very little agreement about what he intended.

Some closest to Dewey—for example, Sam Phillips and George Klein—reject the notion that his speech was bogus. "He just sounded black," G.K. says. "He didn't try to. That was just Dewey." Sam, as usual, offers more: "It was not a conscious effort to come across as a black man. Dewey Phillips could not be . . . what he wasn't." If he sounded country that's because he *was* country. But a twang, Sam is quick to add, had nothing to do with basic intelligence, which, he maintains, Dewey had in spades. "He didn't miss much, man," he says, trying to dispel the popular notion that Dewey must not have been very bright because he slaughtered the English language and talked "down-and-out country." "He had a quick, quick, mind." Even had he wanted to, Sam is convinced he could have put nothing over on Dewey.[16]

Although most concede that Dewey's own unique version of racial ventriloquy was just Dewey being himself on the air, even that causes divergent perceptions of meaning, motive, and intent. Each member of Dewey's intimate circle has their own take on what went on in Dewey's mind while he was doing *Red, Hot and Blue.* Sam Phillips, for example, is persuaded that Dewey hadn't the foggiest idea he would become an overnight sensation; he was as surprised as Gordon Lawhead or anyone else by his huge following. Phillips thinks that Dewey came on the air intent on having a good time but not necessarily seeking black or white listeners specifically. He does, however, concede that Dewey's biggest fans were initially black, probably because Dewey played black artists. "I don't think he thought when he went on the air in the beginning that white people would even listen to him," Sam Phillips maintains. "He really did not. I just absolutely believe that."[17]

Charles Raiteri endorses the idea of Dewey's manner of speech being completely authentic, but he disagrees with the notion that Dewey was surprised by success. Dewey, Raiteri says, was like Elvis in that regard. Both men knew what they wanted and went after it with great enthusiasm. Supporting Raiteri's argument is the fact that Dewey—when still at Grant's—made a concerted effort to promote his R&B records on WDIA before trying to get on WHBQ. Don Kern, WDIA's production manager, reports that Dewey was one of his station's best accounts during the period he was at Grant's. WDIA would write up a spot announcement, Kern would take it to Dewey at Grant's, and Dewey would give Kern a record or two to play on the station, to run with the commercial.[18]

The effort to advertise on WDIA strongly suggests that Dewey was already out to get the black audience before he hit the airwaves. He knew his audience from working at Grant's, and because the black community was familiar with him the transition to the airwaves was quite natural. Beyond that, "He never thought about the color of his audience. He only thought about the music." When it came to the music, Raiteri says, with characteristic tartness, "He didn't care what color the listener was."[19]

Jim Dickinson reinforces that point: Dewey wanted a biracial audience right from the beginning. Dickinson maintains that Dewey's music—like Dewey himself—transcended race. "WDIA was playing black music for black people. WHBQ was playing music for white people." Dewey's favorite term for his audience, Dickinson points out, was "good people." And, Dickinson adds, "He called them that because that's who Dewey was talking to." He was not talking to a black audience or a white one. He "was just talking to 'good people.'"[20]

Cousin Billy Mills disagrees and contends that Dewey's on-air voice was something of a put-on. He insists that some of the confusion about whether the voice belonged to a black or a white man was likely because Dewey was capable of performing an incredible variety of sounds. Whether he was being Dizzy Dean or the scatterbrained Grandma, much of Dewey's success, Mills maintains, was in his ability to imitate almost any voice imaginable. "He spoke the language of the listener," he says.

"He could talk to you in any language that he thought you associated with." Billy, who knew his cousin well since childhood, says Dewey was comfortable talking like a black person. "He could talk country, or he could sound like a backwoods preacher—you name it, he could do it." Significantly, Mills remembers going along to several college fraternity functions that Dewey emceed in the early days. The job called for a fairly traditional announcer, and "Dewey just fit right in. He sounded just like he was supposed to sound."[21] Perhaps adding additional strength to Mills's opinion is that when Dewey did a noon-hour country show in the early 1950s he was not mistaken for being black.

Although it is impossible to determine whether Dewey purposely tried to sound black, it is less difficult, and far more important, to consider his ability to quickly exploit the success he enjoyed with a black audience without alienating a white one. That success was no easy accomplishment. Being a white radio announcer who sounded like a black person was no guarantee of fame and fortune in the South during the late 1940s. There is no question, however, that Dewey, for a few, was a godsend. Musicians like Jim Dickinson grow ecstatic when they speak of him: "I suddenly found that there was this wonderful place on the dial where you could hear this 'stuff' that was what white folks were not supposed to listen to."[22] No matter how enthusiastic the response of hip, young, white males, however, Dewey's act could just as easily have worked to his detriment with the public at large.

Many listeners in the South, noted Sam Phillips, thought Elvis was black when they first heard him—initially at least. That fact badly hurt his chances of being played on white radio stations. Ordinary ears were fooled and so were some musically gifted ones. Even the great Chet Atkins, hearing Elvis for the first time, was unsure. "He sounds black at times and he sounds blue grass [at others]," he said after listening to "Blue Moon of Kentucky."[23] Had audience response been the same with Dewey, he might never have gotten a start. Although Elvis had difficulty finding air play in the South because of confusion about his race, Dewey's radio show benefited from that same confusion.

As soon as he realized that many who heard him thought he was black, Dewey began to capitalize on the idea. Because he and Lawhead were already in hot pursuit of the black audience, Dewey knew full well that capturing at least a significant portion of it would be necessary for success. The unique makeup of his audience in the Mid-South gave him an advantage. White announcers mistaken for being black in other parts of the country were able to acquire large followings. Because the potential for having black fans in Memphis and the Mid-South was enormous, however, Dewey alone was in the uniquely advantageous position of being able to profit from it. The most famous white deejay who managed to fool listeners into thinking he was black was undoubtedly Wolfman Jack (Robert Weston Smith), whose real-life role was reprised in the film classic *American Graffiti*. Yet white crossover disc jockeys who made the most significant cultural impact were not on the West Coast or—like the Wolfman—broadcasting from a clear-channel station in Mexico. Dewey was located in an area of concentrated African American population, the heart of the Southland, the great rural Mississippi Delta. It was that area, due south of Memphis, which suddenly became the focal point for WHBQ's new black programming.[24]

Nashville's powerful WLAC certainly had a shot at the southern audience, but the station seems to have been reluctant to capitalize on it. WLAC demonstrated that both blacks and whites in the South listened to R&B records, even when spun by a white disc jockey, but the station never vigorously pursued its newfound black following. In fact, it seems to have played down the idea. The station's celebrated Hoss Allen, for instance, has confessed in a highly revealing interview that "management was a little embarrassed about this whole thing because they didn't perceive themselves as a black station."[25] No doubt a main reason for WLAC's hesitation was that the station was already a highly profitable business operation, successfully appealing to whites. Apparently, it saw no need to use its new discovery if doing so meant violating the traditional format.

WHBQ, however, at the time *Red, Hot and Blue* was launched, was practically ready to go belly-up. So from the beginning, Dewey's attempt to win over black listeners had strong encouragement from station management, especially from Gordon Lawhead, who was as anxious as Dewey to exploit to the fullest his ailing station's suddenly acquired success with a racially mixed audience. As soon as Lawhead realized that most who heard Dewey thought he was black he began to see WHBQ's economic salvation in Dewey's show. It was Lawhead, his eye on the station's ratings, who understood best the potential money to be made from a broader, black audience. It was obvious to him—indeed, to everyone at WHBQ—that many fans of both races were so instantly turned on to the show that nothing else was important. The station saw no need to fix something that wasn't broken. Dewey was, therefore, given free rein to pursue a black audience. And pursue it he did.

George Klein, at Dewey's side during this time, emphasizes that he went out of his way to appeal to black listeners but emphasizes that Dewey didn't seek African American listeners exclusively. George believes that Dewey intuitively sensed what the black audience wanted to hear and made a conscious effort to solicit that audience. He not only played the best of previously unheard black performers, Klein points out, but also programmed material of specific appeal to the black community. Most important, Dewey—unlike the celebrated Allen, Nobles, and John R. at WLAC—enthusiastically reached out to establish contact with the black community almost as soon as he went on the air.

The best example of the courtship was the strong relationship Dewey quickly established with the Rev. W. Herbert Brewster, whose regular Sunday night church service was carried by WHBQ. Brewster, pastor of the East Trigg Baptist Church, was the best-known spiritual leader in Memphis's black community.[26] Dewey had come to know him not only because the station carried his service but also because of his contacts in the black community on Beale Street. Dewey knew Brewster's name was magic among African Americans, whether spiritually inclined or not.

Brewster's name would soon become equally as well known to white listeners as Dewey began to chat with him nightly on *Red, Hot and Blue*. With Dewey's constant on-air prodding, Brewster began to invite all listeners, black and white, to Sunday night services at East Trigg.

Because Dewey loved to play black gospel music on his show (Sister Rosetta Tharpe and Marie Knight were two of his favorites), a small contingency of white teenagers became interested enough in it to take him up on the invitation. It didn't take long before Brewster had a substantial following of young whites, who, along with Dewey, began to drop by on a regular basis, not so much to hear Brewster preach as to hear some of the best live black gospel music in the city being sung as part of the service.[27]

Dewey Phillips's role in making Brewster's name familiar to white listeners gives further credence to David Halberstam's observation about Dewey integrating the airwaves at night. At the East Trigg church, however, it was not just the airwaves that Dewey helped integrate. For whites who attended regular services there on Sunday nights, it was the closest Memphis ever got to physical and cultural integration in the 1950s. Intended or not, the consequences of Dewey's constant prompting of his audience to visit Brewster's church were definitely interesting. He exposed white teenagers to a segment of black culture many had never imagined, let alone seen or heard. Going to a black church was likely the last thing on their minds. But Dewey piqued their curiosity by playing black gospel music and reinforcing Brewster's Sunday night invitation with the promise of hearing that music live.

The integrated Sunday night assemblies were unprecedented events in the racially stratified city of Memphis before the civil rights era. Even now, many Memphians are shocked to learn that a small but respectable number of white teenagers attended black church services in their city during the early 1950s.

Nonetheless, both of Dewey's loyal gofers, George Klein and Bob Lewis, give firsthand accounts of such gatherings, having helped set up the remote control equipment for Brewster's broadcasts and then monitoring the show while it was on the air. When asked about the seating for the uniquely biracial Sunday night gathering, both men remember that it followed then-conventional customs. It was strictly segregated, but in this instance blacks were at the front of the church and whites occupied the back-row seats. "It was like in reverse," G.K. recalls. "The whites were in the rear." He estimates that the audience was about three-quarters black and one-quarter white. Lewis is more specific: "[Whites] were usually in the left-rear quadrant of the church." Apparently, the idea was for whites to be as inconspicuous as possible because they were very much aware of being outsiders and invited guests. "Nobody bothered us," Klein says. "It was very sacred. You didn't cause any scene."[28]

Most who attended agree that East Trigg services were wholesome experiences because both blacks and whites were happy with the arrangement. Dewey's white listeners could always tune to Brewster's radio show or listen to Dewey babble to Brewster on the telephone, and those same fans now had a chance to sit in on a black church service. Blacks in the congregation seemed equally pleased that young white people were interested in coming to their church for regular worship, even though spiritual solace was likely the last thing on the minds of Dewey's fans.[29]

According to Klein and Lewis, the music, not the ministry, was the prime attraction at the East Trigg church. Brewster had a national reputation as a songwriter and was the author of dozens of spirituals, including "Move on up a Little Higher," Mahalia Jackson's version of which was gospel music's first million-copy seller; "Surely God Is Able," another million-selling record by Clara Ward and the Ward Singers; and "How Far Am I from Canaan?" recorded by the young Sam Cooke, who was still with the Soul Stirrers. Services featured some of the best black gospel groups. Brewster's own group (the Brewsteraires), the Soul Stirrers, and Queen C. Anderson were among those who appeared regularly. Out-of-town guest soloists would also be featured, and it was not unusual for superstars like Mahalia Jackson or Clara Ward and the Ward Singers to make occasional appearances on Sunday nights.[30]

Above all, for Dewey's white teenage followers Brewster's church was one of the few places to hear music other than what George Klein calls the "standard Frank Sinatra, Perry Como stuff on the air." Klein recalls that most of his friends were sheltered from the exciting music of the black church, which made attending services even more alluring. "R&B was just coming on strong," Klein says, "and Dewey had spread the word that you could go to Rev. Brewster's church and hear some dynamite stuff."[31] For G.K. and the other whites in the audience, it was difficult to distinguish gospel from the music of black pop artists featured on Dewey's show. George's description clearly blurs the distinction between the sacred and the profane: "They had a whole band, man! They had guitar and saxes and a drummer. And they were cooking." From Klein's enthusiasm it seems obvious that he considered most services to be not much different from the rock 'n' roll shows he and Dewey would take in on Beale Street. "For us, it was like we were seeing Jackie Wilson, or James Brown or the Drifters or somebody. When it cranked up, everybody got into it."[32]

Bob Lewis, whose father was a Christian minister, breaks into a wry smile as he underscores what enticed whites to the services. Speaking with firm determination to keep the record straight, he emphasizes that few were present for reasons of traditional religious devotion. "It was a groovy 'in' thing to go out to East Trigg Baptist," Lewis says, remembering the mood of the crowd. For a certain segment of the white community, especially Dewey's young teenage listeners, "that used to be date night. A lot of young whites used to come with their dates." The largest crowds would appear whenever a guest soloist was in town. The one Lewis remembers most was Queen C. Anderson: "Big huge woman. She was a tremendous voice."[33]

Music was the primary allure of East Trigg Baptist Church, but most who attended meant no religious disrespect. As might be expected, the law of unintended consequences was at work. Some who came for the music and show found themselves remaining for the entire service, spellbound by Brewster's powerful message and mesmerizing voice. That may have been what Brewster intended. He would often observe, "So many people will listen to a song when they won't listen to a sermon," or, "If singing a song too slow puts them to sleep, pick it up."[34]

Eddie Richardson, known in local deejay circles as "High School Eddie," remembers driving over to the church with a carload of friends to hear the music—the primary attraction at East Trigg. Once there, however, he would frequently experience much more. In retelling the story he sounds a good deal like one of Brewster's parishioners. Regular church, for Richardson, was "an obligation," but at East Trigg "you really felt like you were getting religion—the spirit would move you!"[35]

Brewster's sermons, never completely divorced from the music, were almost always spiked with "exclamations that would come from the organ," Lewis recalls. "You know, ba-loom! when he'd make a point." Brewster was always animated during a sermon, a phenomenon the white, middle-class, teenaged visitors seldom witnessed in their own religious services. "He'd bring the whole church to its feet," High School Eddie remembers. "Put 'em off the air because of people shouting and jumping up and down in the aisle, accidentally pulling plugs out of the wall."[36]

Over the years Dewey and Brewster became close friends. Sunday evening was the only night *Red, Hot and Blue* was not on the air, so whenever possible Dewey and Dot Phillips attended services at East Trigg. Most of Brewster's parishioners were delighted to see them and would crowd around Dewey after the service, treating him like a celebrity. "The church was usually full by the time we got there, and we would just take a seat in the back," Dot Phillips recalls. "But Rev. Brewster would always acknowledge that we were there." She always enjoyed hearing sermons, "and, of course, you just couldn't beat the singing that went on."[37]

At the time, Dewey was by far the most famous white person at the East Trigg Sunday night service, but that was only because a young white teenager in the audience, who spent many a Sunday enjoying the church's gospel choir, was still totally unknown. Elvis Presley, whenever he could do so, attended East Trigg regularly, particularly to hear Queen C. Anderson and the Brewsteraires. He ranked gospel music alongside rock 'n' roll. Some have speculated that he may have even preferred gospel, as evidenced by his love of the music, the songs he would record, and his extensive gospel record collection.

Elvis took advantage of every opportunity to hear black gospel. When younger, he had been drawn to the concerts at Memphis's Ellis Auditorium, where he became devoted to groups like the Blackwood Brothers, the Soul Stirrers, and the Spirit of Memphis quartet. George Klein once called Brother Theo Wade, WDIA's top gospel deejay and also the Spirit of Memphis manager, to arrange for the group to come to Graceland as a surprise for one of Elvis's birthday parties. Plans changed at the last minute, however, and the event never occurred.[38] In order to attend East Trigg Baptist, Elvis would sometimes sneak away from his own church, the First Assembly of God, with his girlfriend Dixie Locke. Even if he had to miss a service he would try to tune in for its broadcast on WHBQ.[39]

Before Elvis could achieve even local fame, however, Dewey would first have to bring the races closer together musically. He would do so not only by continuing to solidify his rapidly growing black audience but also by making the black R&B artists he was so fond of playing into the mainstream music of his many white fans.

The official WHBQ publicity shot of the station's new star. (Charles Raiteri)

Dewey in uniform during
World War II. (Betty Kirby)

Dorothy (Dot) Phillips, high school
graduation. (Betty Kirby)

The photograph that the *Commercial Appeal* ran with its first story on Dewey, June 9, 1950. (Special Collections, University of Memphis Library)

The Chisca Hotel, 272 South Main Street, home of *Red, Hot and Blue* after 1953. (Robert Dye)

Dewey, as emcee, onstage with Lionel Hampton at the Handy Theater, early 1950s. (Dorothy Phillips Collection)

Dewey and Elvis in their favorite store, Lansky Brothers' on Beale. (Bernard J. Lansky Collection)

With Elvis at the Russwood Park concert, July 4, 1956. (Vassar Slate)

Dewey, Elvis, and Joe Cuoghi at Poplar (Pop) Tunes. The date on the box is incorrect; "1953" was written on an older box of records on which they happened to lean. (Dorothy Phillips Collection)

Dewey, Elvis, and Judy Crainer, the Memphis State College yearbook editor, doing their part, trying to obtain university status for MSC, 1956–57. (Special Collections, University of Memphis Library)

George Klein with his high school classmate, Elvis Presley. (George Klein)

Dewey, backstage with Patti Page during her appearance at Lowe's Theater in downtown Memphis, where she was promoting a film. (Dorothy Phillips Collection)

6

Racial Cross-Pollination:
Black and White Together

Getting Elvis and other white listeners to Herbert Brewster's church wasn't the only way Dewey Phillips brought the races closer together. Equally important was strengthening his bonds with the black community by continuing to maintain a strong physical presence in it. Whether appearing at a black baseball league game or attending a musical show on Beale Street (he even liked to leap onstage occasionally at the Hippodrome to introduce an act), Memphis's most popular deejay continued to firm up his following among African Americans by demonstrating that he enjoyed nothing more than being seen on Beale.[1] "Dewey would walk down Beale Street and you would think that the President of the United States was coming," Dot Phillips recalls. As if to confirm his strong following in the black community, she points out that after his first automobile accident, "There were as many blacks as whites who came to see Dewey in the hospital." So many people of both races sent flowers that Baptist Hospital had to call the station and ask fans to stop because there was no more space for the bouquets in Dewey's hospital room.[2]

Max and Betty Carruthers, Dewey's old friends from Adamsville, also remember that black people flocked around him each time he appeared in public. All of this is significant because before his television program, which came later in his career, Dewey acquired recognition strictly from his radio show and frequent appearances at predominantly black functions. "Whenever we'd go out with him to the clubs and restaurants," Betty Carruthers says, "why the black people would always come up to him—they all knew him—and it wouldn't be anytime they'd be swarming all around him." Max Carruthers remembers driving down Beale with Dewey in a convertible, its top down. "Everybody would be hollerin' at him, and he'd be hollerin' at them. Seemed like every black person on Beale Street knew him."[3]

By the early 1950s Dewey's renown on the famous street had achieved near-mythic proportions. Admirers he picked up in Grant's, at Henry's Record Shop, or at Culpepper's made him a familiar figure along the avenue. Once he became a regular on the air—heard as well as seen—he achieved the status of a Beale Street icon, a standing in the black community usually reserved for musical or stage stars.

That *Red, Hot and Blue* had been a mainstay among Memphis blacks since its inception in 1949 is as uncontestable as it is understandable. That it continued to increase in popularity among African Americans even after 1954, however, is astonishing and a dramatic testament to Dewey's staying popularity in the black community. It was in 1954 that WDIA boosted its signal from 250 to fifty thousand watts and extended its day of all-black broadcasting into the evening hours, making the station Dewey's number-one late-night competitor. WDIA's production manager Don Kern, whose job it was to keep a close watch on ratings, likes to brag that after the switch many loyal fans would usually stay with WDIA into the evening hours. Nonetheless, even Kern recognizes that *Red, Hot and Blue* almost always came out on top, a feat even more remarkable considering that Kern put his hottest deejays, Rufus Thomas and Martha Jean "the Queen" Steinberg, on the air opposite Dewey. "He had a tremendous black following. As strong as our station ever got," Kern readily admits, throwing up his arms as if in capitulation. "Dewey Phillips and WHBQ outrated everything that WDIA ever had on at night."[4]

Dewey's continued following on the radio and presence in the black community were symbiotically reinforced each time he made a personal appearance at one of the big musical revues that came to town. After first plugging the revue on his show, he would often check out the last part of its late show personally by heading straight down to Beale Street as soon as he got off the air at midnight, often accompanied by his constant sidekick George Klein. G.K. remembers going many times to black package shows at the Hippodrome (later, the Club Ebony) on Beale Street, where he and Dewey would always be slipped in through the back door.

All-black package musical revues were brought to town by various promoters, whether Robert Henry, one of the record companies, or local theaters, and would feature up-and-coming artists such as Chuck Berry, Little Richard, Ruth Brown, Ivory Joe Hunter, the Coasters, the Drifters,

LaVern Baker, Muddy Waters, Etta James, the Clovers, the Moonglows, Roy Hamilton, or Billy Eckstein. Dewey's reception at the all-black show was usually even more enthusiastic than it was when he appeared in front of white audiences.

"Dewey would be noticed by the promoter almost as soon as we walked in," Klein remembers excitedly, "because he would plug their shows, and they would make a big deal out of that." When the emcee introduced him to the all-black audience he would usually break up the place. "That crowd loved him" so much so that it was difficult getting away after a show. Both G.K. and Sam Phillips remember how time-consuming it was to get into stage shows on Beale Street with Dewey because every black person there wanted to talk to him. After parking the car, Sam recalls, "it would take Dewey a long time to talk to everybody." G.K. adds, "He would just be surrounded by fans hanging out on the street even after the show broke up."[5]

Dewey's connection to Beale Street was not confined to late-night hours. Unquestionably, his highest profile there came after he began to work part time during the day at his favorite establishment, the Home of the Blues Record Shop just a few stores down from the corner of Main and Beale. The Home of the Blues was run by Reuben Cherry, a colorful and somewhat eccentric Jewish merchant who also maintained a close association with the local entertainment community by regularly attending the Variety Club of Memphis, a popular bar frequented by local celebrities and big-name, out-of-town stars who happened to be passing through.[6]

The Home of the Blues was a natural magnet for Dewey Phillips not only because the store was located on Beale Street but also because of its proprietor's oddball personality. Reuben Cherry was another one of a kind, and his unconventional appearance and bizarre behavior made him as fascinating to Dewey as Dewey was to Reuben. The two men were drawn to each other like rowdy youngsters on a playground. They would be lifetime bosom buddies.

Like Dewey, Reuben seemed to have been fabricated by an imaginative Hollywood director. With huge, hornrimmed glasses, a beaming smile, and a constant proclivity for practical jokes and off-color humor, he resembled nothing so much as a poor man's Groucho Marx. His store contained an assortment of relics gathered from the "Fun Shop," the local depository of practical jokes located only a few blocks away on Madison Avenue. He also had a homemade pornography collection featuring nude pictures of downtown prostitutes. On occasion he could make himself the butt of his own jokes. Jim Dickinson, who signed his first recording contract with Reuben's Home of the Blues label, says that Reuben had "one leather-bound book that said 'The Sex Life of Reuben Cherry,' and you opened it up and it was blank!"[7]

The friendship went back to Dewey's earliest days on Beale. Reuben Cherry, like Sam Phillips, was a kind of early mentor and role model for the country boy in the big city long before he became a radio star. Dewey, newly arrived, was still uncertain in Memphis. Reuben strongly encouraged his radio career, and after quitting his job at Grant's Dewey began to hang out with him during the daytime and broadcast on WHBQ at night. "He was sort of Dewey's alter ego at that point in time," Bob Lewis says, recalling that in the early days when he worked with Dewey at the station Reuben was one of the few people who "could come and go as he pleased in the control room."[8]

Even before Dewey, the Home of the Blues Record Shop was common ground for the black and white communities of Memphis because it was one of the few business establishments on Beale frequented by both races. Such mixing, rare in Memphis, was due in part to Reuben's open, easy-going personality and in part because of the record store's location. It was at 107 Beale, half a block off Main Street, the favorite shopping thoroughfare for most white Memphians. By the time Dewey arrived, Reuben had converted the Home of the Blues into a place that reflected the aberrant side of his personality. He carried every record imaginable and even those unimaginable for most Memphians in the 1950s—the obscure and off the wall, the bawdy, and the weird. It was material that all other record stores in Memphis refused to carry. Reuben prided himself on having records not found anywhere else in the city.[9]

Upstairs, older records were still anachronistically displayed inside paper shucks and sorted in old metal record racks—all housed in rooms that had worn walls and sixteen-foot ceilings. But the Home of the Blues wasn't all antiquated. Along with old, strange, and bizarre recordings (most of which were 78s) were ones that were currently hot and presented in the sleek new 45–rpm format. Its ambience earned the store a reputation among the select few who looked for the esoteric, obscure, and lewd, but the hordes that flocked to the Home of the Blues during the early 1950s did so because Reuben also carried the latest up-and-coming R&B music. Little wonder that Dewey was so attracted. The store not only serviced teenaged throngs but it was also where Elvis Presley purchased most of his records.[10]

Furthermore, the Home of the Blues was one of the few stores in Memphis where whites could feel comfortable purchasing black music. There were certainly other record stores, for example, Robert Henry's further down Beale, but even younger white teenagers drawn to the new R&B sounds were more at ease in Reuben's. Most remember it as a place where both races shopped in open comfort, greatly facilitated by the presence of a black employee named Arthur, whose last name is unknown. Although there is some disagreement over Arthur's true function, his commanding demeanor put black customers at ease. The store was integrated in spirit if nothing else. "The closest thing you got to integration in Memphis in the early fifties," says Jim Dickinson, "was the Home of the Blues."[11]

Above all it was Reuben himself, who was in large part responsible for creating a store atmosphere that made for racial harmony. In terms of race relations in Memphis, Reuben Cherry, like Dewey, was far ahead of his time. Also like Dewey, Reuben made a concerted effort to keep a direct line open to the black community. He did so by writing under a regular byline in the *Tri-State Defender,* a black newspaper. Later on the Home of the Blues even had its own record label, which used mostly local black talent such as Willie Mitchell; for a while the label had big-name stars such as the Five Royales and Roy Brown after he left King Records.

The record shop soon became Dewey Phillips's refuge, a sanctuary during the day after an almost always wild night at the radio station. Dewey always got up late; he never ate breakfast before 10:30 at the earliest. He would then go to the Home of the Blues around midday, where he would hang out for most of the afternoon, selling records and pulling together material he would play on his own show later that night. After that he would usually go home to rest for a few hours before returning to the station.[12]

Dewey was always happy at the record shop, attracted as much to Reuben's ever-expanding collection of weird and wonderful records as to the store itself, particularly the many autographed pictures of movie stars. Reuben had made all their acquaintances, frequently helping them raise funds for various causes. He would usually introduce them to Dewey after they had come to town and made a compulsory stop at the Variety Club, which was both men's favorite haunt.

The club offered another rare opportunity for races to mix in this otherwise highly segregated city. Located in the basement of the Gayoso Hotel below the WHBQ studios, it was one of the few places in Memphis in the 1950s to buy a mixed drink (then legal only in private clubs). That enticement plus its juxtaposition to the studio made the club irresistible to Dewey. It became his primary retreat after work, even after the studio moved to the Chisca Hotel. Vassar Slate, the bartender, recalls that Dewey would frequently drop by at midnight, after his show and with a variety of always interesting companions—Reuben Cherry, Elvis Presley, George Klein, Sam Phillips, Jerry Wexler of Atlantic Records, Leonard Chess of Chess Records, or (on occasions Slate remembers best) the entire group at once.[13]

Once Dewey started work at WHBQ, Reuben gave him a job at the record store and paid him a modest weekly salary. Although officially at work, he did little more than make himself available for admiring customers. His name became so well known in Memphis that his presence in the record shop helped attract clientele. As with the radio show, Dewey appealed to both blacks and whites, making him the perfect host in Beale Street's most famously integrated record store. The Home of the Blues was always crowded with customers of both races, looking for "the man on the radio."[14]

Detractors might suggest that the harmonious racial atmosphere created at the Home of the Blues was less about ethnic equanimity than it was the business of selling records. Once again, however, it was a little bit of both. The store's unique exception to Memphis's normally bifurcated racial culture was a congenial one socially, and it resulted in convenient and practical benefits for all involved. Reuben and Dewey profited the most. Reuben had business from both races, and Dewey acquired a feel for shoppers' preferences and thus for what to play on his late-night show. Working daily at the store gave him an opportunity to observe firsthand which records were being talked about and which were being purchased.

But it was not just Dewey's strong identification at the Home of the Blues or his veneration in the local black community that makes him a key figure in the history of Memphis music. Nor is it the instant recognition he receives as being the disc jockey who aired Elvis's first record. Rather, it is the role he played in alerting a huge southern white audience to previously forbidden race music long before Elvis and Alan Freed. WDIA's all-black format captured a small but enthusiastic trickle of young white teenaged fans, but not until the enormous popularity of *Red, Hot and Blue* did that trickle become a flood. Dewey Phillips made black rhythm and blues (soon to be called rock 'n' roll) the new mainstream music for the vast majority of white Mid-South listeners.

There is no accurate, scientific way to measure Dewey's success in integrating the airwaves in the Mid-South; radio surveys didn't ask the race of the listeners they telephoned. Judging from both audience and sponsor response, however, whites as well as blacks were aware of Dewey's R&B records from the beginning.

The sponsors of *Red, Hot and Blue* provide the surest indication of the show's intended audience. Consider, for example, the difference between WLAC and WHBQ. The Nashville station, which enjoys the distinction of beginning black programming in the South, made no effort to cross over the R&B artists it played on its late-night show to a broader white mainstream audience. Instead, during those late hours most sponsors' products (for example, hair straighteners and skin whiteners) were apparently pitched solely to a black audience. WLAC neither expanded black programming beyond its late-night show nor made any attempt to win over the regular white audience with the new R&B sound.[15]

By contrast, Dewey Phillips made a concerted effort to capture the following of both races. He had no sponsors for skin lighteners or hair straighteners. Nashville announcers certainly knew they had a multitude of late-night, white listeners, but their sponsors indicate that those people were not their intended target audience. Dewey's sponsors, however, aimed announcements for products consumed by both races at all those "good people."

Doing so must have worked. From its beginning, ratings for *Red, Hot and Blue* were off the charts, which meant a large white mainstream audience was listening to the R&B artists on Dewey's show along with his black fans.[16] Even without measuring the racial makeup of Dewey's audience through a telephone survey, people (both black and white) in the best position to know emphasize that Dewey's following crossed racial lines. Rufus Thomas, who had the best take on the listening habits of Memphis's black community, put it in language that left no room for ambiguity: "He was just as popular with the black audience as he was with whites." Rufus is equally convinced that Dewey was responsible for easing black artists' transitions to a white audience. "Dewey Phillips played as important a part as anybody," he says, "toward the acceptance of black music crossing the barriers of the races."[17]

At the same time, Bob Lewis, assigned to screen Dewey's telephone calls at the studio in the early 1950s, has no doubt that Dewey had black as well as white listeners from the moment he came on the air. "He had a multiracial audience," Lewis says without hesitation. Although Bob had no precise way of measuring listener color ("blacks were not allowed to actually come up to the studios"), he is certain, using his intuitive—albeit unscientific—method of determining race by sound of voice, that "they [blacks] sure called in." In terms of pure numbers, though, Lewis says with the same certainty, "Most of his calls were white teenage girls. . . . Dewey," he finally concludes, "walked comfortably in both communities, white and black."[18]

The young teenaged crowd always made up the celebrated portion of Dewey's listeners, but judging from the vast numbers of his audience he also attracted older fans, whatever their color. Indeed, his show so totally dominated the ratings that most radio stations all but capitulated. WMPS, for example, a pop music rival, knew full well that it would never be able to attract sponsors during Dewey's nine-to-twelve slot and surrendered completely by refusing to hire a regular announcer during that time period. One keen-eared fan reported that if you listened closely to the music being played on WMPS during these hours, you could pick up the ominous sounds of an automatic record changer, working methodically in an otherwise empty studio.[19]

If additional evidence is needed, more than just Dewey's domination of the ratings confirm his transracial attraction. An excellent barometer of his appeal to white audiences, paradoxically, was the all-black stage shows he and Sam Phillips booked. One of the first they did together was at the all-black Handy Theater in 1951. The men worked with white owner Nate Evans and Robert Henry, the black booking agent. Following the old Beale Street Midnight Rambles arrangement, the regular feature in 1951 was a show intended for black people; a special midnight show was held for whites. Even though the atmosphere encouraged by E. H. "Boss" Crump and Lloyd T. Binford called for strict racial segregation for all public entertainment in Memphis, an all-black cast performing for an all-white audience on Beale Street was, in this instance, apparently socially acceptable given that there were two separate, segregated shows.[20]

Sam Phillips has told Charles Raiteri that black people lined up for blocks for the first show, but white turnout "wasn't that great." Significantly enough, however, when Sam and Dewey booked a show on October 24, 1954, to celebrate the fifth anniversary of *Red, Hot and Blue* with a "Rhythm and Blues" presentation at the Hippodrome featuring the Drifters and LaVern Baker, Dewey's white following was so large that the Midnight Rambles arrangement had to be reversed. By 1954, with Dewey's ever-expanding white audience, as many whites as blacks would appear. Instead of a late-night show for whites, the Hippodrome would have the white show first at about 8 o'clock and then clear the auditorium for a "dance for Negroes" at 10.[21]

All this strongly suggests that after five years of *Red, Hot and Blue* a more conventional white mainstream adult audience had turned on to the black music played on the show. It was that white middle class, not just devoted younger fans, who would be so important in changing America's musical tastes. The cross-pollination of music would never have occurred had the new music not had strong appeal to a much more diffuse white audience.

It would be worthwhile, therefore, to examine the broader Memphis music scene—specifically Dewey's relationship with the rapidly chang-ing record business—on the eve of the city's cultural transformation. The record business is critical to that upheaval, and no one had a greater appreciation of the importance of the industry than Dewey Phillips, whether hawking the new music at Grant's or attempting to proselytize to his ever-expanding white radio audience.

7

The Great Convergence:
Pop Tunes' One-Stop

It was an all-too-typical muggy Memphis summer day that July 11, 1946, when John Novarese and Joe Cuoghi spotted an ad in the *Commercial Appeal* that immediately caught their attention. A record store, Shirley's Poplar Tunes at 306 Poplar Avenue, was for sale, so they went out "the very next day and bought it."[1]

It was a fateful decision. What John and Joe renamed the Poplar Tunes Record Store (almost immediately abbreviated by Memphis fans to "Pop Tunes") would soon become cozily ensconced in the Memphis pantheon of musical history. It acquired that unique distinction because from its beginning it was much more than just a record store and favorite haunt of Dewey Phillips and Elvis Presley (a sign prominently displayed in front of the store once proudly boasted "Elvis Never Left Our Building").

From its inception, Pop Tunes performed a number of jobs simultaneously, servicing a variety of markets and needs for Memphis and the Mid-South. First, in an era before the proliferation of chain stores it was one of the earliest postwar retail outlets exclusively designed for the sale of records. It was no longer necessary to go to Grant's five-and-dime or Schwab's Department Store (or, for that matter, to the grocery or drugstore) to buy vinyl music. Second, it also served a wholesale function as a convenient "one-stop" for jukebox operators and small mom-and-pop record stores, making it one of the largest wholesale and retail record distributors in the South. Finally, the store's most significant contribution to Memphis's music history was perhaps completely inadvertent. While trying to fulfill the needs of local jukebox dealers by affording them an easily accessible, ready-to-use service, Pop Tunes attracted not only Dewey Phillips but also a number of other Memphians who would soon make over the nation's record industry. These people were already turned on to a new sound commonly known to blacks as rhythm and blues and soon to be known to white America as rock 'n' roll.[2]

It all began with that critically important postwar musical apparatus known as the jukebox, which allowed listeners to drop a coin into a slot and hear their favorite record. The jukebox, which was primarily responsible for assisting the record industry's resurgence following World War II, spread prolifically and soon became as prevalent in taverns and drugstores as it was in dance halls and juke joints.[3]

Servicing the records for jukeboxes soon became a cottage industry in Memphis. Before Pop Tunes provided a "one-stop" service, dealers had to go to the various record distributors across town to acquire the latest material. "Most one-stops today are wholesale, not retail," Pop Tunes co-founder John Novarese remembers. "Back then, a man who operated jukeboxes—say he had twenty or thirty of them around town—he would have to make five or six stops to get the latest records from the distributors." With a one-stop, a dealer like Southern Amusement Company, the major jukebox operator in the Memphis area, could stop by Joe and John's new place and pick up everything needed at one time.[4]

More important, after the war Pop Tunes's one-stop not only serviced dealers but also attracted people like Dewey Phillips who were interested in what dealers were buying. Because Pop Tunes carried all the latest new R&B records, Dewey—already seduced by the new sound—had been dropping by "almost every day" since starting at Grant's. After he joined WHBQ he continued to be "in there [Pop Tunes] a minimum of at least three or four times a week, looking for the new releases."[5]

Dewey was always anxious to hear the latest releases but especially eager to check out the newest records of black performers. By this time—the late 1940s—some blacks who enjoyed the luxury of appearing on major labels were frequently being aired on southern radio stations. Almost all who did were the crossovers—artists whose enormous popularity crossed over to a broader white mainstream audience. Already household names—as well known to Memphis audiences as to the nation at large—the stars' fame rested more on their appeal to whites than to blacks. Lena Horne, Louis Armstrong, Nat "King" Cole, Sarah Vaughn, the Ink Spots, Ella Fitzgerald, Count Basie, Duke Ellington, the Mills Brothers, Ethel Waters, and a host of other black celebrities were the conventional entertainers after the war. Record companies enthusiastically promoted them, and radio stations throughout the South played them diligently.

The problem was that record labels almost totally ignored all other black performers, preferring instead to lump the remainder (especially those who did not cross over to the white audience) into a general category called "race music." More often than not, record companies shunned real country, gutbucket music, still considered to be a non-commercial product or at least one difficult to market. Even when new R&B artists managed to get recorded, they were seldom heard by a large audience. Southern radio stations, following the lackluster marketing efforts of record companies, either did little to promote them or ignored them entirely. The result was that the real, down-home sounds of cotton-patch blues were systematically excluded from the conventional white audience.[6]

It was Dewey Phillips who would change all that for most Mid-South listeners once he went on the air with *Red, Hot and Blue* by showcasing that largely ignored black music nightly. Dewey made regular trips to Pop Tunes because he knew the store was beginning to carry the work of new R&B artists, most of whom were starting to appear on new independent labels. These independent labels ("indies"), including Atlantic out of New York, Chess out of Chicago, Modern from Los Angeles, and, of course and a bit later, Sun Records out of Memphis, were beginning to proliferate in large numbers. They sought to capture the black consumer market that increased dramatically following World War II.[7]

Even with the indies producing more black artists, however, until Dewey blasted forth with *Red, Hot and Blue* most radio stations in the South seemed to follow a Catch 22–like logic. They assumed no one wanted to hear race music because the listening habits of the dominant white majority were still keyed to only traditional black crossover artists. Of course, because only traditional black artists were played over the air, white audiences were never exposed to the new music.

Major record companies and white radio station managers seem to have operated on two basically flawed assumptions: black people never listened to the radio and respectable white people did not listen to real, unvarnished, funky blues.[8] In Memphis, Bert Ferguson and WDIA were quickly shattering the first assumption, and Dewey Phillips and WHBQ were about to demolish the second.

Dewey was especially drawn to Novarese and Cuoghi after he began working at the radio station because Pop Tunes kept meticulous track of record sales. Indeed, it was one of the few places in Memphis that reported to *Billboard* and *Cashbox,* and those publications compiled national sales charts from that data. By operating at both the wholesale and retail level, Pop Tunes could affect national charts through the number of records ordered for the store's warehouse. Over-ordering helped push a record onto the charts. If the record sold, Novarese and Cuoghi had plenty on hand; if not, they could return them.[9]

More important for Dewey, however, was the fact that Novarese and Cuoghi kept their own regional charts and published a Pop Tunes Top 40 list. It was this chart that Dewey and a great many other local and regional radio station managers carefully perused on a regular basis. George Klein remembers going to Pop Tunes quite often with Dewey to check the charts. "He and I both researched our own music," says Klein, who continued to hang out with Dewey when in Memphis even after getting his own radio show in Osceola, Arkansas.[10]

When he first came on the air Dewey had used the Home of the Blues to get a ballpark idea of what was hot because—before Pop Tunes—there was no accurate way of assessing which records were being bought locally. He had also managed to get a fairly good notion of what was selling in the black community in the early days by regular visits to Robert Henry's record shop. Once music starting crossing over to a broader white audience, however, it became more difficult to get a handle on what R&B records were being purchased. The Pop Tunes Top 40 list changed all that.

G.K. and Dewey would sometimes first go to the record distributors to find out what material was being released. After that, a quick trip to Joe Cuoghi's Pop Tunes was all but mandatory. Once they took a look at the Top 40 list, G.K. says, "then we knew what to lay on." George is adamant that Dewey prided himself on selecting the right records, something Klein believes was critical to the success of his show. Dewey was particularly fascinated by the R&B performers on the new, independent labels, but even he had to be extremely careful about record selection. "You could be the greatest disc jockey in the world," G.K. says, "but if you weren't playing the Drifters' 'Honey Love,' or you weren't playing the Midnighters' 'Annie Had a Baby,' and the guy across the street was, the kids would go listen to him."[11]

During his heyday in the 1950s Dewey made the now-famous record shop's name as instantly recognizable as his own. Every fan knew it because of the constant prattle about "Jo-Jo" (as Dewey referred to him) Cuoghi and Pop Tunes during his three-hour extravaganzas. He took an instant personal liking to Joe, delighting in his friendship whether frolicking with him in Pop Tunes or babbling about him on the air. Cuoghi, as might be expected, was eternally grateful to Dewey, never failing to acknowledge appreciation for the untold number of customers who flocked into his store with the inevitable "Phillips sent me." Pop Tunes would have succeeded as a business enterprise in the 1950s without the assistance of Dewey Phillips, but it would not have been indelibly stenciled on the minds of practically every late-night listener to *Red, Hot and Blue.*

"Joe always gave Dewey credit for the success of the record shop," Dot Phillips says. "They also just seemed to really hit it off together," and they stayed close all their lives. Randy Phillips remembers that every time his father took him to see Joe at the record store, even though neither of them knew any Italian, he was told to yell out "Paisan" or "Pasquale" as Dewey did on the air almost every time he mentioned Joe's name.[12]

For the Phillips family, New Year's eve became an annual ritual of drinking champagne with Joe Cuoghi at Pop Tunes. Dot says that Dewey always eagerly anticipated the events, which are some of her fondest memories of the era. Over the years Cuoghi came to be thought of as an extended member of the Phillips family. In a strange twist of fate both men died at age forty-two. A picture of Dewey and Joe was prominent in the Phillips living room in Adamsville, Tennessee, until Dot abandoned the home to enter a nursing facility.[13]

On the air, Dewey insisted that fans could conveniently purchase, at either Pop Tunes or Home of the Blues, any record they wanted, a point some thought he hammered home after practically every record played. Both stores advertised on the station, but, as was often the case with Dewey's favorite sponsors, his perpetual plugs, most often during segments when they were not sponsoring his show, were generous to the point of suspicion. Many fans assumed that both proprietors were personally lining Dewey's pocket.

In fact, Dewey's relationship with Pop Tunes was like that with the Home of the Blues. In both instances his presence made for great self-promotion and worked wonderfully well for the businesses. In addition to working there, Dewey also did regular remotes from Pop Tunes, sometimes from a trailer in front of the store and sometimes from a corner of the store itself. The trailer had large windows so people could wave from their passing cars while he broadcasted.[14]

Novarese says that Dewey was never paid an actual salary, but after awhile Cuoghi, like Reuben Cherry, starting giving him a little money. Dot Phillips cannot recall exactly how much he received at either store, but it was a relatively small amount considering the hours he put in before going on the air. One thing is certain: Whether at the Home of the

Blues or Pop Tunes, Dewey was worth far more than a regular salesperson because of the customers he invariably attracted.

"Dewey and Joe had two chairs, sorta like a lounge chair, and they would sit out in front of the store," recalls Frank Berretta. "Like they were movie director's chairs—canvas backs on them. One of them had Dewey Phillips written on the back of it and the other had Jo-Jo Cuoghi." Before Poplar Avenue was widened to its present four lanes the street was cramped, having just two lanes and a narrow sidewalk. Nevertheless, "The buses would come by and people would scream at him, or they would drive by in cars, roll down their windows and holler 'Daddy-O-Dewey.'"[15]

Pop Tunes also came to be a favorite venue for recreational activity when Dewey got off work at midnight. Because *Red, Hot and Blue* had a rock concert–like intensity it was difficult for Dewey and his listeners to shut down immediately after the show ended. It was impossible for him to get to bed immediately after broadcasting, and he would almost always bring people home with him if he came directly to the house. Better still, Dewey loved nothing better than stopping by Joe's place for at least one drink, even if he had his children with him. Randy Phillips remembers visiting his father at the station when he was a toddler and then going to Pop Tunes afterward before going home.[16]

Most of the time, of course, Dewey's children weren't with him, and on those occasions the stopovers usually grew wild. There are all sorts of stories about Dewey's late-night ventures at Cuoghi's, replete with poker games, a lot of drinking, dirty jokes, and, above all, good ol' boy camaraderie. Sun artist and former Elvis girlfriend Barbara Pittman remembers many occasions when she, Elvis, and Dewey went to Pop Tunes at midnight after Dewey's show. Elvis never touched anything, but Dewey and Joe would always rip into the Jack Daniels. "They would start playing music and Dewey would commence to get completely inebriated."[17]

Louis Harris, who along with George Klein frequently accompanied Dewey after hours, remembers going by Cuoghi's the night after "Hound Dog" came out. "We couldn't figure out what Elvis was saying—we couldn't understand the word 'rabbit' when he said, 'You ain't never caught a rabbit and you ain't no friend of mine.'" Harris says, "Dewey kept playing it over and over and over while he and Joe Cuoghi drank Jack Daniels." The more they played it the more they drank and the louder they became. "They couldn't tell whether he was saying hound dog or rabbit or anything," Harris laughs.[18]

Even though Dewey and Elvis Presley did not know each other until that fateful July night in 1954, Elvis, like most teenagers, knew of Dewey from *Red, Hot and Blue.* Both men were regulars at Pop Tunes, and it is even possible that Elvis may have spotted Dewey earlier. All the Pop Tunes people remember Presley coming into the store long before he had his first record hit. Elvis lived in the Lauderdale Courts, only two blocks from the store, and worked at Crown Electric Company just across the street.

Elvis, John Novarese says, would come in during his lunch breaks from Crown Electric or drop by to cash his paycheck. He also liked to hang out at Pop Tunes in the evening. "He became a good friend of Joe's," John says. An old Coke machine stood next to the front door of the shop, and Elvis would stand between that machine and the door." Later on after cutting his first record with Sam Phillips, Elvis liked to "kind of hide out in that spot, and he would have his old working clothes on, and he didn't want Joe to tell people that that was him." The idea, of course, was to watch customers' reactions when they bought his record. Joe was at least partly responsible for encouraging Elvis to quit his job at Crown Electric and start singing full time, John Novarese observes. "He would be working way down in Mississippi or Alabama on Friday or Saturday night, and he would say, 'Man, I could barely get up to go to work.'" Each time Joe cashed Elvis's paycheck he would tell him, "Whatever you are making now, if you go to singing full time, I will guarantee you that you will make twice as much, and if you don't make it, I'll give it to you." Novarese laughs when he reports that Elvis, with now-legendary humility, would reply, "Oh, Mr. Cuoghi, you couldn't do that."[19]

The idea of Elvis and Dewey hanging out in the same store without making contact is fascinating enough, but the Pop Tunes one-stop attracted another regular caller in these early years. This was the man who would play an even more significant role than Dewey Phillips in the coming rock 'n' roll revolution. Sam Phillips was already making regular stops at Pop Tunes to acquire records for his line of work long before he ever opened his now-famous Sun Records studio.

Sam had come to Memphis after the war from Florence, Alabama, via Nashville, having served as a radio announcer in both cities. By the time he started at WREC in Memphis he had picked up a radio engineering license from Alabama Polytechnical Institute in Auburn and was able to feed big-band broadcasts from the outdoor roof of the Peabody Hotel Skyway to the CBS network. In addition, he was in charge of the music library at WREC, which meant he acquired all new records for the station.[20]

It was this latter role that brought Sam to Pop Tunes. In the late 1940s not all record companies had distributors in Memphis, and Sam would often obtain records for the station's library directly from retail outlets. Rather than purchase everything that suppliers offered, he found the best way to determine what was selling was to make weekly trips to Grant's, the Home of the Blues, and Pop Tunes. The one-stop was Sam's favorite because there he could see what was being put into jukeboxes and get a feel for what smaller stores were buying and selling. Jukeboxes were a reliable source of such information because they tallied the number of times each record was played. They were the musical barometer of the nation's taste during the early 1950s.[21]

Although no one, including Sam himself, seems sure of where the first historic encounter between the "Phillips boys" took place, what is certain is that Pop Tunes is where they began to solidify their relationship.[22] Both men had reason to be in the store as often as once a week—quite likely toward the end of each week. Jukebox operators would have been in on Monday, while Tuesdays and Wednesdays were usually when local and outlying retailers bought the newest releases. Sam would usually wait until the end of the week to see what they had purchased.[23] The men also met on other occasions in the downstairs drugstore of the Peabody Hotel on the corner of Union and Second. "We both liked milkshakes a lot, which was about as strong as anything we'd drink in those days," Sam recalls with some intentional irony.

From the moment they got together, Sam Phillips and Dewey Phillips were smitten with each other. Attracted to anyone or anything unconventional—a description that would accurately fit either man—both immediately commanded the other's respect and admiration. As might be imagined, however, two such powerful personalities could also clash almost as frequently as they agreed.[24]

Although Sam often came across as abrasive, arrogant, and self-important (in 1951 he had a "nervous breakdown," was hospitalized for several weeks, and received eight electro-shock treatments), he was also instantly ingratiating.[25] Most people found they couldn't help but like him in spite of his shortcomings. Dewey, however, who got along with nearly everyone, could rattle nerves every now and then, especially when threatened by a personality as dominant as Sam's. Marion Keisker, Sam's secretary, told Peter Guralnick that "Sam and Dewey were so close that she couldn't stand to be in the same room with the two of them." When they got together the atmosphere exuded energy. But more important, things would go ballistic when they disagreed. Disputes rarely got serious, however, because any discord was, more often than not, usually provoked by Dewey, who liked nothing better than prodding Sam every chance he got. "Dewey loved to argue with Sam," Sun artist Dickie Lee observed, "just for the sake of arguing."[26]

Although each man was a one-of-a-kind maverick, each fulfilled the other's immediate needs. Sam, whose ability for spotting talent was famous, recognized Dewey's potential immediately. Dewey, learning of the incredible work Sam planned for the Memphis Recording Service, became as infatuated with his occupation as he was with the man.

Sam hadn't finished the twelfth grade, but he was always eloquent, which made a strong impression on Dewey and Elvis, both captivated by his erudition. "Everything Sam says is a digression upon a digression," Charles Raiteri notes in a more objective appraisal of Sam's oratory. "But if you know that going in and are prepared for that, he'll take you to some interesting places and mesmerize you with his articulation."[27] What intrigued Dewey were those digressions, especially ones on the meaning of existence. When a young man in Alabama, Sam had been a lay preacher, as was his brother, Judd; the two also sang in a church quartet. Dewey, who spent the last years of his life handing out Bibles, seems to have been taken with Sam's ability to expostulate at length on various fine points of scripture.

Dewey may have admired Sam's knowledge, but he never lost his razor-sharp ability to puncture pomposity whenever and wherever he found it. Dickie Lee, for example, recalls one rather long, drawn-out evening when Sam was waxing philosophical about various aspects of religious significance. Dewey, whose hyper-charged personality prevented him from listening attentively for any length of time, soon began to tire of the seemingly never-ending rhetoric. After Sam held forth eloquently for a considerable period, Dewey slowly pulled a rubber band from his pocket, "pulled that sucker back, and popped Sam right in the eye while he was talking." "'Ha,'" Dewey said. "'Gotcha right in the eye.'" Sam was angry, but that didn't last long. "Just a little bit later," remembers Lee, "they were both laughing about the whole thing."[28]

That Dewey and Sam's relationship could withstand such juvenile shenanigans is a testament to their regard for each other. If Dewey was fascinated with Sam, the feeling was reciprocated. Whereas others might have seen Dewey as cocky, Sam recognized the outward brashness as genuine and not a mask for insecurity. What often seemed like awkward, childlike behavior was not an act. It was the real Dewey, having a good time. Sam understood full well that, with Dewey, what you saw is what you got. He was long on craziness but short on hypocrisy. There was not a bogus bone in Dewey's body, and that meant he was Sam's kind of guy.[29]

The two became soul mates for life, although they could be, on occasion, devilishly disruptive as well. Together, the Phillips boys were "a two-man tag team of musical anarchists."[30] They were indeed an outrageous duo if ever there was one, and they instantly struck up what was to become a life-long companionship. Much more important, as a twosome they quickly established a symbiotic musical relationship that would do nothing less than dramatically alter the entire Memphis music scene and in the process help generate a rock 'n' roll movement that would spread across much of the nation.

8

The Phillips Boys:
Soul (Better than Blood) Brothers

If there is a recognized patriarch of the Memphis musical explosion of the 1950s it is unquestionably Sam Phillips, founder of Sun Records, discoverer of Elvis Presley, godfather to the "million dollar quartet," creator of the "rockabilly" sound, winner of a lifetime Grammy Award, and member of all four music halls of fame: rock 'n' roll, country, blues, and rockabilly.

And if one happened to be in the listening range of Sam's bombastic oratory when he was holding forth it was difficult not to be either intimidated or mesmerized. Once Sam Phillips walked into a room, Jim Dickinson says, "the molecular structure of the air would be altered." Once he locked you onto his wave-length, Phillips could be as spellbinding as a foot-washing Baptist preacher. With his drop-dead gaze and riveting, messianic voice he sounded and looked for all the world, as Peter Guralnick observed, "a bit like an Old Testament prophet." When he died at age eighty he still looked young enough to cause one writer to suggest that "he must have made a pact with the devil."[1]

But there was more there than just appearance. Sam Phillips did for popular music what Henry Ford did for the automobile or what Robert Redford's Sundance Film Festival has done for independent films. He helped democratize it. Just as driving an automobile had been restricted to the elite before Ford and making movies had been controlled by the Hollywood studio system before Redford, so music had been confined to a kind of cultural elite before independent record companies. Before Sam and the other indies came along, even so-called popular music, which replaced classical as the plebeian standard, was confined to what was socially acceptable at the time. Some of the early, funky blues he first captured in his studio were definitely not considered as socially acceptable music for a white mainstream audience. Before Sam Phillips captured such music on record and Dewey Phillips played it on his radio show, most white people in the Mid-South thought it should be confined to juke joints and Beale Street dives.

If Dewey Phillips's initial broadcast of *Red, Hot and Blue* on October 10, 1949, marks the beginning of the Mid-South's rock 'n' roll revolution one can find no better second major date than that morning in January 1950 when Sam converted a worn-out radiator shop at 706 Union Avenue into the Memphis Recording Service and opened for business. Both of these now-celebrated acts mark the nearest thing we have to a 1950s' musical genesis, if only because they contrasted so strongly with what immediately preceded them. When Sam leased the tiny storefront recording studio for $150 a month and started filling it with control boards and recording equipment in order to capture the sounds of Delta bluesmen, the South had never witnessed anything like it since the major labels' regional recordings of the 1920s.

Because major labels had to cut back and concentrate on the dominant white market, given the relatively small appeal of black music during the depression and World War II, Sam, along with a host of other independent labels that appeared immediately after the war, had an excellent opportunity to suddenly challenge the majors for that market niche. A major reason for the indies' emergence was that the initial cost of starting a new company had become economically feasible. With the introduction of the studio tape recorder, the recording industry was quickly democratized. No longer was the cost of making a record financially prohibitive to all but the powerful few. Brian Ward has computed that by the late 1940s "a thousand dollars was enough to hire a studio (typically at $50 an hour), book musicians, pay American Federation of Musicians (AFM) dues, have a master tape prepared, and press five hundred singles at 11 cents a shot."[2]

So Sam began his operation on the cheap. In fact, his hole-in-the-wall studio initially served as a way of leasing recordings to other, already established independent labels like the Bihari brothers in Los Angeles (Modern) or Leonard Chess in Chicago (Chess). Recording an artist and then turning the master recording over to another label for pressing and distribution was a cumbersome process that did not maximize profit. Even though Sam didn't set up his own Sun label until 1952, capturing the rich plethora of southern Delta sounds was itself revolutionary. WDIA had begun showcasing black talent, much of it live, but almost no one in the South, let alone in the Delta, had tried to capture that talent on record and distribute it for sale. At the time the local culture precluded doing so. Sam was later fond of saying, with his usual gift for turning a phrase, that all he did was liberate the "musically disenfranchised."

Even so, Sam was relatively late getting into the recording business. By 1950 numerous indies had jumped in. The good fortune for Sam, however, was that there were surprisingly few in the South. Only Nashville (Bullet in the city and Dot in nearby Gallatin, Tennessee) and Jackson, Misssissippi (Trumpet) had labels when he started. His trump card was that he could draw talent from the vastly rich Mississippi Delta. By the time he opened Sun's doors black Delta bluesmen were so eager to be recorded—so anxious for the privilege of being heard for the first time outside their local area—that they expected to have to pay the person recording them.[3] "Jesus Christ, my little ol' studio looked like Radio City Music Hall or something to them—you know what I mean," Sam would yell. "They just couldn't believe that somebody wasn't going to catch them in the door, and say, 'hey, cough up.'"[4] In short, finding and putting on record previously unrecorded blues artists was easy. Sam decided to record Howlin' Wolf, for example, only after a KWEM disc jockey in West Memphis, Arkansas, insisted that he listen to Wolf's regular fifteen-minute segment on that station.[5]

But if recording—converting the sound to disc—was the easy part, it was only half the formula for commercial success in the record business. The remainder was in marketing the product, and here Sam encountered his biggest hurdle. He overcame it only after teaming with Dewey, whose help in showcasing Sam's discoveries proved to be the magic bullet in the latter part of that formula for success. It was Dewey Phillips who became Sam's conduit. It was Dewey who almost single-handedly converted many local artists Sam discovered in his studio into regional, then national, big-name stars.

Even though *Red, Hot and Blue* sizzled on the local Memphis radio dial in 1950, the magnitude of Sam's faith in Dewey's potential to have much wider influence was almost inversely proportional to his actual broadcasting power. WHBQ's signal was a mere thousand watts compared to WDIA's mighty fifty thousand. "Everywhere I went, one of the first things the industry people would want to know about was Dewey," Sam says. "'You mean he's just on a thousand watts and he is making this noise he's making?' I'd say, 'I guarantee if you heard his program, you would understand.'"[6]

If Muddy Waters's observation that "the blues had a baby and they called it rock 'n' roll" was true, then, blues historian Francis Davis says, "Memphis was the maternity ward, and the record producer Sam Phillips was the obstetrician."[7] One is tempted to extend Davis's analogy and suggest that because Memphis and the Mid-South have come to be known as the "cradle of rock 'n' roll," then Dewey Phillips might have been the wet nurse who rocked the cradle. Certainly, Sam thought so. As he often said, he could not have done it without Dewey. He knew that he desperately needed a vehicle to bring his product to market and immediately sensed that Dewey Phillips could fulfill that need.

Sam's initial success was less a contrived effort than the result of a random commingling of two mutually captivated souls, each relishing the other's company. Sam knew that teaming with Dewey in any kind of formal working business relationship would not be easy. For someone not given to following traditional rules, let alone those of a business operation, Dewey would prove a major test of Sam's patience. It was especially tried in the early days before the two ventured together into their first official business operation.

At first, Sam would drop in on *Red, Hot and Blue* at his convenience to absorb the ambience of Dewey at work and hear which new sounds his fans liked. But Sam quickly discovered that he could not only obtain immediate air play on the Mid-South's most important record show but also use Dewey for feedback to assess the quality of the artist he had just recorded.

Sam's decision to work with the always unpredictable Dewey speaks volumes about the way he would later come to exploit talent. His keen knowledge of the record business made him acutely sensitive to a disc jockey's importance in making or breaking a record. If the disc jockey wasn't excited about the recording, you might as well forget it. "Remember the deejay when you first start singing the song," Carl Perkins remembers Sam telling him in the recording studio, "'cause he's gonna' hear it first."[8]

Dewey, of course, wasn't just any disc jockey. He had a track record for spotting hits. Moreover, at this point in their relationship—the early 1950s—he had significantly more power in the record business than Sam, who, in this pre-Elvis era, was virtually unknown outside the Memphis area. Before he established a reputation with the string of stars the Sun label would finally generate he had little, if any, say in determining the final success of any record he produced. Dewey, however, had a mammoth and devoted audience, all of whom were potential record-buyers. In addition, Dewey had record company contacts that Sam would later use, especially in the early days before he started his own label. Sam, for example, initially touched base with the Chess label (so critical in the pre-Sun days) as a result of a happenstance meeting with Leonard Chess, who was making one of his obligatory promotional trips to Dewey's studio.[9]

The only problem was that Sam quickly found that Dewey enjoyed reciprocal visits. This was not always a pleasant experience. For Dewey, visiting Sam at the recording studio was not much different than playing in his own control room, and he began to appear regularly. Sam was left with the unenviable task of dealing with the many hours of idleness that Memphis's most famous late-night deejay had during the day. Doing so quickly became troublesome. It was Sam, of course, who had to capture an artist on tape, but that didn't keep the irrepressible Dewey out of the studio whenever he felt like making an appearance, which, given his restless energy, was quite often. He liked to drop by during recording sessions and would sometimes break into the middle of a live take. Sam might be recording B.B. King, Howlin' Wolf, or Ike Turner, when Dewey, compulsively spontaneous, would charge into the studio unannounced and scream "call Sam." Most of the time the session would end at that point because everyone recognized that little, if anything, productive would be accomplished once Dewey had arrived. Sam didn't care. He knew how desperately he needed Dewey's help. "Dewey could have interrupted the president's cabinet meeting at that time and it would be alright," says long-time Sun sound man Stan Kesler. Sam insists that Dewey was never in the way and would seldom offer advice about cutting a record ("If he did, it was usually on tempo"). He even defends Dewey's middle-of-a-cut arrivals. Those kind of disruptions, he says, "didn't happen on a real frequency basis at all."[10]

One of the biggest of the big names who was getting started in these early days has an interesting take on the relationship between the two men. "All of us used to go over to Sam Phillips studio," B.B. King says. After cutting his initial disc at WDIA, B.B. did some of his earliest work for Sam while he was still leasing out recorded material. "Dewey was hanging out over there," B.B. remembers. "Sam was a little bit introverted, but his brother Dewey was outgoin'."[11]

That the two most famous men in Memphis music during the early 1950s had the same last name caused many to make the same mistake, a mistake made so often that both had fun with the mix-up. "They told people they were brothers," Dot Phillips recalls, "and, of course, people believed them. Well, why shouldn't they?" Why not indeed. Even had

Sam and Dewey not compounded the confusion by their little running joke, it would have been natural to assume that the two men were brothers in blood as well as spirit. Sam certainly thought so: "He and I were brothers in the same belief of what music could do with, for and to, people." After a while the connection was so close that people continued to believe the men were related even when they denied it. "I'd tell people that they weren't any kin," Dewey's sister Betty says, "but it didn't do any good—they wouldn't believe me."[12]

Related or not, they were practically inseparable, personally as well as professionally. Dewey introduced Sam to his favorite haunts on Beale Street—Robert Henry's pool room and Culpepper's—making Sam as much a regular in those places as Dewey was. They were particularly friendly between 1951 and 1955, Dewey already the city's top deejay and Sam still seeking new talent. When they were not working they were socializing.

The mock brothers' relationship even stretched to extended family. "Dewey brought Dot by the recording studio one night," says Sam's wife, Becky, shortly after the two men became friends. "I just accidentally happened by there with [sons] Knox and Jerry." After that both families were frequently at each other's houses, often after Dewey's show. Randy Phillips remembers his father taking him and his brothers swimming at Sam's place on Mendenhall Road when they were quite young. In later years Randy kept in close touch with "Uncle Sam," visiting with him on the telephone and seeing him as often as possible. "I remember the first time my mother told me that he was not my *real* uncle," Randy says. "I started crying. I kept insisting that he was." Not only did the Phillipses seem like an extended family but they also often acted like one. When Dewey was recuperating from an automobile accident Sam kept Randy, then a baby, while Dot visited her husband at the hospital. On another occasion Dewey's entire family lived at Sam's house for about six months while they were having a new home built.[13]

Never one to play his emotional cards close to his chest, Sam becomes almost evangelical when describing his old friend. "He was a genius," he told Peter Guralnick, "and I don't call many people geniuses." And Sam was not the only independent record producer who thought Dewey's gifts were extraordinary. "Dewey was one of those black-voiced Caucasoid poets," Jerry Wexler of Atlantic Records recalled, "a dazzling technician at the turntable, directing comments into the mike for public consumption and, a nanosecond later, off-mike for the delectation of the hangers-on in the control room."[14]

Many might praise Dewey, but it was Sam alone who capitalized on him. Claiming that Dewey had a sixth sense for picking hit records, he shouts (with no regard for qualification), "Dewey Phillips was one of the greatest disk jockeys that's ever been on the air anywhere in this country."[15] That's quite a compliment from a man who spent the best part of his early years in close contact with disc jockeys from Florida to California. In the early days, Sam served as his own record-pusher (as well as studio engineer and producer), driving around the country and promoting his latest releases. "It was my business to know the jocks," he says. None compared to Dewey. "I would consider Dewey as having one of the best quote unquote musical ears I have ever observed," he recalls. As is often the case, Sam is careful to elaborate: "I mean, maybe all of us can hear, or could at one time, hear from thirty cycles, up to maybe ten thousand or twelve thousand, fourteen, but that don't mean you got a great ear, in the sense that I mean."[16]

Little wonder that Sam asked Dewey to join him in his first record financial venture. Although most people are unaware of it, even otherwise well-informed Memphis music veterans, Sam Phillips—after he stopped leasing his material and before he began Sun—started his initial record label in partnership with Dewey. It was a natural choice. The men were already working closely together, if in an unofficial capacity, when the enterprise began. Dewey, along with Ike Turner, was an informal "talent scout" for Sam's studio, even while Sam's artists were still being leased out. Together, Dewey and Ike kept a close watch for anyone whose talent merited an audition and perhaps a shot at a recording career. Turner's Mississippi roots connected him with a great many black artists in the Delta, and Dewey's numerous contacts at the radio station and on Beale Street alerted him to new black talent in the Memphis area.

After a while, so many artists became available to Sam that he decided it was time to stop leasing material and to start his own label. Once that decision was made, who better to do business with than Dewey himself? They called the venture the "Phillips label," no doubt giving rise to further speculation that the two were brothers. It was subtitled the "Hottest Thing in the Country," a phrase Dewey made synonymous with *Red, Hot and Blue*.

Dewey would ultimately provide the indispensable assistance Sam needed, but, unfortunately, it would not be on the newly founded Phillips label. Their ill-fated business venture began and ended with a single record by one performer—Joe Hill Louis. Known as the "one-man band," Louis had been heard regularly on WDIA as the "Peptikon Boy" (Peptikon being an alcohol-laced elixir), a title he long held before it passed to B.B. King, who later joined the station as a singer and disc jockey. The short-lived Phillips endeavor pressed only three hundred copies of Louis's "Gotta Let You Go" / "Boogie in the Park." As Sun Records' historians Colin Escott and Martin Hawkins note, the record was released in August of 1950, but "the label was DOA by September."[17]

Despite its early demise the Phillips label is nonetheless significant because it brought together the two men who would do so much to transform the recording business. Although they would continue to work closely together, it would be on each man's own turf. Sam would soon acquire national recognition with Sun Records. For Dewey, however, the collapse of the Phillips label marked an abrupt halt to his business end of the recording industry. Sam tried to get him to travel with him and distribute records on the "dust bowl circuit" but to no avail. "Dewey," Sam said, "was just married to his program."[18] Fortunately, both men intuitively recognized that it would be best if Dewey's contribution to the Phillipses' enterprise allowed him to maximize what nature so exquisitely prepared him to do. He would continue to be an unofficial, silent partner in the Sam Phillips musical operation until his death.

Dewey served the operation in a dual capacity. He furnished a radio show that provided air time for Sun's early performers and willingly, even enthusiastically, allowed Sam to use and exploit his innate ability to pick potential hits. Dewey would be a one-man sounding board for a never-ending pageant of musical wannabes that paraded through Sam's recording studio.

Every devoted rock 'n' roll fan knows how Sam brought what was to become the holy grail of rock 'n' roll—the acetate disc of Elvis's first hit "That's All Right"—to Dewey to play in July 1954. But airing Elvis's first effort on Dewey's show overshadows what was, by then, a common practice. Bringing "straight-out-of-the-gate" studio dubs to WHBQ for Dewey to spin on *Red, Hot and Blue* before Sam cut the record had become, even before Elvis, standard operating procedure for the two Phillipses.

That procedure was as simple as it was successful. Sam would first capture an artist on tape and immediately cut an acetate disc of the session, right in his tiny studio. Then—before pressing the master—he'd race down to the Gayoso Hotel, where Dewey was stirring the airwaves with *Red, Hot and Blue.* The latest Sam Phillips offering would then blast out instantly to Dewey's captivated audience. It was what might be called a "super-duper, do-or-die Dewey Phillips test." What was being tested was Dewey's personal reaction as well as those of his faithful followers.[19] If a record passed Dewey's trial (the pluperfect reaction was an exuberant "It's a hit. Call Sam!"), then Sam would fire the master off to "Buster" Williams Plastic Products at 1746 Chelsea Avenue in Memphis, which would then produce the actual recording to be sold.

In a near-textbook example of the way it worked, Jack Clement, Sam's righthand man in the Sun studio, recalls that Jerry Lee Lewis's "Crazy Arms" went from audition tape to hit record in practically no time at all. Clement made the tape, but after playing it for his boss Sam immediately made an acetate of it and took it straight down to Dewey. "Dewey started playing it and everyone wanted to buy it," Clement says. "Now, that was when the music business was fun. We make a tape on Thursday, and it's on the radio the next Monday, and on sale in the stores the next Thursday."[20]

"It was a hell of a test," says George Klein, his voice raising to emphasize Dewey's importance to the success of Sam's operation. "Here you are getting a guy in a major media market station playing your new song for you." (He might have added that the guy was also capturing the lion's share of that market). George remembers many nights when Sam would arrive at WHBQ with a freshly cut acetate. The final decision on its success would be determined by Dewey's instant feedback: "Sam would see what kind of reaction he would have" and decide on the spot. "If it was positive, he'd go ahead and press them up."[21]

The test itself was hardly unprecedented. It was common for record companies to give new acetates to deejays to play before pressing copies for retail. The situation in Memphis, however, was unique because of the Sam-Dewey connection. So impressed was Sam by his colleague's ability that quite often a record Dewey personally felt strongly about would be pressed, even if audience reaction was mixed. So assured was Sam by Dewey's ear, says Klein, that if Dewey predicted a hit Sam would race back to the studio and have the record pressed that very night. The symbiosis between the men was so carefully fine-tuned that Sam often estimated the actual number of copies to press merely by the enthusiasm of Dewey's response.[22]

By the time Elvis arrived in 1954 the business of "breaking in" Sam's latest discoveries on *Red, Hot and Blue* had come to be a fairly mundane event for Dewey. He would ultimately introduce to the world not only Elvis but also Jerry Lee Lewis, Johnny Cash, B.B. King, Carl Perkins, Roy Orbison, Charlie Rich, and a host of others. It was Dewey who first played Perkins's "Blue Suede Shoes," Johnny Cash's "I Walk the Line" and "Folsom Prison Blues," and Conway Twitty's "It's Only Make Believe." Dewey was so successful at jumping the gun and being the first to air the work of rockabilly artists that some have speculated, incorrectly, that he was the first to use the term *rockabilly* to describe that battery of Sun stars who combined country music and R&B.[23]

The promotion of so many luminaries, however, overshadows Dewey's contribution to promoting Sam's lesser-known discoveries—black artists whose white listening audience was virtually nonexistent before Dewey launched their careers on *Red, Hot and Blue.* Crossing these artists over to white listeners was the real Sam-Dewey stroke of genius, and it had immense significance for the music industry. Black rhythm and blues performers may not have made the media splash Elvis did, but they are no less important. Their early crossover proved an indispensable prerequisite for Presley's later acceptance. By the time Elvis appeared in 1954, *Red, Hot and Blue* had built an enormous white audience attuned to black R&B artists.

Making the actual crossover was not easy, however, even with Dewey Phillips greasing the skids. From the beginning, Sam understood the problems he faced in selling unknown black performers to white teenagers. His problem was like that Bert Ferguson faced after WDIA's switch to black programming—how to accurately determine the size of the white audience. The received wisdom at the time had it that a great many whites listened frequently to the all-black WDIA but were reluctant to admit doing so when responding to telephone surveys. Sam's knowledge of the record business made him savvy enough to realize that those whites were also reluctant to purchase music recorded by black artists.

Although publicly he liked to play the role of eccentric renegade, Sam was a first-rate businessman who didn't delude himself with expectations of instant success. He assumed from the very start that marketing unknown talent would be difficult and that the audience for black Delta blues was relatively small. "I didn't get into this thing to get rich," he allows, "because I really figured the chance of it commercially succeeding was very limited." He and other early innovators in the field were not certain at first that a white youth market existed for black music. There was even less certainty that it would be a large audience. "Believe me, this is taking nothing away from anybody," he said in a *Rolling Stone* interview in the 1980s, "but it hadn't occurred to too many people that white people would listen to black singers."[24]

Using slightly different language, Jerry Wexler, the legendary head of Atlantic Records, adds, "We were making black records, with black musicians and black singers for black buyers. It never occurred to us in the beginning that there were crossover possibilities. . . . Many people believed that rhythm and blues records sold exclusively to a Negro market up until that time (1953–54)."[25] Although there were a few exceptions, most whites knew next to nothing about R&B. Some hits like Stick McGhee's Atlantic smash "Drinkin' Wine Spo-Dee-O-Dee" (1949) "went white" even in the Deep South, no doubt in part because Dewey played the record incessantly. Those events, however, were rare indeed.

Sam Phillips, like Dewey, was a born-and-bred southerner, which afforded him the experience of making an educated guess that major white resistance was built as much on prejudice against the music as against race. "Gutbucket Southern blues," he loudly exclaims, "was something back in those days that most whites were ashamed of!" As he was about most musical matters, Sam was right. All too many white southerners still associated the blues with uncultured entertainment performed by ignorant low-lifes, primarily for their own amusement. He had to reckon with the strong force of their almost-unconscious resistance. "They liked the music," Sam told Peter Guralnick, "but they weren't sure whether they ought to like it or not."[26] Despite external prejudice, however, there were already early indications. An enthusiastic white crowd, for example, attended Beale Street's all-black Midnight Rambles—moreover, it was a popular southern practice to hire black bands for white dances. Above all, an overwhelming number of whites tuned in to *Red, Hot and Blue.* All such signs helped Sam Phillips realize that white people did indeed listen to the blues, if only "surreptitiously."

In the final analysis, Sam managed to hook the white audience by taking a cue from the Midnight Rambles. That transracial wonder enjoyed enormous popularity in an era of near-total segregation by making the music so attractive that whites suspended prejudices long enough to go to an otherwise (self-imposed) restricted part of town to enjoy it. The same formula that had driven white New York socialites to go to Harlem in the 1920s worked for Memphis and the Rambles, and it would now work for Sam Phillips. He therefore went to Dewey's studio with newly pressed acetates, knowing that *Red, Hot and Blue* had become so popular that whites would be drawn to previously unheard black performers almost in spite of themselves.

Dewey could get away with introducing the white audience to the still-taboo R&B sound on *Red, Hot and Blue* in large part because of the madcap nature of his show. Who could worry about racial boundaries while trying to listen to Dewey Phillips? Who could be uptight about a revolutionary new sound when Dewey's wild shenanigans had people howling between (and during) records? No one had time to think about prejudice during a typical Dewey broadcast. His comedy routines and the show's unpredictable format allowed him to effortlessly integrate the Mid-South's airwaves without so much as a single known voice of resistance.

More important, because Dewey's voice, style, and manner no doubt attracted a white audience that had his same rural, working-class origins, he managed to introduce a lower socioeconomic class of white listeners—those who might be inclined to harbor the strongest prejudice toward blacks—to the still-forbidden music. In this audience were people who, before Red, Hot and Blue, would never in their wildest dreams have imagined listening to black artists singing R&B.[27] It may have been Dewey's slam-dunk success at capturing working-class fans (both black and white) on Red, Hot and Blue that convinced Sam of the necessity of going full speed ahead after what was still an unexplored integrated musical audience. He captured that audience, of course, with a magic combination—a poor, working-class white boy who had the black sound.

Sam may have recorded them, but it was Dewey who excited white listeners about the most important of Sam's early black discoveries—people like Howlin' Wolf and B.B. King, Rufus Thomas and Bobby "Blue" Bland, Ike Turner and Little Milton, Junior Parker and Roscoe Gordon. All these stars subsequently moved from Sun to other labels, causing several detractors to note that Sam had switched to an all-white stable of artists. These same critics later suggested that his actions may have been racially motivated. "Sam discarded all the blacks," Rufus Thomas bitterly complained after Sam stopped cutting his records. "I don't even think the [studio's] wall was black."[28]

Whether or not that criticism is justified, Dewey continued to play and promote all of the black artists with the same enthusiasm he had shown when he introduced their names on the air. But even with Dewey hawking records white acceptability didn't occur overnight. The challenge of broadening the demographic base for new African-American artists was formidable given the uncertainty about the white youth market. It was doubly complicated by the fact that the black audience had to be turned on to the new sound. Initially, as it turned out, Sam's first successes were not because of sales to the now famous white youth market he eventually captured with Elvis Presley but because more affluent postwar urban blacks were beginning to buy the bulk of the records.

Escott and Hawkins maintain that African Americans proved to be the label's biggest buyers in the decade following World War II.[29] That may have been true, but they were reluctant buyers who were finally sold on the notion only through the medium of radio—specifically, by listening to WDIA and Dewey Phillips. Many of the Mid-South's African Americans who were potential purchasers of the records were former sharecroppers who had subsequently moved to the city and achieved a middle-class income. Even after they became more urbanized, they still carried many old, rural-based ideas, so they tended to connect the low-down sounds of new artists with the poorer rural black population they had escaped. Thus they often shunned the music. Like many whites, a number of newly arrived urban blacks, if not embarrassed by gutbucket blues, at least did not cotton to it initially. "It used to be more or less disgraceful to associate yourself with the blues," WDIA's Nat D. Williams wrote. "The blues had to start up from the bottom and came with a lot of dirt on it."[30]

The best black purveyors of the genre had long ago recognized that many newly arrived middle-class blacks looked down on the blues. "It's a pitiful thing," Memphis Slim (Peter Chatman) once observed, but "the black man who owned the blues is still ashamed of the blues." Veteran blues entertainer Rufus Thomas reached the same conclusion after decades of playing the "chitlin circuit." "You have some sections of the blacks that don't really want to associate themselves with it," he observed. But then he quickly adds, "Get these same people behind closed doors and put some records on the jukebox and you got it."[31] Rufus might also have added, "Get them comfortably at home, all alone, listening to their radio, and you got it." What legitimized the sound was radio. WDIA made the blues more acceptable for initially reluctant urban middle-class blacks, and Dewey Phillips strongly reinforced that acceptance for blacks and working-class whites by playing the blues on a white man's show.

Acceptance would be awhile in coming, however, and Sam had to stay in business, which was no small problem. He had virtually no cash flow; borrowing from a bank was impossible, even after Sun's initial success. "The South knew nothing about the record industry," he told *Rolling Stone* magazine, "and didn't believe in it." With his usual awareness of his own role in the bigger picture Sam described the record industry as being "so precarious [that] you can't get financial backing until you don't need it." Going public, of course, was a viable option, but given Sam Phillips's indomitable spirit the possibility was out of the question. He knew the majors had the ability "to eat me alive" and attract any star he might produce. They could afford to "buy all the artists from the independent companies."[32]

In the end, of course, that is precisely what happened. All the Sun stars, including Elvis, went on to bigger labels with more lucrative contracts. After first shunning many of Sam's R&B stars the majors bought them up only after they proved their commercial value. "They didn't [start to] think," Atlantic head Jerry Wexler says, commenting on the Johnny-come-lately attitude of the majors, "until the cash registers started to jingle."[33]

In the process of all this, however, it is important to remember that Sun Records remained independent and was not co-opted by a major label. If late in his life Sam's account of his career sometimes seemed self-aggrandizing (as it often did), it's good to keep in mind that he was not bought out during those early, difficult days when selling out would have been a convenient thing to do. Sun Records remained Sun Records and Sam Phillips remained his own cantankerous independent self until 1966. Only then—nearly a decade after the label was firmly established—did he finally decide to sell it to Shelby Singleton, who also owned an independent label. "It was a sad day," Sam remembered, but then he proudly boasted: "I did not sell out to a major label."[34]

Had it not been for the Sam-Dewey tie during the critical early years it is hard to resist the conclusion that Sam might not have made it without his cohort. Had Dewey not been there, Sam's local stars might have remained just that—local. It is certainly possible that they might have remained forever only dim lights in the brighter firmament. Today it is difficult to imagine Sam's initial prosperity without Dewey's ability to propel unknowns to national prominence. "Dewey made Sam!" Rufus Thomas screams, as if his voice level will somehow ensure the validity of his point. "He would never have come along as much as he did without Dewey pushing those records for him." Sam said essentially the same thing on a television special, even though his language was considerably more opaque: "Dewey Phillips," he said with an uncharacteristic economy of words, "was a part of this whole process."[35]

As *Red, Hot and Blue* grew hotter and hotter Sun's stars grew brighter and brighter. Despite the almost random nature of the Phillips boys' partnership, the synergy between them gave every appearance of having been planned by the gods. The men interacted so well that their ostensibly separate missions seemed to fit each other's goals seamlessly. Sam put the talent on records, and Dewey converted records into hits. It was that simple.

It is easy, of course, to see Dewey's end of all this as a self-fulfilling prophecy. Putting his imprimatur on a record would alone ensure its success; his persistence in predicting a hit would make one. That is what many people think happened. "He'd listen to it, and he'd say, 'That's a hit. You got a hit here,'" recalls Bob Lewis. "And then he'd play it again and again, and of course, half the time it was." Charlie Feathers, one of the early Sun recording artists, remembers how nothing more than Dewey's endorsement of a record would guarantee its success. "If Dewey said the record had it, you could just go on down and start counting your money 'cause it had it. It meant he was gonna play it and that's all it needed."[36] Frank Berretta of Pop Tunes, where the local list of hit records was compiled, also believes the self-fulfilling prophecy. He observed firsthand that Dewey could single-handedly generate enough enthusiasm to turn records into smash hits. "There are a lot of songs that you hear the first time that you shelf it, it's no good," Berretta says, "but Dewey, if he liked the song, I don't give a damn whether you liked it or not, he was going to play it, play it and play it, you are gonna like it!"[37]

This casual disregard about whether listeners liked a record gives further credence to a prophetic predictability: Immediate audience reaction was not Dewey's final critical criterion. "They could call in and say that I never heard anything worse than that, and he didn't care," says brother-in-law Bill Kirby. "He'd always play what he wanted to play and the station couldn't do nothing about it cause he was making all that money for 'em."[38]

Popular wisdom in the music business holds that a hit cannot be made from a dud. A minor hit might be pushed into a major one or a good song might be made more widely known, but a bad song can't be made into a success, even it if is played continually. Many close observers of the record business in Memphis at this time, however, contend that Dewey had the power to convert otherwise lackluster and unknown artists into genuine hits through constant promotion alone. Berretta, who watched sales soar in Pop Tunes after Dewey's endorsement, cites specific examples. Songs like Otis Jackson's "Tell Me Why You Like Roosevelt" or Rosetta Tharpe's "Strange Things Happening Everyday"—obscure efforts that other stations didn't play—became regional and, on occasion, national hits, Berretta argues, because Dewey kept playing them.[39]

Dewey could, of course, miss, and occasionally he did. Robert Johnson remembered how hard Dewey plugged the "Ballad of Bridey Murphy" because he was attracted to the song's weird content (the theme was reincarnation). The record never did much nationally despite Dewey's persistent enthusiasm. Nonetheless, Johnson maintained, "He's right about what will go a lot more often than he's wrong."[40]

With Dewey always on the lookout for the unknown artist and Sam providing a continuous flow of new talent into his studios, it is no wonder that the two succeeded so effortlessly. The Sam-Dewey team was indispensable in making Memphis the birthplace of a music insurrection. Sam's business savvy and Dewey's domination of the airwaves provided the double dose of explosive chemistry needed to propel rock 'n' roll. For nearly a decade together, in Stanley Booth's wonderful phrase, "Sam and Dewey made up the rest of the twentieth century."[41]

9

Red, Hot and Blue:
The Hottest Cotton-Pickin' Thang in the Country

If there was a center of the universe for the "what's-happening-now" rock 'n' roll record scene in the 1950s it had to be the WHBQ studio on the mezzanine floor of the Chisca Hotel at 272 South Main Street in Memphis, Tennessee, every week night between nine o'clock and midnight. That was where *Red, Hot and Blue* was erupting forth for the listening pleasure of Dewey Phillips's local Memphis and Mid-South audience and being taped for later syndication in eleven cities around the country.[1]

Above all, Dewey's tiny, specially constructed control room was the unofficial headquarters for the record industry's new power players. The heads of new, independent record companies all arrived at Daddy-O-Dewey's to promote their newest offerings. "Like Sam [Phillips] is already there with his latest Sun label release," George Klein recalls. "Then Leonard Chess is bringing in Bo Diddley's or Chuck Berry's record." G.K. rattles off record labels and the stars' names associated with each of them: "Jerry Wexler is bringing in the Clovers and the Drifters, or Clyde McPhatter, Big Joe Turner or LaVern Baker, then Don Robey has got Johnny Ace's latest release, or one of the Bihari brothers has something hot from the Modern label."[2]

George says his most exciting recollections of being at Dewey's side during his gofer days at WHBQ concern meeting such notable personalities. Klein would soon become a bit of a celebrity himself because of his association with the biggest of all superstars. He had been a celebrity in his Humes High School class the year it turned out what would be its most famous graduate—Elvis Presley. G.K., one of Elvis's closest friends, would become even more consequential for Dewey's career by being an unofficial liaison between Elvis and Dewey. Even before Elvis arrived on the scene, however, George and Dewey had become instant comrades who played off each other beautifully. Dewey was the star attraction, but Klein was the unofficial station policeman. Like others who worked with Dewey, G.K. was there to make sure the operation ran smoothly. He now laughs about the self-styled babysitting: "I'd sit around and answer the phone, go get him coffee, and generally just make sure he didn't burn the station down."[3]

George might call himself a babysitter, but the relationship between the two men was one of mutual respect. The then-inexperienced Klein was exhilarated and flattered to be given an opportunity to work with Dewey Phillips; to be in the studio with him seemed the fulfillment of a lifelong dream. By the time G.K. arrived at WHBQ he was already a genuine radio groupie, hoping someday to take his rightful place behind a microphone as a full-fledged announcer.

As Dewey's new assistant, however, George had to perform, at least temporarily, a variety of non-announcing chores that made him appear to be little more than a flunky at the station. He endured nonetheless because he knew the work, although hectic, was part of his education. And it did have its moments. He particularly enjoyed determining who would get close enough to watch Dewey perform on the air. No more than a handful of groupies could wedge into the small studio next to the control room and watch the star through a large window, so George would admit them in shifts. "Sometimes I'd have to say, 'I'm sorry but we're full tonight,' because we would have regulars. People would just come up and start hanging around all the time." He had a hard time turning people away though because he remembered the magic he felt when, as a youth, he had trekked to the same studio on warm afternoons after school to watch Bill Gordon, then his idol, do his deejay show.[4]

Serving as control room policemen and absorbing the day-to-day operation of the radio station was not nearly as exciting for George as getting to know the cadre of indie record people who were regulars. Rubbing elbows with Sam Phillips, Jerry Wexler, Ahmet Ertegun, Don Robey, and Leonard Chess gave Klein the same thrill that other people had when they met Elvis. In particular, Klein remembers the early days at the WHBQ studio before indies were big, when labels like Chess and Atlantic were still the mom-and-pop stores of the record industry. Owners did everything on the cheap. "They didn't have the record promo guys then. They would sign the artist, cut the record and then mail it to a small radio station."[5] It was during this period, Muddy Waters recalled, that he saw Leonard Chess "standing on Chicago's Maxwell Street one Sunday afternoon selling records. 'I bought my own record from the man,' Waters chuckled."[6] It would be several years yet before the indie labels that produced most of the monster hits of the 1950s would begin to take on the traits of the major companies. After that, Klein says, they all "developed their own promotion people, and played the game like the big boys."[7]

In the meantime, however, the procedure of mailing new records to stations worked well unless company heads were convinced they had a potential hit on their hands. When that happened they would deliver the record themselves. Because many young, struggling executives believed that success depended on whether Dewey decided they had a hit, paying a visit to the WHBQ studio was an absolute prerequisite when releasing anything that had potential.

The formula was simple enough. When a new disc looked promising, a studio head would hit the road as if on a personal tour. "If they really wanted to work a record," G.K. says, "why mess with the mail? They'd just jump on the plane and fly in to see you themselves." Some record chiefs would visit Dewey if they wanted more air play for a particular artist, whether or not that artist had a new record. Don Nix of the Mar-Keys remembers Jerry Wexler coming to town once to request Dewey's assistance in helping Big Joe Turner make a comeback. Turner, one of Atlantic's superstars with hits like "Shake, Rattle and Roll" and "Flip, Flop and Fly," had a brief slump in the mid-1950s, and Wexler was convinced that a Dewey-assisted promotion campaign was what he needed. Dewey gave a big party, reintroduced Turner to the capacity crowd there, and, sure enough, started him on the proverbial comeback trial.[8]

George's fondest recollections of those days concern the times Leonard Chess came to town. The Chess label, which was out of Chicago, had some of the biggest names in blues and rock 'n' roll—Chuck Berry, Muddy Waters, Bo Diddley, Howlin' Wolf, Etta James, the Moonglows, and Sonny Boy Williamson. For George, however, the best part was the man who ran the operation. Leonard Chess was unquestionably one of the nicest, most colorful characters in the business (and thus he blended perfectly into Dewey's WHBQ studio). "Every other word out of Leonard Chess's mouth was motherfucker," G.K. says. "I really liked him." The feeling must have been mutual. According to one of Leonard's nephews, "If Leonard didn't call you a motherfucker, it meant he didn't like you." "'Hey, G.K., motherfucker,'" Chess would sometimes telephone, "'I'm coming to Memphis to see you and Dewey. Pick me up at the airport.'"[9]

George would pick him up, take him to a hotel, and then drive him to see Dewey at night.

For Leonard Chess, all this was part of a carefully orchestrated agenda. After the Memphis visit George would drive him back to the airport to catch a plane to Nashville, where he'd visit with the hot deejays at WLAC. Sam Phillips would do much the same thing for his Sun label from the Memphis end. Instead of flying, however, he preferred to drive to Nashville, Houston, or New Orleans. That was, of course, after he paid a mandatory visit to his buddy at the WHBQ studio.

Other indie chiefs had to fly into town to get to Dewey, but Sam needed only to take a convenient stroll several blocks from his Union Avenue studio to Main Street to ensure that his newest cut would be given the personal Dewey Phillips test. Even though Sam violated no specific written rules, their powerful and close relationship often gave the appearance of collusion. At best, the scheme worked to the distinct advantage of Sam and his Sun label. At the very least it gave him a competitive edge on the other record producers.

If the other indie heads envied Sam's ideal arrangement, however, no one publicly complained. Nonetheless, because of the importance attached to Dewey's role in converting trial balloons into money-making hits for Sam's label, rumors have developed over the years about possible under-the-table kickbacks in the form of what later came to be called payola. Some suspect that Dewey's remuneration was not so much the joy of seeing his predictions about artists and songs come true as it was more material compensation.[10] Did he, that is, receive a monetary reward for playing Sam Phillips's records or, for that matter, anyone else's?

Before examining the allegation it should be noted that even if Dewey were taking money the practice of doing so was common long before the Alan Freed payola scandal broke at the end of the 1950s. It was unquestionably Freed who brought national publicity to the problem and caused the FCC to tighten its rules. That is not to suggest, however, that most people in the record business were completely unaware of the practice before that scandal broke. As early as 1950, *Billboard* ran a series of articles pointing out that "payola has permeated the field to the core."[11] Testifying in 1960 before the congressional committee investigating payola, Paul Ackerman, the music editor of *Billboard,* recognized that "the line of demarcation as to where legitimate song plugging ends and payola begins has always been difficult to determine."[12] Thus, when Sam Phillips loudly proclaims, "We didn't even know what payola was" in the early 1950s, a charitable interpretation might be that he is arguing that there was nothing illegal about the practice until the Freed scandal changed the rules.[13]

At the time that Sam and Dewey were interacting during the early and mid-1950s the practice was perfectly legitimate, and few, in any, were concerned about it. The word *payola* didn't enter the general public's vocabulary until the infamous Miami deejay convention in the spring of 1959. The expose of that convention, with its now-famous *Miami Herald* headline ("Booze, Broads and Bribes"), caused Congress in February of 1960 to open hearings into payola in the record industry in general and the Miami convention in particular. Alan Freed's conviction, dismissal, and subsequent rush to oblivion was the culmination of that investigation. With Freed's career over, the word *payola* quickly replaced the word *communism* as the dirtiest word in American English.[14]

One should be cautious, however, about reading the present into the past. Before the much-publicized Freed affair the record is clear: Radio stations engaged in all sorts of practices, which, by today's standards, seem shady or highly questionable at best. Remember that Dewey began on WHBQ for no money at all in return for openly plugging his records at Grant's. The custom of allowing artists free on-air plugs in return for their talent was a common occurrence on Memphis radio during the late 1940s, and it didn't stop until years later. B.B. King also started working in radio at WDIA, first singing on the air and then being a disc jockey; he received no salary for his time and effort. Like Dewey, the trade-off for B.B. was the privilege of free plugs for upcoming appearances at various night clubs and juke joints in WDIA's listening area.[15]

The practice was so common throughout the South that it was not unusual for local artists to pay a radio station for the air time during which they performed in order that they might plug their gigs. Small-time performers, especially local gospel groups, relied almost exclusively on that promotional method because radio was the most effective way they had to publicize various church appearances.[16]

The practice of paying deejays to play records dated back to the earliest days of radio.[17] As long as record companies put the payments on their books and disc jockeys reported them on their tax returns, no existing laws were broken. By the early 1950s, however, when Ackerman testified during the congressional investigation, he noted that "one of the banes" of the record and radio business was "the abundance of the product. There were several thousand record companies," releasing "about 130 single records and about 100 LP records" every week.[18] Moreover, small indies—Dewey Phillips's bread-and-butter labels—unlike the majors that could afford to employ professional promoters—often relied on payola as the only means of inducing deejays to play their products. WHHM, the Memphis station that carried Dewey's chief rival, Sleepy-Eyed John Lepley, for instance, had a "play-for-pay" policy. A small cash contribution guaranteed a minimum number of air plays.[19]

It is generally accepted that deejays so often received small favors of one kind or another from promoters that no one thought much of the practice before the Freed affair. Even during the investigations Congress made it clear that it was unconcerned with small-time dishonesty and focused on much bigger bribes. As Oren Harris, chair of the committee, said, "I am not talking about going to lunch with somebody or going to a movie. . . . or a $10 Christmas gift. . . . I am talking about the actual payment of money each month for a particular purpose."[20]

The insignificant freebies Dewey openly received would hardly have qualified under a definition of payola. The Green Beetle, for example, Dewey's favorite local pub, would often send free plate lunches to him in exchange for casual free plugs on the air. He also got a lot of free records. But, says Bill Gordon, it was standard in those days for promoters to give away records or small gifts. "They'd frequently take the deejay out to lunch and maybe slip him a little money to hype a particular record or artist. Nobody thought anything of it because everybody did it," he remembers. It is probably safe to assume that Dewey received the same treatment, Gordon says. "So what's the big deal?"[21]

The big deal, in this case, happens to be the many rumors and later accusations made against Dewey. Because he did so much for Falstaff, making the local bottled beer into the number-one-seller in the Mid-South, there were steady rumors that Herb Saddler, Falstaff's distributor, lined Dewey's pocket frequently. The most highly circulated rumor even had Sadler buying Dewey a new Lincoln automobile. Dewey's brother-in-law Bill Kirby, who was with Dewey day and night, however, says that they were sometimes together when Dewey made payments on the Lincoln.[22]

Other allegations are even harsher. There is still no evidence that Dewey received money from anyone, although Larry Nager, the former music critic for the *Commercial Appeal,* has observed, "Some Memphis music insiders estimate Dewey pulled in as much as $100,000 annually from record companies."[23] Perhaps some "insiders" do feel this way, but who they are or how they reached that conclusion will never be known. The source of Nager's information, unfortunately, is undocumented. Yet an assertion that Dewey lined his pockets with enormous amounts of payola cries out for documentation of some sort. At the very least it deserves closer inspection.

First, Dewey was never called before the congressional committee that investigated payola, apparently because there was no reason to suspect he was taking kickbacks. A great many deejays who were called, however, were at the time receiving thousands of dollars a year.[24] Moreover, beyond the congressional investigation there is little proof to sustain the contention that Dewey took a penny from anyone while he worked at the radio station. The documented evidence on the topic is scant; what is available—although sparse—seems to point in the opposite direction. Conventional wisdom, in this instance at least, doesn't withstand careful exploration. Charles Raiteri, for example, who has compiled what can be called the only real collection of documents on Dewey's years at WHBQ, has but a single letter from a record company offering Dewey money to play records—a $25 check from Bob Shad of Decca Records along with a letter asking Dewey to plug certain records. The letter is dated October 27, 1953—relatively early in Dewey's career and years before the scandalous Miami convention and Freed's subsequent conviction.

Much more important, however, in the same file is a response to Shad's letter from John Cleghorn, the WHBQ general manager whose language strongly suggests that WHBQ wanted no part of this practice. "It has come to our attention that you are forwarding checks to Dewey Phillips, apparently for promoting certain tunes on our radio station," Cleghorn wrote on October 29. "Continuation of this practice will seriously jeopardize Mr. Phillips's position with the station and our attitude toward Decca records." Recognizing that payment was indeed a "common practice" at other radio stations around the country, Cleghorn emphasized, "We do not want it at WHBQ." Finally, in what seems to have been an attempt to ferret out any form of pay-for-play activity at the station—no matter who the culprit—he concluded, "If you have further evidence of any WHBQ artists being given any inducement to play records for any company, I would greatly appreciate being advised."[25]

It is possible, of course, to view the evidence from another angle. One could, no doubt, make a case for an argument that Cleghorn was trying to protect himself by putting into writing an official prohibition on payola yet turning his head to the actual practice. Or, because his letter was written in 1953 and refers to "checks," it could indicate that the practice had gone on for awhile before he caught it or decided to do something about it. Nonetheless, the fact that the file contains no other evidence on the matter seems a strong suggestion that Shad's offer was—if not an isolated instance—at least one nipped in the bud quite early.

What actually happened, of course, can never be conclusively determined. Given its surreptitious nature, trying to accurately assess the final truth about payola (a practice that was almost always undercover) is to negotiate a very slippery slope. Still, some people continue to wonder just how much influence Sam Phillips had on Dewey's decision to play a record. Was Sam, or anyone, putting undue pressure on him? More important, what was Dewey's motive when he willingly, often enthusiastically, played almost every acetate that Sam brought to his show?

Even without a smoking gun it is possible to obtain a sense of what went on at the WHBQ studios during Dewey's reign. Many rumors that have persisted over the years are due, in large part, to Dewey himself, especially his frequent on-air references to being paid. As he did with almost every other topical news item, Dewey converted the Freed scandal into a running joke. Like Jay Leno or David Letterman, he knew a spicy topical subject when it came along and milked it for all it was worth. "That's twice I've played that record tonight," he'd shout on the air. "That'll cost you $20—that's $10 a play." When the congressional investigation got underway he had a field day. "We got so many good records, it's awful. Here's another payola record. Boy, if the FCC catches up with me, I'm gone, you know." Bill Kirby remembers well Dewey's "carrying on" about the payola scandal. "It was all a big joke. He didn't mean any of it, but of course people started believing him."[26]

Whenever Jerry Wexler or Leonard Chess dropped by he went ballistic. Once, when Wexler and Ahmet Ertegun (also of Atlantic) were in the studio, he said, "I got a couple of record companies' thieves from Atlantic down here but I tell you what—they just might as well go home because Leonard Chess has done got it all." Then he would play a Chess record.[27]

Dewey, of course, was not oblivious to the fierce competition for airplay on his show. It doesn't necessarily follow, however, that he was on the take. Indeed, his flippant, light-hearted manner of handling the topic on the air hardly suggests illicit subversion. Moreover, if judged by today's standards, Dewey's constant practice of making out-in-the-open, free plugs for various people and products (with no money being exchanged) was a much greater violation of regulations than taking an occasional gift from a record producer. He constantly plugged the Home of the Blues Record Shop or Joe Cuoghi at Pop Tunes, for example, even during segments of the show they did not sponsor. Sometimes, Dewey talked incessantly about stores such as Schwab's on Beale, even though the famous department store was never one of his advertisers. Lansky Brothers' likewise only rarely advertised but was an endless source of chatter because everyone knew that Elvis bought clothes there. "Get y'all some of these sharp threads they got at Lansky Brothers'," Dewey would shout when he did an actual commercial for the famous brothers. "Do like me, good people, pay for 'em while you're wearing 'em out, or when they catch up with you. De-gaaaw!"[28]

Aside from the open plugs, Dewey no doubt inadvertently added more fuel to the smoldering controversy with the excitement he generated over any artist whose record he wanted to promote. "Whoever he was playing, he thought they were at that moment the greatest person around," says Louis Harris, who is convinced that is the real reason listeners believed Dewey was taking kickbacks. "And he made you feel that way too."[29] It was no doubt his tumultuous enthusiasm, especially the famous "Call Sam" refrain that went up every time Dewey thought he was playing a new hit, that could easily have implied that he was little more than Sam Phillips's pliant puppet and made listeners suspect connivance. Sam himself was sensitive to the suspicions that "Call Sam" generated and feared an audience backlash, especially "since everybody thought we were brothers or cousins. I just didn't want people to think that there was any . . . hanky-panky." Although he tried to stop Dewey's constant cry, his admonitions were of little avail. "He didn't anymore pay any attention to me on that. I mean that 'Call Sam' was his logo and he was gonna do it." After a while, though, the phrase became part of the vernacular of the show, like "Call Elvis."[30]

Nonetheless, the phrase caused Sam some degree of discomfort, and over time he became defensive about accusations of shady deals involving Dewey. It was the notion of paying Dewey hard cash that really triggered his adrenaline. Specifically, "payola" was the buzzword that set him off. "Hell, I never gave payola in my life," he shouts at the top of his voice. The idea of paying Dewey for the privilege of airing a new record on *Red, Hot and Blue* becomes a personal insult. "Ask anybody," Sam says, his voice level at a continuous state of elevation, "if they ever heard me trying to put the hurt on Dewey Phillips to play one of my damned records. I mean ever."[31]

Once he settles down, Sam defends his conviction with what he considers to be his best, most convincing argument: "If Dewey Phillips had wanted to have taken payola, he could have been a millionaire, I mean a millionaire, because he was that important to the industry—instead of dying almost a pauper. No way was he dishonest."[32] Recalling Dewey's sad decline at the end of his life, Sam liked to remind those who made charges of payola just how broke and desperate Dewey was. Sam, who graciously assisted the Phillips family on a number of occasions after Dewey was fired from WHBQ, says, "It was unfortunate in his later years that he had to call on so many people for a little help."[33]

Those not persuaded by Sam's position, of course, like to point out that Alan Freed, who did indeed take many kickbacks, also died a near pauper.[34] But then, judging from Sam's remarks, it becomes apparent that he was as proud of his behavior during this period as he was defensive about charges of favoritism. When arguing a contentious point Sam was famous for attempting to convert listeners to his way of thinking with the missionary zeal of a pious preacher. Nevertheless, despite what often seem like self-serving comments—little more than variations on long-winded rationalizations—Sam, in this instance at least, seems to be speaking the truth: There was never any need for him to resort to payola. For him, the notion of pay-for-play was somewhere between absolutely superfluous and slightly absurd.

This conclusion is drawn not from Sam's loud assertions but from realistic recognition of the mutually beneficial relationship that the Phillips boys had established. It was not a one-way street, owned and navigated by Sam Phillips exclusively. Dewey received a number of reciprocal benefits. He was absolutely delighted, for example, Sam brought his freshly cut acetate test-pressings directly to WHBQ. That enabled Dewey to scoop every deejay in the Mid-South by being the first to preview a new Sun release—no small accomplishment, especially considering the cadre of superstars that Sam was beginning to accumulate on his label. "Dewey was flattered that Sam came to him first," George Klein says. "He not only had first crack at it, but a brand new release, especially a new song by Elvis or Jerry Lee, was a big occasion even for Dewey Phillips on *Red, Hot and Blue*."[35] Moreover, Dewey was more than monetarily compensated by the delight he took in having an opportunity to predict a possible hit even before a record was pressed. Actually, it was Dewey rather than Sam who instigated the practice of Sam bringing new acetates to him first. The proof of this is that Dewey wanted to be first with any new disc, and he and George Klein often made the rounds of record distributors during the day. Sometimes, G.K. remembers, Dewey wouldn't wait for a record distributor to get a record. Buster Williams's pressing plant, which produced records for Sun, Atlantic, and Chess, was located in Memphis on Chelsea Avenue, and Dewey would often go there, trying to wheedle new releases before distributors sent them out. When Sam would bring a pre-press acetate to the WHBQ studio he was doing little more than saving Dewey the trouble of having to run it down.[36]

Dewey with a new acetate was a child with a new toy. "He'd get one of those demo copies," Sun rockabilly superstar Billy Lee Riley says, "and he'd play it until it wore out." The new offering would almost always be a very big deal on the show. "OK, pahd'ner, you are hearing Carl Perkins brand new release *for the very first time* right here on *Red, Hot and Blue.*" If he liked it (as he usually did) he'd add, "I'm predictin' this one will go right to the top of the charts. Yessir! Gonna be the hottest cotton-pickin' record in the country—bar none. CALL SAM!"[37]

Why bother with payola? A casual examination of Sam's arrangement with Dewey—with no extra, under-the-table dealings—reveals that it could not have been any more propitious and opportunistic had Sam planned it personally. Once again he was in the perfect place at the perfect time. His Sun Studio arrangement was so timely that many neglected Delta artists he encountered expected to have to pay him for the privilege of recording their songs. By the same token, his arrangement with Dewey was yet another gift from heaven. Dewey's vast listening audience may have been indispensable to Sam's success, but Dewey didn't necessarily demand anything of Sam. After all, Dewey had earlier been in Sam's employ as a talent scout and had also briefly served as a partner in the record business. Sam didn't have to orchestrate anything. At the very least there was no necessity for a payoff.[38] The bottom line is that Dewey would almost always give nearly any record at least one play before deciding for himself (without money or any other kind of tribute) whether to play it again. He played what he wanted, regardless of what anybody did or said, and everyone—especially Sam Phillips—fully realized that.

George Klein says he can't remember seeing actual money change hands, even though it is unlikely that such a transaction would have taken place in the open. He is nonetheless certain there was none because Dewey's pride was as important as Sam's pocketbook. Convinced as well that if Dewey were receiving kickbacks he would never joke about the topic on the air, G.K. emphasizes the men's symbiotic relationship: "Dewey prided himself on his ability to make this decision, because he knew how much Sam respected his opinion." Moreover, Sam knew that Dewey's reputation was at stake; a great deal of ego was involved on both sides. "Amen!" Sam says when asked the extent of Dewey's pride. "When he picked a damn record, he didn't want to be wrong," he told Peter

Guralnick. "How much bullshit have you got in you, man, and when are you gonna deliver? It so happened, by God, that people believed Dewey, and he delivered."[39]

Finally, George Klein's take on instances when heads of record companies visited Dewey lends finality to what was actually going on. He sums up his recollection of these days by conjuring up an almost textbook innocence of the 1950s, arguing perhaps rather naively that the camaraderie of people in the record business always overshadowed fierce competition or wrong-doing. His impression is that payola, although widespread throughout the industry, was the last thing on people's minds because they were all enjoying themselves way too much.

Whenever out-of-town studio heads came around, Klein knew he was in for a good time because they would usually get together with Sam and Dewey and go out after the show ended at midnight. G.K. is convinced that such events weren't payola so much as it was good public relations—something George saw as an extension of social activity. "They might take me to lunch, or they would hang out with me and Dewey later that night. We'd go out to the Pig 'n' Whistle [barbecue] to get something to eat, or something like that," he says.[40]

On occasion, however, competition in the record business could be fierce and briefly eclipse congeniality. Klein recalls an amicable gathering late one evening after Dewey's show, when visiting record executives got together in a hotel room in the Chisca, where they stayed when they came to town because WHBQ's studio was there. "The conversation got real serious between Sam Phillips and Jerry Wexler of Atlantic Records," G.K. remembers. Where normally such gatherings would include a lot of drinking and convivial discussion, Wexler became serious on this occasion. He turned to Sam and asked bluntly for the magic "trade secret" to his success in the studio. Specifically, Wexler wanted to know how Sam managed to achieve the famous "slapback" effect that most listeners called "echo" and others sometimes confused with the rockabilly sound. "Sam," Wexler asked, "how in the hell do you get that funky sound on Sun Records?" Atlantic was already a big label then, with a lot of monster hits, and even though Sam was already making a big noise in Memphis with Sun, up to that point he had never revealed publicly how he got what was still a highly classified trade secret. Suddenly the mood became solemn. Everyone in the room grew quiet, waiting to see if Sam would be coaxed into finally revealing how he obtained the long-protected, mysterious sound. Slowly and dramatically, Sam paused and cleared his throat. As he tells the story, George also pauses, somewhat melodramatically, and holds the punch line until the final moment: "Sam turned around and faced Wexler, looked him right in the eye and said, 'Well, Jerry, guess what—I ain't gonna tell you.'" If there was tension in the room, that remark broke it. The room exploded in laughter.[41]

10

Dewey and Elvis:
The Synthesized Sound

"If Elvis had consciously sought to synthesize and alchemize blues, gospel, R&B and white country music," *Newsweek* magazine wrote on the twentieth anniversary of Presley's death in 1997, "he couldn't have chosen a better mentor than Sam Phillips." Had *Newsweek* attempted to locate the precise origin of the magic sound that Sam so successfully synthesized it would have included among Elvis's mentors Memphis's other musically famous Phillips. Without question Dewey was as responsible as Sam for laying down the dizzying array of musical sources the young Elvis heard, absorbed, and passed along to much of the world. *Newsweek* did, however, give Dewey a kind of unofficial recognition by pointing out that Memphis, by the time Elvis arrived on the scene, was about the only place where black singers who belted out blues and gospel and white hillbillies who yodeled country and western came together and "rubbed elbows . . . often over the airwaves."[1]

Sam may have created the sound in his diminutive Union Avenue studio, but it was Dewey's wide-ranging broadcasts that were responsible for disseminating that sound and attracting listeners. Without Dewey, Elvis Presley (or, for that matter, any Mid-South teenager in the early 1950s) would never have been conveniently exposed to the jam-packed cornucopia of music—especially the number of seldom-heard black artists who characterized every broadcast of *Red, Hot and Blue*.

When the impressionable thirteen-year-old Elvis Presley arrived in Memphis from Tupelo, Mississippi, in 1948, for example, the best-selling pop records in the country were Nat "King" Cole's "Nature Boy," Dinah Shore's "Buttons and Bows," and "A Little Bird Told Me" by Evelyn Knight with the Star Dusters. Memphis airwaves were also filled with the sounds of "Mañana" by Peggy Lee and "Now Is the Hour" by Margaret Whiting as well as various versions of "On a Slow Boat to China." On the lighter side was the Art Mooney version of "I'm Looking over a Four-Leaf Clover," Spike Jones's "All I Want for Christmas (Is My Two Front Teeth)," Kay Kyser's "Woody Woodpecker Song," and Arthur Godfry's late-1940s' attempt at humor, "Slap Her Down again Paw."[2] But all wasn't inane and innocuous. The standard country and western charts were led by Eddy Arnold, Cowboy Copas, and Hank Thompson. More important, some previously unheard black artists were beginning to cross over to the mainstream market and disturb the existing order. Fats Domino had just recorded "The Fat Man," and John Lee Hooker had produced what would become a million-seller, "I'm in the Mood."

But it was Louis Jordan, the legendary black performer from just over the Memphis-Arkansas bridge in Brinkley, Arkansas, who made a name for himself by producing what were still awkwardly referred to in official trade publications like *Billboard* as "race records." His "Run, Joe" was the most frequently played record in that category in 1948. On June 25, 1949, however, just months before Dewey Phillips was to break out with *Red, Hot and Blue, Billboard* replaced its clumsy "race" designation with the more descriptive "rhythm and blues." In that new category the number-one best-seller was Jordan's blistering version of "Saturday Night Fish Fry." (Even after the designation of race ceased, however, things were still slow to change. WREC announcer Fred Cook remembers going into record stores in Memphis in the 1950s and seeing a category marked "race" among the 78s.)[3]

Jordan was to dominate *Billboard*'s ratings during the 1940s with twenty-one number-one songs on R&B, country, and pop charts during the decade. From 1942 to 1951 he had an incredible fifty-seven R&B hits. Indeed, Jerry Wexler coined the term *rhythm and blues*, but it was Jordan who popularized its musical expression. Even though Jordan recorded for Decca, a primary label, the majors were already following the new musical direction started by the up-and-coming indies. Jordan turned out a monster hit, "Caldonia," and was also responsible for some of the best of the early crossover music. He did minor R&B classics like "Ain't Nobody Here but Us Chickens"; "Beans and Cornbread" (used by Spike Lee in the film *Malcolm X*); and the number B.B. King used for years to open his shows, "Let the Good Times Roll."[4] In addition to being one of the best R&B black crossover performers Jordan was also one of Dewey's favorites, which meant that Mid-South listeners, including the newly arrived Elvis, were exposed to him early. "I made just as much money off white people as I did colored," Jordan liked to brag. "I could play a white joint this week and a colored next."[5]

Black crossover R&B stylists like Jordan were not the only entertainers who appeared regularly on a typical Dewey Phillips show. This was Memphis, which meant that country singers were listened to as well as black artists. Red Foley's "Tennessee Saturday Night" on Decca was one of the biggest country hits of 1948, one that many consider to be a forerunner of the famous rockabilly sound that most music authorities say Sam Phillips did not arrive at until the early 1950s. Although there is considerable disagreement about the matter, at least some argue that Sam's "Rocket 88" (by Ike Turner in March 1951) was the first rock 'n' roll song.[6]

What is now the frequently imitated Sun Records sound—which came to be conveniently labeled as "rockabilly"—is generally defined as a combination of two broad musical genres, country and R&B. It is what one writer cleverly tagged "black and backwoods."[7] That definition has been repeated so often that it is accepted as gospel. The fact is, however, that the sound so closely associated with Elvis and others in the battery of stars whose work Sam produced at Sun Studios was nothing less than a synthesis of a huge and variegated amalgamation of music that had been heard around Memphis and in the Mid-South for years—most of it on a typical Dewey Phillips broadcast.

There is no question, however, that black and backwoods made up the kernel of the sound. "It was a giant wedding ceremony," was the way Elvis's co-discoverer, Marion Keisker, put it, referring to the way black and white had to connect in order to merge these great musical traditions. "It was like two feuding clans had been brought together."[8] The clans may not have feuded, but each had certainly claimed its own turf.

It was not just those two sounds. The final rockabilly product was a carefully blended combination drawn from a virtual smorgasbord of music—rhythm and blues, gospel (both black and white), country, jazz, boogie-woogie, and even bluegrass—all of which seemed to have converged in Memphis during the late 1940s.[9] The melding of these sounds at this particular time was no doubt due to a number of factors, not the least of which was the uniquely fortunate geography of Memphis itself. The city, at the crossroads of the Mid-South, drew talent from various directions. Pete Daniel, who has emphasized the rural origins of many 1950s' black performers, has pointed out that the vast number of African American artists that Sam Phillips put on his Sun label—"B.B. King, Joe Hill Louis, Rufus Thomas, the Prisonaires, Junior Parker, Roscoe Gordon,

Jackie Brensten, Ike Turner, James Cotton, and Howlin' Wolf"—all grew up in an area that was just a few hours' drive from Memphis.[10]

Serving as the musical capital for the confluence of diverse cultures meant that the city's sound always had two major groupings at its core, but even that uniqueness is difficult to isolate. Attempting to draw a clear distinction between "black" and "backwoods" can often lead to trouble. The entities were never entirely isolated from one another, and an effort to separate them can be as misleading as it is frustrating. How can one totally segregate black music from country? Specifically, why should black people's music—designated as R&B—preclude it from being labeled country as well? The backgrounds of many African American R&B musicians, especially those who came from the heart of the Delta, were, after all, rural. "If you took a [white] Southern country person and a Southern black," Sam Phillips used to argue, "they were damn close together."[11] Even if a more urbane southern black was beginning to emerge after the war, many black artists who would contribute significantly to the early, influential Sun sound during the 1950s were recent transplants to the city, and their style was deeply rooted in the country soil.

B.B. King, for example, like Dewey Phillips, also listened faithfully to the *Grand Ole Opry* as a young teenager. In an interview conducted at the Center for Southern Folklore in the early 1980s, King pointed out that in his youth he was as taken with country and western music as with the blues. As a boy in Indianola, Mississippi, he listened to the *Opry* over the same WSM out of Nashville that Dewey Phillips tuned to in Adamsville, Tennessee. He recalled, "I was familiar with Roy Acuff and Minnie Pearl and people like that—Merle Travis, Bill Monroe—all these people I knew very well from [WSM] radio."[12]

Despite its complicated origin, however, country and western music— often disparagingly referred to as "hillbilly"—was invariably a favorite of white Memphians. Most local radio stations in the late 1940s devoted at least some portion of their programming to it. Memphis music, in other words, even immediately after the war, was still uniquely southern. There was Hank Williams and Eddie Arnold as well as Frank Sinatra, Perry Como, Peggy Lee, Jo Stafford, and Guy Lombardo. Before Dewey, many Memphians still fortified themselves with the innocuous twangs of country and western, mixed with the latest pop offerings and spiced with an occasional black R&B artist such as Louis Jordan.

But country and western sounds hardly had the potential for a musical revolution. In fact, country music has always been considered tradition-al—the closest thing the nation has had to a "standard American" variety.

Perceived as music of the working class, its whining tones and homiletic messages have made it palatable to a mass audience of all ages.[13]

As evidence of just how conservative country and western music is, its southern variety has often been mixed with traditional local politics. In Memphis there is no better example of that than the Tennessee governor's race during the hotly contested election year of 1948—the year Dewey Phillips arrived at Grant's and began worrying Gordon Lawhead to let him broadcast on WHBQ.

The very week in October that Nat D. Williams broke the color barrier by becoming the South's first publicly recognized black deejay on WDIA, another event was taking place that would warm the hearts of local country and western fans not inclined to listen to WDIA's all-black fare. They needed only to wander down to Court Square in the center of town and hear Roy Acuff and his Smoky Mountain Boys kick up their style of what the *Commercial Appeal* labeled a "hillbilly jamboree" for free. Acuff, already a country and western superstar, was one of the regular favorites on the *Grand Ole Opry*. A free concert itself would be treat enough, but this particular extravaganza offered more than just Acuff's music. Roy himself was the GOP candidate for governor of the state of Tennessee in 1948. His music, alas, was apparently more appealing than his politics. He lost the race to Gov. Gordon Browning by a substantial margin.[14]

If country music was traditional, the other current gushing into the Memphis confluence, the Delta blues, was much more culturally threatening. Stemming from the interior of the Deep South, these sounds were potentially much more disturbing to a white mainstream audience. The artists were predominantly black, and the blues' style and message a sharp departure from the norm. Rolling up from the Mississippi Delta through the conduit of Beale Street (and, thanks to WDIA and Dewey Phillips, starting to saturate the airwaves), the blues' soulful rhythms were fraught with rudimentary sounds that would later, in the words of one music critic, "shake teenagers out of their white skin gentility."[15]

A large number of white teenagers who lived in Memphis had parents who had distinctly rural roots. They had already been lured to the new, synthesized sound of black and backwoods through the corn-fed antics of the incorrigibly countrified Dewey Phillips. Dewey shook up the peculiarly southern variety of those white teenagers, and he did so long before the most important teenager of all, Elvis Presley, made his appearance. Before Elvis gathered the sounds into one that transformed the musical landscape, Daddy-O-Dewey was serving up ingredients that went into the final product. By the time Presley arrived, Dewey had systematically trained a younger generation of listeners to appreciate the innovative sounds of black artists. "When Elvis came along, everybody says we were listening to Kay Star, Patti Page, and Perry Como," says High School Eddie Richardson, a former Memphis freelance disc jockey who specializes in 1950s' parties. "We weren't. We were already rock 'n' rollers. By listening to Dewey," says Richardson, who like most Mid-South teenagers was a devoted *Red, Hot and Blue* fan, "we were already turned on to the sounds of the Clovers and Drifters and Hank Ballard and the Midnighters and Chuck Willis."[16]

Not only would most white teenagers never have heard the black sounds, but, more important, they would have missed a great many other musical genres as well because Dewey wasn't playing black music exclusively. He turned on Memphis audiences to Little Richard, Chuck Berry, LaVern Baker, Howlin' Wolf, T-Bone Walker and Muddy Waters, but he played them all—R&B, country and western, gospel, standard pop, and always a bit of genuinely weird, off-the-wall material. Even though his first love was country music and he came to be identified with R&B, it was the variety of music that *Red, Hot and Blue* managed to extend.

On any given night listeners got what might be called a Dewey Phillips's amalgamated hodge-podge. Only on *Red, Hot and Blue* could you have Dean Martin's "That's Amore" followed by Big Mama Thornton's "Hound Dog"; Patti Page followed by Howlin' Wolf; Mahalia Jackson's "Move on up a Little Higher" preceding Lloyd Price's "Lawdy, Miss Clawdy"; and then Hank Williams and Rosetta Tharpe back to back. Only by listening to Daddy-O-Dewey did you hear everything from B.B. King's "Three O'Clock Blues" to Muddy Waters's "Hoochie Coutchie Man." And just about the time that you thought Dewey had slipped totally out of the mainstream he'd throw Frankie Laine's "That's My Desire" on the turntable.[17]

It is true that any one of these artists, black or white, could have been picked up elsewhere on other Memphis radio stations in the 1950s. It was only on *Red, Hot and Blue,* however, that it was possible to hear this great variety of sound on a single program. Even though most local stations were starting to gradually change their programming, the little diverse music that did exist was all over the Memphis dial—until Dewey.[18] The popular Sleepy-Eyed John Lepley, for example, had a three-to-five afternoon slot on WHHM filled with the latest country and western sounds. Taking his theme song from Merle Travis's record ("Sleepy-Eyed John /

better get your britches on / Sleepy-Eyed John / better tie your shoes"), John had a lock on the city's hardcore country and western audience. Those who wanted to hear hillbilly music made it a point to listen to Sleepy-Eyed John. The difficulty, for some people, however was that he programmed nothing but country and western.

People who wanted to hear the latest in R&B or funky Delta blues could tune to WDIA, and because fully half of that station's record fare was devoted to black gospel music, you could also pick that up as well. Once again, however, WDIA carried nothing but black programming, to the exclusion of everything else. Almost without exception the station's complete format—all music, news and variety shows throughout the day and night—was pitched strictly to the black community. It is true that WDIA, right from its beginning, had a strong appeal to a small number of whites, especially young teenagers like Elvis who were fascinated by previously unheard black artists. Even though the station made no pre-text of appealing to anyone but the black community, whites certainly listened, if only surreptitiously.

Nonetheless, even these hip young whites inevitably grew tired of the steady diet of all-black programming. Compounding this tendency was the fact that at least some whites who were strongly attracted to the black music were still constrained enough by their traditional prejudices to feel uncomfortable listening to an all-black station, especially in the presence of others or when called on a phone survey.[19]

Seen in this light, Dewey's part in selling black music to a white audience becomes even more important to the birth of rock 'n' roll in the Mid-South. It was certainly not an easy sell. Nelson George has suggested that the term *rock and roll* was used by whites in the 1950s "to camouflage its black roots" that were sunk deep in rhythm and blues, itself a term born in the 1940s "as a description of a synthesis of black musical genres."[20] A white man playing the black music, however, was perfectly legitimate for whites, especially those who might be reluctant to listen to an all-black station or too embarrassed to admit they did. For that reason Rufus Thomas gives Dewey nearly as much credit as Elvis for popularizing black music. Most whites, he insists, "didn't pay attention" when blacks sang their own music; as whites, though, Dewey and Elvis "gave black music an injection like it had never had before."[21]

Doing for whites what WDIA had done for blacks, Dewey legitimized the black sound for a white audience and made it all the more palatable by mixing the music on his show, synthesizing black and white, country and blues, gospel and pop. He did even more. Ironically, WDIA, which was still afraid of alienating white listeners (especially when it initially changed its format), tended to avoid gutbucket blues artists. According to David Evans, an authority on Memphis music, "WDIA often played the more urbane blues, while Dewey would get down and play the funkier stuff."[22] But Dewey's smorgasbord of selections interested not just white people. He had an impact on black performers in Memphis as well, especially those whose friendship he made even before going on the air: B.B. King, Rufus Thomas, Bobby "Blue" Bland, Edward "Prince Gabe" Kirby, and a host of other Beale Street musicians.

Once those black performers began to listen to his show, they got the full treatment. Many of the African American musicians whose names have since become synonymous with the blues absorbed other styles of music early on, much of it from Dewey's mixture of musical entries. Bland told Memphis newspaper reporters Margaret McKee and Fred Chisenhall that he wasn't interested in hillbilly music until he came to Memphis and began to listen to the radio. Like most black musicians, he was a regular fan of *Red, Hot and Blue* and picked up Dewey's steady flow of country and western. "I still know more hillbilly tunes than I do blues," Bland reported. "Hank Snow, Hank Williams, Eddie Arnold—so much feeling, so much sadness."[23]

Finally, and most important, Dewey's three-hour quintessential mixture had its longest-lasting historical impact on one of his biggest fans, an aspiring musician who had just arrived from Tupelo. The fans of Elvis Presley emphasize that he picked up the influential black sound in the early days by listening to WDIA. Barbara Pittman, Elvis's close friend at the time, even suggests that he listened to WDIA even more than to Dewey. WDIA, she says, was "his favorite station." Both the much criticized Albert Goldman biography of Presley and Peter Guralnick's highly praised study recognize the radio station's influence. I went to high school with Elvis and later worked at WDIA. At one point I brought him to a WDIA *Goodwill Revue,* and he said that he was a regular fan of the station, listening as much for the gospel music as he did for R&B.[24]

All that is true enough. It could also, however, be argued with equal certainty that Elvis heard the same black performers with a greater degree of regularity by faithfully listening to Dewey on *Red, Hot and Blue.* And listen he did. Elvis may have never made his initial record for Sun had it not been for Dewey. Sam Phillips maintains that Elvis managed "to get up the courage to come into the studio" and record only after listening to Dewey's show. "He told me right here in this room," Sam told Norm Shaw during an interview at Sun, "that the thing that really got him interested in Sun Records was he loved 'Mystery Train' that I cut with Little Junior Parker. He loved that on Ol' Dewey's show."[25]

It is almost impossible to measure the impact that *Red, Hot and Blue* had on the young Elvis. Evan "Buzzy" Forbess, one of Elvis' closest friends, lived with him in the Lauderdale Courts during those early formative years after Presley arrived in Memphis. Forbess, who didn't enjoy the black music as much as Elvis did, says Presley was so tuned into Dewey that he had little choice about the influence he had on him: "Dewey Phillips had his radio show and played a lot of records by black entertainers. . . . It's not a case of liking or not like." Presley was so locked into Dewey's show that "he just sang what was."[26] "What was," of course, was the multitude of sound emanating from the WHBQ dial.

Elvis may have been initiated into rhythm and blues by listening to all-black WDIA, but an even stronger influence on his singing career was the broad range of musical talent he encountered when he listened to Dewey. Elvis's musical tastes, Sam Phillips says, "ran the gamut." And where else could Elvis hear that gamut of sound on a single show except *Red, How and Blue?* Elvis liked Dean Martin's work as much as B.B. King's. He was as enamored by the sounds of Rosetta Tharpe as by Howlin' Wolf and liked Hank Snow and Eddie Arnold as much as Jackie Wilson and Clyde McFadder. Many of his fans are often surprised to learn of his fondness for traditional fare. "I like Crosby, Como, Sinatra, all the big ones," he once told Robert Johnson. "They had to be good to get there."[27] When Presley left for the army he stopped by Joe Cuoghi's Pop Tunes to collect an armload of records, and Johnson faithfully reported each of his choices (most of which would seldom have been heard on WDIA): "Dean Martin's 'Return to Me,' Nat Cole's 'Looking Back,' Pat Boone's 'Too Soon to Know,' Jo Stafford's 'Sweet Little Darling,' Don Gibson's 'I Can't Stop Loving You,' and the Chantelles' 'Maybe.'"[28]

Dewey's influence was inescapable. Elvis, like most Memphis teenagers, had passed an inordinate number of hours listening to *Red, Hot and Blue* long before that fateful night in 1954 when Sam Phillips brought the acetate recording of "That's All Right, Mama" to the WHBQ studios and Dewey conducted the celebrated first live interview with the future king of rock 'n' roll.

11

Dewey Introduces Elvis
to the World

As unauthenticated stories surrounding the life and career of Elvis Presley
continue to grow, so does the degree of difficulty in trying to sort truth
from fiction. The notion, for example, of a young Elvis Presley hitting
the night spots and juke joints of Beale Street shortly after arriving in
Memphis in 1948 has become part of the Presley folklore. The concept,
however, like much of the Presley legend, is impossible to verify from
reliable sources. More important, in this instance at least, it strikes most
knowledgeable Memphians as well as more recent serious scholars as
being totally unrealistic.[1]

It is conceivable that a very young Elvis, thirteen and fresh out of
Mississippi, might have ventured down to Lansky Brothers shortly after
arriving to try on clothes. Bernard Lansky, for instance, remembers that
"Elvis used to work at the Lowe's [State] Theater around the corner [from
Beale] and he used to get off for lunch and walk around."[2] That would
have been sometime after the fall of 1950, when Presley first started
working at the movie theater. But even had he frequented Lanskys' before meeting Dewey (the store was in the first block of Beale Street) it
was in an area often visited by as many whites as blacks. The clubs and
joints—those places where Beale came to life musically—were further
down the street in the third or fourth block.

Most authors who make the mistake of placing a very young Elvis further south on Beale also emphasize that he started listening to WDIA and
WHBQ almost as soon as he arrived in 1948. The latter part of that argument is, of course, true.[3] Elvis eagerly listened to black music, whether
on the air or recorded, very soon after moving to the city. But listening
to music and going inside clubs were two entirely different things. For

a young white teenager from Mississippi it was a quantum leap from flipping on a radio dial or dropping a needle on a turntable to physically walking toward the end of Beale Street and realizing that you were the only young white person for blocks around.

Informed Memphians are convinced that Elvis's first exposure to this area of Beale Street (the one most white people considered off limits at the time) likely came only after Dewey Phillips introduced him to it in 1954. Those closest to Dewey and Elvis agree that the two did not formally meet until that year.[4] George Klein, the closest of all to both men during this period, has said that Dewey "did not know Elvis until Sam brought that acetate to the studio in July of '54." Moreover, Dewey's widow, Dot, and his two sisters, Marjorie and Betty, cannot recall their brother knowing Elvis previously. When Presley was eighteen, Dewey was twenty-seven. "Elvis was just a young boy, and Dewey was an older man," says Dewey's sister Betty Kirby. "He would have had no reason to know him."[5]

Even though Elvis had never met Dewey, he knew of him from the radio show and was, without question, one of Dewey's biggest fans. Elvis listened faithfully to *Red, Hot and Blue* from shortly after coming to Memphis in 1948. It is also possible that Dewey may have seen Elvis earlier than 1954. Dewey told his friend, the writer Stanley Booth, in 1968 that before Elvis made his first record he "hung around" the WHBQ studio practically "every night" while Dewey was doing his show. That memory, however, makes Elvis little more than a typical groupie, waiting for the right moment to make contact with Dewey.[6]

It is also possible that Elvis might have seen Dewey at Pop Tunes or the Home of the Blues but had not met him. Some have also suggested that Elvis might have met Dewey at the Sun studio before his first recording session, but Sam Phillips says they were unacquainted with each other before Elvis recorded "That's All Right, Mama." "I think [Dewey] may have seen Elvis hanging around the studio [just before the recording]," he recalls, "because Scotty and Bill were in and out. But that was it."[7]

Another possibility for an early meeting between the two men would have been at the Chickasaw Ballroom in the basement of the Chisca Hotel. Herbie O'Mell had booked Elvis there a number of times on Saturday nights in 1953, a full year before Dewey spun his first record. Herbie, the same age as Elvis, remembers the year exactly because he was a senior at Central High School. He rented the ballroom, paid Elvis $100, charged admission, and usually "picked up a couple of hundred dollars every Saturday night." Dewey, he says, would "drop by sometimes after his show" (WHBQ moved its studios there in 1953). He was, however, usually "just passing through and didn't stay long." O'Mell candidly admits having "no recognition of Dewey actually meeting Elvis" or of Dewey being present when Elvis performed.[8]

Stories nonetheless persist of a young Elvis hanging out in the barrelhouses and juke joints of Beale during the late 1940s and early 1950s before he met Dewey. The stories still strike Memphians who know the city's history as being absurd. Jim Dickinson, probably the best long-time observer of the Memphis music scene, still becomes exercised over what he considers as wild distortion of fact. "The first block, maybe block and a half, is where white people could go *in the day time* because it just wasn't OK to be there," he shouts.[9]

Significantly, Peter Guralnick, after characteristically exhaustive research, has reached essentially the same conclusion. Guralnick has trouble placing a young Elvis on Beale before his rise to fame locally and finds "it far more likely that he would start going down to the clubs once he had achieved a certain measure of confidence and respect." Guralnick points out that Robert Henry's often-cited claim—reported in Margaret McKee and Fred Chisenhall's *Beale Black and Blue*—of taking Elvis to the Hotel Men's Improvement Club (later the Flamingo Room) on Hernando just off Beale should be taken with Henry's later, critical qualifier: "I met him through Dewey Phillips."[10] Further investigation of McKee and Chisenhall's transcript of the interview with Henry in 1973 makes it quite clear that Elvis didn't get to Beale Street until he met Dewey. On the tape, Chisenhall asks Henry, "Now, let me understand. It was Dewey Phillips, the disc jockey who [was] personally acquainted with Elvis, who first brought [Elvis] to you. Is that right?" Henry responds, "Yes."[11] Henry also told Charles Raiteri essentially the same story much later in his life. Henry, then eighty-seven, recalled Presley's first appearances in the black community: "He used to come down to a colored [nightclub] on Hernando" to watch black performers. "I showed him how coloreds worked." When Raiteri asks him how Elvis got there in the first place, Henry replies that Dewey Phillips brought him.[12]

Other Beale Street regulars give voice to the same story. Both Andrew "Sunbeam" Mitchell and Robert Henry's wife were interviewed in 1983 by the Center for Southern Folklore in Memphis. Sunbeam remembers Elvis occasionally sitting in on a session with Bill Harvey and his band. Before that first appearance, however, he also recalls "Dewey Phillips coming around and telling me about Elvis." When Robert Henry's wife was asked if she could recollect whether Elvis "would ever sit in at any of the clubs," she replies that she saw nothing like that, remembering only Elvis coming to Henry's record shop on several occasions by himself because "[Dewey] Phillips sent him down there." She remembers Dewey telling Elvis, "'Go down there to Robert Henry's.' I guess he did it out of curiosity that they were playing music and such as that, well, I guess that he wanted to be there."[13]

Robert "Honeymoon" Garner, a jazz pianist and later a WDIA disc jockey, recalled young Elvis jamming at the Flamingo Room. "Yeah, he always came up there with Dewey Phillips. I met him a couple of times." B.B. King did not encounter Elvis until long after meeting Dewey on Beale in the late 1940s. In an interview at the Center for Southern Folklore in 1981, B.B. was asked if he ever jammed with Elvis. By the time he met him at Mitchell's Hotel, B.B. responded, Elvis had begun to make a name for himself. "He and some other guys had heard about us playing, and they came around."[14]

Finally, another frequently cited quotation used to claim that Elvis was on the Beale Street music scene very early after his arrival in Memphis is Nat D. Williams's comments, taken also from his interview with McKee and Chisenhall. Before becoming WDIA's first black disc jockey, Nat for years emceed Amateur Night at the famous Palace Theater on Beale. Reflecting on those experiences he says, "Elvis Presley on Beale Street when he first started was a favorite man."[15] The observation sounds authentic and authoritative, especially coming from one who knew Beale Street so well. The problem, however, is that McKee and Chisenhall interviewed Nat in 1973 after the first of what would be several strokes. I worked closely with Nat for five years at WDIA during the 1950s and appreciated and respected his razor-sharp mind. McKee and Chisenhall interviewed him during his later years, however, and the interviews are suspect because of Nat's uncharacteristic and confused ramblings. He talks, for example, about Elvis appearing on Beale Street while Nat was emceeing Amateur Night. "So when he had a show down there at the Palace, everybody got ready for something good. Yeah. They were crazy about Presley," Nat said. Nat stopped emceeing Amateur Night, however, in 1940, when the five-year-old Elvis still lived in Mississippi.[16]

In sum, until he was well known locally there are no documented instances of Elvis jamming in Memphis clubs. Even though there are frequent references to sightings of him on Beale Street during these early years, whether at the Home of the Blues, the Hotel Improvement Club, or Robert Henry's record shop, Dewey Phillips was already close by his side.

Clearly, it was Dewey who introduced Presley to Beale Street's juke joints and night spots, and he did so only after making him instantly famous on July 10, 1954, by spinning his first record and interviewing him on the air. What many claim are authentic Elvis sightings occurred only after that date. Presley's greatly increased presence on Beale occurred only after he began to keep company with Dewey following the celebrated interview.[17] Peter Guralnick reports that Elvis told his then-girlfriend Dixie Locke that he and Dewey often went to Beale together. It was only then that he met B.B. King, saw "a nattily dressed Lowell Fulson at the Club Handy," and checked out Calvin Newborn, who was doing "the splits while he was playing the guitar at the Flamingo Lounge."[18]

One thing that is certain: Dewey and Elvis became friends almost immediately. Dot Phillips, for instance, remembers Elvis being a regular caller in the Phillips household very shortly after his initial appearance on *Red, Hot and Blue.* "The first time I saw him, he was a striking good-looking boy," she recalls. She pinpoints the date of their first acquaintance even more precisely. It was only a few days after Dewey interviewed Elvis "when Dewey brought him out to the house and gave him some of his clothes. They were real nice clothes, 'cause Dewey didn't wear nothing but the best." Dot Phillips also remembers the first time she heard Elvis sing in a live performance. Again, it was a short time after the interview and at the Bon Air Club at Summer and Mendenhall Road in Memphis. Dot is specific about time and place because that is where Dewey had taken her in 1954 to celebrate their sixth wedding anniversary. Elvis was a spectacle to behold. He sang "Old Shep," "That's All Right," and "Blue Moon of Kentucky." She remembers not only his voice and every song he sang but also being impressed with how neat and well dressed he was and, of course, the courteous, deferential manner he assumed in front of older people. "He was quite shy and the most mannerly young man I had ever met. Everything was 'yes ma'm' and 'no ma'm.'"[19]

Dorothy Phillips's most vivid memory, however, concerns a fortnight earlier, when Dewey introduced Elvis, if not to the world, at least to his Memphis and Mid-South audience on *Red, Hot and Blue.* Among Elvis fans, that event ranks as one of the best-known interviews in the history of radio. Even though Dot is certain that neither she nor Dewey knew Elvis before that night, she does remember thinking that this was someone who would soon become very important.

Neither Dot (nor most of the world, for that matter) was aware of it at the time, but Dewey's involvement in what would be one of the quintessential events in American popular music—the airing of Elvis's first acetate recording had started almost twenty-four hours earlier. Dewey, as was often the case, had stopped by Sam Phillips's recording studio the previous night after *Red, Hot and Blue*. He was not actually present when Elvis recorded "That's All Right." Sam had made the tape of it a few days earlier but had not yet decided to cut the acetate disc. It was about 12:30 when Dewey appeared. Sam sat him down, poured him a beer, and let him listen to the tape. Dewey was fascinated and, according to Sam, uncharacteristically quiet. As Sam told Peter Guralnick, "He was reticent, and I was glad that he was." Had he said, "'Hey, man, this is a hit, it's a hit,' I would have thought Dewey was just trying to make me feel good." After listening to the tape repeatedly on into the wee hours of the morning, both men decided to go home and sleep on it. Sam was surprised by a telephone call from Dewey early the next morning. "I didn't sleep well last night, man," he said, "because [I] kept thinking about that record." Those were the magic words Sam needed. When Dewey told him he wanted two copies for his show that night and concluded, "We ain't letting anybody know," Sam had no more doubts about what to do with the tape. He immediately went to the studio and cut both acetates.[20]

The first play went out on Dewey's show, and all hell broke loose. Dewey's wild ravings about "That's All Right" generated so much excitement that Sam had nearly six thousand back orders before the record had been cut for sale in Memphis let alone released in any market outside the city. As Elvis's guitarist Scotty Moore said, "Dewey Phillips had played it on the radio, creating such a stampede" that there was an immediate crisis, requiring Sam to work with Elvis several nights in a row trying to record a B side.[21]

Sam Phillips, in a rare, abstruse moment, becomes uncharacteristically speechless when describing that memorable first-play evening: "Dewey put the damn thing on the turntable in the control room and really—   ." Dot Phillips's account is much more precise. She remembers talking to her husband over the telephone during the course of the chaos. "In between all the phone calls and telegrams that started pouring in, he'd call me and say, 'They're driving me crazy with these requests.'" Even the normally frenetic Daddy-O-Dewey himself was visibly and vocally shaken by the frenzy. Each time he played the record he'd call Dot and say, "'I'm having to play it again,'" as though each time came as a surprise. Dot says she "will remember that night as long as she lives."[22]

She also remembers what happened several days later. The Phillipses were going out of town, and Dewey, as usual, was furiously flipping the dial of the car's radio while driving. Finally, he tuned to Sleepy-Eyed John

Lepley, whose afternoon fare of country and western music on WHHM made him one of the few Memphis deejays whose popularity approached Dewey's. Sleepy-Eyed John still had hordes of devoted pure country fans who wanted no part of rock 'n' roll and thought Elvis Presley sounded entirely too black. He was, Dot says, "just going on and on about how he'd heard everybody say that 'That's All Right' was supposed to be such a great record, 'but I'll tell you what I think about it,' he said, and then you heard a sound like the record hitting the inside of a garbage can." She adds, "After Elvis got so big, Sleepy-Eyed John tried to say that he had been the first one in Memphis to play the record."[23]

That's Dot's take. Sam Phillips's version is that John didn't play either side until some days—maybe weeks—later and then it was only "Blue Moon of Kentucky," which he would "proceed to make fun of. He would do nothing but pan the record and make fun of Elvis." Things got so bad, Sam says, that Vernon Presley grew angry. "Now, Vernon very seldom got mad, but he came by my studio and said, 'I'm going up and whip this son-of-a-bitch's ass.'" Strong language to be sure. In truth, Sleepy-Eyed John was taken with the more countrified sound of "Blue Moon of Kentucky" and therefore played what proved to be the flip side of the monster hit "That's All Right."[24]

Lepley was a highly talented individual whose misfortune it was to be a contemporary of Dewey Phillips. He, too, was an interesting character, and he often drew dissimilar reactions from people. Lepley probably boosted Elvis's country following as much as anyone save Dewey. After Presley's initial popularity, for example, he was responsible for booking several gigs for him at the Eagle's Nest, a local nightclub where he frequently promoted bands.[25]

Sleepy-Eyed John's reaction aside, it was the fans' immediate response to the record that proved important. Stories surrounding it have become part of the Presley liturgy, recited from memory not just by diehard Elvis fans but by others who enjoy popular music in general. Not surprisingly, however, the story has as many variations as individuals to recount them; trying to make an accurate determination of what actually happened that night is difficult. How many times, for example, was the record played? Numbers abound, but a sprinkling of estimates affords some idea of the spread.

The most often cited figure, that given in *The Elvis Encyclopedia* and now passed along during the official Sun Studio tours, is fourteen times. Dewey, however, told Stanley Booth that he "played the record thirty times. Fifteen times each side." George Klein is probably the original source for another frequently quoted (although more modest in sum) number: seven plays in a three-hour period.[26] Dot Phillips maintains that there were eleven separate playings, and Cousin Billy Mills employs a southern colloquialism: "Forty-'leven times."

No matter what the exact number, everyone close to Dewey agrees that he was ecstatic about the record. George Klein echoes Dot's impression and says that Dewey was as enthusiastic as Sam. Sam, always sensitive to the charge that he had a heavy hand in personally promoting records through Dewey, likes to emphasize that the event—and Dewey's reaction—were completely spontaneous happenings. "No hype was done, absolutely," he vows. As if to answer criticism that Elvis may have planted fans in the audience to telephone in an unprecedented number of requests, Sam reminds people that the singer, at this time, "really, had very few friends." Dewey kept playing the record, according to Sam, only because of the reaction it received. Dewey, he maintains, would never repeat a selection unless it excited him. "He would not have done that except for the response."[27]

Elvis, recalling the evening, particularly the famous incident when Dewey interviewed him live on the air without Presley knowing it, said, "I was scared to death. I was shaking all over when I heard what had happened. I just couldn't believe it but Dewey kept telling me to 'cool it,' it was really happening." Later, when Elvis realized he been interviewed without being aware of it, "he broke out in a cold sweat."[28]

Dewey's claim to the distinction of introducing Elvis on his show (and identifying him as a Humes High graduate to ensure that listeners knew he was white) is no small achievement, but it is in some ways unfortunate because it detracts from his importance in the broader picture of American popular music.[29] Almost everything written about Presley's early years manages to mention Dewey's initial effort, yet very little is said about his subsequent role in helping propel Elvis's career. That is distressing because Dewey's involvement encompassed much more than the now-familiar stories of spinning the first disc, surreptitiously interviewing Elvis without his knowledge, and generating the initial excitement. Launching Elvis was just the first phase; securing him firmly in orbit required a struggle that went far beyond that celebrated first effort. Unlikely as it now seems, establishing Elvis Presley as a major recording star was a formidable task, even given the combined endeavors of Sam and Dewey Phillips.[30]

Sam, for example, has repeatedly described the difficulty of trying to get the unusual and highly innovative Elvis air-play in the South, even after the initially successful first record was distributed. Although it is difficult to imagine now, he says, "At the time, believe me, Elvis was a strange creature. They didn't know whether he was fish or fowl." The problem, as Sam relates it, was that R&B deejays felt "he shouldn't be played after the sun comes up" because he sounded way too country. Country deejays throughout the South, however, said that they "would get run out of town because he sounds too black." And, of course those who played the usual pop material said, "We have got to have our Perry Como, we got to have our Eddie Fisher, people like that." A great many radio stations outside Memphis refused to put "That's All Right" on the air.[31]

Some feel that negative reaction was strong enough to indicate that a few in the business had conspired to keep Elvis off the national charts. "There were certain guardians of the culture who came to New York in groups," trying to stop him as Jerry Wexler has said, recalling the initial reaction to the unconventional Elvis. Wexler, a former *Billboard* writer who knew the recording business from a New York perspective, says there were indeed those who tried "to persuade *Billboard* not to put Elvis Presley's music in the charts because this was the kind of music best described by a Southern expletive we don't use in polite company."[32]

By the end of July, even though Elvis had blasted up to number three on local charts he was still virtually unknown outside the WHBQ listening area. During the months immediately following Dewey's first-time play, Presley had been compelled to continue driving a truck for Crown Electric. Calvin Newborn, for example, remembers that Elvis still wore a uniform when he and Dewey dropped by the Flamingo Room near Beale and Hernando. Elvis's refusal to quit his day job in spite of spectacular local success indicates that no one, including Elvis, was certain that his name would spread beyond the range of *Red, Hot and Blue.*

Sam Phillips immediately hit the road with the record, and provides the most reliable source for corroborating Presley's limited regional appeal. He grew frustrated and depressed on what he labels (incorrectly) the dust bowl circuit, trying to persuade distributors and disc jockeys in Florida and Texas to play "That's All Right." At this stage Sam had only forty distributors for his Sun label, and even they were not enthusiastic about Elvis. "Now, it was an immediate hit in Memphis," he liked to recall. "But on the road, it drug my ass out." He "didn't threaten them and say: 'Well, you wait and see,' 'cause, hell I didn't know myself. I didn't know for sure." Yet Dewey, he says, did know for sure. Elvis was not just a "novel thing" to him; he recognized immediately that "Elvis had a feeling about him." Sam Phillips says that others, including himself, might have had doubts, but, "Dewey, if it felt good to him, . . . he really didn't have any inhibitions about playing Elvis."[33]

Jerry Schilling, a member of the "Memphis Mafia" and co-producer of Sam Phillips's biography for A&E television, picks up on Marion Keisker's observation on the documentary that Elvis "could not have walked into any other recording studio in the country" and had that opportunity. Jerry observes, "I don't think there was any other radio show in America besides Dewey's that Sam could have walked in and get Elvis played like that."[34]

It was such persistence that marked what was perhaps Dewey's major contribution to Presley's success. If everything started with Elvis, as John Lennon once proclaimed, then Dewey's perseverance at this critical moment was even more important. "There would never have been an Elvis without Sam," Jim Dickinson asserts, but one could just as easily argue that there would never have been an Elvis without Dewey. If Sam was the discoverer, Dewey was the first promoter. If Sam was the patriarchal parent, Dewey was the family elder. Although it is difficult for some of Elvis's fans to grasp, without Dewey's loud proselytizing on *Red, Hot and Blue* it is hard to imagine Presley's success in the Mid-South. Sam has no reservations about giving Dewey full credit for prescience. In magnanimous moments he recognizes his namesake's importance in launching Elvis. In 1972, when the Memphis Music Festival presented the first Dewey Phillips Memorial Award to George Klein, Sam made the presentation and declared that he would not be where he was had it not been for Dewey. "Yes sir," he exclaimed on another occasion. "Dewey was responsible for Elvis."[35]

He no doubt remembered quite well just how bleak the prospects were for getting Elvis played outside Dewey's listening range. After making his usual station-to-station circuit in a number of states, Sam was all but ready to give up. When he returned to Memphis, however, he found that Dewey had made the record the hottest thing in the Mid-South. In addition to hawking Elvis's music on *Red, Hot and Blue,* Dewey continued to evangelize about the newly discovered sensation at several of Presley's personal appearances. These early promotional activities away from the WHBQ studios, not as well known as Dewey's radio assistance, were just as important for Elvis's budding career. It is a cliché of Memphis music history to say that Dewey's career grew locally as Elvis's did nationally. Such thinking, however, assumes that Dewey was then relatively unknown. The fact was that Dewey's star status provided a ready audience for Elvis's initial work. The same could be said of Sam. Before Elvis became a major star, he and the mostly Mid-South regional label on which he recorded were known to very few outside the confines of Sun's narrow distribution. As John King, a Memphis record collector, puts it, "In New York, no one knew diddly fuck about Sun Records."[36] At this stage of their careers, Elvis and Sam were not recognizable name brands let alone pop-culture icons.

After Elvis's fame spread nationally, of course, he and Dewey would benefit from one another. For now, however, it was Dewey who was the prominent member of the team and the unknown Elvis who received assistance. At this early stage of Presley's career being seen with Dewey on Beale Street helped considerably in gaining recognition in the local black community. "With Dewey he visited the clubs on Beale," Peter Guralnick has noted, "where Dewey was still hailed as a conquering hero and this white boy who sang the blues was readily accepted as yet another of Dewey's crazy ideas."[37]

Elvis's local fame quickly spread, of course, far beyond Beale Street as Dewey alerted his vast audience to any and all personal appearances. The success of that early exposure is important and owes a great deal to indispensable aid from Dewey's hard-hitting air plugs. He was trying so hard for name recognition at one point that he performed at local shopping centers. There is a famous picture, for example, of the young Presley, leaning on a Chevrolet and decked out in black pants and a pink shirt, at the opening of the Lamar-Airways Shopping Center. Significantly, Opal Walker, the photographer, says the only reason she came to see Elvis was because she was curious "after listening to Dewey Phillips radio show." At this point, "Nobody knew who Elvis was."[38]

During this critical early period Dewey distinguished himself almost alone among Memphis and Mid-South deejays by making certain that his fans knew who Elvis was. Both on the air and off he frequently complained about the amount of flack he caught from radio colleagues for hyping the unknown Presley. With the exception of Sleepy-Eyed John, who quickly recognized Elvis's country appeal, the initial response of most Memphis deejays to the King's off-the-wall style was negative. They not only refused to play his records but also made it abundantly clear that they considered Dewey to be misguided in promoting him.[39]

Even other deejays at Dewey's own station were forbidden to play Elvis at first. Wink Martindale, who was running WHBQ's morning show at the time, says, "Only Dewey Phillips could play E's [Elvis's] records in the early days or at least for the first couple of weeks after [Sam] brought it to the station." Not until Dewey created his prerequisite pandemonium on *Red, Hot and Blue* did the station lift its prohibition. "Then the whole station started playing it," Wink points out, "because then the dam gates broke open and everybody played Elvis."[40]

In addition to using his on-air power, Dewey was also instrumental in putting Elvis's name before the public by using his connections with acquaintances in the print media. Both Dewey and Marion Keisker used their influence to get his good friend Robert Johnson to arrange for Edwin Howard, who wrote the popular "Front Row" column for the *Memphis Press-Scimitar,* to conduct Elvis's first local newspaper interview. At last people who didn't listen to *Red, Hot and Blue* could learn something about Dewey's latest discovery.[41]

Just as important in putting Elvis's name before the public were the frequent appearances Dewey made with him in and around the Memphis area, whether at high schools or local record hops. Don Nix remembers Dewey bringing Elvis to Memphis's Messick High School in 1955. Don, who was in the eighth grade, says that although Elvis was the star attraction ("I had never heard girls scream for someone like that since Frank Sinatra"), he was just as excited at seeing Dewey Phillips. "Dewey was considered to be a big celebrity by everyone of the kids in the audience," he says. For regular listeners to *Red, Hot and Blue* the event provided a double dose of star power.[42]

Dewey also held frequent record or sock hops featuring Elvis as a "special guest" on several occasions. Usually called "Red, Hot and Blue Dances," they were often held in the Chickasaw Ballroom of the Chisca Hotel. Dewey had begun them during the early 1950s, long before Elvis (and long before Alan Freed popularized the idea). On those occasions Dewey's appearance alone was sufficient to guarantee a huge throng of screaming teenagers. Even the legendary deejays at WLAC never had platter parties to promote innovative black artists they introduced on the air.[43]

Dewey's persistence paid off soon enough. It can best be seen in the throngs gathered for Presley's initial big shows in Memphis. One of the first occurred just weeks after Dewey played Elvis's first record. Presley opened a program for Slim Whitman at the Overton Park Shell on July 30, 1954. Dewey plugged the show incessantly. Even though Whitman was the headliner and newspaper advertising only mentioned Elvis (misspelling his name), at least part of the unusually large turnout must have come from Dewey's widespread radio audience. Indeed, some fans readily acknowledged seeing Elvis for the first time because of Dewey's plugs. The notable Memphis photographer Robert Dye, for example, who would capture for posterity some of the most famous shots of a very young, still relatively unknown Elvis Presley, decided to attend Elvis's appearance at the Overton Park Shell a year later, on August 5, 1955, because Dewey had made "such a fuss" about him on his show.[44]

Much more important than that first 1954 Overton Park Shell program in boosting Elvis's celebrity status was his first appearance at Ellis Auditorium in downtown Memphis on February 6, 1955.[45] His name appeared at the bottom of the program, under those of the well-known country stars Faron Young and Ferlin Huskey. Dewey related the night's events to his friend Stanley Booth. Elvis was quite nervous, he said, and requested that Dewey be with him for the matinee. "But Sam and I were out at my house, drinking beer, or we had something going," Dewey would confess to Booth, "and I missed the afternoon show. Elvis came looking for me, mad as hell." He had tried singing "Old Shep" and "That's How My Heartaches Begin" but apparently was unable to get much response from the audience. Dewey accompanied Elvis to the evening show and strongly suggested that he forget the hillbilly routine and open with "Good Rockin' Tonight." Dewey not only served as emcee but also stayed onstage while Elvis performed, even breaking out in an impromptu duet with him, an event captured in a Robert Dye photograph. "He went into 'Good Rockin',' started to shake, and the place just blew apart," Dewey remembered. "The people wouldn't let him leave."[46]

Even after Elvis achieved national fame Dewey decided to bring him to WHBQ's television studios for an appearance on Wink Martindale's locally produced *Dance Party.* The show, a version of Dick Clark's *American Bandstand,* was extremely popular with Memphis teenagers in the mid-1950s. Martindale, pleased to have the new star on his show, chatted briefly with both men before doing an in-depth interview with Elvis. Because Dewey seemed uncomfortable with a new, still unfamiliar medium both he and Elvis appeared to be slightly stilted, nervous, and even a bit awkward.

After profusely thanking Dewey for bringing Elvis, Wink made an effort at banter: "You were really one of the guys who helped to get this fella started, weren't you?" he asked Dewey. Dewey, already bored by the question, replied with a throw-away line: "I helped a little." When Wink asked whether Dewey was the first to play Elvis's records, Dewey, always avoiding a serious response, quickly threw the question to Elvis, who at first replied "Nahhhh!" (which was greeted with laughter) and then playfully pretended that he must grudgingly admit it was indeed his friend Dewey: "I guess he was the first one in Memphis to play my record."[47]

Then, in a moment of rare seriousness, Dewey described how Sam brought the acetate to the studio and how, after listening, he said, "Man, one of 'em has to go! That 'Blue Moon' and 'That's All Right.'" Next he carefully explained what has become a faithfully memorized ritual among Elvis fans everywhere—his call to the Presley family, who contacted Elvis in the Suzore movie theater. Once Dewey had Elvis in the station, he said, "We cut loose with that record."[48]

Apparently, Dewey and Elvis had planned to harmonize on a few verses of "Money, Honey" to try to break the ice before Martindale started questioning Elvis. Like most of Dewey's anticipated performances, however, this one didn't come off as planned. He kept asking Elvis whether he was ready to sing, but Elvis responded with non sequiturs. Dewey, never one to let the dead air go on for too long, finally launched into a brief solo of "Money, Honey" ("Well, the landlord ran my front door bell, I let it ring for a long, long spell"). At last he turned his newfound discovery over to Wink in a typical switch from spontaneous lunacy to "Dewey the Professional Announcer": "Martindale, [I] want you to meet one of the nicest guys in show business, Elvis Presley. He's a clean boy [applause]. He's one of the hottest guys that's ever hit show business."[49]

Dewey may have carefully orchestrated Presley's moves in Memphis, but he could do little for him in early New York appearances. After the *Steve Allen Show* on July 1, when Elvis was spruced up in white tie and tails, Dewey was agitated by the fact that Elvis not only had to appear without his guitar but also had to stand still while he sang. Elvis telephoned Dewey immediately after the show, expecting congratulations. "You better call home and get straight, boy," Dewey responded. "What you doing in that monkey suit? Where's you guitar?"[50] Dewey was so disturbed that he decided Elvis needed to make a hometown appearance to reassure fans that he had not sold out to New York television "big shots." Convinced Elvis needed to let loyal followers know that the *Steve Allen Show*—presented as the best in "clean family entertainment"—would not be the future for the coming king of rock 'n' roll, Dewey encouraged Elvis to perform at home as soon as possible.

What followed was the Russwood Park show on July 4, 1956. Dewey again served as emcee and was apparently in top form. Robert Johnson reported that he was "cotton-pickin' cute," especially when he did an

impression of "old Elvis" and "new Elvis," demonstrating for the enthusiastic crowd how restrained Elvis had been on the *Steve Allen Show* and
telling them that he would now perform, swiveling hips and all. That is
precisely what Elvis did, and, of course, he brought down the house.[51]
Dewey was vindicated. Once again, all was right with the world.

The usually supercharged Dewey in one of his calmer moments. (Dorothy Phillips Collection)

The Home of the Blues Record Shop on Beale Street, facing east from Main Street, late 1930s or early 1940s. (Robert Dye)

The original Poplar Tunes on Poplar Avenue. (Robert Dye)

Sam Phillips at Sun Studio. (Robert Dye)

Dewey, Wink Martindale, and Elvis on Wink's *Dance Party*. (Courtesy of Wink Martindale)

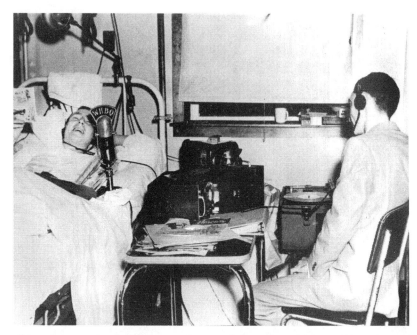

Although recovering from his second automobile accident, Dewey still broadcast from Kennedy Veterans Hospital in Memphis; the engineer is unidentified. (Dorothy Phillips Collection)

During television show, Harry Fritzius (center, in ape mask) frightening guest Jane Russell. (Dorothy Phillips Collection)

Cavorting with Harry Fritzius, who appeared with Dewey on the *Pop Shop* television show. (Special Collections, University of Memphis Library)

Killing time, a favorite practice on *Pop Shop*. (Special Collections, University of Memphis Library)

The Holy Grail of rock 'n' roll, Elvis's first record. (Robert Dye)

12

The King and His Court Jester:
Men-Children in the Promised Land

Elvis Presley would not be the only Sun Studio artist Dewey would help convert into a superstar, but he was one of the first, and Dewey took a fancy to him right away. But if he was attracted to Elvis immediately, it is also safe to say that Presley was even more enamored of Dewey. How could it have been otherwise? Presley may have been stereotyped as an explosive, swivel-hipped rocker, but close friends well knew that personally he was the quiet boy next door. In reality, Elvis was always shy and reserved. Dewey, however, was nothing if not a human dynamo. How could an unpretentious youngster from Mississippi not help but be attracted to the top deejay in the Mid-South, who also just happened to be one of the most outrageous and colorful characters in the city?

Because both hit it off famously from the start it is not surprising that they took even more delight in each other's company after Presley's reputation began to soar. The men not only had a good time together but also admired and respected each other professionally. There was never competition between the two, no jockeying for ego supremacy. This was particularly apparent in the way Elvis related to Dewey. No matter how quickly Presley's popularity spread, Dewey, for Elvis, was still the man who started his career, the celebrity deejay with the name recognition.

That is not to say that Elvis was one of Dewey's obsequious groupies—not by a long shot. Even though he remained something in awe of the man who had given him the biggest break of his life, he never related to him as a fan or underling. Until Dewey's public behavior worsened at the end of his life, he and Elvis remained close, and Presley constantly sought his company. Sam Phillips says that Elvis "was just totally fascinated by Dewey" because "he entertained him all the time; Dewey was just fun to be around."[1]

Cousin Billy Mills watched the relationship and says that Elvis was comfortable with Dewey because he "wasn't trying to work him." After Elvis achieved stardom, it seemed that "everybody else was trying to get something from him, whereas Dewey just liked being around him." Elvis always appreciated that, friends report, noting that he was drawn to Dewey like a long-lost relative. Stanley Booth is probably correct in saying that Dewey, at this very early stage of Elvis's career, was "as close to him as anyone except his mother Gladys."[2]

As for Dewey himself, he was in hog heaven with his newly discovered headliner. He delighted in showing him off to the public and chumming with him in private. He could never be accused, in Billy's phrase, of trying to "work" Elvis, but he liked nothing better than showing off his prize product to close friends and relatives. "He'd just ride up and down the road sometimes in Adamsville, yellin' Elvis is going to be here at 5 o'clock this afternoon," Max Carruthers remembers. "Then there'd be a crowd start circling our house, and I'd have to tell them that Elvis wasn't really going to be there." Max's wife, Betty, quickly adds, "But still, the traffic in this block around our house would get so that you couldn't get near here, just wanting to see Dewey himself."[3]

Billy Mills and Bill Kirby recall several instances when Dewey casually invited them to drop by the house and Elvis "just happened to be there," visiting. Moreover, whenever old Adamsville friends were in town Dewey rarely missed an opportunity to take them to Elvis's home. The Carruthers spent an entire evening on several occasions watching Dewey and Elvis play pool.

Finally, whenever some of the crowd from back home would settle in Memphis, Dewey's preferred way of reconnecting was to take them to Graceland for a social call. Bill "Bear" McClain, the Selmer High School basketball star who became one of Dewey's best friends, remembers just such an occasion. "He called one Christmas Eve, and said, 'Let's go to Elvis's tonight.'" Bear, who thought Dewey was joking, was shocked when he picked him up and took him to Graceland. "Elvis just met us right at the front door," McClain says. "Never have I been treated as nice in my life. We all went down and played pool the whole evening."[4]

It was during these early, crony days that Dewey bought Elvis an old Lincoln sedan for $450 so he could go out of town on gigs. Moreover, several close sources report learning from Dewey that Elvis had asked him to be his manager. Before Colonel Parker arrived on the scene, Dewey told Stanley Booth, Elvis wanted him. Dewey declined, however, telling Presley that he "didn't know anything about managing." James Parks, who often hung around the Sun Studio, confirms this story, saying that Dewey told him the same thing but then added that he "didn't want to do that because he would have had to quit the radio station."[5]

Dewey, of course, would have been a disaster as Elvis's agent, evidenced by the fact that he couldn't manage his own affairs. Because Dewey never had an agent he had to be his own business manager, which was the cause of a great many of his later problems. "He was being paid very well, but he was spending every penny of it," says Bob Lewis. "He just didn't have a good business sense. It's too bad." Even though Colonel Parker exploited Presley, the singer, Lewis believes, needed him. "If Elvis had been his own business manager, he would have probably ended up the way Dewey Phillips did."[6]

Dewey may have turned down the request to be Elvis's agent but he continued to play a predominant role in Presley's life, even after Parker came on as manager. It was apparent to all close friends that both Phillipses—Sam and Dewey—were Elvis's early role models and surrogate fathers, not the Colonel. June Juanico, one of Presley's early girlfriends, has argued that Elvis listened to the Phillipses more than the Colonel even after the latter came on board. When Elvis's mother died, for example, Elvis insisted on going to the funeral home with the body for the embalming. When he refused to leave her, Sam and Dewey stayed there with him all night, not the Colonel. Sam, who knew he had a formidable task in persuading Elvis to give up Gladys Presley's body, also realized Dewey's importance in Elvis's life. "To make sure that I got through to Elvis," he said, "I went and got Dewey."[7]

Dewey probably remained closer to Elvis than he would have had he become his agent. Their association was always more about pleasure than duty. In the early days it was not unusual for Presley to arrive at Dewey's home with his band after midnight, when *Red, Hot and Blue* had ended.[8] Elvis continued to appear regularly at Dewey's place, even after national fame made privacy impossible for him to achieve. Once reaching superstardom, especially after he began making movies, Elvis's appearances almost anywhere guaranteed an instant crowd, caused a media frenzy, and eliminated any semblance of solitude. All Dewey had to do, for instance, was to announce that Elvis was in the WHBQ studio and there would be mass confusion that began with the instant appearance of hysterical teenagers and ended only after the police were called and Elvis was smuggled out through the back door.[9]

Elvis learned quickly that Dewey's residence was one of the few places he could find shelter from the maelstrom of constant public attention. "Elvis could not go anywhere," Dorothy Phillips remembers, "and our house was where nobody would bother him." She worked hard to maintain Presley's seclusion. Eventually, of course, it became a major production for him to leave Graceland, but sometimes—with a little planning and a little luck—he could still escape. There was the night, for example, that Elvis and a Hollywood friend, Nick Adams, came to the Phillipses for supper. They had to stop at a service station en route, which drew an instant crowd. In no time at all so many people were following them that Elvis had to call Dewey and alert him to their arrival. Preparations were made so that once at the Phillipses he could quickly dart inside and escape the ever-increasing crowd. For the rest of the evening, Dot says, people came to the door. She made them wait, however, until everyone finished supper. "It was raining and I hated to make them stand outside in the rain, but that's what they did."[10]

What took place inside the Phillipses' home when Memphis's famous twosome got together? The favorite pastimes were playing the pinball machine, shooting pool (a constant), or watching movies (according to rumor, some of them pornographic) in the garage. Pool was also the main order of business whenever Dewey and Elvis were at the *other* Phillips household. Sam's wife, Becky, recalls that "Dewey wanted to beat Elvis more than anything, and sometimes he did."[11]

Billy Mills thinks it significant that one of the first things his cousin bought as soon as he could afford it was a pinball machine, which he kept in his living room. Dewey had loved the game as a boy but frequently could not afford to play, let alone buy a machine.[12] The pinball machine soon morphed into bumper pool and finally into what Dewey considered as the ultimate accessory of a sybaritic life-style: an actual pool table.

Stories have circulated for years about the fierce competition generated by Dewey's pool table. Johnny Cash, another Sun star, at one time lived only about three blocks from the Phillips home and enjoyed coming over frequently and spending time with Dewey. Randy Phillips remembers playing catch with him and also that Cash and his father always shot pool when they got together.[13]

But life was more than playing pool. Dewey liked to take Elvis swimming at McKellar Lake. Later, after Elvis got a house with a pool, Dewey and his children would often go there and swim. In fact, Randy says that Elvis may have saved Dewey's life. On one occasion while Dewey, who was clowning, tried to do a flip from the diving board, he hit his bad leg on the board. "Elvis saw he wasn't coming up," Randy says, "so he jumped in and pulled Dewey out."[14]

Whether swimming, shooting pool, or hanging out, Dewey never wavered from his role as the proverbial big kid. In that regard he found a mirror image in Elvis. Both possessed that rare faculty for understanding the child in us all, which is why he and Elvis were constantly playing practical jokes on each other. When together the two were little more than grown-up juveniles, each a man-child concerned only with maximizing newfound fame and fortune through absolute gratification. Neither outgrew adolescence, and each was attracted to the innocent, boyish charm of the other. Whenever they got together, life was like it was for most adolescents—little more than practical jokes and a headlong rush in the pursuit of pleasure.

Perhaps a major reason they never seemed to tire of what often appeared to adults as immature, foolish behavior was that their expectation levels were on the same plane. Despite the monetary means for acquiring untold material goods from their newfound fortunes, both men contented themselves with the basics. Elvis's idea of a good time was to take friends to the movies or a skating rink. Dewey, too, was able to rejoice in what can only be described as the creature comforts. After closing his always hectic, three-hour show, for example, he could think of no better way to end an evening than gathering Elvis, George Klein, Louis Harris, and a small coterie of other friends and going home to enormous quantities of Memphis's most famous miniature comestibles, half-dollar-size Krystal hamburgers.

Krystals were an integral part of late-evening entertainment for Dewey and Elvis's crowd. When asked to recall "wild parties" that the two men might have had at her home after *Red, Hot and Blue,* what Dot Phillips remembers most are Krystal hamburger parties. "It wasn't anything for Dewey to call at twelve midnight and say that there was a bunch coming out to the house." When she asked what she should prepare the answer was always the same, "Don't bother, honey, me and Elvis'll jest stop and pick up some Krystals." Dewey would then call the Krystal at Second and Union, directly across the street from the Peabody Hotel, and order a hundred of the diminutive burgers, to be picked up by Elvis and G.K. just before Dewey's show ended. "It wasn't too long then, maybe an hour later," Dot chuckles as she remembers a frequently repeated scene, "the crowd would arrive. They'd come walking in the front door with both of 'em carrying just sacks full of those durn things." Randy Phillips recalls "many a morning, when we had [leftover] Krystal hamburgers for breakfast."[15]

Just as the underprivileged Elvis, fresh from an indigent Mississippi past, never felt more magnanimous or affluent than when he rented the Madison Theater or the Memphis Fairgrounds for a night of fun with friends, so, too, Dewey Phillips, the poor country boy from Crump, Tennessee, never felt more opulent than when he brought home sacks of Krystal hamburgers for his buddies to enjoy. Billy Mills, who had witnessed Dewey's childhood deprivation and his relative affluence as one of the South's highest-paid disc jockeys, resorts to a favorite theme when explaining what made Dewey happy: "He liked the Krystal hamburgers better than the big thick, juicies, because he'd never had the big thick juicies. He was eating high on the hog just having those Krystal hamburgers."[16]

Although both Phillips families enjoyed the company of Elvis in their homes, some of Dot's fondest memories concern the times Elvis reciprocated and had her family over to his place. Her happiest recollections are of those times the entire family would visit the Presleys on Audubon Drive, where Gladys Presley would serve ice cream and cookies to the little ones. Most of these visits were on Sunday afternoons, one of the rare opportunities for Dewey to spend time with his children. "There was no finer person than Gladys Presley," Dot says. "Elvis worshipped his mother and she did him." Dot remembers clearly how painful it was to see Elvis after his mother died. "Elvis was setting on the steps [outside the funeral home] when I got there," she recalls. "He just said, 'Miss Dot, what are we going to do?'"[17]

Over the years Dot and Gladys became good friends. Their contacts were infrequent at first but included some interesting moments. On one occasion Dewey telephoned from New York, where Elvis had flown him for Presley's second appearance on the *Ed Sullivan Show*. Elvis had been trying to call his mother (something he did almost every night when out of town) but had forgotten the recently acquired unlisted number. Dot went to the Presleys the next morning and gave Gladys her son's hotel telephone number in New York so they could connect.[18]

Paradoxically, as Dot and Gladys saw more of each other the time that Dewey and Elvis spent together grew progressively shorter. Free time for America's most famous celebrity soon became a precious commodity. His fame, which continued to grow far beyond even Dewey's expectations, inevitably meant the endless repetition of Hollywood movies, which meant much less contact with people at home.

Yet Elvis made a concerted effort to stay close. No one knew better than he how much of his initial success could be attributed to Dewey, and he took every opportunity to show gratitude, particularly during the early years of his career when they were closest. Just after his first appearance on the *Ed Sullivan Show,* for example, he literally tried to pay Dewey for everything he had done for him. He held one of his "Red, Hot and Blue" dances from the Chisca ballroom and gave the proceeds of the event to Dewey.[19] Moreover, he treated Dewey the way he treated all very close friends, showering him with gifts whenever there was a holiday or he had occasion to do so. Billy Mills remembers Dewey showing him twelve or fourteen watches—all elaborate and expensive—that Elvis had sent over the years, always with an inscription on the order of "Thank you, 'Red, Hot and Blue.'"[20] Much more important, when Dewey endured troubled times Elvis helped him financially on a number of occasions. It wasn't necessary, however, to lavish Dewey with tangible rewards to demonstrate gratitude; Dewey was well aware of it. One reason Elvis respected his former mentor, George Klein says, was that Dewey "never threw the part he played in his career in his face. He didn't have to say it," Klein quickly adds. "Elvis knew it."[21]

Presley would try to demonstrate appreciation in more subtle ways as well. Later on, even after unprecedented fame, he would still drop by the WHBQ studio whenever he was in town, always when the hour was late, because *Red, Hot and Blue* went until midnight. These were, Billy Mills says, primarily social calls, but professional as well. "He'd always sit down with Dewey and talk about 'what's my good and what's my bad.' Not many people asked Dewey for advice, but Elvis did. When Dewey responded, it wasn't telling him what to do, it was strictly 'this is what I think.'"[22]

More often than not George Klein would be with Elvis when he dropped by the studio. Often during those years he was also around when Dewey and Elvis got together after *Red, Hot and Blue* shut down. No doubt Dewey and Presley would have continued their intimate association had George never been Dewey's gofer at WHBQ, but George's close association with Dewey at the time Elvis became popular guaranteed that the threesome would remain connected. G.K. and Elvis had known each other ever since 1948, when they were both in an eighth-grade music class at Humes High School. Although they were what George describes as "cordial friends from the eighth grade on," they were not yet truly close. They saw each other mostly at school, or they might occasionally go to the Memphis Fairgrounds together, where, George remembers, "We used to slip over the fence so we wouldn't have to pay the 50 cents to get in." They did not become close, however, until their senior year.[23]

George's association with Elvis, like his association with Dewey, was tightly woven during the early, formative years. Once he replaced Bob Lewis at WHBQ, and even after he became one of Memphis's best-known radio and television personalities, G.K. would always be, to Dewey, a gofer, the man who brought him coffee and grabbed his telegrams. For Elvis, however, George would remain the president of the Humes High senior class, a person whose stature and importance demanded eternal respect. Thus, even at the pinnacle of his fame Elvis liked nothing better, especially when George was present, than to point to the high school class picture he kept on his wall and ask those present to guess whose face was at its summit. According to Memphis Mafia member Alan Fortas, when guests were unable to make out the identity of the tiny presidential head, Elvis would proudly announce, "That's George Klein. He was one of the few guys who was nice to me in school."[24]

Dewey all but adopted George and Elvis. The paternalistic role (if not of a father then at least of a protective big brother) meant Dewey shouldered almost complete financial responsibility whenever the three were together, especially in the early days. He never failed to pick up a bill when they ate out, a custom he seems to have developed with many up-and-coming stars. Sun recording artist Dickie Lee, for example, says that whenever he and Dewey went out together at the beginning of his career Dewey delighted in grabbing the check. With George and Elvis it went even further. In addition to buying Elvis a car, Dewey frequently supplied him with his own clothes and the essentials necessary for stage appearances. Moreover, Dot says that although Elvis seldom slept at their house, Klein frequently did, especially in the early days when the two were practically inseparable.

G.K. recalls many after-hour gatherings when he, Elvis, and Dewey would hang out after Dewey signed off the air. These were golden years in the lives of all three men. Elvis had achieved unimagined fame, Dewey was at the peak of his popularity, and even George was establishing himself as the "other" rock 'n' roll deejay in Memphis. After a brief stint in Osceola, Arkansas, Klein had come back to Memphis to join the much more prestigious WMC, where he did a show called the *Rock 'n' Roll Ballroom* in the three-to-six afternoon slot. Together, they were having the best time of their lives and not doing much of anything except having fun.

The usual procedure after Dewey got off was to go to one of the popular local drive-ins (Kay's or Pig 'n' Whistle were the favorites). Teenagers would be "screaming at Dewey as much as Elvis" from their cars, George says. Later, if Dewey wanted to imbibe (and he usually did), they would go to the Variety Club in the basement of the Gayoso Hotel because it stayed open until three in the morning.

One of George's favorite recollections of the Variety Club concerns a gathering there one night shortly after Elvis signed with RCA. There was a piano, and when they arrived Elvis announced that he was going to play a new song he was getting ready to record in Nashville. He then played "Heartbreak Hotel." The club's doors were closed, making the gathering a late-night private party. "It was just me and Elvis and Dewey and the bartender, Slate," George fondly recalls. "We knew right away that it would be a smash. We said, 'Yeah, man, that sounds great!' And then he told us that a school teacher down in Florida wrote it for him."[25]

After shutting down the Variety Club, nowhere else was still open in the city. Unless they felt like driving over to West Memphis to the Plantation Inn or Danny's Club they would usually go to an all-night restaurant or maybe to Sam Phillips's house. If all else failed they would buy Krystals and go back to Dewey's.

These years were as ephemeral as they were glorious—destined to be short-lived as Elvis's popularity continued to draw him to Hollywood to make what proved to be a string of seemingly never-ending movies. At first he tried hard to stay in touch. While working on his first picture, for example, he telephoned Dewey on a regular basis, complaining about the long hours and hard work of making a motion picture. "This place isn't anything but a workshop," Elvis protested, pointing out that he had to get up at 5:30 for makeup and often didn't finish until 8:30 at night.[26] Once the Hollywood motion picture mill began grinding out Presley films, however, even the telephone calls became less frequent, and his drop-ins to the WHBQ studio during Dewey's show even rarer.

George was to go his own way as well. When he graduated from Memphis State University in 1957, WMC let him go. He traveled around with Elvis for nearly a year until Presley went into the army in the spring of 1958. George then returned to radio in Memphis. By the time Elvis got out of the army some two years later his relationship with Dewey had begun to show signs of strain as Dewey's substance abuse began to worsen. The threesome never retrieved the salad days of the mid-1950s, when life was still relatively uncomplicated and each could share the other's enormous success.

During those good years Dewey never failed to applaud Elvis's attributes, whether on the air and in the always news-hungry media. In an interview in *TV Guide* in 1956 he chastised critics who found fault with his good friend, especially those "who think Elvis is getting a little 'uptown,'" completely ignoring the fact that, on the air, Dewey always labeled Elvis as "'bout as far uptown as you can git." He reassured fans that Elvis's phenomenal success had not changed him. He was still a "good boy," Dewey said, and he pointed out that "Elvis worries a lot about people thinking he's got the big head." In a rare serious moment Dewey gave fans an opportunity to share the closeness he enjoyed with Presley: "I don't think they know the things that boy has on his mind. He's always afraid he'll hurt somebody's feelings."[27]

Elvis's time was always rationed, and the times the men got together in Memphis inevitably became media events, which in those days meant careful coverage by local newspapers. On one occasion, for example, the two were having dinner together at the State Café, just off Main and Beale and across the street from Memphis's Malco Theater (now the Orpheum). The cafe was one of Dewey's favorite restaurants, and he would often eat dinner there and visit with Dino Grisanti, the colorful owner. Like Dewey, Dino had been discharged from the army at the end of the war. Both loved to get together with other Beale Street veterans like Abe Schwab or Bernard Lansky and exchange war stories over drinks and food. The cafe's exclusive dining room was reserved for people like Dewey, and of course, Elvis whenever he was in town.[28]

It was 1956. Elvis had just returned from Hollywood, and, as was their custom, he and Dewey were in their special room at Dino's. Already the news media was out in full force. The *Press-Scimitar* faithfully reported on its front page that Elvis had just had caps put on "to make his teeth look prettier" for movies but noted, "They aren't worn during meals." During the course of the dinner Presley apparently placed the caps in a folded handkerchief. Somehow during the commotion "which is inevitably present," the paper pointed out, "wherever Elvis is," they were knocked off the table. Both men crawled around on the floor, looking for them, but found only one. Dewey, always quick to keep a crowd entertained whenever the two appeared publicly (especially if the media was present), scrupulously reported that "someone had stepped on the other one." Knowing Presley's fans to be fascinated by the minute details of his life, including what was perceived to be his enormous wealth, he casually announced that it was too bad the one cap "was in little bitty pieces. Cost $150, too."[29]

But all was not lighthearted frivolity. Even with both men on their best behavior—as they always were when they appeared together in public—adversity was beginning to raise its ugly head. Before Dewey's decline there was almost never open friction between the two. The single important exception occurred in June 1957, when Dewey visited Elvis while he was filming *Jailhouse Rock* in Hollywood. The flare-up was a relatively minor one. It was, however, a public feud—scrupulously covered by long-time Dewey watcher Robert Johnson in the *Press-Scimitar*—and an ominous foreshadowing of what was to come. The incident stirred strong feelings that would finally become irreparable during Dewey's last days, when he alienated nearly all who had once been his friend.

The early difficulty began when Presley decided to bring his Memphis friend out to see the movie capital of the world and give him an Elvis-guided personal tour. Brandishing his 1957 superstardom, Presley paid all expenses for Dewey's trip, including putting him up in his personal suite at the Beverly Wilshire Hotel. It was quite a gesture, considering that various members of the Memphis Mafia were always set up in their own rooms when they traveled with the King.[30]

It all began pleasantly enough, with Elvis asking Dewey to appear on the MGM lot with him. He assumed that Dewey, like everyone else, would be fascinated by the opportunity to observe firsthand the making of a major motion picture. That, according to Robert Johnson, apparently was not to be the case. Once on the set Dewey hung around only about fifteen minutes and then grew "bored, nervous and left."[31]

Elvis was surprised but not really upset—yet. He moved off the MGM lot and took his guest to the Hollywood dentist who had been responsible for the recent work on his own teeth. He had gold caps made for Dewey's teeth and picked up the $450 bill. Next on the itinerary was the compulsory visit to the stars' homes. They inspected Robert Mitchum's and Wendell Corey's before retiring to their favorite pastime, shooting pool, this time on a table Elvis had erected specially in the Beverly Wilshire suite.

Minor troubles started that night when the Presley entourage attended the Moulin Rouge. Elvis, of course, was immediately recognized as he entered, and the management asked if he would acknowledge an introduction and perhaps sing a song. Always graceful and cooperative,

Presley agreed. As soon as the announcement was made and a spotlight hit the table, however, Dewey rose, stood in front of Elvis, and began to make ostentatious bows.

Dewey's drinking—almost always a factor when he partied—had not yet reached serious proportions, so the entire business seems to have been nothing more than Dewey being Dewey after a few drinks, never passing a chance to disturb the natural order if opportunity presented itself. He never intended to hurt anyone, but he caused a great deal of embarrassment nonetheless. Elvis was flustered by the incident, although not so much so, Robert Johnson sympathetically reported, that he failed to pick up the $175 check.

More serious difficulties erupted the next day when Dewey returned to the lot, where he was introduced to Yul Brynner, who was filming *The Brothers Karamazov*. Dewey, more than six feet tall, was apparently surprised to meet the veteran actor and realize his height. As is often the case when famous incidents occur without impartial witnesses, there are various versions of what was said when the men shook hands. Most agree that the general idea Dewey managed to convey was that the superstar's stature was far below what Dewey expected. "You're a short mother, ain'tcha?" was what most heard. Robert Johnson, however, reported that Dewey insisted he said, "My gosh, you look shorter than you do in pictures." Afterward, trying to explain the incident, Dewey pointed out that he had been trying to tell Brynner that "he wasn't near as big as I thought of him." Nonetheless, Elvis was reportedly extremely upset and immediately apologized to Brynner.[32]

Once again, unfortunately, the worst was yet to come. Elvis, who had just recorded "Teddy Bear," decided to bring a rare acetate copy of it with him to Hollywood and preview it for close friends. He specifically warned Dewey not to take it back to Memphis and play it on his show because RCA Victor had not yet released the song for air play. An early release, especially of anything by Elvis, caused problems because the recording company was not prepared to supply the always necessary copious copies to distributors. Dewey, however, apparently remembering his part in previewing Elvis's first acetate, could not resist the temptation to try doing so again. He slipped the copy into his suitcase when he left and, of course, as soon as he got home he began to play it on his show.

"Elvis was furious," Robert Johnson reported. Dewey had seriously taken advantage of Presley's confidence, so his anger was certainly justified. Even Dewey knew it. Johnson gave no further details other than to tell readers that Dewey had apologized and the two then "spent a happy night of reunion together." Johnson, almost always inclined to put a positive Dewey spin on any controversy concerning his close friend, left readers with the impression that the feud was healed.[33]

Despite all outward appearances, however, all was still not quite right. Apparently, Dewey had gone too far. When asked if the rift might be permanent, Presley responded, "I got no argument with him. I guess people think that because I don't go up to his program anymore." Johnson reported that Elvis had confided in Billy Leaptrott, a *Press-Scimitar* photographer and former Humes High schoolmate, that he "didn't want Dewey to get hurt." Despite that guarded exchange of words Johnson ended the story on his inevitably optimistic note by pointing out that Leaptrott "didn't say so, but it is very probable that Elvis, like Dewey, wants to be friends again."[34]

Nonetheless, when Elvis stopped dropping by the WHBQ studio, as was his usual practice, Dewey began to take it personally. Feeling slighted, he decided after getting off the air one night to make an unannounced appearance at Graceland. He did so, however, only after first fortifying himself by visiting his old friend Joe Cuoghi at Pop Tunes. Dewey's drinking was becoming a problem, and he and Joe managed to dispose of a considerable amount of liquor. When he arrived at his final destination he was, according to the local newspapers, drunk. After being refused admittance at the gate he climbed the fence and shouted at the top of his voice, "I'm through with you, Elvis."[35] The police were called. When the story broke, Elvis's explanation for keeping Dewey out was that his mother had been nervous since an earlier incident brought harm to Liberace's mother.

Several days after the publicity generated by the incident Dewey was profuse with apologies to the public. In a lengthy interview with Robert Johnson he reviewed the various episodes, starting with Hollywood. His behavior there he chalked up to the fact that he had gone to the movie capital "to have a good time." He was flippant in dismissing the Moulin Rouge matter ("I was just feeling good, playing around. They put the spotlight on Elvis, and I jumped up and waved my hand. I was on vacation"). As far as the Yul Brynner incident was concerned, he made every effort to make it seem innocuous ("I didn't realize I was embarrassing anyone"). When Elvis introduced Brynner, he reported, "All I said was 'How you getting along, old buddy?' just as I would to anyone." He didn't think the actor had been at all upset by his observation about height. Brynner had responded, "'That's how they put the cameras, Phillips,' and that's all there was to it."[36]

The incident at the Graceland gate, however, was much more serious and called for a more elaborate explanation. Dewey claimed that he didn't go over the fence. "I walked right through the cotton-pickin' gate. The guard left it open." He maintained that it was only about 1 A.M. and insisted that the hour was not a late one because "Elvis stayed up late almost every night." Dewey had just gotten off work and, he claimed, there were several "other girls" with him who wanted to see Elvis. He readily admitted to consuming "two or three beers" but insisted that he "wasn't drunk." Furthermore, he had a valid reason for being there. Sam Phillips had given him a Polaroid camera for Christmas, and he had let Elvis have it. He wanted it back because "I was going to take the rest of my vacation at Pickwick and I would need the camera."[37]

Barbara Pittman, who was close to both Dewey and Elvis, was in the car with Dewey that night and readily admits that he had been drinking heavily but says that the business about climbing the fence was an exaggeration. She saw him slide through the gate, which was slightly ajar, after Elvis's Uncle Vester (who was working the gate that night) refused to call the house and ask whether to admit Dewey. According to Pittman, Dewey limped up the hill to Graceland's front door and banged on it until the police were called. "He could never have climbed over that wall with his bum leg." Then he walked back down the hill, where the police were waiting to arrest him.[38]

More troubling than the obvious embarrassment caused by this incident was the fact that Dewey was beginning to lose control. This was 1957, a year before he started coming apart after his dismissal from WHBQ, so such behavior could be excused as a one-time-only event even as it foreshadowed the gruesome days ahead. Drinking heavily and trying to crash the gate at Graceland constituted bad conduct, but he could still recognize his wrong-doing and feel remorse. He admitted publicly that he "said some things I shouldn't have said" and tried to let everyone know that he felt no hard feelings toward Elvis. "I still love that boy like a brother," Johnson's column reported. "Or maybe it would be better to say like a son."[39]

Thus it was still hard, at this stage, for Dewey and Elvis to stay mad at each other very long. Elvis, at least for now, continued to be open to Dewey's friendship; Dewey, open for sure, nonetheless had a harder time. His carefree personality seemed to nurture an infantile, innocent charm by which he was able to convince himself that he had done nothing wrong. Commenting on the Yul Brynner incident, Dickie Lee says that Dewey would probably ask, "'Golly, why are you mad at me? What did

I do? It was like you hurt my feelings, you're mad at me and I have no idea why.'" You could sense, Dickie Lee says, all that from him "without him actually saying it. He'd be sulky. Just like a kid would be, just kinda clam up."[40]

Robert Johnson also picked up on that aspect of Dewey's personality. Over the years he spent a great deal of time with his friend; the two became close enough that they often visited in each other's homes or had drinks and dinner together. Dewey was, Sam Phillips says, one of the few people who could make Johnson laugh. "Bob was such a laid-back cat in his way that the only time I ever saw him smile was when Dewey would get him laughing. He'd actually laugh out loud and that was a rarity."[41]

Underneath his hyper exterior, Johnson noted, Dewey was, like Elvis, "basically shy." Johnson argued that when in his element—clowning in front of a microphone or behind a studio glass before a group of teenagers—Dewey could be manic. But "put him in a group of several people he doesn't know and he'll retire quietly to a corner. Either that or [apparently attempting to explain his actions toward Elvis] suddenly become very noisy and extrovertish in an attempt to compensate."[42]

Whatever the explanation for Dewey's unpredictable conduct, his brief feud with Elvis seemed to temporarily cease. Johnson reported that Elvis had taken the initiative by dropping in on Dewey at the WHBQ studio one night when he was doing *Red, Hot and Blue*. After the show a crowd of people led by Elvis and Dewey went to Sam Phillips house, where they spent the evening playing records and having a good time.[43]

Following that evening, differences between the two seemed to die down. Dewey continued to shout Presley's praises every night on his show and often pretended that Elvis was in the studio even when he was not. One of his favorite practices was to sign off the program by saying, "Elvis is gon' be here tomorrow and sing his newest record for ya'—live right here in the studio." Superficially at least all seemed much as it had been in the old days. When the King went into the army in 1958, for instance, Dewey was emotionally moved and acted for all the world like a proud father.

They made one last public appearance together, just before Elvis left for the service, at Joe Cuoghi's Pop Tunes. "A lot of misunderstanding fell way as they talked," Johnson happily reported. Dewey announced that he would devote the last two hours of *Red, Hot and Blue* on the coming Saturday night to playing just Elvis's records. There were sixty-two songs at that point, enough for more than three hours of music. Dewey

promised to play as many of them as he could "as a salute to Elvis."
Perhaps remembering his own service to his country during World War
II, Dewey said he was pleased that Presley did not request preferential
treatment but allowed himself to be drafted like everyone else. "That guy
could have gotten out of that," Dewey later told Cousin Billy. But "he
was over there riding them tanks. There is a real American for you."[44]

13

"Red Hot at First . . .
Blue at the Very End"

When Dewey Phillips's decline began sometime during the mid-1950s he was probably at the peak of his power. Before his descent, *Red, Hot and Blue* could not have been more red or more hot. Daddy-O-Dewey, whose local popularity continued to profit by Elvis's growing fame, enjoyed mastery of the airwaves.

Exhilarated by their lion's share of a rapidly growing youth market now turned on to the new rhythm and blues sound, station management decided to strike while Dewey's iron was hot. Not only was their superstar receiving attractive offers from other stations but there was also talk of going national with his show—coast to coast over the Mutual Network. It was during this period that Dewey repeatedly turned down much more lucrative offers in other cities because he did not want to leave Memphis.[1] The station realized that the best way to exploit Dewey's increasing renown was through the powerful new medium of television. The thinking was that Dewey's loyal radio following would switch over to television. Because that was where the big money was, that's where he should be.

Still, WHBQ knew the risk involved. The station had never been entirely comfortable with the always potentially troublesome Dewey—Robert Johnson once said "it was easier to deplore than ignore him"—and television was a fresh venture. Station management figured that Dewey's radio audience had always been limited to those who had made a deliberate choice to follow him. Television, however, was a new medium with a mesmerized following. Many tuned in just to see what was on. Management was undoubtedly more anxious about Dewey's unsettling antics in front of this wider and largely unexplored audience than with what he said to devoted followers on the radio.

The best example of that anxiety can be seen in the station's decision to have a one-night-only trial program before putting Dewey on television permanently. On August 25, 1956, WHBQ-TV first presented Dewey to a television audience on a Saturday night show at 8, *Phillips and His Phriends*. It followed the *Lawrence Welk Show*, causing Robert Johnson to caustically remark that Dewey would be a "sort of beer chaser for the champagne music." The *Commercial Appeal* later reported that this single show caused a "minor explosion" of telephone calls, even though the "vast bulk of calls were highly enthusiastic." Nonetheless, Dewey did not appear on television again on a regular daily basis until December 31, more than four months later.[2]

On the very last day of 1956, WHBQ-TV permanently placed Dewey in a favorite late-afternoon slot—3:30 to 4:30, a move obviously designed to catch the teenaged after-school crowd, evidenced by the fact that Elvis would be his special guest on the first show.[3] The program was called *Pop Shop* and was to be "simulcast" with radio. Dewey would presumably continue to do his regular thing, just as he had done on *Red, Hot and Blue*—play records and be Dewey.

Because he was being seen as well as heard, however, the new medium presented the biggest challenge of his career. Dewey had acquired his reputation solely on being unique, a faceless disc jockey. Some critics were quick to express the notion that he should have stuck to his original medium.

The format of the *Pop Shop* was essentially the same as for *Red, Hot and Blue*—perhaps best described by Robert Johnson as "casual pandemonium"—but television was not always complimentary to Dewey. Welton Roy, the WHBQ engineer who had constructed the special studio just for Dewey's radio show, also arranged separate accommodations for him for television. The show was conducted live from a permanent set isolated on the second floor in an area originally designed as a storage place for the station's other sets. *Pop Shop* usually opened with the star cozily ensconced behind a large desk, surrounded by turntables on each side. Spread out on the desk were various kinds of noise-making paraphernalia (his favorite was Myrtle the Cow), affording Dewey endless opportunities whenever there was a lull in the action. "We made up the show as we went," says Durrell Durham, *Pop Shop*'s director. "Dewey was in charge of the music, but nothing else. While one record was playing, he'd sit there and flip through the 45s and pick out the next record—*all on camera.*"[4]

Some who had grown up with him on radio didn't relish the idea of watching their star "invent things to do" on the new medium, no matter how absurd or amazing they might be. To them he seemed at times awkward, looking for ways to kill time while records were spinning. To others he seemed "restless." Many close to Dewey think he was much more at ease on radio than television. As Sam Phillips said, "He got to you through your ears and not through your eyes."[5]

Despite these problems, however, Dewey's television ratings paralleled those of his radio show, which meant, Robert Johnson noted, that *Pop Shop* "had by far the best ratings in the time period." Nonetheless, Johnson also reported that WHBQ-TV was under fierce pressure from its network affiliate, ABC, to carry Dick Clark's sensational new show in that same time period. (Memphis was later in getting *American Bandstand* than the rest of the country.) Dewey would be moved out of the choice afternoon slot to late evening, Johnson announced, because Clark's show had "piled up amazing popularity ratings in cities where it is seen." On January 9, 1958, just a little over one year after Dewey's television show had begun, WHBQ-TV decided to transfer *Pop Shop* to 11:30 P.M.[6]

Joining Dewey on the evening show—renamed *Night Beat*—was an art student named Harry Fitzius, who continued doing what he had been doing on the afternoon show, wander aimlessly around the set without uttering a word. Harry was as disheveled as he was mysterious, always appearing in a trench coat and an apelike mask, behind which he could hide his more outrageous shenanigans.

One of those shenanigans managed to get Dewey fired from the show. Although details of incident vary, there is agreement that Harry performed what was considered in the 1950s to be an obscenity with a life-sized photograph of Jayne Mansfield brought to the studio to promote her new movie, *The Girl Can't Help It*. As often happens with stories of a scatological nature, people seem to embroider it slightly at each telling. According to one version, Harry lay on top of the photograph in what was described as a "horizontal grope session," fondling, among other things, the cardboard Mansfield's breasts.[7]

What actually happened should best be recalled by Durrell Durham, who was, after all, the director of the show at the time it occurred: "Harry pinched [the cardboard cutout] on the butt. He then turned his back to the camera, unzipped his pants and tucked his shirt in. Then he zipped his pants back up. That was it!"[8]

A party was held the night of the Mansfield incident—January 12—ostensibly to celebrate the new evening time slot for the television show, which had been on for only four nights. The party was held at the home of Gene Roper, the television station's manager, who used the occasion to announce that the show would be dropped. "Dewey was about as low as I've seen him," recalls Durham. "Gene called Dewey into a separate room and he came out and said, 'It's all over.'"[9]

By today's standards the Mansfield incident hardly seems shocking, but such behavior violated socially acceptable practices of the electronic media in the 1950s. "He is very talented. If he could just discipline his talent," said WHBQ-TV manager Bill Grumbles, explaining to the press why the decision had been made to drop Dewey's show. Grumbles tried to play down the Mansfield incident by maintaining that he had mixed feelings about scheduling Dewey on television in the first place. "I let my emotions rule my thinking" was his polite way of putting it. The station's official explanation for the dismissal was that because Dewey's program began at 11:30 at night, thirty minutes had to be edited from the late show, which previously had run until midnight. Because WHBQ-TV had invested more than $1 million in movies, Grumbles maintained, the late-night show "was very expensive in overtime." Moreover, he recognized that Dewey's television show had "interfered" with *Red, Hot and Blue* (the implication being that his star had been unable to devote sufficient attention to both programs). Dewey would definitely continue doing his regular radio broadcast from 9 until midnight.[10]

Robert Johnson, as always, covered the story for the *Press-Scimitar* and carefully noted that Dewey's official reaction was "one of relief." The new show, Dewey told him, "had been burdensome." If that sounds like sour grapes, Johnson's next statement was more telling: "He was enthusiastic at first, and then some people started telling him he would lose his teenage viewers. He ended up not happy."[11]

News of the firing certainly did not please Dewey, but it would not carry the same devastating weight as his dismissal from radio in 1958. It was radio, not television, that warmed his heart, kindled his spirit, and stoked his engine. As long as he continued the show that started it all he was still in his element. It was removal from *Red, Hot and Blue* that proved to be a death knell for Daddy-O-Dewey.

The finale was not pretty. The heady flight to celebrity disintegrated into a bewildering disarray of liquor and pills. Dewey's decline went on for about ten full years, and in the end he was, in a much more exaggerated way, like Elvis—all but a parody of his former self, a pathetic caricature in a tragic stupor.

Those inclined to a more positive reading of Dewey's descent like to say it was his addiction to the enormous quantity of pain pills he had to consume that caused him to go into his final phase of self-destruction. Certainly, only the most callused cynic would fail to sympathize with what seems to have been a desperate effort to ease the near-constant pain in his left leg caused by two nasty car accidents, one in 1950 and the other in 1952. It is equally obvious, however, that he had a problem with alcohol even before the massive doses of pills. Many suspect (although it cannot be confirmed) that alcohol contributed to both of Dewey's accidents. Either way, it was a sad ending for the man who made an incalculable contribution to the Memphis and Mid-South music scene.

There was plenty of blame to go around, but his outrageous conduct afforded critics endless opportunities to further discredit him. By the time it was all over, Dewey in the final stages of dissipation had become as infamous as Dewey in all his glory had been famous. As Charles Raiteri, commenting on Dewey's plight at the close of his life, observes, "It was red hot at first, but blue at the very end."[12]

Although the last ten years of his life—the period Dorothy Phillips refers to euphemistically as "when he was on the skids"—appears not to have begun until he was fired in 1958, the groundwork for his serious personal troubles began in 1950 with the first automobile accident, a tragedy of monumental proportions. Two people were killed. One, a woman from Arkansas, was in the car of a man who survived. Much more important was that the second woman, a passenger in the car with Dewey, was an attractive, unmarried, nineteen-year-old named Doris Petty. Both women were killed instantly.[13]

Dewey's role in the tragedy over the years was further compounded by rumor and hearsay about his drinking problem. Because of the endless number of horror stories concerning substance abuse later in life, many have assumed that Dewey must have been under the influence in 1950. The assumption, however, cannot be tested and might very well be incorrect. Abuse of pain pills did not come until after a second accident in 1952, and there is no hard proof that Dewey was drinking at the time of either incident. Alcohol was not mentioned in either accident report, but many have speculated, largely because of his later reputation, that Dewey's drinking must have been the real cause in both events.

Toward the end of his life, when he unquestionably had a serious drug problem that was exacerbated by abusive drinking, it was natural to assume that the happy-go-lucky Dewey had trouble with the bottle from the beginning. The difficulty, however, of determining whether Dewey's drinking was a problem before his drug abuse is, in some way, similar to the difficulty of trying to separate his on-air persona from his real personality.

Dewey was Dewey twenty-four hours a day, which meant his manic personality seldom shut down, with or without liquor or drugs. On the air Dewey was unrestrained madness, and many have inferred that he must have been high on something—liquor or pills—during most of his broadcasts. One author even has Dewey openly drinking while on the air. "It was a common sight to see someone hand Dewey a bottle of whiskey and a record through WHBQ's special booth at the Old Chisca Hotel," writes Arnold Dewitt.[14]

Such accounts have circulated widely over the years, no doubt expanded with each telling. They are, however, often apocryphal, as seems to be the case here. First, everyone who worked closely with Dewey at WHBQ is adamant that they never saw him take a drink while on the air. Even later, after he worked at other stations once he was fired from WHBQ—during the period he abused alcohol—there are still no credible accounts of him drinking while actually doing a show.

When Jack Parnell, a contemporary who worked with Dewey on WHBQ, was asked if he ever saw him drunk on the air, his telling response was that Dewey "never appeared to be strung-out on his show because he was strung-out all the time—that's just the way he was; he didn't *need any alcohol. I've never seen him when he wasn't on."* Durrell Durham is even more specific. "We thought that Dewey was always drunk," he says laughingly. "He seemed high as a kite all the time." That, however, "was just part of his personality. But he would never drink before he went on the air, I can assure you."[15]

Even though no one ever saw Dewey partake while doing a show, he certainly could have, given his disregard for rules. Almost all agree that Dewey, from the beginning, certainly liked his liquor. Stories abound of drinking bouts with Joe Cuoghi, Sam Phillips, and other old friends. No matter where (or with whom) he imbibed, he made no pretense of being a bastion of sobriety. His favorite watering holes were the Variety Club, Joe Cuoghi's all-night card games, and the Green Beetle down the street from the Chisca Hotel. Dewey obviously drank early and drank often—he was what one might call an enthusiastic drinker.[16]

In fact, on special occasions Dewey and Sam could be seen drinking publicly. Nate Evans, owner of the Handy Theater, says that at the Rocket 88 show, the only one Dewey and Sam booked together at his theater, "They got really carried away celebrating out in the lobby and got drunk right there."[17] Nonetheless, Sam still insists that "Dewey himself never was a heavy drinker." Of course, Sam, who liked iced tea glasses of vodka and has been described by Jim Dickinson as "a full speed ahead drinker," had his own definition of what might be termed "a heavy drinker." By contemporary standards it could be argued that all Dewey's friends and drinking companions were in a major state of denial. Regular consumption of alcohol, critics would suggest, indicates a serious, if not an addictive, problem. Those who contend that Dewey had no difficulty early in his career refuse to see the obvious.[18]

Nonetheless, almost everyone—friends and family alike—agree that Dewey's worst period did not come until the final years of his life. Dot Phillips does not try to hide her husband's problem but says it worsened toward the end of his life, mostly because of the pain pills. At one point, for example, he welcomed new neighbors while the Phillipses lived on Perkins Street by taking a fifth of Jack Daniels and going next door. "Hi," he said. "I'm Dewey Phillips, let's have a drink." He and the neighbors began to drink, and, Dot Phillips says, the woman has "been drinking ever since. Poor thing," Dot moans, without hint of irony or a sliver of sarcasm, "she turned into an alcoholic."[19]

Everyone seems to have a story about Dewey's drinking. The bottom line seems to be that without the pills, his liquor habit was reasonably under control for a long time, likely until after the second accident. The question of whether alcohol was involved in either of the accidents cannot be answered with certainty. Making matters more difficult, the query is complicated by Dewey's tarnished reputation as a driver.

Dewey already had acquired notoriety for being wild at the wheel—even when sober—long before either accident. Abe Schwab says that Dewey drove the way he ran his show, which is why he had the accidents. Even Sam Phillips confesses that he was afraid to ride with Dewey, even when sober. "He scared the hell out of me. He was just so crazy when he was driving. He would be talking to you and just not really paying any attention to the road." Dewey liked to frighten people, and he did so until Sam caught on. "He would reach over and hit the dash and holler real loud," Sam says, "just to shake you up. If he knew you didn't trust his driving, that would just wind him up more. Even backing out of the driveway, when he found anything about you that he could get next to you with, he'd do it just to watch you jump."[20]

"Amen!" says Dot Phillips to Sam's observations. Dewey would do ninety miles an hour down the middle of Main Street "if he took a mind to it." Once, while returning home from Alamo, Tennessee, she objected to his speeding so much that he slowed to nearly twenty miles an hour.

That angered Dot so much that she grabbed the keys and threw them through the car window. Dewey crawled on the ground for nearly an hour before finding them.[21]

What really happened in the accidents may always be a mystery. The fact that alcohol was not mentioned in contemporary official reports or newspaper accounts does not rule out the possibility that it was present. The true stories behind the tragedies may not have been told.[22] What is certain, however, is that whatever did occur was played down considerably by a 1950s' press far less probing and vigilant than the press of today. The press bore little resemblance to the frenzied media circus that often accompanies celebrities' wrongdoings today. A press not engaged extensively in investigative journalism, coupled with a police force that often coddled the Mid-South's most famous disc jockey, meant that the story was tempered considerably if not kept from the public view entirely.

The first accident followed his always-wild Saturday night show and occurred in the early Sunday morning hours of September 3, 1950, one mile west of the Critten–St. Francis County line in Arkansas. It left Dewey with a compound fracture of the left thigh as well as chest, head, and internal injuries. He was listed in critical condition, remained in a coma for several weeks, and then spent a few more recovering in Campbell Clinic in Memphis. The badly mangled leg left Dewey with a lifetime of pain and a crippled gait.

Although Memphis's major newspapers, the *Commercial Appeal* and the *Press-Scimitar,* gave the incident front-page coverage, both stories were significant in what they failed to say rather than in what they said. Each pointed out only that Doris Petty (the woman in the car with Dewey) had moved to Memphis from Booneville, Mississippi, about six weeks earlier and had applied for a job in Memphis. They further pointed out that she was temporarily living with her aunt, who was staying at the Chisca Hotel. (The WHBQ studios were at this time still in the Gayoso Hotel.) Although the *Commercial Appeal* ran a picture of Petty, no mention was made of why she was with Dewey. Nor was there any comment on the fact that a married man with two small children was alone in his car after midnight with a teenaged female, in the process of driving with her into another state when the accident occurred. Perhaps the newspapers felt it best to leave sordid details to the reader's imagination.[23]

The radio station reacted with striking reticence and self-restraint. The only official public announcement WHBQ made was that Dewey would be a while recuperating and that his show would be temporarily taken over by Lee McEachern, the station's production director. Even more significant, the announcement added that "as soon as Phillips improves sufficiently, the station plans to let him broadcast from the hospital." Then, as promised, after only a matter of weeks he began doing his show, first from his hospital bed in the Campbell Clinic and then while recuperating at home for another six weeks.

Not only did the station abstain from any reprimand, but it also left the impression that its sole concern was to reassure listeners that Dewey's accident would not cut off the star from his fans. He would be broadcasting again, the implication was, as soon as he could function long enough to be propped in front of a microphone. The station made no mention of how or why the accident occurred or of either woman. Billy Mills, reflecting on the fact that so little was said about the incident, remarked, "The radio station tap danced around that one."[24] Sam says that Dewey talked about the wreck very little, but he is certain that it bothered him a great deal and that he carried a great deal of guilt about Doris Petty's death. Nonetheless, despite having a number of opportunities to discuss the incident, he offered no explanation.[25]

Dot's reaction to the incident speaks volumes about her tolerance of her husband's wandering ways. She admits that Dewey didn't talk to her for quite awhile about the other woman in the car. Moreover, had he not been the first to speak, it is unlikely that she would have. Dot was, of course, well aware of Dewey's after-hours carousing, but apparently, she resigned herself to the idea that his most ardent fans were star-struck teenage females and let things go at that. According to Sam's wife (and Dot's close friend) Becky Phillips, she didn't "waste a lot of energy" worrying about Dewey and other women.[26]

Recognizing that her husband had every opportunity to see other women if he wanted, Dot apparently adopted a "don't ask, don't tell" attitude. Dewey, therefore, had little difficulty maintaining an appearance of propriety. Dickie Lee, whose admiration of his hero no doubt clouds his objectivity, offers an ambiguous assessment: "He was a womanizer, but if he ever cheated on Dot, I don't know anything about it." Lee, who spent many after-work hours hanging out with Dewey, says he had "fun with women," as he did with men, but "never got raunchy or anything like that."[27]

His wife may have been patient and understanding most of the time, but there were other occasions when even she would draw the line, especially if she suspected that Dewey might be serious about someone else. One telling story involves another woman at the Variety Club, where it was not unusual for her husband to be seen having drinks with other females. Over the years Dewey's good friend Vassar Slate, the club's bartender, would cover for him. It worked for a while, but apparently Dot learned about the clandestine practice—at least in one instance. One night, after repeated suspicions, she called the club, looking for Dewey. Slate told her he wasn't there, but she had a bellhop summon him to the telephone, saying she was his sister. He had been there all along, she found, and with someone else. Fearful that he was seeing the woman regularly, Dot became even more distrustful after Dewey insisted that she visit her mother in Alamo. She then hired a private detective to follow him and confronted him with the details when she discovered that he was indeed seeing a woman from Mississippi on a regular basis. "That broke up that affair quick," she said.[28] Apart from that isolated incident, however, Dot seems to have stood by her man almost until the end, when his substance abuse finally forced her, however reluctantly, to move out of the house.

Dewey's second accident occurred in March 1952, about a year and a half after the first. His unmatched enthusiasm for local basketball frequently took him back to his old hometown to watch the teams there as often as possible. (He even tried to take his vacation to coincide with the state prep tournament to make sure he could see all the games.) Traveling alone in the car this time, he had gone to Adamsville earlier in the evening to try to get tickets for the Region 8 high school basketball tournament that was being held in Henderson, Tennessee. It was a game that held special fascination because one of the players was his friend Bill "Bear" McClain. [29]

When he reached Adamsville he found that Max and Betty Jo Carruthers had been unable to get him tickets for the sold-out game. He turned the car around and was headed back to Memphis when he had an accident near Bolivar, Tennessee. Dewey's 1950 Dodge sedan tore through a steel guard rail, plunged down an embankment, and turned over several times before it came to rest upside down and 150 feet from the highway. Not only did the hood rip through the windshield but the front seat tore free from its mounting and slid under the dashboard, pinning him in the car until several passersby could right the vehicle and free him. Had there not been a car immediately behind him to witness the accident he probably would not have survived it. So badly demolished was the Dodge that a photograph accompanying the newspaper story reveals only one thing clearly visible in the otherwise mangled heap of metal—a WHBQ sign over Dewey's license plate.[30] He was immediately rushed to Kennedy Veterans Hospital in Memphis in critical condition with a compound fracture of the lower left leg, a fractured right thigh, a severe abdomen wound, and lacerations of the chest and face. They operated from ten that night until about four the next morning. Things were, Dot says, "just touch and go."[31]

According to the *Memphis Press-Scimitar*'s account, the Tennessee Highway Patrol said Dewey's car "was traveling at high speed" on a downhill S-curve when the accident occurred. The weather was good, the two-lane concrete highway was dry, and no other automobile was involved. No mention was made of alcohol. Dewey's statement to the press was that the car "went out of control on a sharp curve" because his injured leg, which still had a pin in it from the first accident, "had failed to function properly" as he attempted to apply his brakes. The wreck occurred on a Saturday evening around 7:30, and once again WHBQ announced that an effort would be made to continue Dewey's broadcasts without interruption. This was initially accomplished easily enough because his Saturday night show had already been recorded ("previously transcribed" was the phrase) and there was no regularly scheduled show on Sunday.[32]

By the following Monday it became apparent that Dewey would need a considerable period for healing this time, so it was decided to let Gordon Lawhead run the show temporarily until WHBQ could devise something else. As it turned out, Lawhead had to pinch-hit only for a relatively short time—just long enough to convert the Kennedy Hospital room into a kind of portable broadcasting studio that could operate easily from Dewey's bedside. He was in a partial body cast, with his injured leg in a harness that hung from the ceiling. Bob Lewis, Dewey's gofer, had the task of going to Kennedy Hospital every day and setting up the "studio." "He had two turntables," Bob recalls. "I played the record, and he did the thing from his hospital bed."[33]

The hospital broadcasts went on for about six weeks, but Dewey didn't miss a show, even during a long convalesence at home. The radio station transferred all its portable equipment from the hospital to the Phillips household. *Red, Hot and Blue* managed the switch from the WHBQ studios to Kennedy Hospital to the Phillips home without losing a single lucrative minute of air time.

Dewey and Dot were living with his sister and brother-in-law at the time, and the family had to accommodate to the new arrangement. Brother-in-law Bill Kirby remembers how surprised he was when WHBQ set Dewey up to broadcast from the house. There was Dewey, flat on his back, leg still in a huge cast suspended in middle of the air in its harness, and the WHBQ microphone poised by his side. Kirby smiles as he recalls how unprecedented the arrangement was. "We couldn't believe at first that he was really going to broadcast right from the bed. I remember we all had to be quiet the whole time he was on the air." Betty Kirby and Dot would take turns taking Randy, then a baby, outside during the show so that his crying wouldn't be picked up during the broadcast.[34]

Once well enough to return to the station Dewey did so, but only with the assistance of a wheelchair that transported him into the studio via the hotel elevator. When he reached the control room he rolled himself up to the microphone. "It was never necessary for him to leave that wheel chair," Bob Lewis says. "He did the whole show from right there."[35] Even while convalescing, however, he never stopped clowning. Being confined to a wheelchair while trying to do a hectic deejay show for three hours would have been difficult enough for most, but wheeling down the hall to the toilet between records proved a near impossibility. Or so Dewey believed. He convinced himself that during his temporary on-the-air incarceration he could never relieve himself and get back to the studio in the brief interval of a three-minute record. Whenever nature called, therefore, he chose to urinate into an empty pop bottle. Then, at the end of the evening, Dewey being Dewey, he could not resist the temptation to carefully line the bottles on the console for the next day's disc jockey to deal with. "That's one reason why they built that special control room for him," Charles Raiteri says.[36]

The first accident was wretched enough, but the second one proved more disastrous still. It not only reinjured his already badly shattered leg but also, and more important, marked the beginning of a long slide toward narcotic oblivion. Because there is no indication of drug abuse before either wreck, it is easy to presume that reinjuring his leg started Dewey on the pain pills that in turn led to his final annihilation. "Demerol and Dilaudid were the main drugs," says Sam Phillips. "After the second wreck Dewey was never really out of pain." Sam, who is convinced that this is when Dewey became dependent, says that he "got to where he used the pain as a crutch to get drugs. Dewey was never an alcoholic; he was a pillaholic, I guess."[37]

Just how much Dewey's substance abuse contributed to the decision to dismiss him from the station is difficult to determine. It might have been a factor, but much of the evidence seems to suggest that it was not the primary one. It is true that the dismissal, which devastated him, exacerbated an already existing drug problem, but the fact that he was retained at the station until 1958 indicates that substance abuse alone was not the sole reason for his release.

WHBQ deejay Jack Parnell, who was around when Dewey was fired, says the station may have "already been upset with him about other things anyway—the drugs, the wreck, etc., but the radical change to the Top 40 format was the precipitating factor." Jack supports this idea by pointing out that he was hired several months before Dewey's dismissal. "I think they had it in mind when they hired me." More important, he notes that Ray Brown, another WHBQ deejay, was also released at the same time as Dewey, giving support to the notion that both firings, and the subsequent hiring of new personnel, came about because of the program shift.[38] Contrary to all conventional wisdom concerning Dewey's problems with drinking and pills, had it not been for the format change he might never have been dismissed. The real culprit was that Dewey did not fit into WHBQ's switch-over. Ground zero for Daddy-O-Dewey was Top 40 radio.

The transformation began when WHBQ was purchased in 1954 by General Teleradio, a large corporation in New York that owned other stations around the country. In essence, the Memphis takeover by a large radio conglomerate meant that WHBQ became another entity in the expansive GenTel system. The immediate result was a loss of local autonomy; decisions concerning which format policy to implement were now made by the parent company rather than at each local station in the chain.[39]

By the time GenTel took over, playing only the Top 40 hits was the wave of the future for radio entertainment in America, and the new owners were convinced they had to ride the crest of that wave. Top 40's characteristic trait was a lot of music and very little talk. The focus was on the records and not the deejay. One reason for the format change was undoubtedly the shift taking place in the music itself. Subtle though it was, that shift had at least some part in Dewey Phillips's decline.

The initial luster of early 1950s' rock 'n' roll (or at least Dewey's unique version of it) was beginning to wear thin by mid-decade. The Top 40 list had to be filled with a lot of rock 'n' roll but not Dewey Phillips's rendition of it. It is certainly true that musical tastes were changing; *Red, Hot and Blue,* however, was still commercially successful. But equally true was the fact that the time had long since passed when Dewey anchored the station financially. WHBQ's new management was convinced that a radical adjustment in its basic format was as necessary by the late 1950s as the former management had been when they made a more revolutionary

187

decision during the late 1940s to experiment with the totally unknown Dewey Phillips.[40]

The first station in Memphis to go Top 40 was WMPS in 1955. That switch and the station's subsequent climb in ratings made GenTel's decision to change the WHBQ format even more compelling although it would take several years before the switch over was complete. In the meanwhile, as WMPS and WHBQ headed into the late 1950s the stations played a ratings game with each other, carefully following the delicate, albeit significant, shift that was slowly taking place in the musical preferences of the audience.[41]

Alex Ward, Memphis deejay and a long-time record collector, is a student of the city's music during the 1950s and likes to point out that, by 1958, "You are no longer getting the real raw rock and roll." Beginning in about 1956, WHBQ was starting to follow WMPS. "'Q' actually got softer as WMPS did—they are both *quieting down* the music" as Top 40 came to dominate everything. "Before it is over," Ward concludes, "WHBQ ends up even quieter than 'MPS. 'HBQ is playing Andy Williams and Mitch Miller—'MPS is at least playing Fabian."[42]

The change, of course, had to affect Dewey Phillips and *Red, Hot and Blue.* Don McLean's immortal statement that this was "the day the music died" referred to Buddy Holly being killed in a airplane crash, Elvis going into the army, Little Richard becoming a minister, and Jerry Lee Lewis marrying his thirteen-year-old cousin. By the late 1950s a little bit of Dewey Phillips died as well. At the very least he was no longer at the peak of his powers.

The changing tastes of audiences already had an impact on Dewey's television show, which aired in 1956. He found it necessary to play more traditional Top 40 hits for his television audience and exclude artists such as Rosetta Tharpe, Marie Knight, "Brother" Dave Gardner, and a host of other nonmainstream musical eccentrics characteristic of the early *Red, Hot and Blue.* Even the television show's theme song, Tommy Dorsey's version of "Opus One," conformed perfectly to a more broadly anticipated audience. Perhaps of even greater importance, WHBQ-TV had begun to air Dick Clark's *American Bandstand* in 1956. "Everything is a little cleaner now," Ward noted, emphasizing that the less offensive and more socially acceptable Clark appeared more attractive to WHBQ than the worrisome (and by now not quite as profitable) Dewey. "It is summer of 1958, and they are bringing in younger jocks," observes Ward. "Dewey simply does not have the clout he had earlier."[43]

John Fry, one of Memphis's top record producers, also argues that

Dewey was done in by the fundamental change in the music. "As the music got more sophisticated" it didn't seem right that songs were being played by Dewey Phillips. "The records weren't raw anymore," Fry says. There was suddenly gross inconsistency between Dewey and the music. "It was kind of funny to hear somebody screaming and pounding on the table, and then this intricately produced record comes on; they just didn't go together."[44]

All that is true enough. Still, in the bigger picture, Dewey's demise was the actual format itself. Deejays, who were expected to stick closely to the Top 40 playlist, became automatons, little more than cogs in a machine, dispensing only essential information about the record, time and temperature, and, of course, the sponsor's product. There were no more disc jockey "personalities." Dewey Phillips's legendary career, like those of many other top deejays around the country, was over. What critics then called "assembly line rock" took all the fun, if not soul, out of the work of older, star-studded deejays who were now told, in essence, to keep their mouths shut, follow the station format, and play the records.

Dewey Phillips keep his mouth shut? The very thought was anathema to him and his fans. For him to follow a format, Jack Parnell says, "would be like trying to get Jonathan Winters [or perhaps Robin Williams] to follow a format. To try to get Dewey to do that, you might as well tie him up and put tape over his mouth." Most fans listened as much (if not more) to his wild, unexpected voice-overs as to the music.[45]

To rigidly lock him into a formatted straightjacket was to eliminate what Dewey Phillips was all about. Commenting on how out of place he would be in such a system, Bill Burke, a local *Press-Scimitar* writer, put it perfectly when he observed that Dewey would have been "a Gen. George S. Patton without a war; a Don Quixote without windmills."[46] To borrow one of Dewey's phrases and put the matter colloquially, he had about as much chance of surviving the Top 40 format as "a one-legged man at a kickin' contest."

The official shift took place in the fall of 1957 when WHBQ announced that it was dropping affiliation with the ABC network and going to "a restyled programming format based on local music-personality appeal." Although not strictly following the Top 40 format, it indicated it would now feature the Top 56 tunes (WHBQ's frequency was 560 on the dial) "based on a survey conducted by the station among its listenership on the basis of requests to disk jockeys." No specific announcement was made at the time, but it appeared that Dewey would be phased out slowly. Bill Grumbles pointed out that although the *Pop Shop* television show would continue, the station was ending its simultaneous radio broadcast "because of technical difficulties in coordinating it."[47]

It took WHBQ nearly another year to switch over totally, but it held on to *Red, Hot and Blue* until the change was complete. It did so because Dewey—who no longer totally dominated ratings—still had a significantly large audience. The decision may have been motivated less by an altruistic desire to assist the fallen star then by a selfish decision to wean fans away from him slowly, allowing them time to adapt to Top 40. Nonetheless, the new owners' determination to have the station conform to their chain's policy overrode efforts to keep him on the air permanently. Sam Phillips believes that no attempt was made to have Dewey adapt to the new system because management knew he could not or would not do so. "They knew there was no way that Dewey could become a Top 40 monkey," he says, "just sitting there playing the records."[48]

In fact, contrary to Sam's opinion (and those of most who supported Dewey)—indeed, contrary to what now would seem to be common sense—the station did make an effort, albeit a brief and half-hearted one, to adjust Dewey to the new format. He was kept on, at least for awhile, unlike Ray Brown, who apparently was dismissed without much warning. Brown would later claim that he realized he was fired when he heard, while driving to work one morning, that someone else would be doing his show.[49]

Larry Caughlin, an engineer employed by WHBQ in 1957, about the time the station was switching to Top 40, spent a great deal of time in his first year at the station trying to record some of Dewey's commercials as part of the attempt to make the transition. The station had him pre-tape Dewey's spots, with the hope that tape would eliminate the famous ad libs and move Dewey toward a more formal presentation. The attempt, however, was not only hopelessly futile but it also drove Caughlin wild. Although he would try to have Dewey make a one-minute commercial, it would often last as long as five minutes while Dewey rambled on, occasionally about a different product. In the middle of a furniture commercial, for example, he would add "freeze it and eat it," which he used exclusively for Falstaff Beer. Dewey also walked around the microphone while he was talking or stood on a chair and played with the ceiling. On rare occasions things might progress as far as the last line before Dewey would blow a recording with some outrageous outburst. In the end, the commercials had to be taped piecemeal by finding a word here and there in a great many takes and then splicing the whole thing together.[50]

Dewey vociferously complained during this period about having his freedom restricted, seeing no reason not to continue with what had always been a magic formula. Several of his loyal sponsors also complained, arguing that their favorite disc jockey had his hands tied. Some were so concerned that they threatened to remove their commercials unless something was done. Still, the station's response was at best lackluster. It made a few concessions, temporarily giving Dewey a bit of slack, but they were only futile reprieves from the final, inevitable retreat. WHBQ gradually had to accept the fact that there was no way Dewey would fit in with the new format. Even Dewey Phillips, it seems, could not stop the Top 40 tidal wave now engulfing the entire country.[51]

When the decision was finally made to terminate, it was no doubt as big a surprise to Dewey's fans as it was to him. Don Nix remembers well the night Dewey broadcast his last show. Nix and a friend were double-dating in a 1955 Ford. Both couples in the car had begun to go together while listening to Dewey's music, and they all were crying, especially when he played his final song, "Goodnight My Love," and signed off. Nix and his friends went downtown, where cars were lined up around the Chisca Hotel. People were driving up and down Main Street, blowing the horns of their automobiles. It was a hot July night, and almost everyone had their car windows down, listening to the broadcast, the sound of which spilled out into the street. All eight of Memphis's high schools were represented on Main Street, and, Nix says, everyone was sobbing.[52]

Apparently Dewey gave no indication over the air that he had been fired—only that he was leaving the station for good. It was, Sam Phillips says, Dewey's style not to apologize and certainly never to ask for sympathy. "He'd rather silently steal away." Nix is convinced that people thought he was leaving of his own accord. Had they known he had been fired, he is certain that there would have been protests. Indeed, there were some, albeit on a minor scale. Jim Dickinson remembers seeing teenagers lined up in front of East High School, carrying signs that read "Bring Back Dewey."[53]

WHBQ might have assumed that fans would gradually accommodate to life without Red, Hot and Blue, but for Dewey there could be no adaptation or adjustment. When the dismissal occurred the news hit him like a tank. Brother-in-law Bill Kirby was with Dewey the day the ax fell and remembers the incident all too well. The news was as unexpected as it was devastating. "They didn't really have much to say. He talked to them a while, and that was it," Kirby remembers. Dewey sat in the outer office for a short period, apparently stunned, then slowly rose and walked out. After a few minutes he stumbled back inside and asked if management would reconsider. When they said no he left again.[54]

"Man, that really tore him up," Kirby says. "It just took everything out of him because he knew that all he worked for was there and it was all destroyed." Barbara Pittman spent time with Dewey the day he got fired. They went to see Joe Cuoghi at Pop Tunes and then went all over town. She was too young to drink, but Dewey, she says, "got totaled." She thinks they ended up at the Sun Studio and Jack Clement had to take Dewey home.[55]

Sam Phillips, reflecting on it all much later, says he saw the inevitability of Top 40 radio and remembers trying to explain it to Dewey. "This was a format thing," he told him. "If you could have done a format, you'd still be there, but you'd have been shot if you had tried it!"[56] Sam tried to emphasize to Dewey that he was "not fired, just let go—there is a difference." Nonetheless, the termination wiped him out. "Dewey's pride was his greatest asset and his greatest liability," Sam observes. "He was a very proud person."[57]

14

The Final Descent:
"If Dewey Couldn't be Number One,
He Didn't Wanna Be"

Although the Phillips family still speaks of Dewey in positive, if not glowing, terms, none have any problem with openly discussing his terrible decline toward the end—when, as Dot Phillips sometimes puts it, "He was just a mess." She, for example, is quick to emphasize that Dewey's drug habit started as a desperate effort to relieve his suffering. Most people, she says, do not realize the severity of the damage done to his left leg; after the second accident he came very close to death. "He'd lost a lot of blood," she recalls. "The whole six hours they were operating on him, we didn't think he'd make it." Sam Phillips says that anybody else would have been dead in such an accident. "He was *re-broken* all to pieces."[1]

Unfortunately, the second accident was just the beginning of never-ending misery with his leg. Before it was all over Dewey had a total of fourteen operations, most of which involved surgery on his shin and scraping the bone. Each time, the leg became a bit shorter. Army doctors at the Kennedy Veterans Hospital advised that the leg should be amputated. When he chose not to, he committed himself to a lifetime of pain.[2]

After leaving the hospital following the first accident, a specially built shoe allowed Dewey to walk at first without a noticeable limp. Later, however, when some of the pins were removed, he developed a distinct and irregular gait that never left him even though he wore the shoe. Once he started to appear on television, the discernible hobble soon became as familiar a characteristic to fans as his spitfire sentences had been on the radio. Dewey always seemed to move a little faster than would be expected, apparently trying to compensate for the bad leg that inevitably dragged behind, giving him an idiosyncratic lope.

The medical term for his problem is "osteomyelitis," an acute bone infection that develops from badly shattered bones. "Dewey's wound would heal from the outside in, but it wouldn't heal from the inside out," Dot laments. "It might heal for a while, but then it would get worse." The sore was deep in his leg, causing the wound to fester, so it was purposely left open to permit drainage from time to time and thus never allowed to completely heal. Bill Kirby tried to get him to "stop picking at it," which did no good. For well over a decade Dewey walked around with an open leg wound.[3]

Randy Phillips tries to remain composed as he poignantly recalls the grief his father suffered. On some days the leg would hurt more than others. "A lot of times, after getting into it with Grandpa [Dot's father] over the pills, Dewey would go outside on the front porch and sit down and rub his leg," Randy remembers. His father would pull up his pants, pull back the brace ("like a polio brace"), show him the hole in his leg, and "say 'This is why I have to take those pills.'" Initially, he had pins in the leg as well, which Randy says Dewey felt constantly. As he grew older he would sit with his father and try to talk to him—"You know, try to soothe him a little."[4]

The only real soothing Dewey ever had from pain, however, came with pills. Perhaps it might have been predicted (given Dewey's normally erratic behavior), but his reliance on them for relief was almost immediately out of control. Sam Phillips says that before Dewey came to rely on drugs he never complained about pain because he thought doing so was "sissy." Later, however, after he became strung out, "He'd go out to Kennedy and tell them how bad he was hurtin'. And no doubt he was," Sam adds. After all that complaining, "He usually didn't have much trouble getting almost anything he wanted."[5]

Dewey's drug addiction at the end invites an almost melodramatic comparison with Elvis Presley's substance abuse problem. The similarities are striking. Both men were celebrities who abused drugs, had easy access to them, and had virtually no one around to say no. Both were superstars whose shortcomings were, at best, often tolerated. At worst, and on many occasions, both were coddled and pampered like spoiled children. Close friends often found it difficult to refuse the requests of either man.

Before becoming too judgmental, however, one should always be cautious about reading current values into the past. It is good to remember that America's modern "drug problem" was virtually nonexistent during the 1950s. At the very least, information concerning the harmful effects of excessive medication in no way commanded the glaring attention it does now. Things like drug prevention counciling, de-tox programs, and support groups were almost nonexistent. The conventional way to handle substance abusers was to place them in either a mental institution or the psychiatric wards of hospitals. Thus, without condoning their actions it is easy to view people like Dewey and Elvis as tragic figures who perhaps should be pitied rather than scorned. If nothing else, their rocket rides to stardom and easily accessible drug supplies were not accompanied by the abundance of drug treatment programs afforded most celebrities today.

Dewey, however, must be held at least in part accountable for his downfall. His drug abuse was not simply an inevitable result of an indifferent society. He alone was the architect of much of his misery. Liquor and drugs are a lethal combination, and when mixed with the already ballistic personality of a Dewey Phillips it is difficult to resist the conclusion that the outcome had to be fatal.

It should be recognized that close friends and associates, always with the best of motivations, sometimes seemed to contribute significantly— even if unintentionally—to Dewey's catastrophic descent. At a minimum their compliant accommodation to his self-destructive life-style made the unfortunate process a great deal easier to accomplish. His behavior was tolerated by those who could (and certainly should) have done something about it. To use modern jargon, he had many enablers.

There were, for example, the law enforcement agencies in Memphis. The Memphis police were if not totally intimidated by Dewey's enormous popularity then certainly cowed by it, especially later, after he became the man who not only launched the careers of Jerry Lee Lewis and Johnny Cash but also was best friends with his excellency, the king of rock 'n' roll. It would not be inaccurate to say that the police could not have pampered Dewey more had he been the chief's own son.[6] Until close to the end, a great many people on the force discreetly looked the other way when his abusive behavior caused problems. "The police gave Dewey a lot of slack," says friend Dickie Lee. "They might clock him at eighty miles an hour down Poplar Avenue and after a brief scolding, say, 'Now, Dewey, be careful.'"[7]

Once the behavior was tolerated there was no end to the abuse. If stopped for any infraction, many of the Memphis police force were almost apologetic if they had to make so much as a mild reprimand. Jerry

Phillips, Dewey's younger son, says that the pattern became so commonplace that his father would carry records on the back seat of his car. "When a cop stopped him, he'd just reach back and hand him a record. I can remember he showed me the records he kept up there after he told me that story."[8]

Although not excusable, such behavior becomes more understandable considering the cozy nature of Dewey's association with the police during this time. On one side of the coin it was practically impossible for a law officer (or anyone for that matter) to live in the city of Memphis during the 1950s and not know Dewey Phillips—if not on sight than at least by reputation. The flip side was that Dewey, a classic "good ol' southern country boy," came to know most members of the force. And—until the last years of his life—very few, if any, were willing to chastise, let alone arrest, him for intoxication, drugs, or disturbing the peace.[9]

After all, Dewey was chums with the highest-ranking members of the department. He often joked on the air about Police Chief James McDonald, who would frequently be the butt of some of his bawdiest gags. Joe Gagliano, one of his closest friends, was a plainclothes detective on the force. So well known was his connection with the police that it carried over to friends and family members. Dot Phillips, for example, was once ticketed but later found out that it was because she was in a borrowed car. The police apologized to her afterward. Had they recognized the car and realized she was Dewey's wife, they said, they would never have given her the ticket in the first place. There were many nights, Dot remembers, when the police brought Dewey home and never a word was mentioned about an arrest. She unmindfully and inadvertently indicts her own complicity by acknowledging that most of the time she was "grateful just to have him returned safely." Sadly, such occurrences became more frequent as Dewey's dependency on drugs worsened. At the end, some behavior was frightening, even by the standards of the always frenzied Dewey.[10]

Robert Johnson, who continued to stay close to his friend, even during his desperate last years, says that at the end he "popped pain killers like pop corn."[11] By all accounts Dewey selected drugs indiscriminately, although his preference was for Darvon and Codeine. Tales abound of him walking into strangers' homes, going to their medicine cabinets, and swallowing whatever was available. Indeed, there are so many "Dewey-in-decline yarns" that they might seem to be invented. Unfortunately, numerous witnesses recollect an uncomfortable kernel of truth in all too many of them.

It seems as if everyone has a story about Dewey's never-ending quest for a fix. The most frequently circulated ones have him (a) surreptitiously obtaining huge amounts of Codeine from various druggists; (b) picking up stacks of records from distributors and then trading the records for drugs; or (c) acquiring any kind of pill imaginable from an unnamed black dentist in South Memphis.[12] His suppliers, anyone from a local druggist or dentist to a devoted fan or friend with an available medicine cabinet, were seemingly as generous as they were ubiquitous.

By all accounts, some of these stories seem true. Although family members don't deny any of them, they point out that most of the time Dewey had to go no farther than to a corner drugstore for his supply. He could, Dot says, walk into nearly any store in town and find someone who knew him. Perhaps the saddest commentary of all on the generally permissive attitude that all too many in the city of Memphis had toward this superstar is reflected in Dot's claim that "Dewey could get his pills almost anywhere, anytime." The ease with which he could obtain them meant that at any given moment a seemingly never-ending supply was available. She has, she remembers, "probably flushed a small kitchen of pills down the commode."[13]

He generally didn't even need a prescription. Most druggists would fill his empty, unlabeled medicine bottles or pass along free samples of whatever he wanted. Jerry Phillips was a senior in high school before he found out that his father was on pills. He wasn't surprised, however, when he found all sorts of "complementary samples and prescription drugs" when cleaning Dewey's room at the time of his death.[14]

Dewey's sisters go even further. The pills, Marjorie Phillips Barba says, "were in all colors, all sizes, all shapes. He didn't know what he had." Betty Kirby happened to be living in Millington, Tennessee, at the time Dewey joined that city's radio station following his dismissal from WHBQ. At one point she watched Dewey walk behind the counter of a drugstore in Millington and "put a handful of pills in his pocket." When she confronted the druggist, both he and Dewey claimed the incident never happened.[15] "I would call the drugstore and tell them not to give them to him," Dot recalls angrily, "but they'd tell me 'If we don't somebody else will, and those might kill him.'" She throws up her hands in bewildered acquiescence: "You know, it was *safer* just to let him get them from the druggist."[16]

It is not only heart-rending but also understandable that the Phillips family, watching their loved one suffer through these awful years, might want to blame an outside force for Dewey's behavior. Observing his daily, constant pain and the devastating reaction to it would no doubt convince them that there had to be some villain—a sympathetic druggist, a tolerant police force, or a lackadaisical press—responsible for his downfall. They all make suitable devils and perhaps convenient scapegoats.

Also understandable is the animosity that some family members hold toward the radio station that abruptly dismissed Dewey after he had originally helped to financially resurrect it. Their anger is vented not so much on the reason for the dismissal but on how they believe the station may have contributed to Dewey's drug habit. Voicing the concerns of those who feel he was pressured to continue broadcasting after both accidents, Betty Kirby says, "When he was in the hospital recovering, WHBQ wanted him on the air, regardless." She is convinced that this is what did it and blames the station for insisting on keeping his show going while he convalesced.[17] According to her scenario, the station anxiously pressured the hospital to get Dewey sufficiently functional to broadcast. In order to do that it was necessary to give him so much medication that he became addicted to pain pills.

There is no real proof, of course, that this took place. It is true that when Gordon Lawhead became Dewey's replacement after the second accident the results were probably as predictable as they were inevitable. Without Dewey it was a matter of déjà vu. Gordon said he was losing the audience just as he never gained an audience when running the show himself. If Dewey wasn't doing *Red, Hot and Blue,* very few bothered to listen.

It was at that point that the decision was made to have Dewey broadcast from his hospital bed. "One way they had to do that," Charles Raiteri argues, "was to pump him up with morphine." Dot observes when he was doing his show from the hospital "he took Demerol before he went on the air and then he took it again right after. He was in constant pain."[18] There is no way to know whether the station suggested heavier medication or the hospital responded. What is certain is that the station wasted no time getting Dewey back on the air and that when he did return he was so heavily medicated that he was nearly incoherent.

Robert Gordon has managed to obtain a copy of Dewey broadcasting from Kennedy Veterans Hospital, and it is included as part of a CD entitled *Red, Hot and Blue: Dewey Phillips Live Radio Broadcasts from 1952–1964.* Make no mistake about it; Dewey was strung out on something. Should there be any doubt, Dewey announces, "I got a morphine shot in me and I can't see very good here."[19] Of course, one could argue that the story of Dewey ranting about payola is analogous to the previous statement. If it were true, would he have talked about it on the air? The difference is that in this instance it is obvious to even the most casual listener that the already wild Dewey is much more spaced out than usual. He is thick-tongued, and his speech is slurred. Moreover, the quantum jump in his normally rapid-fire delivery makes it difficult to follow even familiar phrases. Thus, it is difficult for even an ardent fan of Dewey's to listen to the CD and not conclude that he was flying high.

Still, given the station's bottom-line financial interests one can easily recognize that WHBQ wanted to get Dewey back on the air as quickly as possible. Moreover, the station capitalized on his accident by actively promoting his heroic effort to continue broadcasting while in the process of recovery. Not only was there a lot of media attention (newspaper photographs of Dewey broadcasting from his hospital bed), but Jerry Phillips also recalls that the station printed promotional matchbooks showing his father lying in bed, microphone beside him on a small table and head back, grinning the familiar Dewey grin.[20]

Not all family and friends blame the radio station. Dot Phillips, for example, gratefully recognizes that "WHBQ probably did the right thing. He never missed a paycheck when he was in the hospital."[21] Rather than fault the station, some feel that Dewey, like Elvis, had become a victim of his own superstardom. Both men had become bigger-than-life figures, and it was almost impossible to refuse either of them anything they wanted. An avalanche of admiration buried any effort at admonishment. That meant not only turning a blind eye toward the drug problem but also creating a permissive attitude toward behavior in general. For whatever reason, both headliners were often pampered, which made it increasingly difficult to say no to them or correct any perceived wrongdoing.

Durrell Durham complained that it was painfully embarrassing to try and tell Dewey anything on his television show. "Every once in a while, people would come in and say, 'Don't let Dewey do that on TV anymore,' I'd say, 'OK, you tell him not to do it. He's not gonna listen to me. He don't even know my name. *I'm just the Director of the show!* He's the star. He can do almost anything he wants to.'"[22]

With little or no external restraint, therefore, Dewey's reaction to his dismissal from WHBQ was a near-textbook example of how not to escape one's problems by numbing through drugs. Even though the firing desolated him, he seems to have repressed anger and resentment by going his merry way. At the height of his popularity he had turned down far more lucrative offers from stations in other cities. After dismissal from WHBQ he bitterly resented having to leave the city he loved, especially having to do so involuntarily. Although it was apparent that he was upset, good-time Dewey had to continue, happy-go-lucky as ever; he had created an on-air persona that was often difficult to shut down.

For Dewey, the trouble with this blurred, seamless mixture of on-air and off-air personality was that outside observers had no way of knowing what his actual reality was. It was just as hard for friends and family to tell from his general behavior how much he was hurting as it must have been for Dewey himself. He must have been indignant about having to leave Memphis, which had become his adopted home. Because he had to continue working somewhere, however, and he made a living by having an eternally happy radio personality, it was necessary to continue projecting that Pollyanna-ish facade. Inasmuch as he would not consider the possibility of any other line of work, he had little choice. Every other radio station in town had jumped on the fashionable Top 40 bandwagon. Dewey was caught in a kind of radio cul de sac.

He left Memphis and went first to KXLR in Little Rock, Arkansas, a station that had made him an earlier offer while he was still at WHBQ. He joined them on August 15, 1958, doing a nightly radio show from 8 to midnight. As he had done in Memphis, he also broadcast a ninety-minute television show with Harry Fitzius on Saturday afternoons. Now, however, the show was a completely separate entity, not simulcast with radio. The television show was carried by a completely different Little Rock station, KHTV, Channel 7.

Little Rock is fewer than 150 miles from Memphis, but for Dewey it could have been on another planet. Dot says it was all that she could do to drag him out of town kicking and screaming. Some of his bitterness over having to leave can be subtly detected through Robert Johnson's column in the *Press-Scimitar:* "I'll be making more money to start than I have in ten years in Memphis radio," Dewey uncharacteristically bragged. "In case you are wondering what that might be," Johnson reported, echoing his own indignant boasting, "it runs comfortably into five figures."[23]

The money might have been better in Little Rock, but it afforded little compensation for a man who had practically owned the entertainment industry in Memphis for a decade. Dewey considered himself to have been unmercifully banished and talked of nothing but returning to Memphis. He even failed to move his family to Little Rock. After the Phillips house in Memphis was sold, Dot and the boys moved in with Sam Phillips, supposedly on a temporary basis until they could find another place, presumably in Little Rock. That move, however, never happened.[24]

After only a couple of months Dewey desperately begged Sam for a spot on WHEY, the small new station Sam co-owned in Millington, which was just outside the Memphis city limits. Even though its weak signal failed to reach most of the metropolitan area it brought Dewey much closer to where he wanted to be. He jumped at the opportunity as soon as Sam offered it.

He may have felt like he was back in Memphis, but the embarrassment that accompanied his new job did little to salve his already badly damaged ego. Dewey came on the air at WHEY at 2 in the afternoon, which meant he immediately followed George Klein, now a hot deejay on the same station in the 1 to 2 o'clock slot. In case Dewey needed an introduction to the notion that he had come down a notch or two in the world, sharing the microphone with the man who had once opened his telegrams and fetched his coffee no doubt afforded a daily reminder of his plight. Indeed, he had competed with George several times before. When Dewey was at the height of his power, his *Pop Shop* television show aired at the same time that G.K.'s popular afternoon radio show was broadcast from WMC.[25]

Dewey managed to stick it out at WHEY for nearly a year, until August 1959, but by then his frustration had turned to anguish. In desperation, he grew so lonesome one night that he again called Sam Phillips to see whether he could do anything for him. "Dewey didn't cry easy, and he was crying on the phone," Sam says, remembering just how frantic his friend was to get back to his beloved city. At the time Sam had an all-female radio station, WHER, in Memphis, so he couldn't put Dewey to work there. He did, however, help him get a job at WHHM in Memphis by talking to Harlan Hill, the former professional football player who spent time with the Chicago Bears. Hill, who had become a part owner of WHHM, decided, with Sam's prodding, to give Dewey the shot he wanted.[26]

It worked wonderfully well. Not only did the job get Dewey back inside the city of Memphis, but also, and much more important, he also had a chance to reprise *Red, Hot and Blue* when WHHM put him in an 8 to midnight slot. Dewey was deliriously excited at what seemed like a shot at a comeback, if not on the same station than at least in the same city and with the same show. "I'm going to tear this town up," he told Robert Johnson. Never one to hide his feelings, he let everyone know how much he wanted to be back. "I was so hungry to be back in Memphis," he said, "I was ready to change my name to Maybelline and go with [the all-women station] WHER."[27]

WHHM itself was no less enthusiastic about the possibility of reviving Dewey and the early 1950s' radio format. Slipping badly in the ratings, the station decided to chuck the Top 40 playlist and return to the glorious days of yesteryear. At the time it hired Dewey the station also re-hired the highly popular Sleepy-Eyed John Lepley, who had originally been with WHHM but left to go to West Memphis's KWAM.[28] Like Dewey, he wanted to get back to Memphis but for a different reason. His lifelong ambition to become a physician could be realized by entering the University of Tennessee Medical School, which was located in the city.

Both men had huge followings, practically personifying the "personality" deejay, so the move was an obvious effort to reverse the clock to the heady days when a deejay alone was not just the star of a show but the reason for its existence. By combining two disc jockeys who at one time had controlled the Memphis airwaves the station made it clear that it was trying to resurrect the era that had faded so rapidly and hoping to reprise earlier ratings. Most important, it was Dewey's long-awaited big shot. Even though his language was not explicit he strongly suggested that he was ready at last to put his disreputable past behind him and reform. Without mentioning liquor or pills specifically, he dramatically announced in Johnson's column, "I'm going to get plenty of sleep and feel good when I go on the air. And I'm going to have this city right where I had it before. This is what I've been waiting for."[29]

Despite the enthusiasm, however, the much-anticipated comeback never occurred. Neither Dewey nor Sleepy-Eyed John ever came close to acquiring their old followings. That was particularly unfortunate because many of Dewey's followers are convinced that he did some of his finest radio work while at WHHM even though his personal life was already well into a final, fast descent.[30] In fact, Dewey's sun had already set. Radio broadcasting had undergone a sea change. Top 40 radio had a lock on the city's audience, and personality deejays like Dewey and Sleepy-Eyed John who had been wiped out by its unfriendly format were doomed to an oblivion reserved for all who fall victim to the whims of fashion. Radio's fickle listeners now made Dewey's insane style of behavior behind the microphone as far out of fashion as it had once been in.

Perhaps Dewey intuitively sensed all this. Perhaps he realized that his glory days were behind him—that he could never again capture those magic moments of the early 1950s when he was king of the musical hill, forever on top and riding the crest of the rock 'n' roll tidal wave.

From this point on his life became little more than a mockery of what it had once been. As it slowly became obvious that the much-hoped-for comeback would never materialize, Dewey began, full-throttle, a mad rush toward self-destruction. His personal problems began to escalate in almost direct proportion to his ever-expanding substance abuse.

While Dewey was still at WHHM his drinking problem was beginning to be noticed. The Memphis police, for the first time, began to arrest him on charges of drunkenness and reckless driving. Robert Johnson, commenting on the sad spectacle Dewey had become from about 1960 onward, remarked much later that he was a "confused and lonely man with the heart of a boy, living in the past."[31] No doubt the reality of being unable to resuscitate his career had begun to set in while he was still at WHHM.

Sadly, the greater the realization of his plight, the harder he tried to change his fate. He tried to alter everything, that is, except an increasing reliance on pills. It was during this period that he began showing up at rock 'n' roll shows in the area, any place he thought he could appear and be recognized. He'd get onstage at these shows if he were allowed (more often than not, given his condition, he was turned down), somehow hoping he could work the wizardry that would bring back the stardom he once enjoyed.

The frustration that seems to have grown in direct proportion to an inability to control his life was becoming more obvious to those around him. Bob Lewis says that Dewey could never understand why things couldn't be just like they once were. "Bless his heart, his fame was just bigger than he was. He had no way of handling it."[32] It was Dewey's youngest son, Jerry, though, who summarized his father's fate: "If Dewey couldn't be number one . . . he didn't wanna be."[33]

Inevitably, he was fired from WHHM in 1962. Even though his substance abuse continued to increase, he was dismissed at about the same time that most of the other deejays were dropped. This seems to suggest that, once again, it was not entirely due to his personal behavior. Rather, Dewey, like the others, had become expendable as the Top 40 steamroller continued to take its toll. WHHM, failing to revitalize the old 1950s' format, went bankrupt and left the air in a short while after the dismissals.

Following another period of disorientation Dewey was rehired in 1963 by the same station (now with new call letters) in Millington, where he had earlier been employed. WHEY had also gone broke and left the air but subsequently reorganized as WGMM. Unfortunately, its low-watt signal was so weak that it could barely be picked up in nearby Memphis. Located near the Millington Naval Air Station inside a dingy, makeshift trailer that was itself inside a sprawling shopping center, WGMM is where the once renowned Daddy-O-Dewey—mentor and career launcher for Elvis Presley, Johnny Cash, and Jerry Lee Lewis—would spend his last broadcasting days.[34]

As his drug problem grew inexorably more serious, Dot could do little more than try to cope with daily life. Although the police were starting to pick up Dewey on a regular basis, even at this rapidly declining stage he could usually avoid jail time. Apart from becoming an ever-increasing embarrassment for Dot, he was still on reasonably good terms with the majority of the police force, and they usually could talk him into letting them take him home without serious damage being done to anyone except himself.

Sometimes, however, it was not the police who brought him home. Often, after a night of wild carousing, others would deposit him. "He'd always resist going home," says Stan Kesler, a Sun Studio musician who very often took Dewey home after he'd drop by Sam's studio very late at night. Dewey wanted, Kesler says, to be taken anywhere except his house. "'Let's go down to see Elvis,' he'd say," but Stan would point out that it was the middle of the night. "I know that," Dewey would argue, "but I called him a while ago." Stan, who knew that was not the case, would refuse to go. Dewey would then ask to be taken to Sam's house, and again Kesler would point out that it was late. "Aw, Sam don't never go to bed," Dewey would argue. Finally, he would reluctantly give in and be talked into going to his house. Even then, however, it wasn't over. "No telling how many times he'd walk away from the house after he was let off," Stan Kesler says.[35]

As might be expected, such abuse began to take a nasty physical toll. James Parks, who hung around the Sun Studio a lot during these years, remembers seeing Dewey "coughing up blood, and in a lot of pain. He was taking Darvons, and always acted like he was on speed." He was still coming into Sam's studio almost every day, though, and often enough Sam would be tolerant. Parks remembers, however, that they now kept the studio door locked during recording sessions, which was unusual. It was likely done, he thinks, so Dewey wouldn't come in when someone went out. "They still respected him," he says. "He was an institution, but everybody began to wonder why he hung around there so much."[36]

It was also during this period that Dewey began to shuffle in and out of psychiatric wards for short periods, shortness of duration being the operative term. The process began after he had been stopped on several occasions, suspected of driving while intoxicated. The police had begun to arrest him now on a regular basis.[37] Following one arrest Sam talked to a psychiatrist at Kennedy Veterans Hospital and persuasively argued before the court that Dewey needed to be under the care of a physician in a hospital rather than in jail. Once the court agreed, the two made brief visits to psychiatrists at various local hospitals, and he was admitted. By the time he died Dewey had spent time in several psychiatric wards. The law, however, would not allow the family to commit him permanently, and that, Dot Phillips maintains, was the essence of the problem.[38]

Because Dewey had to commit himself, he could also decide when he could leave. The difficulty was not so much getting him to go but keeping him there. He could sign himself out of a facility anytime he wanted, which, to Dewey, of course, meant whenever he was starting to feel well again. After a brief stay he'd release himself but would be back in a matter of weeks.

It was during this period that Dot began to show signs of being unable to cope with Dewey's behavior. She once had to call the police at 4 in the morning after trying to put him to sleep, which, according to the police report, had been "ever since [his arrival] at midnight. His speech was incoherent and muttled [sic]," the report indicated, and "his eyes were very glassy" because "he had been eating tranquilizer pills by the handful."[39]

Dot is convinced that her husband would have been all right (or at least well on his way to full recovery) had the various institutions been able to retain him. Better than anyone else, however, she also recognizes that the institutions' problems were exacerbated by Dewey himself, especially his ongoing efforts to keep those around him perpetually entertained. Even in these darkest moments he was always on, constantly engaged in being a private, one-man show for the exclusive benefit of his constantly captive audience. Betty Kirby recognizes that hospitals were sometimes willing to dismiss her brother because he managed to persuade them that there was nothing wrong with him. "He'd have them all laughing at him five minutes after he checked in."[40] Nonetheless, Dewey was in trouble, and he knew it. He would not have temporarily committed himself if he didn't. Because of the pejorative stigma attached to the name *psychiatric ward,* however, he not only shunned assistance from there but was also ashamed when he did.

Those closest to him knew he was in trouble, too. They also knew Dewey well enough to know that he would do what he wanted, no matter how distressed he was and no matter what he thought or said. Billy Mills, who read his cousin's personality like a book, thoroughly appreciates the degree of difficulty involved trying to get Dewey straight. He tried on a number of occasions to speak with him about his problem but to no avail. "At first, he would actually get serious, but before you quit talking, he was back to the same ol' Dewey." Mills now has enough detachment to laugh when he remembers how hard it was to keep Dewey on a serious topic for any length of time. No matter how much you pleaded, he says, "didn't make a big rat's ass difference anyway. Hell, if Dewey went to an AA meeting, he'd end up selling 'em the liquor."[41]

15

"Goodbye, Good People"

Dewey loved to joke about his problems in front of friends and strangers alike, but his flippant attitude often masked turmoil. Hopelessly confused by a bewildering reality and baffled by his continued tumble from stardom, he was already floundering badly when his last real hope for turning the corner toward stability finally collapsed. In 1963, after a great deal of soul-searching, his wife decided to leave him for good.

Dot had been struggling for a number of years with the knowledge of how bad Dewey's problem was. In 1959 she accidentally discovered his abuse of pain pills. After her own surgery, she had been given a prescription for pain. Her suspicions were originally aroused when, after taking only a few pills from her bottle, she noticed that the level had dropped dramatically. She realized that Dewey was the culprit when she hung up his coat one day and found a pill bottle in his pocket, her name on the label. He had called her doctor and filled the prescription without her knowledge. After that, she remembers, he deteriorated rapidly. Nonetheless, despite his increasingly erratic behavior, Dot somehow managed to stay with Dewey through some of his most difficult years. As his substance abuse increased, however, so did his anger and violence. When that happened she realized she had to get out. "I had three boys," she says, "and when Dewey would get bad off, I couldn't tell what he'd do." The first time she sensed he might physically harm the boys she knew she had to leave.[1]

Until that point, most of his loved ones looked on Dewey as a relatively good family man and a loving father. He even relished the family role, always insisting that his children call him daddy. Randy, for example, remembers being spanked more than once as a small child for calling his father Daddy-O-Dewey. He also recalls being taken to the radio station frequently as a small boy and even being dragged along to some of Dewey's sock hops in schools. His father did so, Randy thinks, because he "had to be away so much and didn't get to spend as much time with us kids as he wanted to."[2]

Unfortunately, all that changed as Dewey's mood worsened. The flash point occurred when he exploded in one of his all too frequent outbursts and threw something at their youngest son, cutting his leg badly. There had also been another occasion when he became uncontrollably angry and slapped one of the boys on the forehead. Dot let her husband discipline their children with spankings, but she would not tolerate him using other kinds of physical force or violence.

When he cut their son's leg she became enraged and began to wield a butcher's knife. When she did, Dewey's mother (with whom the family was living), calmly told Dot to put down the knife. Odessa Phillips then walked over to Dewey and, as Dot said, "slapped the fire out of him." At that point he apparently realized what he had done. He sat down, cried, and then apologized. No matter, however. Dot had decided that was it. She made up her mind at that moment to leave him, knowing full well that she would have to take care of the youngsters herself, which she did.[3]

Without question Dot's departure proved to be the decisive blow for an already badly strung-out Dewey. The day she left, Barbara Pittman talked to him. He was, she says, totally destroyed in mind and spirit. "He kept saying over and over, 'I've lost everything . . . I've lost everything.'" Pittman tried to comfort him by telling him it was not necessarily the end of the world, but he refused to hear her. "No Barb," he said, "I know I am a dead man now."[4]

Marjorie sensed the same reaction from her brother. "After Dot left him, he just didn't care anymore," she recalls sadly. "I think that he just gave up at the end." She remembers that Dot, at Dewey's funeral, felt guilty about separating from him. She said, "If I hadn't left him, he'd still be alive." Marjorie replied that she could not have prevented his death and that it was crazy to blame herself. Nonetheless, she thinks Dot always carried that guilt.[5] Dewey's other sister, Betty, also sensed that he was "pretty hopeless at the end." She never lost her love for him or gave up on him, but she admits that was there was little anyone could do.[6]

After Dot's departure Dewey either lived with his mother or stayed with other family members and friends who continued to entertain the rather forlorn notion that somehow he would suddenly get his life together.

He remained close to his mother until the end, but for almost everyone else staying connected was an increasingly difficult task. Friendships were severely tested as his grotesque behavior began to grate on almost all around him. Sam Phillips continued to show an amazing degree of tolerance for Dewey's now-frequent appearances at Sun Studio, even when he broke in, as he often seemed to do, in the middle of a recording session.

Not all, however, were so tolerant. Barbara Pittman, one of Sun's few female recording artists, was in awe of Dewey ("To me he was like 'an institution'") but vividly remembers him accidentally erasing a full day's session at Sun Studio after he appeared there late one night with a bottle of Jack Daniels. "We were all listening to the master cut in the control room when Dewey started pushing buttons and managed to erase it," she recalls. They had been at work nearly thirteen hours. Sam became upset, and "I went for Dewey's throat." After that, she confesses to being relieved when the staff at Sun came to realize they would have to run Dewey out of the studio—and fast—in order to accomplish anything after he'd appeared.[7]

Despite his sometimes abysmal behavior a handful of people still tried to provide at least moderate assistance. Estelle Axton, co-owner of Stax Records in Memphis, whose son, Packey, became friendly with Dewey at the end, occasionally let him sleep upstairs above the Stax Studio. Joe Cuoghi and Robert Johnson also stuck close by him. But it was Sam Phillips who proved to be Dewey's best and most loyal friend. Sam was in a much better position to help than the others, and he did so magnanimously.

At first he assisted Dewey financially on numerous occasions, but like the Memphis police and other close friends who did more harm than good in trying to help, Sam gradually realized that he was enabling Dewey to continue his habit. To his great credit, however, Sam did not give up once he saw what was happening. He continued to provide financial assistance to Dot and the children. By giving the family money—which he did frequently—he knew he was helping them and allowing Dot to decide how to use it to help her estranged husband. More important, Sam provided increased support in other practical ways. Whenever Dewey got into serious trouble (which, in the last years, he did with a depressing degree of regularity) Sam always seemed to be there.

Elvis, of course, was the other source of support for Dot and the children toward the end; like Sam, he assisted the family financially while distancing himself from Dewey. Dot cannot put a precise figure on the amount Elvis gave her but says he was "always helping out, usually at Christmas time." Randy Phillips recalls that when he was still young (probably sometime in the early 1960s) George Klein delivered a $500 check from Elvis at Christmas, and he is certain that Elvis helped the family even more after his father's condition worsened.[8]

This practice speaks well of Elvis's character, because his former mentor was definitely becoming a constant source of embarrassment. Dewey's favorite trick, for example, was to get whacked out and show up at Graceland in the wee hours of the morning. Elvis tried to be understanding at first, but he, like everyone else who had been close—seeing the hopelessness of the situation—inevitably had to capitulate. He was finally forced to keep Dewey out no matter what time of the day or night he arrived. Sam Phillips could still laugh when he remembered how persistent Dewey was after Elvis gave explicit orders to never let him get past the front gate. "Dewey didn't want Elvis telling him 'no,' or even looking like he wasn't glad to see him, day or night."[9]

Nonetheless, Sam recognizes that Elvis had no other course of action. "It got to where Dewey was doing so damn bad and everything, and maybe Elvis wasn't ready for him that night." He also argues that had Dewey not been in the shape he was Presley would have gladly moved him into Graceland along with other members of the Memphis Mafia. "Elvis was just totally fascinated by Dewey. He got a hell of a kick out of him," Sam maintains—except for the drugs. "Hell," Sam says, "he woulda' had Daddy-O-Dewey out there entertaining him all the time cause Dewey was funny. Just fun to be around." In the end, it caused Presley a great deal of emotional anguish to refuse to see Dewey. George Klein says that Elvis, like so many others, felt guilty for having to treat Dewey as he did.[10]

Jack Parnell remembers a situation that speaks volumes about the final days of the Dewey-Elvis friendship. He encountered Dewey one morning at a Gridiron Restaurant near Graceland. Jack was working the early morning shift at WHBQ, which put him on the air at 5 o'clock, so he recalls that the meeting would have been about 4 in the morning. Dewey was with Elvis's close friend and bodyguard Red West, and Jack was surprised at how well he looked. He hadn't seen Dewey for a long time and noticed how much he had improved. As he says, "The last I had run into Dewey, he was like warmed over death." After complimenting him on his appearance, Parnell asked what had happened. "Dewey said that Elvis told him, 'If you will stay straight, you don't ever have to worry about anything in your life. You can live at Graceland; I'll take care of you; you can be an advisor to me." Dewey broke out in a huge smile and, for a brief moment, looked like the Dewey of old. "'I'll give you spending money,'" he said Elvis promised, "'just stay straight.'" Dewey continued, beginning to bubble excitedly, "'You get back on the booze and the pills though, and you are out.'" After relating this story, Parnell says Dewey looked him straight in the eye and said, "'I'm never gonna' go back on that stuff again. I'm clean and I'm straight, and I'm havin' a good time. I've got it made now.'" Parnell shrugs and looks dejectedly at the ground as he hits home with the fatal punch line: "Well, that lasted just a short while and Dewey got back on the pills or booze or whatever. And Elvis kicked him out."[11]

Even in his darkest moments, however, Dewey never lost his sense of humor. Robert Johnson saw him in 1961, after he had gone into Gailor Memorial Psychiatric Hospital for an evaluation. "Day after he got out, he came to see me," Johnson recalled. "'Got no one to blame except myself,' he said. Then grinned: 'Guess what? I made 100 on my brain wave test.'"[12]

Somehow, in the midst of all this, Dewey continued to enjoy his favorite recreational activity, attending basketball games. Over the years he had become close friends with most of the Memphis State basketball team, even having some players as guests on his show. Randy Phillips remembers his father playing basketball in their backyard with members of the famous MSU team of 1959 that went all the way to the finals of the National Invitation Tournament. His most avid interest, though, was high school basketball, especially the fortunes of the Treadwell team coached by Bill "Bear" McClain.

He may have kept his sense of humor and interest in sports, but Dewey's behavior was becoming more bizarre. His increased intake of amphetamines, friends say, made him speed all the time. One night in 1961 the police picked him up for drunken driving and hitting a sign post. He was taken to jail and this time detained. While awaiting trial he was freed on $350 bond, but when he didn't show up for the trial the judge ordered the bond to be forfeit. A few minutes later, when he did appear, the trial was reset and the bond was increased to $1,000. Unable to post additional bond money, Dewey was thrown back into jail. There, he managed to overdose on pills he had hidden in his shoe. (Apparently, the police had not yet become concerned enough to search him thoroughly.) He had to be rushed, unconscious, to John Gaston Hospital, and his stomach was pumped. After a brief stay in jail he was finally charged with DWI and fined $50.[13]

211

Following this incident Dot once again tried to have him committed, but City Court Judge Beverly Boushe would not do so unless Dewey signed himself in. Dot, furious, "told the woman judge that he would keep this up until he killed himself or somebody else." The judge replied, "'Well let him do that. Then he can be put where he belongs.'" Dot sighs with frustration when telling the story and adds, "That was her attitude. What could I do?"[14]

Dot's warning almost proved prophetic. Dewey didn't kill anyone, but he did manage to involve himself in an ugly fracas that turned violent. In the summer of 1963, according to the *Memphis Press-Scimitar* account, he walked into a drugstore and asked the druggist, Joshua Meshew, for "some narcotics, without specifying any particular kind." When Meshew told him he had none, Dewey reportedly "lunged at him." Meshew "then picked up a club from behind the drugstore counter, knocked the disc jockey down, called police and had Mr. Phillips arrested." Charged with "disorderly conduct," he avoided jail time, but apparently there was enough damage done that Dewey walked around for several days with a bandage on his head. Judge Boushe was now willing to dismiss the charges if the family indicated that "arrangements had been made for psychiatric treatment."[15]

Relentlessly, the downward spiral continued. In that same year Dewey was picked up at the Majic Grill and held in protective custody "at the request of relatives." Much worse, he had previously been reported "missing."[16] According to the newspaper account of the incident, he was found, after an exhaustive search, aimlessly walking the street, by two plainclothes policemen cruising the area. Bad enough that he was picked up, but the fact that someone in the family had earlier reported him missing and then placed him in protective custody was all too indicative of his now-sorry state.[17]

Incredibly, through it all Dewey somehow continued to do his regular show on WGMM in Millington, even developing a new generation of young followers who had never heard him on WHBQ. During this period, Randy Haspel of Memphis's "Randy and the Radiants" remembers large crowds of teenagers attending station-sponsored Saturday night dances at the YMCA in East Memphis. Dewey, who had acquired a "living legend" status, could still make hundreds of youngsters ask for his autograph.[18]

Despite the crowds (or perhaps because of them) he continued to fantasize about an eventual return to the glory days in Memphis. Bill Thomas, the Millington station manager, remembers that Dewey always shouted on the WGMM show, "'Hey, Gordon Lawhead—man, I'm sounding good. You need me back on WHBQ!'"[19] It was all to no avail, of course. Once again, unavoidably and perhaps inexorably, the Millington station finally had to recognize Dewey's drug problem and let him go.

The next time the police picked him up on a disorderly conduct charge his general demeanor had deteriorated badly. Someone had stolen his shoes, and he was barefoot at the time of the arrest. Nevertheless, "good ol' Dewey" (or maybe it was "famous ol' Dewey") apparently seemed harmless enough to be released yet again.[20] This time, in desperation, Judge Boushe turned him over to Jimmy Stroud, a popular and colorful Memphian who ran the Union Mission, a religious organization which, together with Calvary Colony, the mission's alcoholic rehabilitation center, worked with the down-and-out derelicts of society "who have almost lost hope."

Stroud was able to take advantage of Dewey's name recognition by assigning him the job of going to nearby towns and arranging with service clubs and civic groups to schedule a film, *The Open Door,* which tried to demonstrate the Union Mission's work. After about a month it seemed that the hoped-for miracle had actually occurred. Robert Johnson announced that Dewey "looked better than I've seen him in several years." In his regular column he faithfully reported that Dewey had told him, "Mr. Johnson, I've been saved, and this time it's for good." Dewey's pattern of behavior with Stroud, however, followed closely his experience in the psychiatric wards. Initial, highly touted success was soon followed by a sudden and dramatic downturn. All together, while working for Jimmy Stroud he stayed off drugs for not much more than two months.[21]

The Stroud failure was the last dead-end street for Daddy-O-Dewey. At the close of his life he took on all the characteristics of a homeless person, having no direction or purpose, showing up briefly at familiar spots, and then suddenly vanishing without a trace. The only time George Klein had contact with him during this period is when Dewey would be stranded somewhere and call G.K. for a ride home. He could almost always catch a ride from favorite haunts such as Sun Studio, Pop Tunes, and Select-O-Hit Records, but sometimes he couldn't and Klein would have to retrieve him.[22]

It was during these last days that friends report endless accounts of Dewey's dissipated behavior, each one more pathetic than before. Most stories have to do with him babbling incoherently in a drugged-out stupor or answering questions with non sequiturs—always finishing with the assurance he'd be "back on 'Q' Monday" or that "Elvis will be picking me up soon." His favorite practice was to pretend to call Elvis and then tell whoever would bother to listen that he had just talked to the King and everything was going to be OK. "I think he was just fantasizing," says Dickie Lee. "Everybody knew that he was just lying—pretending that Elvis was on the other end of the phone."[23]

Reuben Cherry remembers the last time he saw Dewey, a crumpled figure sitting on the curb outside his store, so disheveled that Cherry barely recognized him. When he realized it was Dewey, he asked what he was doing there. Reuben says Dewey's last words to him were, "Waiting for Elvis."[24]

Friends also remember Dewey's physical as well as mental deterioration. The person they had formerly known was no longer there. Bettye Berger, who had been friends with Dewey since the early days, was shocked by his appearance as she watched him pathetically trying to get into the Sun Studio one day. "At first, I didn't even recognize him! He was just pounding on the studio door—screaming and hollering something awful. Then he stumbled down the stairs. I could hardly talk to him."[25] Other close observers who saw Dewey at the very end tell similarly dismal stories. "He'd look right past you," Billy Lee Riley laments. "He'd look around you, over you; his mind was just gone."[26]

Local deejay Alex Ward saw him in the summer of 1968, only a few months before Dewey died, and his account of this last encounter is perhaps the saddest comment of all on what Dewey Phillips had become at the end of his life. Ward, who grew up listening to Dewey and later had the top afternoon show on WHBQ, now runs the popular *Pig 'n' Whistle Oldies Show* on Memphis radio. Like most Memphis deejays he had elevated Dewey Phillips to iconic status. It was therefore shocking for him to realize that the person he encountered one day in Hot Line Record Distributors was indeed Dewey Phillips. "I hear this old decrepit man, hollering over another album that was playing," he recalls. Johnny Keyes, who was running the place at the time, was trying to deal with Dewey, who was ravaged by years of substance abuse. "I didn't realize it was him," Ward says. "I didn't know who this guy was." Upon closer examination, however, the worst soon became apparent. Ward's voice drops into a lower range, dramatizing the pathos of the moment. "It was Dewey. Man, he was rumpled; he was dirty; he smelled really bad. His mouth had white stuff all over it, and his eyes were glazed. It was horrible."[27]

Keyes was doing everything he could, politely, to get Dewey out of the building without creating an incident. He asked Alex if he would mind taking Dewey to Pop Tunes and turning him over to Joe Cuoghi. "Here comes Dewey in these horrible dirty, clothes, smelling awful," Ward says. "'Hey, how you doin'? What'd you say your name was?' He didn't even know who I was." Worse still, it was difficult to understand what he was saying. "He gets in the back seat of my car, and he is just sputtering—just leaning over and just spittin' every time he tried to talk." When they got to Pop Tunes, Dewey pulled Ward by the hand through the back door. Without talking to anyone he moved with Ward behind the counter. Ward was uncomfortable, for he could see that Joe Cuoghi, who did not recognize Ward by sight, was upset and wondering who he was and what he was doing there.

"Dewey immediately says: 'Oh, yeah, he's with me—this is my friend— what is your name again?'" While he was talking, Dewey picked up the records behind the counter and handed them to Alex. "'This is good stuff, play this on your show,'" he advised. "And," Ward continues, "I'm looking at Joe Cuoghi, and he is looking at me, and I start putting records back on the counter, and Joe kinda nods at me like, 'Good boy' [laughs]." Alex and Joe continued to pacify Dewey by letting him repeat this process for a while. "Here is another one, and I just take it from Dewey and hand it over to Joe and finally say, 'Look, Dewey, I've got to run.' Dewey says, 'Yeah, man, good to see you. What did you say your name was?' That was my last contact with Dewey Phillips."[28]

On Christmas Day, Dewey had made it a ritual to visit both Robert Johnson and Sam Phillips. Later, after Dewey died, Johnson reflected in one of his columns about one of the final Christmases. "He came with a crutch and a cab. I had to pay the cab," Johnson recalled. "Dewey wasn't in shape to visit anyone. I drove him home and he had forgotten how to get there."[29]

By the very end, he seemed to have forgotten almost everything. His difficulty in separating himself from his old deejay role on *Red, Hot and Blue* now extended to an inability to separate reality from fantasy. It is hard to determine whether his frequent references to Elvis's imminent appearance were hallucinations or whether Dewey actually believed that Elvis was about to appear in the next instant. In time, he not only called everyone Elvis (man or woman) but also began to refer to himself that way. Jerry Wexler has recalled the following Dewey-babble in one of their last conversations: "'Elvis,' he'd tell me on the phone, 'this is Elvis. Elvis is coming to New York.'"[30]

Dewey continued to drop by the station periodically until his final days. There was a big window in Wink Martindale's office overlooking

Main Street, Jack Parnell recalls, and "without warning, Dewey goes over, raises the window and hollers out loud into the thin air, 'Whatcha' say, Elvis?'"[31]

Perhaps the most telling example of Dewey's total collapse was that even his mother finally recognized the hopelessness of his situation. Their love for each other was as strong as ever, but Odessa Phillips, like everyone else, apparently had resigned herself to the futility of trying to straighten out her only son. "He had gotten to the point where even she wasn't able to take care of him," Betty Kirby says. "Nobody could help him, really."[32]

The saddest day for Randy Phillips was his father's final Christmas. Everyone was at his grandmother's house for dinner except Dewey, and Randy was given the job of going out and trying to locate him. After checking the local drugstore where he often got pills, Randy finally ran him down, talking to friends in a service station. He overheard Dewey asking them for a loan so he could buy Christmas presents for his children. The group laughed at him because they were convinced he would use the money to buy pills. What hurt Randy the most was that when they walked away, one shouted at Dewey, "Why don't you go to your friend Elvis and borrow some money from him?" Randy "saw tears in his [father's] eyes, and remembers thinking if it had been the other way around, Dewey would have given that guy the money."[33]

Even more vivid is the memory of the weekend his father died. Both Phillips boys had continued to spend several weeks with Dewey every summer after their parents split, and Randy was living at his grandmother's house with Dewey. "He seemed to be better, and in pretty good spirits," Randy says. They had breakfast, and "I told him me and my fraternity brothers wanted him to go to the game with us in Knoxville." Memphis State was playing the University of Tennessee, and Randy wanted Dewey to ride along with them. Dewey declined, however, saying that "he had some things to do." In retrospect Randy might see that refusal as an omen given his father's normal enthusiasm for a Memphis State ballgame. Dewey would be dead by the time Randy got back from Knoxville.[34]

The day before Dewey died, Sam Phillips saw him at Sun Studio. He had just been to Millington to see a doctor he had known for some time and told Sam he had "chest trouble." The doctor told him to come back, but he never did. Dewey also told Sam that he believed he had pneumonia. "And I think he did have pneumonia," Sam adds. "He had gotten in a very run-down condition, looked extremely bad, and weighed practically nothing."[35] WHBQ deejay Ron Meroney also recalls how terrible Dewey looked at the very end. When he learned that Dewey was only forty-two at the time of his death Ron was shocked. "I always thought he was much older than that," he observed. "He was run hard and put away wet too many times. He certainly looked much older."[36]

When Barbara Pittman saw Dewey for the final time she was startled to see blood around the corner of his mouth. Apparently, he had a tendency at the end to bite his tongue. When that happened the blood would dry and cake without him being aware of it. They talked about the past, the good old times, and Dewey began to cry. "He seemed to be going over his life and saying, 'How did I end up like this?'" Pittman says.[37] Despite his often soiled and rumpled appearance, however, Dewey still made an effort to present himself in the best possible light. He always carried a pocket comb and would quickly pull it out whenever acquaintances appeared. Then he'd comb his hair back and say, "Eat your heart out, Elvis."[38]

Dewey's death, in contrast to the majority of events surrounding his life, was as undramatic as it was uneventful. His mother told reporters that he was sober for the entire day before he died, and he talked to her "seriously" that night. Dewey saw Claude Cockrell, a friend who worked with him in Millington, and then came home early to listen to a high school football game. He apparently fell sleep with the radio on. Odessa Phillips talked to him for a few minutes the next morning about 10, when she heard the radio was still on, and "he was in good spirits." But then, she told reporters, "I went back at 5 P.M. and found him dead." He was forty-two. Odessa's first call was to Marjorie. "I want you to come here," she said matter-of-factly. "I've just found Dewey dead in the bed." Although Marjorie means no disrespect for her brother, she was relieved for her mother's sake that it was finally over. Odessa had been "through so much with him" at the end.[39]

When reporters contacted Sam Phillips for a quotable reaction, he stated publicly what he always maintained privately: Dewey had "played a very important part in the careers of some of the world's great recording artists in the 1950s." As usual, Sam minced few words when praising the person who had been so important to his own career. "Few men had the respect in the industry that he held both from the artists and record producers."[40]

For almost all his close friends, the immediate reaction to Dewey's death was not only remorse but also guilt and frustration at not having done more to help him. Jim Dickinson says that when Dewey died,

"Sam [Phillips] was more upset than I have ever seen him. He wanted to know whose fault it was." Sam had adamantly maintained that it "had to be somebody's fault that everyone let him get to that stage." Sam's son, Knox, thinks "we all let him down real bad because as much as he did for all of us, we should have cut him much more slack than anybody else."[41]

For a while Dickie Lee uses the same language—"We let him down. We should have done something that we didn't do"—but then he recognizes the desperation of such sentiments. "He was in a state where if you just made yourself available to him, you were makin' a bad mistake, because he was gonna take advantage of that."[42] Dewey's bottomless descent at the very end became a somber parable of his hopelessness as well as his helplessness.

The media immediately solicited reactions from all who had been on the cutting edge of the rock 'n' roll revolution, and it was mostly a clarion cry of praise for Dewey. Each superstar carefully acknowledged the importance of the man who had played the key role in the early development of their careers. Elvis was quick to recall the famous night Dewey played the first record. "We were very good friends," Elvis said, "and I have always appreciated everything he did for me in helping me in my career in the early days. I am awfully hurt."[43]

Johnny Cash, who had lived only blocks from the Phillipses' home, recalled that his children had played with Dewey's children as youngsters and allowed that Dewey was one of his closest, best-loved friends. Above all else, like so many others he felt that Dewey was critical in launching his career. "Dewey probably did more for newcomers in the record business than any disc jockey in the country," said a grateful Carl Perkins. Dewey had not only aided Perkins but also other young performers on the Sun label like Roy Orbison and Bill Justis when they were beginning. It was difficult, Perkins recalled, to get other stations to play the new R&B music.[44]

Even those who never made it big remembered how much Dewey had pushed them along while trying. When a friend called Barbara Pittman, who was performing in Los Angeles, with the news of his death, she says, she felt "like a piece of my life had gone."[45] Jim Dickinson adds his own bittersweet memory of his longtime childhood idol. "Dewey died of a broken heart. And this was a man who had one of the biggest hearts you have ever seen." Dickinson, who recognizes that Dewey "had been the walking dead for a long time," doesn't let his love for him interfere with a realistic assessment of what he meant for people. "Now he was crazy.

He was all the things they say he was. But he had this other quality of humanity that caused him to reach out. Just like Elvis giving away the cars."[46]

Despite wide media coverage of Dewey's dissipation (Memphis newspapers carefully reported every detail of his misadventures at the end), the news of his death came as a shock to many who had been unaware of his plight. Sam Phillips remembers a lack of acknowledgement for Dewey's relevance, which he rightly attributes to Dewey's awful state before he died: "Now regardless of how he went down, he was a damned institution here. When somebody like that dies, like Elvis, you still think you're dreaming—there for a little while until you wake up to the reality of it later on."[47]

Dot turned instinctively to Sam for assistance in making funeral arrangements. Once again she found herself leaning on the strong arm of the man who had been so helpful to her family while Dewey was alive. And Sam, to his credit, was just as essential at his death. He assisted Dot with picking out a casket and then stayed by her side from the time of the death Friday afternoon until the final burial. He remembers "just staying over at the house until very late that first night. After that, I came home to get a little nap and then back over there again—like that the whole weekend. It was pretty rough."[48]

Funeral services for Dewey were held at the Memphis Funeral Home and then the body was taken to Crump, Tennessee, his birthplace, for burial. His family and close friends followed the hearse to the tiny hamlet, where a separate, open-casket service was held at graveside for those who could not attend the service in Memphis.[49] Although Sam was supposed to record the event, Dot thinks he forgot to turn on the recorder. He did send a wreath, however, draped with the magic words that for many were emblematic of Dewey Phillips's life: "Red, Hot and Blue." Claude Cockrell, who was with Dewey the day before he died, sent a gold-sprayed wreath in the shape of a heart. He told Dot that he felt it was the best way he could express his sentiments: "Dewey had a heart of gold."[50]

Pallbearers, in addition to Sam and George Klein, were Dickie Lee, Claude Cockrell, and both of Sam's sons, Knox and Jerry. Dickie, Claude, and Sam's boys drove from Memphis to Crump together, stopping along the way to eat and arriving after the service had started. Embarrassed, they later apologized to Dot. "I told her I hated for this to happen," Lee says. "But you know he would have loved it." Dot looked at him and said, "You know you're right." Their mistake was a fitting one, Lee observes.

"Screwed up right down to the very last you know. Dewey would have just laughed."[51]

The Memphis service was a modest one. The eulogy was delivered by the Rev. Don Taylor, pastor of the Methodist church Dewey's mother attended. Betty requested that "The Old Rugged Cross" be played because she remembered that Dewey had frequently sung that "with a great deal of spirit" while in the bathroom shaving. The version for the service, however, was played, not sung, and was "just terrible," Betty maintains. "Why, Dewey," she observes, "would have gotten up and walked out."[52]

Elvis sent word by a friend that he wanted to come to Dewey's funeral but (anticipating the frenzy that always occurred when he appeared anywhere) he would not do so if the family thought that would create too much confusion. Dot replied through the friend that it would be "perfectly alright" if he attended, and Elvis did indeed show up at the Memphis Funeral Home along with Priscilla Presley, his father, Vernon, and several members of his entourage. He sent a wreath shaped in the form of a large horseshoe inscribed with Dewey's favorite expression when he played a new record he thought would hit big: "Call Sam." When Presley arrived, Dot recalled, "he came over to me and hugged my neck." She then introduced him to Odessa Phillips, whom he had never met. "He sat between me and [her] during the service." Dot was moved when she saw Elvis cry.[53]

In *Elvis, What Happened?* Red West provides an account of Elvis having the giggles at Dewey's funeral, a story some have circulated to suggest Elvis's lack of proper respect for a man who had played a major role in his early career. Like all Elvis stories, this one has expanded over the years, especially by unkind critics who know that relations between Elvis and Dewey were strained at the end. Family members strongly reject West's interpretation, however, and are quick to set the record straight. Once Elvis arrived, there was legitimate fear that he might be mobbed, so he and his entourage were put into a small room at the funeral home, set off to separate them (and the immediate family and very close friends) from others. Once the service was over a curtain was drawn. Then Elvis and the family, along with other loved ones, sat around and told stories about Dewey, which no doubt brought about an occasional howl of laughter. "Elvis was not being nasty. He meant no disrespect," says Randy Phillips, emphasizing that the atmosphere at the funeral was courteous and refined "They got to talkin' about the old times. Fun times," Randy adds. "Things Daddy and Elvis used to do, and they got to laughing about it.

After a while, we were all laughing a little about the crazy things they did back in the early days."[54]

Dot also feels strongly about Elvis's appearance at the funeral and says that if anything untoward did happen she didn't know about it. "That was the biggest lie that was ever told," she says flatly, referring to West's book. "If I had heard anything disrespectful, I wouldn't have let it go on in the first place. I would have said something then or said something later." Moreover, she "doesn't believe that Elvis would have said anything bad anyway. He came to pay his respects. I was just pleased that he came. And I'm sure that really would have pleased Dewey that he came." Afterward, Dot told Presley just that and reiterated that Dewey would have wanted him there. "He said, 'Miss Dorothy, Dewey was my friend.' He then told me in a real convincing way that he appreciated everything that Dewey had done for him." Then, she says, "He told me that I was also his friend and that he hoped that he would always be my friend." Dot had always considered Elvis to be very polite; moreover, "He was always so appreciative of how much good Dewey had done him. I don't think that ever changed." Although Elvis and Dewey had lost almost all contact at the end, Dot had "nothing but the highest respect for him always." She doesn't comment much on the final split between the men but observes, "Elvis never lost touch. Elvis helped me when I needed help and I didn't have to ask him. He found out and just knew. He was a good friend and I feel fortunate to have known him. That's all I want to say."[55]

16

The Legacy:
The Next Generation and Beyond

Despite the enormous amount of media attention devoted to Elvis Presley, Sam Phillips, and the origins of rock 'n' roll, the significant contribution Dewey Phillips made in helping launch Presley's career and turning on the southern white audience to previously forbidden race music is hardly mentioned. Fortunately, however, that is beginning to change. Gradually, if belatedly, Dewey's role is being acknowledged, best evidenced by his inclusion in a permanent exhibit of 1950s' deejays in Cleveland's Rock 'n' roll Hall of Fame, in a display at the Rock 'n' Soul Museum in Memphis, and in a televised biography of Sam Phillips.

Although we are some distance from the beginnings of rock 'n' roll, Dewey's legacy is still felt because his show made such a huge impact on young listeners who became the next generation of Memphis musicians. Steve Cropper says he and Duck Dunn (along with the Stax generation of performers) "kinda grew up on Dewey Phillips." Singer and songwriter Sid Selvidge would drive to Clarksdale, Mississippi—the closest spot he could pick up Dewey on the dial—to hear him. Memphis's most articulate musician, the legendary Jim Dickinson, who grew up listening to *Red, Hot and Blue,* is convinced that Dewey's is the untold story of the history of rock 'n' roll. Dickinson arrived in Memphis from Chicago in 1949, the famous "it" year. He was only eight, but because he would spend his entire life in music, he is firmly convinced that it was more than serendipity that caused him to arrive in Memphis the year WDIA went all-black and Dewey Phillips began *Red, Hot and Blue.*

Jim became the leader of Atlantic Records' house band in the 1970s and played piano for such luminaries as the Rolling Stones, Aretha Franklin, and Ry Cooder. He is still going strong. In case evidence is needed of Dewey's link (through Jim) to cutting-edge music, Dickinson plays keyboard on Bob Dylan's Grammy award–winning release "Time Out of Mind" (Dylan personally thanked Jim when he received the award).

When discussing his propitious arrival in Memphis in 1949, Jim borrows a page from Sam Phillips and speaks with the fervor of a Baptist preacher: "God sent me here. I firmly believe it!" He speaks of Dewey's impact on his life in tones that sound religious in nature. "He radically changed my life. Musically I had no idea what was goin' on at the time. Here is this crazy guy teaching me how to think."

As for Dewey's impact, Jim says, "Here is a man who is barely literate and just competent enough to run a console and he is changing the cultural history of this city." Dewey created a mind-set that not only shaped his own destiny but also changed a generation's way of thinking. Dickinson believes that Dewey musically "opened doors" for him, something that would not have happened had he not had the good fortune to hear *Red, Hot and Blue* in the early 1950s. He credits his early musical success to the head start he got by hearing the kind of music Dewey played. "When I went to college in Texas and started talking to musicians there, most of them had never heard of the stuff I was playing," he says. Just listening to Dewey's show gave Dickinson a repertoire that other people didn't know about. "In Waco, Texas, in 1961 I had a hell of an act, courtesy of Dewey Phillips. All I had to do was to remember a few songs. They thought I was a genius!"[1]

That heartfelt observation leaves little doubt about Dewey's importance to future musicians from a city that calls itself "the Home of the Blues" and "the Birthplace of Rock and Roll." But this Memphis disc jockey carved out a niche for himself in the pantheon of popular musical history in a much more significant way. He may have made at least a partial contribution to racial cross-culturalization at a critical moment, one that would ultimately have an impact on the entire nation rather than just on the Mid-South.

When Dewey Phillips first hit the Memphis airwaves with *Red, Hot and Blue* in 1949, the blacks and whites in his audience still inhabited two entirely separate and distinctly unequal worlds. By the time he left that show in 1958, the most important of the barriers separating those worlds were already beginning to crumble. Although no one would dare suggest that Dewey alone can take credit for the collapse of these obstacles, one could argue that he made more than a modest contribution to their downfall. "The importance of rhythm and blues music on radio was that it was heard by integrated audiences," radio historian J. Fred Mac-

Donald has observed. In the privacy of one's home, musical integration was as close as the radio dial. In an age that still segregated races by law, "rhythm and blues was a black-and-white enterprise." It was not until black music crossed over into the white mainstream that it "helped to change the course of American cultural and social development."[2]

In less academic language, Rufus Thomas—commenting on the often-made assertion that white people stole black music—argues that "Elvis would never have gotten started had it not been for the black man's type of music." But then Rufus quickly adds, with usual streetwise, down-home perception, "'Course it works the other way. Had it not been for Elvis, the blues as of today wouldn't be as big."[3]

Rufus's remarks reveal a deeper, more profound truth: The mainstreaming of black music was, in the long run, mutually beneficial to both races, especially in an era marked by rigid segregation. "Thank God for Elvis Presley!" the legendary Little Richard once shouted, also recognizing the critical role the King had in bringing the black sound to a popular audience. The "cover" arrangement, whereby mainstream whites covered black artists, helped promote black music and culture. "Paradoxically," Brian Ward has noted, "nothing did more than the [white] cover phenomenon to facilitate a mass market for R&B and extend the opportunities for black artists, writers and entrepreneurs."[4]

Dewey Phillips's achievement, if less obvious, was no less important. The civil rights movement in the Mid-South was still nearly a decade away when *Red, Hot and Blue* was at its peak. Even though the enormous gap in race relations that he helped close was only a musical one, Dewey's work, quietly and subtly, was already scrambling racial identities and attitudes. Still, legal desegregation—tearing down racial walls in public accommodations—as well as employment and educational opportunities for the majority of Memphis and Mid-South blacks would not come until years after the movement began.

Nonetheless, Dewey's predominantly teenaged listening audience (the term *teenager* came into vogue sometime during the mid-1950s) would soon mature into the "youth" generation that would lead the civil rights movement of the 1960s. Integration of the airwaves did not inevitably lead to integration of other public facilities, but by making Mid-South listeners more racially conscious, by reducing the worst kind of racial stereotyping, Dewey contributed in his own way to laying the groundwork for future racial progress. Peter Guralnick, a long-time observer of the Memphis musical scene, put it best: "Dewey Phillips' nightly radio show unified Memphis, black and white, in a way that no formal institution could."[5]

This is not to suggest that the introduction of black music on the airways instantly converted white racists into integrationists. Sam Phillips, for example, is convinced that had there been no Elvis Presley (or someone "with the same feeling as a black person") the entire music industry would still be segregated. That speculation certainly might be true if confined only to the music industry. Beyond that, it becomes much more difficult to demonstrate the integrationist spirit of rock music. Pete Daniel has argued that it would be wrong to conclude that the confluence of black and white music eliminated segregation. "Some of the same white youths who cheered Louis Armstrong, B.B. King, Little Richard, or Chuck Berry," Daniel has concluded, "also enthusiastically cheered segregationist politicians." Daniel does argue, however, that the musical upheaval was nonetheless worthwhile and productive. He points out that when "black and white musicians gained immense fame and influence . . . they undermined a wide spectrum of racial stereotypes."[6]

Dewey's contribution to the destruction of those stereotypes can no longer be ignored. Remember that he was exposing the Deep South to black artists five years before the Supreme Court declared segregation illegal. Once these previously unheard black performers began to infiltrate the Mid-South airwaves, falling on black and white ears alike, racial attitudes were inevitably challenged. By the time the Court handed down its historic decision in 1954, "rhythm and blues [had] evolved into rock 'n' roll," Daniel has pointed out, "and soul music rode the wave of civil rights triumphs and failures."[7]

It is difficult sometimes to recall the overwhelmingly white world of the South at the time *Red, Hot and Blue* made its musical debut. "I went on the air on a Saturday morning with a news bulletin that some black people were entering the library" in Memphis says Bob Lewis, expressing disbelief in the recollection. "How could I have been so ignorant? Can you believe that? Black folks going into *our* library. It was actually a news bulletin!" Jerry Schilling remembers vividly his own antiquated attitudes. "Before Dewey played the music," he says, "my only knowledge of black people was someone who worked as a maid in somebody's house, or maybe cut somebody's grass." Jerry, who later joined Elvis's entourage as a member of the Memphis Mafia, recalls listening to Dewey as a youngster. "Dewey playing all those black artists suddenly put all of us on an equal basis."[8]

The bottom line is that Dewey helped create a more tolerable atmosphere for bringing about the change at a time when it desperately needed it. "Rock 'n' roll," Michael T. Bertrand has concluded in his study of the impact of the music on the culture, "exemplified and established an environment conducive to racial indifference, tolerance, and eventual acceptance." Putting it in more simplistic language (and perhaps making it more applicable to Dewey's contribution), other observers have noted that "all music is colorblind" and "it became more difficult to hate someone whose music you loved." "Out of respect for the blues," said another, "came the first tentative gropings toward respect for the people who played them."[9]

But if it can be argued that racial progress was made through Dewey's work it is important to recognize that such progress may not have been his original intention. Halberstam's observation about Dewey integrating the airwaves at night is on target, but no evidence indicates that racial integration was Dewey Phillips's objective.

William Barlow, for example, a historian of black radio, has been justifiably critical of Dewey's behavior, viewing his role on the air as "shallow, adolescent rebelliousness, without moral or political conviction." Barlow contrasts Dewey with other white deejays who were civil rights activists and argues that Dewey was responsible for "no social or political action. Phillips was nothing like Zenas Sears; he never publicly spoke out on race relations, marched on a picket line, or voted in an election."[10] It is certainly true that Dewey was totally unlike Barlow's example. Zenas "Daddy" Sears, Atlanta's white crossover deejay, fought for racial equality and became an activist in the civil rights movement while broadcasting from WGST.

Barlow's criticism, although undeniably correct, seems somewhat harsh. He faults Dewey for a sin of omission rather than commission, and, after all *Red, Hot and Blue* left WHBQ in 1958. What is often referred to as the 1960s protest movement didn't truly explode until the middle of the decade, and by that time Dewey's substance abuse had all but destroyed him. But Barlow's observation contains an important kernel of truth. Dewey could have cared less about politics and had little inclination to join a picket line or become involved in any serious cause, let alone a civil rights movement. Although he enjoyed violating customs, like many poor white southern stars he so enthusiastically promoted (e.g., Elvis, Carl Perkins, Johnny Cash) Dewey at least partially reflected his times. He accepted more of the South's racial mores than he attempted to change, especially laws guarding social and political structure.

The prevailing code of racial etiquette in Memphis carefully promoted segregated facilities. The notion of challenging laws protecting that arrangement never crossed Dewey's mind. If it did, he did very little to act on it. Sam Phillips held a studio party at the Memphis Holiday Inn, for example, and invited all the record distributors, two of whom, George and Ernie Laymen, the owners of United Distributing out of Chicago, were black. He and Dewey went to the Holiday Inn to eat with them after the event but were told that the restaurant's policy was not to serve black people. Even though Sam and Kemmons Wilson, owner of the Holiday Inn, were close friends and business associates, both he and Dewey were quite willing to leave the restaurant without protest rather than create a scene. (To their credit, however, they then had a private meal with their guests, which in itself certainly violated the racially acceptable practices of 1950s' Memphis).[11] It is thus safe to say that Dewey never crusaded for racial justice; nor did he have any kind of prearranged subversive agenda. Indeed, little evidence exists to suggest that he wanted to improve the harsh reality of daily life for African Americans or was particularly concerned about "social uplift" for black people.

Having said all that, however, it is important not to lose sight of what he did accomplish without in any way being politically committed. In addition to musically integrating the Mid-South's airwaves, he undoubtedly served as a positive role model for a great many rural, working-class southern whites who without him would have had virtually no exposure to black performers and black culture. Again, he seems to have fulfilled that role without intention, perfectly content, grooving on the music and thumbing his nose at white mainstream culture.[12]

Dewey was perfectly comfortable going into black clubs, churches, and juke joints, places other white Memphians at the time carefully avoided. Moreover, he regularly entertained black friends in his home. Randy remembers the constant presence of black people in the Phillips home when he was a small child in the 1950s. In Memphis, such racial mixing put Dewey at the cutting edge of changing race relations. With the working-class credentials of a poor country boy from the hinterlands of Crump, Tennessee, this behavior in itself was abnormal for its day. Stanley Booth says Dewey was frequently called "nigger lover" but that didn't bother him. "He was one of the most non-discriminating people I ever met," Booth adds.[13] Dewey's innocent, color-blind attitude, evident by frequent appearances on Beale Street, at black music shows, or at dozens of other all-black activities, made him a powerful (if almost accidental) destroyer of accepted racial custom.

Thus, whatever racial changes that occurred because of Dewey Phillips's radio show could serve as a near-textbook example of the law of unintended consequences. White racists might have seen in black-oriented music a vile conspiracy to subvert popular culture and encourage racial integration, but that was certainly never the intent of artists who made the music or individuals like Dewey who played and promoted it.

Like Bert Ferguson at WDIA, Dewey did not take to the airwaves to scramble race relations. That just happened to be a consequence of both men's actions. Ferguson had followed the dollar signs; with Dewey it was a case of following the music. By carefully avoiding political activism both men pursued a practice common to most of radio's racial innovators. Almost everyone associated with early black-oriented radio, especially in the Deep South, was careful not to offend the sensibilities of either white listeners or sponsors by promoting racial protest.[14]

One thing is certain: If the political system did not change immediately, the music did. By the time Dewey left WHBQ, musical segregation had already collapsed. Whether the political consequence was intended or not, the old musical order had died, been given a proper burial, and endured the last nails being firmly driven into its casket. By the end of the 1950s the biracial youth market had crested. Driving home this point, Brian Ward has concluded that 204 of the 730 Top Ten songs on *Billboard*'s best-seller list between 1957 and 1964 were by black artists. "This was arguably," Ward concludes, "the most racially integrated popular music scene in American history."[15]

Even if Dewey had no social or political agenda he still shook up the racial status quo. He was able to do so only because his showmanship and infectious behavior on *Red, Hot and Blue* made blacks as well as whites captive to his charms. Change occurred only because his outlaw style made him irresistible to listeners. Dewey alone achieved huge success in crossing all musical barriers of race because he was what might be called unavoidably entertaining. His seductive personality allowed him to revolutionize and integrate the airways without so much as an ounce of resistance. He was turned on to the music, his audience was turned on to him, and the rest is nothing short of a cultural revolution.

But more than Dewey's maverick style was at work. Something else was going on and that was the music itself. Neither Dewey Phillips nor any individual alone can claim responsibility for the shift in musical tastes and the cultural changes that followed. Most listeners felt that Dewey's on-air presence alone was fireworks enough. The music he played was an added bonus, icing on the entertainment cake. In reality, however,

Dewey was doing little more than subversively selling a tantalizingly new product—the still-unheard music of black America.

Certainly, his style was inimitable; the likes of him has yet to be seen. Yet in the final analysis, it was not his personality but the music that bridged the racial gap and shook up popular culture. The music alone had this quality. It was subversively subtle, with no pressing need to cry out for social revolution and racial change. It needed neither violent protest nor peaceful picket lines. It helped shatter Jim Crow's cultural barriers without firing a shot or lifting a protest sign. More important, its power transcended the confines of not just the rural South but of the entire country. "You can go anywhere else on earth outside the U.S. and rock 'n' roll music is symbolic of freedom," Jim Dickinson has observed. "Not democracy, not Christianity," Jim shouts, with his usual gift for hyperbole. "Rock 'n' roll music, which succeeded where both politics and religion failed to spread the American culture for good or bad to the rest of the world." Sam Phillips himself, as might be expected, makes the same kind of assertion: "Rock 'n' roll has done more to bring the world together than any one single thing that I know of."[16]

In the final analysis, then, Dewey Phillips was little more than the appropriate vehicle for conveying the musical sounds that would soon make this sea change possible. As the seller of the music, he was pitch-perfect. Dewey's medium was the message, and that message was the music. Were he still alive, Dewey would be the first to recognize that, above all, it was the music he loved so deeply and spent his life promoting with great proselytizing fervor that was responsible for bringing the races closer. It was also responsible for whatever social upheaval followed. Without the music, Dewey would have been practically unheard of. Indeed, the music was what Dewey Phillips was all about.

Epilogue

Coming to terms with Dewey Phillips is not easy. He was neither monster nor angel, neither devil nor saint, but an unpretentious, kindhearted, self-absorbed, and, ultimately, self-destructive soul who wanted nothing more than to spread the gospel of the new rhythm and blues sound to a captivated audience. That he certainly did. For better or worse the music he helped so much to change has become a key part of the way people now live. A great part of that change is reflected in the huge transformation that took place in popular culture during the last half of the twentieth century.

But even accounting for the racial progress that may have been helped as a result of the music, any objective appraisal of this period cries out for an awareness that there are at least some mixed feelings about how much lives changed at the millennium. Even those who proudly participated in protest demonstrations fighting for civil rights must recognize the unintended changes that took place completely apart from the rewards of racial advancement. The most forceful fan of rock 'n' roll becomes nostalgic when recalling the nonracial aspects of the years immediately preceding the upheaval that the music helped bring about. The music of an era—old or new—does that. While we can hope that the racial transformation is permanent, in the long eye of history rock 'n' roll may be only one more cycle in shifting musical tastes.

During my many hours of interviews with Dorothy Phillips she always remained quietly tranquil, speaking softly, seldom animated, and rarely displaying deep-felt emotion when recalling the early days with Daddy-O-Dewey. The one, misty-eyed exception was a recollection of a quiet Memphis evening in the backyard of Sam Phillips's home during the Easter weekend of 1955. Elvis had gained popularity, and the whole gang—Dewey, Sam, Elvis, and everyone's families—was sitting around Sam's swimming pool relaxing and enjoying life. The fierce Memphis summer lay ahead, and the cool, early evening breeze by the side of the pool provided a refreshing comfort before the heat arrived.

The year 1955—the heady days of Elvis's early superstardom—was the period when he and Dewey seemed to be almost joined at the hip. Presley had not yet been crowned the king of rock 'n' roll, but already the evangelical efforts of his court jester had helped spread his fame from the confines of his provincial beginnings to a much larger Mid-South audience. Basking in the crew-cut complacency of the peace and prosperity promised by the Eisenhower years, the country—after several dismal decades of depression and world war—was bubbling over with wide-eyed optimism. It was difficult to find anyone not convinced that the best was yet to come. It would be years before his claim to the title of "the King" was uncontested, but already Elvis was at least a prince, no doubt aware that the most exciting part of his early fame was in the pursuit itself. All was indeed right with the world.

On this particular evening in Sam's backyard, everyone, including Elvis, seemed to be in a particularly pensive mood. Whenever the crowd got together—especially Dewey and Sam—there was always "lots of hollering and carrying on," but this night seemed different. The evening had started late, and after a while "things just seemed to quiet down and everybody got kind of comfortable in their favorite chairs." Before anyone realized it, the first light of an Easter sunrise began to break. At that point Elvis, without provocation or request, ambled over to his guitar and started strumming slowly. "Just as the sun was coming up, he began singing 'Take My Hand, Precious Lord,'" Dot says as she stares outward, apparently seeing the picture now as vividly as then. "And I think it was the most beautiful moment I can remember in my whole life."

As Dot relates the incident, it is difficult to picture that frozen image without thinking of how the story ended. It is hard to conjure up the instant without seeing it from this side of the sadness and sorrow that accompanied the stratospheric rise and fall of both Elvis Presley and Dewey Phillips. It is impossible to isolate that single mental picture without thinking about the awful declines that lay ahead for both of these extraordinary men. Those old enough to remember the wonderful years between the moment Dot remembers and the final fall perhaps become misty-eyed as well. Nor can we help but be drawn to the conclusion that the nice, quiet evening in Memphis in Sam Phillips's backyard during Easter of 1955 might have been the final, fading moment of American innocence.

Notes

Introduction

1. There is no precise definition of the Mid-South. In Memphis the term is generally used to define west Tennessee, eastern Arkansas, and northern Mississippi. The city's leading newspaper, for example, the *Memphis Commercial Appeal*—advertising itself as having "the largest distribution in the Mid-South"—circulates in these areas as well as in small portions of Alabama and the Bootheel of Missouri.

2. Barlow, *Voice Over,* 157–92.

3. Freed did not leave Cleveland to join WINS in New York until 1954; not until 1958 did he go on the network outlet station there, WABC. Freed, "I Told You So," 44; *New York Times,* May 20, 1960, 1, 62; Jackson, *Big Beat Heat,* 65–69.

4. Clements, "'Phillips Sent Me,'" 12.

5. Interview with Jim Dickinson. Unless otherwise noted, all interviews are by the author.

6. Sid Selvidge, cited in Van Wyngarden, "Redefining the Memphis Sound," 43.

7. Marion Keisker on "Sam Phillips: The Man Who Invented Rock 'n' Roll."

8. Halberstam, *The Fifties,* 460.

Chapter 1: Programmed Chaos: Dewey Phillips on the Air

1. Burke, "Dewey Phillips Set for Shiloh Honor"; interview with Charles Raiteri; interview with Sam Phillips. Unless otherwise noted, all interviews are by the author.

2. Haspel, "Tell 'Em Philips Sencha," 134–42.

3. Johnson, "TV News and Views," Aug. 22, 1956, 24.

4. Interview with Fred Cook.

5. Interview with Bob Lewis; interview with Sam Phillips; Raiteri interview with John Fry.

6. Raiteri interview with Laddy Hutchinson.

7. Raiteri interview with Stanley Booth.

8. Interview with Bob Lewis.

9. Jack Parnell in *Rock 'n' Roll Invaders.*

10. Clippings from Dorothy Phillips collection.

11. Interview with Sam Phillips.

12. Raiteri interview with Stanley Booth. In fact, Wexler was well aware of (and fascinated by) most of Dewey's scams and recorded as much in his autobiography. Wexler and Ritz, *Rhythm and the Blues,* 124–25.

13. Interview with Billy Britt Mills; interview with Louis Harris.

14. Interview with Charles Raiteri.

15. Johnson, "TV News and Views," Aug. 22, 1956, 24.

16. Interview with Jim Dickinson.

17. Interview with Betty Jo Carruthers, May 28, 1996; Raiteri interview with Sam Phillips; Guralnick, *Last Train to Memphis,* 98.

18. Dewey is quoted on *Red, Hot and Blue.*

19. Raiteri interview with Billy Lee Riley.

20. Gordon Lawhead in *Daddy-O-Dewey.*

21. Clements, "'Phillips Sent Me,'" 12.

22. There is no evidence to indicate that such a song was ever written. "The People's Choice," *Radio-TV Mirror* (n.d.), Dorothy Phillips Collection, Crump, Tenn.; Dewitt, *Elvis, the Sun Years,* 136; Clements, "'Phillips Sent Me,'" 12.

23. Clements, "'Phillips Sent Me,'" 12.

24. Haspel, "Tell 'Em Philips Sencha," 137.

25. Clements, "'Phillips Sent Me,'" 12.

26. Phillips in *Daddy-O-Dewey;* Nager, "Dewey Took Giant Steps," C1.

27. Raiteri interview with Dorothy Phillips; interview with Bill Kirby.

28. Raiteri interview with Charles Caughlin (quotation); Raiteri interview with Don Nix. Nix was an original member of a Memphis group, the Mar-Keys.

29. Interview with Dorothy Phillips, June 11, 1993.

30. Interview with Bob Lewis.

31. "Dewey was already anticipating 'Señor Wences' on the *Ed Sullivan Show,*" Jim Dickinson says. "Remember, how he'd go, ''S ok? 'S a' right'?" Interview with Jim Dickinson.

32. George Klein in *Daddy-O-Dewey.*

33. Ibid.; Raiteri interview with Welton M. Roy; George Klein on "Sam Phillips: The Man Who Invented Rock 'n' Roll."

34. Whisenhunt, "Weary Engineers Move WHBQ Overnight," 7.

35. Interview with Jack Parnell.

36. Clipping (n.d.), Alex Ward Collection, Memphis; interview with George Klein, June 7, 1989; interview with Bob Lewis; interview with Irvin Schatz.

37. Interview with Alex Ward.

38. Gordon Lawhead in *Daddy-O-Dewey.*

39.Raiteri interview with Welton M. Roy.

40. Interview with Durrell Durham.

41. Interview with Dorothy Phillips, June 11, 1993.

42. Interview with Durrell Durham; interview with George Klein, May 28, 1996.

43. Pond is cited in Gordon, *It Came from Memphis,* 19.

44. Interview with John Fry.

45. Russell's remarks are taken from Raiteri interview with John King.

46. Interview with Bill Kirby, May 28, 1996.

47. Interview with Louis Harris.

48. Interview with Harv Stegman.

49. Interview with Billy Britt Mills.

50. Interview with Fred Cook.

51. Nager, "Dewey Took Giant Steps," C1; interview with Sam Phillips; Raiteri interview with Sam Phillips. Official ratings of Dewey's show were conducted by the Hooper polling organization, but unfortunately there are no extant records of these. The radio station has nothing, and the Library of Congress says, "We do have Hooper ratings for network programming from old time radio but not for regional radio shows." Patrick Timony, Library of Congress email to author, Dec. 22, 20003.

52. Interview with Ron Meroney.

53. George Klein in *Daddy-O-Dewey.*

54. Interview with Gordon Lawhead, emphasis added.

55. Howard, "Profit Sharing Announced by WHBQ," 11.

56. Ibid. The plan called for periodic division among staff members of one-third of all profits above $36,000 annually. The figure represented a "reasonable return" of 5 percent ($25,000) on their investment plus a "reasonable allowance" ($11,000) for depreciation and improvements.

57. Interview with Durrell Durham.

58. Interview with Jim Dickinson.

59. Interview with Gordon Lawhead.

60. Moore, *That's Alright, Elvis,* 62.

61. Interview with George Klein, May 5, 1990.

62. For a wonderful account of Binford's doings, see Magness, "Era of Film Censorship."

63. Significantly, Binford was careful to make certain that blacks were always portrayed in subservient roles. He censored movies, one observer noted, "in which roles are depicted by [N]egro actors or actresses not ordinarily performed by members of the colored race in real life." He therefore prevented the stage version of "Annie Get Your Gun" from being performed in Memphis because one of the parts featured a black person as a railroad conductor. "We don't have any Negro conductors in the South," Binford carefully explained, arguing that he was only "maintaining community racial standards." Blinded by his own personal self-righteousness, he concluded: "Of course, it can't show here. It's social equality in action." The quotations are from the *Pittsburg Courier,* Sept. 15, 1956, 22; and

Magness, "Era of Film Censorship"; see also Melton, "Blacks in Memphis," 205; Shelton, "Lloyd T. Binford"; and Tucker, *Lieutenant Lee,* 145–46.

64. Interview with Alex Ward.

65. Interview with Jack Parnell; interview with Bill Kirby, May 28, 1996.

66. Interview with Alex Ward.

67. Interview with Dorothy Phillips, Aug. 8, 1995; see also Gordon Lawhead in *Daddy-O-Dewey.*

68. Guralnick, *Last Train to Memphis,* 97.

69. Raiteri interview with Dickie Lee; interview with Betty Phillips Kirby, July 11, 1996.

Chapter 2: Before the Storm: Dewey Arrives at the Five-and-Dime

1. Interview with Gordon Lawhead. Unless otherwise noted, all interviews are by the author.

2. Johnson, "TV News and Views," Aug. 22, 1956, 24.

3. Dewey's power to turn records into hits before they caught on nationally was not limited to Elvis and the other local stars he promoted so enthusiastically for Sam Phillips's Sun Records label. According to Berretta, record promoters from all over the country, especially the new rhythm and blues independents like Leonard Chess of Chess Records and Jerry Wexler of Atlantic, knew that when they came to Memphis they had to see only one man—Dewey Phillips. Interview with Frank Berretta.

4. *Memphis World,* June 9, 1950, 4.

5. Many states at this time had laws that dictated that public school teachers could not be married.

6. Interview with Betty Phillips Kirby, May 28, 1996.

7. Ibid.; Betty Jo Carruthers to the Editor, July 2, 1981, clipping from the Selmer, Tenn., newspaper, n.d., Charles Raiteri Collection, Memphis.

8. Interview with Billy Britt Mills.

9. Interview with Marjorie Phillips Barba.

10. Interview with Billy Britt Mills; interview with Jewell Phillips Tyler.

11. Wolff, "To Make a Shining Light," 113.

12. Johnson, "TV News and Views," Aug. 22, 1956, 24.

13. Dewey "just 'passed through' Tech High School," grins Cousin Billy, who adds, understandably, that it was not unusual at the time for youngsters to drop out of school, especially if their families were in need of money, as Dewey's certainly was. Interview with Billy Britt Mills; see also Ellis, "Music Kingmaker," F1, F4.

14. Interview with Betty Phillips Kirby, May 28, 1996; Booth, *Rhythm Oil,* 48; Ellis, "Music Kingmaker," F1, F4.

15. Interview with Billy Britt Mills.

16. Interview with Dorothy Phillips, June 11, 1993; interview with George Klein, May 5, 1990.

17. Johnson, "TV News and Views," March 7, 1961, 10; interview with Betty Phillips Kirby, May 28, 1996; Raiteri interview with Marjorie Phillips Barba; interview with Billy Britt Mills.

18. "The People's Choice," Dorothy Phillips Collection, Crump, Tenn. The Memphis College of Music was later incorporated into Southwestern College and later became Rhodes College.

19. Raiteri interview with Marjorie Phillips Barba.

20. Interview with Gordon Lawhead.

21. Interview with Betty Phillips Kirby, May 28, 1996.

22. Interview with Billy Britt Mills. Germantown is today a predominantly up-scale, lily-white suburb and Tennessee's eleventh-largest municipality.

23. *Memphis World,* June 9, 1950, 4.

24. The store's name was officially W. T. Grant, but almost everyone in Memphis referred to it as "Grant's," as I have here.

25. Interview with Billy Britt Mills; Clements, "'Phllips Sent Me,'" 12; *Memphis World,* June 9, 1950, 4.

26. Raiteri interview with H. E. Van Meter.

27. Interview with Frank Berretta; interview with Billy Britt Mills.

28. Interview with Frank Berretta; Raiteri interview with Abe Schwab.

29. Raiteri interview with H. E. Van Meter.

30. Ownby, *American Dreams in Mississippi,* 124–29.

31. Van Meter is quoted in Clements, "'Phillips Sent Me,'" 12.

32. Vassar Slate in *Daddy-O-Dewey.*

33. Raiteri interview with Bill Thomas; interview with Betty Phillips Kirby, May 28, 1996.

34. Interview with Billy Britt Mills.

35. Ibid.

36. Gordon Lawhead in *Daddy-O-Dewey;* interview with George Klein, May 5, 1990.

37. Raiteri interview with Bill Thomas; Raiteri interview with H. E. Van Meter.

38. Raiteri interview with Marjorie Phillips Barba.

39. Interview with Dorothy Phillips, July 8, 1994.

40. Ibid.

41. Raiteri interview with Marjorie Phillips Barba; interview with Bill Kirby, July 11, 1996; interview with Betty Phillips Kirby, July 11, 1996; interview with Billy Britt Mills.

42. Johnson, "TV News and Views," Aug. 22, 1956, 24. The call, Johnson remembered, came in the middle of the night.

43. Ibid.; Johnson in the *Memphis Press-Scimitar,* June 20, 1972.

Chapter 3: The White Brother on Beale Street

1. Interview with Charles Raiteri. Unless otherwise noted, all interviews are by the author.

2. Raiteri interview with Bernard Lansky.

3. *Memphis Commercial Appeal,* July 12, 1959. For a long time Beale Street was officially Beale Avenue (all Memphis streets running east and west are avenues). After it became famous, the city finally changed the street's name to what everyone was already calling it.

4. Its eastern end became a suburb for the wealthy. Raichelson, *Beale Street Talks,* 1.

5. Faragher and Harrington, *Memphis in Vintage Postcards,* 37; Palmer, "Sam Phillips: The Sun King," 36.

6. This had come about largely as a result of the city's dreadful yellow fever epidemics of the 1870s. The prevalence of the disease in Africa produced a partial immunity to its most harmful effects among African Americans, making whites much more likely to contract it. Melton, "Blacks in Memphis," 29–31; Hutchins, "Beale Street as It Was," 57; Raichelson, *Beale Street Talks,* 2; Sigafoos, *Cotton Row to Beale Street,* 97–98; Capers, *The Biography of a River Town,* 198–99; McKee and Chisenhall, *Beale Black and Blue,* 13.

7. "Parents may well have been worn out by depression and war," Pete Daniel says, "but their children were hungry for adventure." Daniel, *Lost Revolutions,* 123. See also Evans, "Goin' Up the Country," 81, and Cantor, *Wheelin' on Beale,* 137–53.

8. *United States Census of Population, 1950; U.S. Censuses of Population and Housing, 1960;* Lemann, *The Promised Land.* For the impact of the new moneyed urban black workers on Memphis, see Melton, "Blacks in Memphis," 292–96.

9. Raichelson, *Beale Street Talks,* 1.

10. Burnett, "The Blues," H5; quotation from Van Wyngarden, "Redefining the Memphis Sound," 34–45. The petition to Congress was the work of blues scholar Harry Godwin and blues great Memphis Slim (Peter Chatman). Nager, *Memphis Beat,* 219.

11. Famed folklorist Alan Lomax once ornately described the Mississippi River as "southern America in liquid form." Lomax, *The Land Where the Blues Began,* 3; see also Kirby, *From Africa to Beale Street.*

12. Raichelson, *Beale Street Talks,* 3–4.

13. Miller, *Mr. Crump of Memphis,* 292–335; Tucker, *Memphis since Crump,* 40–78; Tucker, *Lieutenant Lee,* 139–42; McKee and Chisenhall, *Beale Black and Blue,* 81–86; see also Melton, "Blacks in Memphis," 263–69; Lewis, "Fifty Years of Politics," 75–76, 166–71; and Jalenak, "Beale Street Politics," 18, 25, 142.

14. Williams wrote nationally syndicated columns for black newspapers. "Nat D. Williams: Tan Town Disc Jester."

15. Boyle's comments made the front page ("Boyle Keeps Eyes on Nineteen Negroes"); see also Hurley et al., *Pictures Tell the Story,* 113. Crump is quoted in

Tucker, *Memphis since Crump,* 19–20. See also Withers, *The Memphis Blues Again,* 8; McKee and Chisenhall, *Beale Black and Blue,* 82; Tucker, *Memphis since Crump,* 30; Tucker, *Lieutenant Lee,* 124–37.

16. Memphis won the unfortunate distinction of "Murder Capital of the U.S.A." in 1912, when a statistician for the Prudential Insurance Company computed that the city had eighty-nine murders per hundred thousand citizens during the thirty years studied. *Memphis Commercial Appeal,* July 12, 1959.

17. Peiser, McDaniel, and Allen interview with B.B. King, Center for Southern Folklore Archives.

18. Interview with Jim Dickinson.

19. Interview with Billy Britt Mills.

20. Guralnick, *Last Train to Memphis,* 507.

21. Lee, *Beale Street,* 13. Black Hall of Fame photographer Ernest Withers, one of the best recorders of the Beale Street scene, estimates that "maybe fifteen or twenty" black merchants were on Beale Street and "the other ten or twelve [were] off on Hernando and Fourth Street." Allen and McDaniel interview with Ernest Withers, Center for Southern Folklore Archives.

22. Raiteri interview with Abe Schwab.

23. Peiser interview with Jake Salky, Center for Southern Folklore Archives.

24. Ibid.; Raiteri interview with Bernard Lansky.

25. Raiteri, liner notes for *Dewey Phillips.*

26. Interview with B.B. King; Raiteri interview with B.B. King.

27. After singing on Nat D. Williams's regular afternoon program *The Tan-Town Jamboree* for about three months, B.B. was given a small time segment of his own. His first separate listing appears in the *Memphis Commercial Appeal*'s radio time schedule as March 26, 1949, but not until mid-April 1949 did he get a daily fifteen-minute slot. *Memphis Commercial Appeal,* March 27, 1949, sec. 4, 9; *Memphis Commercial Appeal,* April 18, 1949, 28.

28. Raiteri interview with Sam Phillips.

29. Raiteri interview with B.B. King.

30. Interview tapes with Mrs. Anselmo Borasso, Memphis Room, Shelby County Public Library and Information Center.

31. McKee and Chisenhall, *Beale Black and Blue,* 66–67.

32. B.B. King in *All Day and All Night.*

33. Raiteri interview with B.B. King.

34. Guralnick, *Last Train to Memphis,* 6.

35. Kirby, *From Africa to Beale Street,* 71.

36. Raiteri interview with B.B. King; interview with Rufus Thomas, June 12, 1995; Rufus Thomas in *Rock 'n' Roll Invaders;* Gordon, *It Came from Memphis,* 15–16; Ellis, "Music Kingmaker," F4.

37. Thomas's color quote is cited in Halberstam, *The Fifties,* 459. Rufus was perhaps subconsciously paraphrasing WLAC's John R., who popularized the expression "music knows no color."

38. Raiteri interview with B.B. King.
39. Clements, "'Phillips Sent Me,'" 12.
40. Interview with Charles Raiteri.
41. McDaniel interview with Mrs. Robert Henry, Center for Southern Folklore Archives.
42. Interview tapes with Robert Henry, Memphis Room, Shelby County Public Library and Information Center.
43. McDaniel interview with Mrs. Robert Henry, Center for Southern Folklore Archives.
44. "He loved barbecue," Mrs. Henry recalls. "He was crazy about Culpepper's, too." Ibid.
45. The segregated arrangement didn't stop others, however. Johnny Mills' was so popular a late-night stop that it was not unusual to find whites overcoming their usual aversion to the area, milling outside and waiting for an open spot on their half of the counter. Coppock, "Mid-South Memoirs," G7.
46. Interview with Dorothy Phillips, July 8, 1994.
47. Interview tapes with Robert Henry, Memphis Room, Shelby County Public Library and Information Center.
48. Ibid.; *Tri-State Defender,* Aug. 29, 1953, 1–2.
49. McDaniel interview with Andrew "Sunbeam" Mitchell, Center for Southern Folklore Archives.
50. Interview with Rufus Thomas, June 12, 1995. Memphis had the reputation of being one of the few places between Chicago and New Orleans where black entertainers could find decent accommodations. Walter interview with Nat D. Williams, Oral History, Memphis Room, Shelby County Public Library and Information Center.
51. Andrew "Sunbeam" Mitchell in *All Day and All Night.*
52. Raiteri interview with Abe Schwab.
53. McKee and Chisenhall, *Beale Black and Blue,* 248; McDaniel interview with Andrew "Sunbeam" Mitchell; Raichelson, *Beale Street Talks,* 34–35.
54. Peiser, McDaniel, and Allen interview with B.B. King, Center for Southern Folklore Archives.
55. Interview with Dorothy Phillips, July 8, 1994.
56. Interview with Fred Cook.
57. Clipping, n.d., Alex Ward Collection, Memphis.
58. Interview with Bob Alburty.
59. Clipping, n.d., Alex Ward Collection, Memphis.
60. Johnson, "TV News and Views," Aug. 22, 1956, 24.
61. Interview with Dorothy Phillips, July 8, 1994.
62. Interview with Bob Alburty.
63. Interview with Abe Schwab, May 28, 1995; see also Raiteri interview with Abe Schwab.
64. Ibid.

65. By this time WHBQ—like several other Memphis stations—was experimenting with black gospel music. The Spirit of Memphis Quartet started appearing nightly on WHBQ in 1947.

66. Interview with Dorothy Phillips, Aug. 8, 1995.

67. Interview with Gordon Lawhead.

Chapter 4: The New Memphis Sound: The Birth of Black Programming

1. Cantor, *Wheelin' on Beale*. WDIA's influence was truly revolutionary. In December 1947—on the eve of the station's switch— *Ebony* magazine could find only sixteen blacks among the estimated three thousand deejays employed in the entire country. *Ebony,* Dec. 1947, 41.

2. This information is based on my extensive interviews with Bert Ferguson for Cantor, *Wheelin' on Beale,* 13–24.

3. Because he was introduced on the air as "the first Negro announcer in the South," public recognition set Williams apart from those other blacks who might have been on the air in the South before him but were not identified as being black.

4. Ward, *Just My Soul Responding,* 139.

5. Ibid. Until someone writes a much-needed study of WLAC, the best synthesis can be found in Barlow, *Voice Over,* 160–64. See also the interview with Allen in Williams, "William T. 'Hoss' Allen," 30; Chaffin, "DJ: First Soul Brother"; and Smith, *Pied Pipers.*

6. Hoss Allen is cited in the film *Rock 'n' Roll Invaders.* Barlow, *Voice Over,* 160–64. WLAC was not only heard around the country but also in the Caribbean. George, *Death of Rhythm and Blues,* 54.

7. Cantor, *Wheelin' on Beale,* 154–72.

8. "The Forgotten 15,000,000," 25.

9. Cantor, *Wheelin' on Beale,* 85–86

10. "The Forgotten 15,000,000," 25.

11. John Pepper and Bert Ferguson, "But Can You Buy Loyalty?" Chris Spindel Collection, Memphis; *Memphis Commercial Appeal,* June 20, 1954, 2, 6; Sigafoos, *Cotton Row,* 216. For the impact of the new moneyed urban black workers on Memphis, see Melton, "Blacks in Memphis," 292–96.

12. "Mother Station of the Negroes," in Mike Leadbitter, *Delta Country Blues,* David Evans Collection, Memphis.

13. Nat Williams frequently used the expression in his regular by-line columns. Melton, "Blacks in Memphis," 187; Fox, "Beale Street and the Blues," 137–53. WDIA was able to make its 10 percent claim by roughly estimating the black population of the country at fifteen million (10 percent of the total population) and then claiming to reach 1.5 million blacks in the Mid-South, or 10 percent of that total.

14. For earlier efforts to exploit the commercial black market see Cantor, *Whee-lin' on Beale,* 18–20.

15. Interview with Gordon Lawhead; Gordon Lawhead in *Daddy-O-Dewey.* Unless otherwise noted, all interviews are by the author.

16. Lawhead was not the only one who saw the potential to be had after WDIA signed off. Sam Phillips also applied for a twenty-four-hour, all-black station but was turned down by the FCC, at which point he started an all-women's station in Memphis, WHER. "Sam Phillips: The Man Who Invented Rock 'n' Roll."

17. Interview with Gordon Lawhead.

18. Ibid.; Gordon Lawhead in *Daddy-O-Dewey*

19. Interview with Don Kern.

20. Gordon Lawhead in *Daddy-O-Dewey.*

21. Although there is no evidence to support the claim, Lawhead maintains that the name was originally borrowed from Cole Porter's Broadway show *Red, Hot and Blue,* which was staged in 1936. There was also a film by the same title in 1949. Interview with Gordon Lawhead.

22. Ibid.; Gordon Lawhead in *Daddy-O-Dewey.*

23. Interview with Charles Raiteri.

24. Gordon Lawhead in *Daddy-O-Dewey;* interview with George Klein, Aug. 3, 1988.

25. Gordon Lawhead in *Daddy-O-Dewey;* see also Clements, "'Phillips Sent Me,'" 12.

26. Alex Bonner in *Daddy-O-Dewey.*

27. Gordon Lawhead in *Daddy-O-Dewey.*

28. Interview with Bob Lewis.

29. Interview with Gordon Lawhead; Gordon Lawhead in *Daddy-O-Dewey.*

30. Ibid.

Chapter 5: "What in the World Is That?" Is This Guy Black or White?

1. Interview with Gordon Lawhead. Unless otherwise noted, all interviews are by the author.

2. Raiteri interview with Gordon Lawhead.

3. Ibid. A document in Charles Raiteri's file marked "Acceptance and Payroll Deduction Authority" shows Dewey's employment beginning on October 24, 1949, but Dewey didn't sign the document until the end of the following year, December 4, 1950. The signing was not an error because when Dewey signed he listed as a dependent his son Randy (born in December 1949) in what appears to be preparation to begin receiving pay starting on January 1, 1951. That suggests that Dewey may have worked from October 24, 1949, until well into 1950—perhaps the entire year—without pay. Gordon Lawhead says he is uncertain but to his best recollection Dewey worked until May or June 1950 without pay. Raiteri Collection, Memphis.

4. Interview with Gordon Lawhead; Gordon Lawhead in *Daddy-O-Dewey; Memphis World,* Aug. 6, 1958, 5; Clements, "'Phillips Sent Me,'" 12; Nager, "Dewey Took Giant Steps," C1.

5. Interview with Bob Lewis; interview with Gordon Lawhead.

6. Ibid.; interview with Fred Cook; interview with Durrell Durham.

7. Interview with Dorothy Phillips, Aug. 8, 1995.

8. Johnson, "TV News and Views," Aug. 22, 1956, 24. This conclusion was drawn from newspaper sources and by talking to scores of Dewey's early fans.

9. Clements, "'Phillips Sent Me,'" 12.

10. Ibid.; *Memphis World,* June 13, 1950, 3.

11. The *World*'s original story on Dewey, without his picture, appeared in the weekly on June 6, 1950. They ran the same story the next week and included his picture, as if to clarify readers' curiosity about Dewey's color. *Memphis World,* June 6, 1950, 4; *Memphis World,* June 13, 1950, 3.

12. Cantor, *Wheelin' on Beale,* 164; Smith, *Pied Pipers.*

13. Barlow, *Voice Over,* 139; see also MacDonald, *Don't Touch That Dial!* The practice was also quite common among singers. Salem, *The Late Great Johnny Ace.* On the original minstrel shows, see Toll, *Blacking Up.*

14. The strangest of all racial ventriloquy stories related by Barlow is that of Vernon Winslow, who was not allowed to announce on WJMR in New Orleans because he was black but was given permission to train a white deejay to sound black. The show was very successful until Winslow attempted one night to broadcast on his own. He was fired, but the station continued the practice of white surrogates. Barlow, *Voice Over,* 165–66; George, *Death of Rhythm and Blues,* 52–53; see also Smith, *Pied Pipers,* 121–24.

15. John R. in *Rock 'n' Roll Invaders.*

16. Interview with George Klein, May 5, 1990; interview with Sam Phillips.

17. Raiteri interview with Sam Phillips; interview with Jewell Phillips Tyler.

18. Interview with Don Kern; interview with Charles Raiteri. For the manner in which Elvis pursued fame, see Guralnick, *Last Train to Memphis.*

19. Interview with Charles Raiteri; Raiteri interview with Sam Phillips.

20. Jim Dickinson on "Sam Phillips: The Man Who Invented Rock 'n' Roll."

21. Interview with Billy Britt Mills.

22. Interview with Jim Dickinson.

23. Raiteri interview with Sam Phillips; interview with Sam Phillips; Atkins on *Sun Days with Elvis.* For a more elaborate discussion of the early response to Presley, see Bertrand, *Race, Rock, and Elvis,* 199–204

24. "The Forgotten 15,000,000," 24–25. For a thorough discussion of Wolfman Jack, see Barlow, *Voice Over,* 182–86.

25. Allen is quoted in Williams, "William T. 'Hoss' Allen," 32.

26. Guralnick, *Last Train to Memphis,* 75. For information on W. Herbert Brewster, see Reagon, ed., "William Herbert Brewster Sr." and Heilbutt, *The Gospel Good News.*

27. Interview with Roy Neal; Lornell interviews with Ford Nelson, Theo Wade,

and Shirley and Jet Bledsoe, Special Collections, University of Memphis Library; Lornell, *Happy in the Service of the Lord.*

28. Interview with George Klein, June 7, 1989; interview with Bob Lewis.

29. Interview with Roy Neal.

30. For Brewster's contribution to music, see Reagon, ed., "William Herbert Brewster Sr."

31. Interview with George Klein, June 7, 1989.

32. Ibid.

33. Interview with Bob Lewis.

34. Brewster is quoted in Hazen and Freeman, *Memphis Elvis-Style,* 52–53.

35. Raiteri interview with Eddie Richardson.

36. Ibid.; interview with Bob Lewis.

37. Interview with Dorothy Phillips, June 11, 1993; interview with Roy Neal.

38. Interview with George Klein, Aug. 3, 1988; Dewitt, *Elvis, the Sun Years,* 85–86.

39. Ibid.; see also Guralnick, *Last Train to Memphis,* 75.

Chapter 6: Racial Cross-Pollination: Black and White Together

1. Dewey emceed the Negro Southern League All-Stars battle against the Memphis Red Sox in July 1950, and he was "brought back by popular demand" for another guest emcee spot in August. *Memphis World,* July 7, 1950, 7; Aug. 18, 1950, 5.

2. Interview with Dorothy Phillips, June 11, 1993; interview with Betty Phillips Kirby, July 11, 1996; interview with Marjorie Phillips Barba. Unless otherwise noted, all interviews are by the author.

3. Interview with Max and Betty Jo Carruthers, July 16, 1996.

4. Interview with Don Kern.

5. Interview with George Klein, Aug. 3, 1988; Raiteri interview with Sam Phillips.

6. Interview with Vassar Slate.

7. Interview with Jim Dickinson.

8. Interview with Bob Lewis.

9. Interview with Natalie Frager; interview with Steve Leibowitz.

10. Peiser interview with Ida Cherry, Center for Southern Folklore Archives.

11. Raiteri interview with Jim Dickinson; Peiser interview with Ida Cherry, Center for Southern Folklore Archives.

12. Peiser interview with Natalie Frager, Beale Street Tape Transcript; interview with Dorothy Phillips, Aug. 8, 1995.

13. Interview with Vassar Slate.

14. Interview with George Klein, Aug. 3, 1988; interview with Dorothy Phillips, June 11, 1993.

15. The only successful effort to reach the white mainstream audience was a spinoff of WLAC's efforts. Randy's Record Shop in nearby Gallatin, Tennessee, one of Gene Nobles's early sponsors (the show soon came to be known as *Randy's*

Record Shop), sold R&B records on WLAC through the country's first mail order record business. Initially recording mostly black artists, Dot began to specialize in white cover versions of black artists. Dot Records were also manufactured at the Plastics Products Company in Memphis, which produced the records for the Sun label. *Rock 'n' Roll Invaders;* Barlow, *Voice Over,* 160–64; "First Soul Brother of the Airwaves," M1, M4.

16. Interview with Gordon Lawhead; Gordon Lawhead in *Daddy-O-Dewey.*

17. Rufus Thomas quoted in *Memphis Commercial Appeal,* Sept. 28, 1993.

18. Interview with Bob Lewis.

19. Haspel, "Tell 'Em Philips Sencha," 134.

20. Allen and McDaniel interview with Phil Zerilla, Center for Southern Folklore Archives. Even though no official public ordinance prohibited integrated entertainment, the intimidating climate provided by Crump and Binford often had the same effect. *Code of Ordinances City of Memphis, Tennessee;* Klewer, *Memphis Digest.* For a discussion of the racial impact of Binford and Crump on the musical culture see Dowdy, "Censoring Popular Culture," 98–117.

21. Raiteri interview with Sam Phillips; see also *Memphis Commercial Appeal,* Sept. 28, 1993, C3. Information about the Hippodrome show comes from a newspaper clipping, n.n., n.d., Charles Raiteri Collection, Memphis.

Chapter 7: The Great Convergence: Pop Tunes One-Stop

1. Interview with John Novarese. Unless otherwise noted, all interviews are by the author.

2. Ibid.; interview with Frank Berretta.

3. "The jukebox quickly became ubiquitous," says blues historian Francis Davis. Part of the blues mythology had Muddy Waters installing one in his shack in Mississippi. Davis, *History of the Blues,* 140. Although there is no evidence that Waters put in a jukebox, the legend nonetheless continues. Gordon, *Can't Be Satisfied.*

4. Interview with John Novarese.

5. Ibid.

6. Major record companies had set up temporary regional recording centers throughout the South during the 1920s and produced more than five hundred race records annually, resulting in literally millions of records sold. The market died, however, during the Great Depression and World War II. Charters, "Workin' on the Building"; Davis, *History of the Blues,* 64; Dickerson, *Goin' Back to Memphis,* 44, 47; Evans, "Going Up the Country," 58; George, *Death of Rhythm and Blues,* 10–11; Oakley, *Devil's Music;* Spottswood, "Country Girls," 88–99.

7. On the critical importance of the independents in the rock 'n' roll revolution, see Escott and Hawkins, *Good Rockin' Tonight;* Gillett, *Making Tracks;* Gillett, *The Sound of the City,* 67–118; Kennedy and McNutt, *Little Labels;* Mabry, "The Rise and Fall of Ace Records," 411–50; and Shaw, *Honkers and Shouters.*

8. As late as World War II the listening audience for Delta blues' artists was

confined almost exclusively to a handful of the white elite. Even after John Lomax found Leadbelly in jail and Muddy Waters on the Stovall Plantation near Clarksdale, Mississippi, the audience was still limited mostly to devotees of Library of Congress recordings and professional academicians and scholars who prided themselves on their esoteric knowledge of the performers. Filene, *Romancing the Folk;* Porterfield, *Last Cavalier.*

9. David Less, former Pop Tunes's employee and later executive director of the Blues Foundation, says, "In those days of unlimited returns" the companies took a chance. "With Poplar Tunes rolling the dice, the record companies were willing to gamble." Nager, "The Unknown Record Man," 24–25.

10. Interview with George Klein, June 7, 1989. According to Novarese and Berretta, who kept the store files, as late as the mid-1950s *Billboard* still got local data from white record shops only. Interview with John Novarese; interview with Frank Berretta.

11. "Growing Up with Elvis," 32.

12. Interview with Dorothy Phillips, July 8, 1994; interview with Randy Phillips, Jan. 29, 2000.

13. Ibid.

14. Interview with Frank Berretta; Raiteri interview with Jim Dickinson; Raiteri interview with John Fry.

15. Interview with John Novarese; interview with Frank Berretta.

16. Interview with Randy Phillips, May 31, 1994.

17. Raiteri interview with Barbara Pittman.

18. Interview with Louis Harris.

19. Interview with John Novarese.

20. Escott and Hawkins, *Good Rockin' Tonight,* 7–10

21. Ibid., 57; see also Raiteri interview with Sam Phillips.

22. Sam told Charles Raiteri in 1977 that he met Dewey at Grant's before he had gotten to WHBQ, but he told me in 1993 that Dewey was already on the air when they met. Interview with Sam Phillips; Raiteri interview with Sam Phillips; interview with Harv Stegman. Stanley Booth says, "They met while Dewey was working at Grant's and Sam was announcing at WREC" (*Rhythm Oil,* 49).

23. Interview with Frank Berretta.

24. Raiteri interview with Sam Phillips.

25. "Sam Phillips: The Man Who Invented Rock 'n' Roll."

26. Keisker and Lee are cited in Guralnick, *Last Train to Memphis,* 98.

27. Interview with Charles Raiteri.

28. Raiteri interview with Dickie Lee.

29. Raiteri interview with Sam Phillips; interview with George Klein, June 7, 1989.

30. Whitmer, *The Inner Elvis,* 94.

Chapter 8: The Phillips Boys: Soul (Better Than Blood) Brothers

1. Dickinson on "Sam Phillips: The Man Who Invented Rock 'n' Roll"; Guralnick, "Million Dollar Quartet," 30; Baker, "We Flat-Ass Changed the World," 19–20.

2. Ward, *Just My Soul Responding,* 21; see also Escott and Hawkins, *Good Rockin' Tonight;* Kennedy and McNutt, *Little Labels;* and Shaw, *Honkers and Shouters.*

3. Escott, *Sun Records,* 33; Salem, *The Late Great Johnny Ace,* 35. Although Trumpet was short-lived, (1950–55) it produced the classic "Dust My Broom" by Elmore James as well as Sonny Boy Williamson's early recordings. George, *Death of Rhythm and Blues,* 28.

4. Interview with Sam Phillips. Unless otherwise noted, all interviews are by the author.

5. Petreycik, "Interview with Sam Phillips," 58; Raiteri interview with Knox Phillips; Cohodas, *Spinning Blues into Gold,* 63; Humphrey, "Bright Lights," 189.

6. Phillips is quoted in Ellis, "Music Kingmaker," F4; see also Petreycik, "Interview with Sam Phillips," 58; and Escott and Hawkins, *Good Rockin' Tonight,* 20.

7. Davis, *History of the Blues,* 44.

8. Carl Perkins on "Sam Phillips: The Man Who Invented Rock 'n' Roll."

9. Cohodas, *Spinning Blues into Gold,* 58.

10. Raiteri interview with Stan Kessler; Raiteri interview with Sam Phillips.

11. Raiteri interview with B.B. King.

12. Interview with Dorothy Phillips, June 11, 1993; Sam Phillips on "Sam Phillips: The Man Who Invented Rock 'n' Roll"; interview with Betty Phillips Kirby, May 28, 1996; Raiteri interview with Sam Phillips; interview with Jim Dickinson.

13. Raiteri interview with Becky Phillips; interview with Randy Phillips, Jan. 29, 2000; Raiteri interview with Dorothy Phillips; Raiteri interview with Randy Phillips.

14. Guralnick, *Last Train to Memphis,* 98; Wexler, *Rhythm and the Blues,* 124–25.

15. Phillips is quoted in the *Memphis Commercial Appeal,* Sept. 29, 30, 1968.

16. Raiteri interview with Sam Phillips (quotation); see also *Memphis Commercial Appeal,* Sept. 28, 1993, C3.

17. Escott and Hawkins, *Good Rockin' Tonight,* 20–21; see also Floyd, *Sun Records,* xiii; and "Sam Phillips: The Man Who Invented Rock 'n' Roll."

18. Raiteri interview with Sam Phillips.

19. Escott and Hawkins, *Good Rockin' Tonight,* 36.

20. Clement's quotes are taken from Dickerson, *Goin' Back to Memphis,* 106; Smith, *Pied Pipers,* 57.

21. Interview with George Klein, June 7, 1989.

22. Ibid.; interview with Sam Phillips; see also Kaye "The *Rolling Stone* Interview," 85.

23. "Dewey Phillips, Forty-two, Disk Jockey, Dies," 32. Apparently it was Carl Perkins who credited Dewey with coining the term *rockabilly*. Nager, "Dewey Took Giant Steps," C1.

24. Interview with Sam Phillips; Kaye, "The *Rolling Stone* Interview," 85.

25. Wexler is quoted in Fox, *In the Groove,* 127. See also Kramer, "Atlantic and R&B Trend Developed," 24, 38, and Ertegun, "Great Sound Is No Great Secret," 24, 39.

26. Interview with Sam Phillips; Escott and Hawkins, *Good Rockin' Tonight,* 18–19; Guralnick, *Last Train to Memphis,* 96.

27. Even if the documents of Dewey's Hooper ratings existed, and they do not, it would be impossible to verify the class makeup of his listeners because class identity was never asked for during telephone surveys. Nonetheless, scholars have long maintained (even in antebellum days) that lower-class whites, who had the most to lose socially and economically by the rising status of black people, often felt a greater threat from African Americans and hence often exerted greater prejudice. Bloom, *Class, Race and the Civil Rights Movement;* Roediger, *The Wages of Whiteness;* Stokes, *Race and Class.*

28. Rufus Thomas on "Sam Phillips: The Man Who Invented Rock 'n' Roll." In fairness to Sam, it should be noted that whites as well as blacks left Sun, most thinking that they could do better with a bigger label.

29. Escott and Hawkins, *Sun Records,* 33.

30. Nat D. Williams, "Down on Beale," *Pittsburgh Courier,* Janurary 21, 1950, 21. Williams wrote a regular "Down on Beale" column for both black newspapers in Memphis, the *World* and the *Tri-State Defender.* Occasionally, his articles were picked up by the *Chicago Defender* and the *Pittsburgh Courier.*

31. Memphis Slim is quoted in Dickerson, *Goin' Back to Memphis,* 65; Rufus Thomas interview, Aug. 9, 1994; see also Walter interview with Nat D. Williams, Memphis Room, Shelby County Public Library and Information Center.

32. Kaye, "The *Rolling Stone* Interview," 88; *Memphis Commercial Appeal,* March 22, 1992, G1; Nager, *Memphis Beat,* 160.

33. Wexler on "Sam Phillips: The Man Who Invented Rock 'n' Roll."

34. Sam later tried to form a group of independent labels because he recognized that indies were selling out to the majors, but it was all in vain. Sam Phillips on "Sam Phillips: The Man Who Invented Rock 'n' Roll"; see also Nager, "Forty Years of Sun," G1–2.

35. Interview with Rufus Thomas, Oct. 8, 2000; Phillips on "Sam Phillips: The Man Who Invented Rock 'n' Roll."

36. Interview with Bob Lewis; interview with Jim Dickinson. Feathers is quoted on a private videotape in the possession of Bettye Berger.

37. Interview with Frank Berretta.

38. Interview with Bill Kirby, July 11, 1996.

39. Interview with Frank Berretta.

40. Johnson, "TV News and Views," Aug. 22, 1956, 24.
41. Booth, *Rhythm Oil,* 47.

Chapter 9: *Red, Hot and Blue:* The Hottest Cotton-Pickin' Thang
in the Country

1. Dewey was to be heard over stations ranging from WNJR-Newark, New Jersey, to WJAK-Jackson, Tennessee. "Rhythm 'n' Blues Ramblings," April, 1955, clipping, Dorothy Phillips Collection, Crump, Tenn.
2. Interview with George Klein, Aug. 3, 1988. Unless otherwise noted, all interviews are by the author.
3. Ibid.
4. Ibid.
5. Ibid.
6. Waters is quoted in Dewitt, *Elvis, the Sun Years,* 131.
7. Interview with George Klein, May 5, 1990.
8. Ibid. Raiteri interview with Don Nix.
9. Interview with George Klein, May 5, 1990. The nephew is quoted in Cohodas, *Spinning Blues into Gold,* 28.
10. See, for example, Nager, *Memphis Beat,* 129; Raiteri interview with Sam Phillips.
11. "Hungry DJ's a Growing Headache" (quotation); Wexler, "R. and B. Jockeys Ride Payola."
12. U.S. Congress, House Committee on Interstate and Foreign Commerce, *Responsibilities of Broadcasting Licensees,* pt. 2, 900; see also Eliot, *Rockonomics;* Jackson, *Big Beat Heat,* 257–59; and Segrave, *Payola in the Music Industry.*
13. Raiteri interview with Sam Phillips.
14. *New York Times,* May 20, 1960, 1, 62; Jackson, *Big Beat Heat,* 307–27; Selby, "They Knocked the Rock"; *Rock 'n' Roll Invaders;* Smith, *Pied Pipers,* 1–51; "Thirty Years of Payola," 1–29.
15. Cantor, *Wheelin' on Beale,* 81.
16. WDIA—attempting to raise the standard of gospel groups appearing on the station—broke a precedent during the early 1950s by refusing to take money for putting groups right off the street on the air. WDIA was the exception, however, because both small-time artists and record promoters continued to pay stations for air time to promote live appearances. Interview with Don Kern.
17. U.S. Congress, House Committee on Interstate and Foreign Commerce, *Communications Act Amendments,* pt. 1, 9–87; Eliot, *Rockonomics.* Many think that payola was not a problem until rock 'n' roll permeated American culture. It was legal, "but to those who viewed rock'n'roll as a corrupting influence, payola was a sure sign that evil forces were at work to capture the minds of white middle class America." Williams, "William T. 'Hoss' Allen," 109.

18. Ackerman, U.S. Congress, House Committee on Interstate and Foreign Commerce, *Communications Act Amendments,* pt. 2, 903.

19. This practice—not much different from openly buying commercial time—was quite common. Many record companies had contracts with various stations to pay a specific amount a week for a specific number of record plays. One even gave Christmas presents regularly, using lists marked from A through D based on amount of time played. "The ones in the high [i.e., A] category got the larger sums, and those in the lower category got the smaller sums." U.S. Congress, House Committee on Interstate and Foreign Commerce, *Communications Act Amendments,* pt. 1, 413–19, 632–36; interview with Don Kern; interview with George Klein, Aug. 3, 1988; interview with Gordon Lawhead.

20. Oren Harris, Congress, House Committee on Interstate and Foreign Commerce, *Communications Act Amendments,* pt. 1, 331.

21. Dewitt, *Elvis, the Sun Years,* 131; Raiteri interview with Don Nix; interview with Bill Gordon.

22. Interview with Bill Kirby, May 28, 1996. Dewey did receive a "talent fee" from Herb Saddler beyond his regular salary. It was and still is, however, a common (and quite legal) practice for sponsors to pay extra money to ensure that their product is advertised by a specific deejay. Thus, the payment is not considered payola. Interview with Gordon Lawhead.

23. Nager, *Memphis Beat,* 129

24. U.S. Congress, House Committee on Interstate and Foreign Commerce, *Communications Act Amendments,* pt. 2, 1148–52.

25. Bob Shad to Dewey Phillips, Oct. 27, 1953, and John Cleghorn to Bob Shad, Oct. 29, 1953, both in Raiteri Collection, Memphis.

26. Dewey Phillips in *Daddy-O-Dewey;* interview with Bill Kirby, May 28, 1996.

27. Dewey Phillips on *Red, Hot and Blue;* interview with Jim Dickinson; Raiteri interview with Stanley Booth.

28. Dewey Phillips on *Red, Hot and Blue;* Raiteri interview with Abe Schwab.

29. Interview with Louis Harris.

30. Raiteri interview with Sam Phillips.

31. Interview with Sam Phillips.

32. Sam Phillips in *Daddy-O-Dewey.*

33. Ibid. Dorothy Phillips confirms that Sam did indeed generously help the Phillips family. Interview with Dorothy Phillips, July 8, 1994.

34. Jackson, *Big Beat Heat,* 307–27.

35. Interview with George Klein, Aug. 3, 1988.

36. Ibid.

37. Raiteri interview with Billy Lee Riley.

38. Jack Parnell, a contemporary deejay, is convinced that Dewey never took payola because he was content with his financial situation at the time. Parnell attributes Dewey's lack of wealth to his unwillingness to ask the radio station for more money. "Dewey was extremely naive. I don't think he knew how popular

he was," Parnell says. If he had, "he probably would have lost his ability to be Dewey Phillips straight." Jack Parnell in *Rock 'n' Roll Invaders.*

39. Interview with George Klein, June 7, 1989; Guralnick, *Last Train to Memphis,* 99. Guralnick contrasts Dewey with Alan Freed, who was "as flamboyant as Dewey and as opportunistic in business as Dewey was lacking in business sense" (176).

40. Interview with George Klein, Aug. 3, 1988.

41. Ibid.

Chapter 10: Dewey and Elvis: The Synthesized Sound

1. Gates, "Good Rockin'," 54–55.

2. Mattfeld, *Variety Music Cavalcade,* 572; Murrells, *Million-Selling Records.*

3. Ibid. *Billboard* kept its new name designation until 1957, when the column labeled "Rhythm and Blues Notes," was renamed "On the Beat—Rhythm & Blues—Rock and Roll." *Billboard,* Jan. 26, Feb. 16, 1957; Fred Cook interview. Unless otherwise noted, all interviews are by the author.

4. George, *Death of Rhythm and Blues,* 26. Jordan still ranks fourth among R&B artists in terms of record sales and chart longevity. Chilton, *Let the Good Times Roll;* Koch, "Jordan."

5. Jordan's quote is cited in George, *Death of Rhythm and Blues,* 19–20; see also Barlow, *Looking Up,* 334–35.

6. Another popular choice is Wynonie Harris's 1947 hit "Good Rockin' To-night." The debate still rages, but the Rock 'n' Soul Museum in Memphis, which houses the Smithsonian Institution's "Rock 'n' Soul: Social Crossroads" permanent exhibition, labels "Rocket 88" as the first rock 'n' roll song.

7. Pichaske, *A Generation in Motion,* 37; *Memphis Commercial Appeal,* Sept. 28, 1993; Morrison, *Go Cat Go!*

8. Marion Keisker cited in Marcus, *Mystery Train,* 170–71.

9. For good discussions of the complicated origins of rockabilly, see Morrison, *Go Cat Go!* and Tucker, "Rethinking Elvis," 19–28.

10. Kaye, "The Memphis Blues Again," 75ff.; Daniel, *Lost Revolutions,* 132

11. Sam Phillips is quoted in Palmer, "Sam Phillips: The Sun King," 36.

12. Peiser, McDaniel, and Allen interview with B.B. King, Center for Southern Folklore Archives.

13. Malone, *Country Music U.S.A.;* Tosches, *Country;* Cobb, *The Most Southern Place,* 299.

14. *Memphis Commercial Appeal,* Oct. 21, 1948, 1.

15. Christgau, *Any Old Way You Choose It,* 279.

16. Raiteri interview with Eddie Richardson.

17. Raiteri interview with Jim Dickinson; interview with Charles Raiteri.

18. Interview with Jack Parnell.

19. Don Kern, WDIA's production manager, says the station was certain whites

were listening because sponsors frequently reported whites responding to the commercials run on the station. Interview with Don Kern.

20. George, *Death of Rhythm and Blues,* xii. On the connection between rhythm and blues and rock 'n' roll, see Redd, *Rock Is Rhythm and Blues.*

21. Rufus Thomas on *Sun Days with Elvis.*

22. Interview with David Evans.

23. Bland is quoted in McKee and Chisenhall, *Beale Black and Blue,* 249; see also "Bobby Bland," 42; Raiteri interview with B.B. King; interview with Rufus Thomas, June 12, 1995; and interview with Robert "Honeymoon" Garner.

24. Interview with George Klein, May 28, 1996; Raiteri interview with Barbara Pittman; Goldman, *Elvis;* Guralnick, *Last Train to Memphis.*

25. Shaw, "Sam Phillips Interview," 6.

26. Forbess is quoted in Morthland, "Elvis: The King Remembered," 45.

27. Johnson, "TV News and Views," May 4, 1956, 25.

28. Johnson, "TV News and Views," March 18, 1958, 19.

Chapter 11: Dewey Introduces Elvis to the World

1. For a good summary of the current status of the debate, see Guralnick, *Last Train to Memphis,* 507n147.

2. Guida interview with Bernard Lansky, Center for Southern Folklore Archives; see also Dewitt, *Elvis, the Sun Years,* 75, 91–95, 103, 141.

3. Cantor, *Wheelin' on Beale,* 190 (author's note).

4. Interview with George Klein, May 5, 1990; interview with Sam Phillips; interview with Gordon Lawhead. Unless otherwise noted, all interviews are by the author.

5. "Growing Up with Elvis," 30; Freeman, "Interview with George Klein," 18; interview with Betty Phillips Kirby, May 28, 1996. Hazen and Freeman, *Memphis Elvis-Style,* speculates that Dewey may have emceed a show for Elvis at the Eagle's Nest, a nightclub located in the Clearpool entertainment complex, as early as 1953. The story is based on only one eyewitness account, however, and even Hazen and Freeman acknowledge its shaky verification. "Because the story is undocumented," they point out, "its truth may be in doubt" (74).

6. Booth, "A Hound Dog to the Manor Born," 48.

7. Raiteri interview with Sam Phillips; Escott and Hawkins, *Good Rockin' Tonight,* 62.

8. Interview with Herbie O'Mell. O'Mell says he continued the gigs until Elvis announced that he could get $150 for playing Saturday nights at the Eagle's Nest.

9. Interview with Jim Dickinson.

10. Guralnick, *Last Train to Memphis,* 507n147.

11. Interview tapes with Robert Henry for "Beale Street Black and Blue" transcripts, Memphis Room, Shelby County Public Library and Information Center.

12. Raiteri interview with Robert Henry.

13. McDaniel interview with Andrew "Sunbeam" Mitchell, Less interview of Andrew "Sunbeam" Mitchell, and McDaniel interview with Mrs. Robert Henry, all Center for Southern Folklore Archives.

14. Interview with Robert "Honeymoon" Garner; Peiser, McDaniel, and Allen interview with B.B. King, Center for Southern Folklore Archives.

15. McKee and Chisenhall, *Beale Black and Blue,* 95.

16. Interview tapes with Nat D. Williams for "Beale Street Black and Blue" transcripts, Memphis Room, Shelby County Public Library and Information Center.

17. Peiser, McDaniel, and Allen interview with B.B. King; Peiser and McDaniel interview with B.B. King; McDaniel interview with Mrs. Robert Henry.

18. Guralnick, *Last Train to Memphis,* 147–48.

19. Interview with Dorothy Phillips, July 8, 1994; Guralnick, *Last Train to Memphis,* 105.

20. Guralnick, *Last Train to Memphis,* 99–100; see also Moore, *That's Alright, Elvis,* 62.

21. Moore, *That's Alright, Elvis,* 63; Johnson, "TV News and Views," Feb. 5, 1959. Sun Records' Jack Clements reports the same response after Dewey's initial play: "Dewey Phillips had played it the night before on his show and. . . . everybody in town was talking about it." Jack Clements on "Sam Phillips: The Man Who Invented Rock 'n' Roll."

22. Raiteri interview with Sam Phillips; Raiteri interview with Dorothy Phillips.

23. Raiteri interview with Dorothy Phillips.

24. Raiteri interview with Sam Phillips; Johnson, "TV News and Views," Feb. 5, 1955, 9; Moore, *That's Alright, Elvis,* 64–65.

25. Moore, *That's Alright, Elvis;* Hazen and Freeman, *Memphis Elvis-Style,* 74, 77; Dewitt, *Elvis, the Sun Years,* 301.

26. Stanley, *The Elvis Encyclopedia;* Booth, "A Hound Dog to the Manor Born," 48; "Growing Up with Elvis," 30.

27. Interview with Dorothy Phillips, June 11, 1993; "Growing Up with Elvis," 30; Nager, "Dewey Took Giant Steps," C3; interview with Billy Britt Mills; interview with Sam Phillips.

28. Elvis is quoted in *Memphis Commercial Appeal,* Sept. 29, 30, 1968, 2:6; see also Booth, "A Hound Dog to the Manor Born," 48.

29. The first person to report that Dewey had purposely asked Elvis where he went to school in order to verify his race was Stanley Booth ("A Hound Dog to the Manor Born," 48). Dewey told Booth that story toward the end of his life, when the men were very close.

30. Johnson, "TV News and Views," Feb. 5, 1955, 9.

31. Sam Phillips comments are taken from Raiteri, liner notes for *Dewey Phillips;* Sam Phillips in *Daddy-O-Dewey* and private videotape in the possession of Bettye Berger. Elvis's reception in the black community was equally unenthusiastic.

"They talked about him something terrible," Little Milton Campbell has said. "They treated him terrible. A lot of people say he stole [black music]." Campbell on "Sam Phillips: The Man Who Invented Rock 'n' Roll"; see also Bertrand, *Race, Rock, and Elvis*, 199–204; and Dewitt, *Elvis, the Sun Years*, 150.

32. Jerry Wexler on "Sam Phillips: The Man Who Invented Rock 'n' Roll."

33. Freeman, "Interview with Calvin Newborn," 16. Sam Phillips's comments are taken from Raiteri, liner notes for *Dewey Phillips*.

34. Interview with Jerry Schilling; Marion Keisker on "Sam Phillips: The Man Who Invented Rock 'n' Roll."

35. Jim Dickinson on "Sam Phillips: The Man Who Invented Rock 'n' Roll"; Sam Phillips in *Daddy-O-Dewey;* Raiteri, interview with Sam Phillips; see also Johnson, "Good Evening," June 20, 1972, 7.

36. Raiteri interview with Sam Phillips; Raiteri interview with John King.

37. Guralnick, *Last Train to Memphis*, 205–6.

38. Walker is cited in Hazen and Freeman, *Memphis Elvis-Style*, 76–77.

39. Interview with Fred Cook; interview with Sam Phillips; interview with George Klein, May 5, 1990.

40. Wink Martindale on *Sun Days with Elvis*.

41. Howard, "The Front Row," 23. Howard, the editor's son, says that Robert Johnson was his mentor and frequently asked him to cover various assignments such as interviews and reviews for him. Interview with Edwin Howard; Guralnick, *Last Train to Memphis*, 108–9.

42. Raiteri interview with Don Nix.

43. Williams, "Willilam T. 'Hoss' Allen," 32.

44. Guralnick, *Last Train to Memphis*, 108–11; Guralnick and Jorgensen, *Elvis Day by Day*, 18–19; Nager, *Memphis Beat*, 155; Dewitt, *Elvis, the Sun Years*, 153; Ringel, "A Star Is Born," 75. Dye's photos of the later 1955 concert can be seen in Ringel, "A Star Is Born," 74; and Guralnick and Jorgensen, *Elvis Day by Day*, 44.

45. Guralnick, *Elvis Day by Day*, 31.

46. Dewey's quotations are taken from Booth, "A Hound Dog to the Manor Born," 48.

47. Osborne, *Elvis*, 34–40.

48. Ibid.

49. Ibid.

50. Booth, *Rhythm Oil*, 64.

51. Johnson, "TV News and Views," July 5, 1956, 19; Booth, "A Hound Dog to the Manor Born," 49–50.

Chapter 12: The King and His Court Jester: Men-Children in the Promised Land

1. Raiteri interview with Sam Phillips.

2. Interview with Billy Britt Mills; interview with George Klein, June 7, 1989; interview with Dorothy Phillips, Aug. 8, 1995; Raiteri interview with Barbara Pitt-

man; Booth, "A Hound Dog to the Manor Born," 108. Unless otherwise noted, all interviews are by the author.

3. Interview with Max and Betty Jo Carruthers, July 16, 1996.

4. Interview with Bill "Bear" McClain.

5. Raiteri interview with Dickie Lee; Booth, "A Hound Dog to the Manor Born," 48, 108; Booth, *Rhythm Oil*, 63–64; Raiteri interview with James Parks.

6. Interview with Bob Lewis.

7. Juanico's account is from Whitmer, *The Inner Elvis*, 218–19; Raiteri interview with Sam Phillips; Escott and Hawkins, *Good Rockin' Tonight*, 90.

8. Raiteri interview with Jerry Phillips; Raiteri interview with Randy Phillips.

9. Interview with George Klein, June 7,1989; interview with Bob Lewis.

10. Hazen and Freeman, *Memphis Elvis-Style*, 66; interview with Dorothy Phillips, Aug. 8, 1995.

11. Raiteri interview with Becky Phillips; Raiteri interview with Randy Phillips.

12. Interview with Billy Britt Mills.

13. Interview with Randy Phillips.

14. Ibid.

15. Ibid.; interview with Dorothy Phillips, Aug. 8, 1995; see also "Growing Up with Elvis," 34.

16. Interview with Billy Britt Mills.

17. Interview with Dorothy Phillips, Aug. 8, 1995.

18. Ibid.; Guralnick and Jorgensen, *Elvis Day by Day,* 89. Dewey almost didn't get to see Presley perform on the Sullivan show. He telephoned his friend Robert Johnson from New York to report that the demand for tickets made them "almost impossible to get. . . . even with Elvis and Col. Parker doing all they could for him." Later, Dewey telephoned Johnson again and said a "miracle had been worked and he was in." Johnson, "TV News and Views," Oct. 30, 1956, 25.

19. Interview with George Klein, June 7, 1989; interview with Herbie O'Mell.

20. Interview with Billy Britt Mills.

21. Interview with George Klein, June 7, 1989.

22. Interview with Billy Britt Mills.

23. Interview with George Klein, June 7, 1989; see also "Growing Up with Elvis," 34.

24. "Growing up with Elvis," 34; Fortas, *Elvis: From Memphis to Hollywood,* 58.

25. Raiteri interview with Dickie Lee; interview with George Klein, June 7, 1989.

26. Presley is quoted in the *Memphis Press-Scimitar,* Sept. 1, 1956.

27. [Untitled], *TV Guide,* Sept. 22–28, 1956, 19, Dorothy Phillips Collection, Crump, Tenn.

28. Raiteri interview with Abe Schwab.

29. Johnson, "TV News and Views," Oct. 17, 1956, 1.

30. Johnson, "TV News and Views," June 7, 1957, 13.

31. Ibid.

32. For a good summary of what happened while Dewey was visiting Elvis in Hollywood, see Johnson's account, "Those Reports True," 15, 30; see also Raiteri, liner notes for *Dewey Phillips;* and Guralnick and Jorgensen, *Elvis Day by Day,* 105.

33. Johnson, "Those Reports True," 15, 30.

34. Ibid.; see also Raiteri interview with Don Nix; Raiteri interview with Sam Phillips; Raiteri interview with Jim Dickinson; and Guralnick, *Last Train to Memphis,* 419, 424–25.

35. Johnson, "Those Reports True," 15, 30.

36. Ibid.

37. Ibid.

38. Raiteri interview with Barbara Pittman.

39. Johnson, "Those Reports True," 15, 30.

40. Raiteri interview with Dickie Lee.

41. Raiteri interview with Sam Phillips.

42. Johnson, "TV News and Views," Aug. 22, 1956, 24.

43. Johnson, "TV News and Views," March 7, 1961, 10.

44. Johnson, "TV News and Views," March 18, 1958, 19; interview with Billy Britt Mills.

Chapter 13: "Red Hot at First . . . Blue at the Very End"

1. Johnson, "Good Evening," Oct. 1, 1968, 5; Sam Phillips on "Sam Phillips: The Man Who Invented Rock 'n' Roll"; "Rhythm 'n' Blues Ramblings," clipping dated April 1955, Dorothy Phillips Collection, Crump, Tenn.

2. Johnson, "TV News and Views," Aug. 22, 1956, 24; Mitchell, "New Dewey Phillips TV Show," 10. For viewers' comments on the show, see Johnson, "TV News and Views," Aug. 29, 1956, 22.

3. Mitchell, "New Dewey Phillips TV Show."

4. Interview with Durrell Durham. Unless otherwise noted, all interviews are by the author.

5. Raiteri interview with Sam Phillips; interview with Billy Britt Mills; interview with George Klein, May 28, 1996.

6. Johnson, "TV News and Views," Jan. 3, 1958, 19; interview with Gordon Lawhead; Gordon, *It Came from Memphis,* 22–23.

7. Haspel, "Tell 'Em Philips Sencha," 139; Gordon, *It Came from Memphis,* 23; Lance Russell in *Daddy-O-Dewey.*

8. Interview with Durrell Durham; *Memphis Press-Scimitar,* Jan. 14, 1958, 5. Durham told Robert Gordon essentially the same story (*It Came from Memphis,* 23).

9. Ibid.

10. Grumbles comments are quoted by Johnson in the *Memphis Press-Scimitar,* Jan. 14, 1958, 5.

11. Ibid.

12. Interview with Charles Raiteri.

13. *Memphis Commercial Appeal,* Sept. 4, 1950, 1–3; *Memphis Press-Scimitar,* Sept. 4, 1950, 1–2, Sept. 5, 1950, 5. The man in the other car accused Dewey of causing the accident, sued him, and settled out of court for about $2,500.

14. Dewitt, *Elvis, the Sun Years,* 148.

15. Interview with Jack Parnell; interview with Durrell Durham.

16. Interview with Gordon Lawhead; interview with Jack Parnell; interview with Sam Phillips; Raiteri interview with Dickie Lee.

17. Raiteri interview with Nate Evans.

18. Raiteri interview with Sam Phillips; Raiteri interview with Jim Dickinson.

19. Raiteri interview with Dorothy Phillips.

20. Raiteri interview with Sam Phillips; interview with Abe Schwab, May 28, 1995.

21. Raiteri interview with Dorothy Phillips.

22. Accounts of the accident have been gathered from the *Memphis Commercial Appeal* and the *Memphis Press-Scimitar.* Official records are unavailable. According to both the Arkansas and Tennessee Highway Patrol it was then "normal procedure to destroy old records after a certain period of time." This procedure was verified by John Dougan, archivist at the Memphis Shelby County Records Office, who told me on March 15, 2003, that, "The Highway Patrol Office [both Tennessee and Arkansas] usually do not keep their records long at all."

23. Silver, "Six Dead," 1, 3; Porteous, "Three Memphians Die," 1–2; "Dewey Phillips Still Critical," 5.

24. "Dewey Phillips Still Critical," 5; interview with Billy Britt Mills.

25. Raiteri interview with Sam Phillips.

26. Raiteri interview with Dorothy Phillips; Raiteri interview with Becky Phillips.

27. Raiteri interview with Dickie Lee.

28. Raiteri interview with Dorothy Phillips.

29. Interview with Bill "Bear" McClain.

30. "Disk Jockey Phillips Badly Hurt Again," 1; interview with Betty Jo Carruthers, July 16, 1996.

31. Raiteri interview with Dorothy Phillips.

32. "Disk Jockey Phillips Badly Hurt Again," 1.

33. Interview with Bob Lewis.

34. Ibid; interview with Bill Kirby, July 11, 1996; Raiteri interview with Betty Phillips Kirby.

35. Interview with Bob Lewis.

36. Interview with Charles Raiteri.

37. Interview with Sam Phillips.

38. Interview with Jack Parnell.

39. *Memphis Press-Scimitar,* July 19, 1954, 24, July 28, 1954, 15; interview with Gordon Lawhead; interview with Ron Meroney.

40. *Memphis Press-Scimitar,* July 19, 1954, 24, July 28, 1954, 15; interview with Jack Parnell; interview with Sam Phillips.

41. *Memphis Press-Scimitar,* July 19, 1954, 24, July 28, 1954, 15; interview with Gordon Lawhead; interview with Alex Ward.

42. Interview with Alex Ward.

43. Ibid.

44. Raiteri interview with John Fry.

45. Interview with Jack Parnell.

46. Burke, "Dewey Phillips Set for Shiloh Honor," 5.

47. Grumbles is quoted in Johnson, "WHBQ Radio Will End Affiliation," 25; interview with Jack Parnell.

48. Raiteri interview with Sam Phillips.

49. Interview with Jack Parnell.

50. Raiteri interview with Larry Caughlin.

51. Ibid.

52. Raiteri interview with Don Nix.

53. Raiteri interview with Sam Phillips; Raiteri interview with Don Nix; interview with Jim Dickinson.

54. Interview with Bill Kirby, July 11, 1996.

55. Ibid.; Raiteri interview with Barbara Pittman.

56. Sam Phillips is quoted in Ellis, "Music Kingmaker," F4.

57. Raiteri interview with Sam Phillips.

Chapter 14: The Final Descent: "If Dewey Couldn't Be Number One, He Didn't Wanna Be"

1. Raiteri interview with Dorothy Phillips; Raiteri interview with Sam Phillips.

2. Interview with Betty Phillips Kirby, May 28, 1996; interview with Marjorie Phillips Barba. Unless otherwise noted, all interviews are by the author.

3. Interview with Dorothy Phillips; interview with Bill Kirby, July 11, 1996.

4. Interview with Randy Phillips, May 31, 1994.

5. Raiteri interview with Sam Phillips.

6. Interview with Betty Phillips Kirby, July 11, 1996; interview with Marjorie Phillips Barba; interview with Dorothy Phillips, Aug. 8, 1995.

7. Raiteri interview with Dickie Lee.

8. Raiteri interview with Jerry Phillips.

9. Interview with Marjorie Phillips Barba.

10. Interview with Dorothy Phillips, Aug. 8, 1995.

11. Johnson, "Good Evening," June 20, 1972, 7.

12. Raiteri interview with Stanley Booth; Raiteri interview with Jim Dickinson; interview with Jim Dickinson; interview with Dorothy Phillips, Aug. 8, 1995.

13. Interview with Dorothy Phillips, Aug. 8, 1995.

14. Raiteri interview with Jerry Phillips.

15. Interview with Marjorie Phillips Barba; interview with Betty Phillips Kirby, May 28, 1996.

16. Interview with Dorothy Phillips, Aug. 8, 1995.

17. Interview with Betty Phillips Kirby, May 28, 1996.

18. Interview with Charles Raiteri; interview with Dorothy Phillips, Aug. 8, 1995.

19. Robert Gordon says that Bill Quigley found an old acetate recording at a yard sale and taped a copy of it for him. The CD contains much of the material on the vinyl LP *Dewey Phillips: Red, Hot and Blue,* plus the Kennedy broadcasts.

20. Interview with Gordon Lawhead; interview with Jack Parnell; interview with Jerry Phillips.

21. Interview with Dorothy Phillips, Aug. 8, 1995.

22. Interview with Durrell Durham.

23. Johnson, "TV News and Views," Aug. 7, 1958, B4.

24. Interview with Dorothy Phillips, Aug. 8, 1995.

25. Interview with George Klein, June 7,1989.

26. Raiteri interview with Sam Phillips.

27. Johnson, "TV News and Views," Aug. 7, 1959, B4.

28. For a thorough discussion of WHHM's plan, see Johnson in the *Memphis Press-Scimitar,* Aug. 7, 1959. KWEM had changed its call letters to KWAM.

29. Ibid.

30. "He probably did his best radio shtick at WHHM," says Alex Ward, who has monitoried Dewey's career closely. "And nobody" he concludes in frustration, "has got so much as a tape on him during this period." Interview with Alex Ward.

31. Dewey Mills Phillips, Record of Arrests, Nov. 25, 1959, March 3, 1960; Johnson, "Good Evening," Oct. 1, 1968, 5.

32. Interview with Bob Lewis.

33. Raiteri interview with Jerry Phillips.

34. Raiteri interview with Bill Thomas, WGMM station manager interview.

35. Raiteri interview with Stan Kesler.

36. Raiteri interview with James Parks.

37. Dewey Mills Phillips, Record of Arrests, June 26, 1960, Feb. 16, Oct. 13, 1961.

38. Dewey Mills Phillips, Record of Arrests, Feb. 16, 1961; Raiteri interview with Sam Phillips.

39. Dewey Mills Phillips, Record of Arrests, Feb. 16, 1961.

40. Interview with Betty Phillips Kirby, May 28, 1996.

41. Interview with Billy Britt Mills.

Chapter 15: "Goodbye, Good People"

1. Dorothy Phillips interview, June 11, 1993. Unless otherwise noted, all interviews are by the author.

2. Raiteri interview with Dorothy Phillips; interview with Randy Phillips, May 31, 1994.

3. Interview with Betty Phillips Kirby, May 28, 1996; interview with Randy Phillips, Jan. 29, 2000; interview with Dorothy Phillips, June 11, 1993. Dot and Dewey's youngest son, Michael, died at twenty-four from colon cancer.

4. Raiteri interview with Barbara Pittman.

5. Interview with Marjorie Phillips Barba.

6. Interview with Betty Phillips Kirby, May 28, 1996.

7. Raiteri interview with Barbara Pittman.

8. Interview with Randy Phillips, Jan. 29, 2000.

9. Interview with Sam Phillips.

10. Interview with George Klein, June 7, 1989; Raiteri interview with Sam Phillips; Raiteri interview with Don Nix; interview with Randy Phillips, Jan. 29, 2000.

11. Interview with Jack Parnell.

12. Johnson, "Good Evening," June 20, 1972, 7.

13. Dewey Mills Phillips, Record of Arrests, March 6, 1961; Johnson, "TV News and Views," March 7, 1961, 10.

14. Raiteri interview with Dorothy Phillips.

15. Memphis City Court, Judges Trial Docket, Criminal, Dewey Phillips Docket no. E38297, 477–78. There may have been some previous history between these two. Dot thinks the druggist may have been one of those she "threatened to have arrested if he gave Dewey any more drugs." Interview with Dorothy Phillips, Aug. 8, 1995; "Pharmacist Accuses Dewey Phillips," 29.

16. Dewey Mills Phillips, Record of Arrests, Oct. 3, 1963.

17. *Memphis Press-Scimitar,* Oct. 4, 1963, 14.

18. Haspel, "Tell 'Em Philips Sencha," 142.

19. Raiteri interview with Bill Thomas; see also Rufus Thomas in *Daddy-O-Dewey.*

20. Johnson, "Good Evening," Oct. 1, 1968, 5.

21. Ibid.

22. Interview with George Klein, May 5, 1990.

23. Raiteri interview with Dickie Lee.

24. Raiteri interview with Reuben Cherry.

25. Interview with Bettye Berger, May 30, 1994; see also Raiteri, liner notes for *Dewey Phillips.*

26. Raiteri interview with Billy Lee Riley.

27. Interview with Alex Ward.

28. Ibid.

29. Johnson, "Good Evening," Oct. 30, 1968, 5.

30. Interview with Ron Meroney; Wexler, *Rhythm and the Blues,* 126.

31. Interview with Jack Parnell.

32. Interview with Betty Phillips Kirby, May 28,1996.

33. Raiteri interview with Randy Phillips.

34. Ibid.

35. Raiteri interview with Sam Phillips; Raiteri interview with Marjorie Phillips Barba.

36. Interview with Ron Meroney.

37. Raiteri interview with Barbara Pittman.

38. Interview with Ron Meroney; Raiteri interview with Barbara Pittman.

39. Kingsley, "Dewey Phillips Is Found Dead," 6; "Rites Tomorrow for Disc Jockey," 30; "Dewey Phillips, Forty-two, Disc Jockey, Dies," 32; Raiteri interview with Marjorie Phillips Barba.

40. Sam is quoted in Kingsley, "Dewey Phillips Is Found Dead," 2:6.

41. Jim Dickinson and Sam and Knox Phillips are quoted in Kingsley, "Dewey Phillips Is Found Dead," 2:6.

42. Dickie Lee is quoted in Kingsley, "Dewey Phillips Is Found Dead," 2:6.

43. Elvis is quoted in Kingsley, "Dewey Phillips Is Found Dead," 2:6.

44. Johnny Cash and Carl Perkins are quoted in Kingsley, "Dewey Phillips Is Found Dead," 2:6.

45. Raiteri interview with Barbara Pittman.

46. Interview with Jim Dickinson.

47. Raiteri interview with Sam Phillips.

48. Raiteri interview with Sam Phillips.

49. Memphis/National Funeral Home records file, Memphis Room, Shelby County Public Library and Information Center.

50. Interview with Dorothy Phillips, June 11, 1993.

51. Raiteri interview with Dickie Lee; Memphis/National Funeral Home records file.

52. Interview with Betty Phillips Kirby, July 11, 1996.

53. Raiteri interview with Dorothy Phillips.

54. West, *Elvis, What Happened?* 159.

55. Interview with Dorothy Phillips, July 8, 1994; Raiteri interview with Dorothy Phillips.

Chapter 16: The Legacy: The Next Generation and Beyond

1. Bowman, *Soulsville,* 23; interview with Jim Dickinson; Ellis, "Music Kingmaker," F1, F4; Nager, "Dewey Took Giant Steps," C1. Unless otherwise noted, all interviews are by the author.

2. MacDonald, *Don't Touch That Dial!* 368.

3. Interview tapes with Rufus Thomas, Memphis Room, Shelby County Public Library and Information Center.

4. Little Richard is quoted in *The* Rolling Stone *Interviews,* ed. Fong-Torres, 371. Ward, *Just My Soul Responding,* 44–45.

5. Peter Guralnick on "Sam Phillips: The Man Who Invented Rock 'n' Roll."

6. Sam Phillips on "Sam Phillips: The Man Who Invented Rock 'n' Roll"; Daniel, *Lost Revolutions,* 174. On black music breaking down white racial stereotypes, see also Ward, *Just My Soul Responding,* 50–52.

7. Daniel, *Lost Revolutions,* 148; see also Ward, *Just My Soul Responding.*

8. Interview with Bob Lewis; interview with Jerry Schilling.

9. Bertrand, *Race, Rock, and Elvis,* 121; *Rock 'n' Roll Invaders;* Neill, "Beale Street Remembered," 8, David Evans Collection.

10. Barlow, *Voice Over,* 168–71, 176. For a more elaborate discussion of the unusual hybrid of black and white deejays that produced rock 'n' roll, see George, *Death of Rhythm and Blues,* 39–57; Gillett, *Sound of the City,* 39–49; and Hoskyns, *Say It One Time,* 60–62.

11. Interview with Sam Phillips.

12. Because of disillusionment over the failure of the civil rights movement to achieve full racial integration in America, many have played down the importance of the races coming together musically as a prelude to integration. For a strong argument supporting music's importance, see Ward, *Just My Soul Responding.* On the more general connection between music and political protest, see Street, *Rebel Rock.*

13. Raiteri interview with Stanley Booth.

14. MacDonald, *Don't Touch That Dial!* 333–34; Ward, *Just My Soul Responding,* 33, 103.

15. Ward, *Just My Soul Responding,* 124.

16. Jim Dickinson on "Sam Phillips: The Man Who Invented Rock 'n' Roll"; Petreycik, "Interview with Sam Phillips," 56.

Bibliography

Interviews by the Author

All interviews conducted in Memphis, Tennessee, unless otherwise noted; the tapes are in the author's possession.

Alburty, Bob, July 22, 1994.

Barba, Marjorie Phillips, May 26, 1996.

Berretta, Frank, May 31, 1996.

Berger, Bettye, June 4, 1993; May 30, 1994.

Carruthers, Betty Jo, May 28, 1996 (Adamsville, Tenn.); July 16, 1996 (Crump, Tenn.).

Carruthers, Max, May 28, 1996 (Adamsville, Tenn.); July 16, 1996 (Crump, Tenn.).

Cook, Fred, July 11, 1997.

Dickinson, Jim, March 10, 1996.

Dougan, John, March 15, 2003.

Durham, Durrell, Feb. 23, 2000.

Evans, David, Aug. 11, 1990.

Frager, Natalie, June 10, 1996.

Garner, Robert "Honeymoon," May 5, 1995.

Gordon, Bill, by telephone, Oct. 9, 1997.

Harris, Louis, Aug. 2, 1996.

Howard, Edwin, by telephone, Dec. 11, 2001.

Kern, Don, July 18, 1989.

King, B.B., Aug. 30, 1990.

Kirby, Bill, May 28, July 11, 1996.

Kirby, Betty Phillips, May 28, July 11, 1996.

Klein, George, Aug. 3, 1988, June 7, 1989, May 5, 1990, May 28, 1996.

Lawhead, Gordon, June 8, 1994.

Leibowitz, Steve, May 4, 1996.
Lewis, Bob, May 21, 1996 (Jackson, Tenn.).
McClain, Bill "Bear," Feb. 16, 2000.
Meroney, Ron, June 3, 1995.
Mills, Billy Britt, Sept. 28, 1996 (Dayton, Ohio).
Neal, Roy, May 9, 1989.
Novarese, John, Jan. 4, 1994.
O'Mell, Herbie, Sept. 18, 2002.
Parnell, Jack, Aug. 1, 1996.
Phillips, Dorothy (Dot), June 11, 1993, July 8, 1994, Aug. 8, 1995 (all Crump,
    Tenn.).
Phillips, Randy, May 31, 1994, Jan. 29, 2000.
Phillips, Sam, May 28, 1993.
Raiteri, Charles, July 22, 1993.
Schatz, Irvin, by telephone, April 15, 2003.
Schilling, Jerry, Nov. 2, 2000.
Schwab, Abe, July 8, 1994, May 28, 1995, June 9, 1996.
Slate, Vassar, May 29, 1995.
Stegman, Harv, Aug. 4, 1996.
Thomas, Rufus, Aug. 9, 1994, June 12, Dec. 29, 1995, Oct. 8, 2000.
Tyler, Jewell Phillips, July 16, 1996 (Crump, Tenn.).
Ward, Alex, Nov. 3, 1999.

Interviews by Charles Raiteri

Transcripts are in Raiteri's possession

Barba, Marjorie Phillips
Booth, Stanley
Caughlin, Larry
Cherry, Reuben
Dickinson, Jim
Evans, David
Fry, John
Henry, Robert
Hutchinson, Laddie
Jackson, Wayne
Kesler, Stan
King, B.B.
King, John
Klein, George
Lansky, Bernard
Lee, Dickie
Nix, Don

Parks, James
Phillips, Becky
Phillips, Dorothy (Dot)
Phillips, Knox
Phillips, Jerry
Phillips, Randy
Phillips, Sam
Pittman, Barbara
Richardson, Eddie (High School)
Riley, Billy Lee
Roy, Welton M.
Schwab, Abe
Thomas, Bill
Thomas, Rufus
Van Meter, H. E.

Special Collections

Center for Southern Folklore Archives, Memphis, Tenn.

Andrew "Sunbeam" Mitchell. Interview by George McDaniel, March 16, 1983.
———. Interview by David Less, June 6, 1979.
B.B. King. Interview by Judy Peiser and George McDaniel, May 7, 1983.
———. Interview by Judy Peiser, George McDaniel, and Ray Allen, April 1, 1981.
Bernard Lansky. Interview by Louis Guida, Feb. 15, 1983.
Ernest Withers. Interview by Ray Allen and George McDaniel, June 12, 1981.
Ida Cherry. Interview by Judy Peiser, Aug. 11, 1994, Beale Street Tape Transcripts.
Jake Salky. Interview by Judy Peiser, Feb. 10, 1983.
(Mrs.) Robert Henry, widow of Robert Henry. Interview by George McDaniel, Feb. 10, 1983.
Natalie Frager. Interview by Judy Peiser, Aug. 11, 1994, Beale Street Tape Transcripts.
Phil Zerilla. Interview by Ray Allen and George McDaniel, June 17, 1981.

Memphis Room, Shelby County Public Library and Information Center

Interview tapes with Mrs. Anselmo Borasso for "Beale Street Black and Blue" transcripts, Sept. 4, 1973, box 60, 12, Oral History Collection.
Interview tapes by Nat D. Williams for "Beale Street Black and Blue" transcripts, Feb. 2, 1973, box 60, 1–39, 1–37, Oral History Collection.
Memphis/National Funeral Home records file.
Oral history interview with Nat D. Williams by Ronald Anderson Walter, Sept. 13, 1976.

Interview tapes with Robert Henry for "Beale Street Black and Blue" transcripts, Oct. 15, 1972, box 60, 40, Oral History Collection.

Interview tapes with Rufus Thomas for "Beale Street Black and Blue" transcripts, Oct. 9, 1973, box 59, 12, Oral History Collection.

Special Collections, University of Memphis

Kip Lornell interviews with Ford Nelson, Theo Wade, and Shirley and Jet Bledsoe, Special Collections, University of Memphis Libraries.

Private Collections

Bettye Berger, David Evans, Dorothy Phillips, Charles Raiteri, Chris Spindel, and Alex Ward.

Other Sources

Baker, Jackson. "We Flat-Ass Changed the World." *Memphis Flyer,* June 8–14, 2000, 19–22.

Barlow, William. *Looking Up at Down: The Emergence of Blues Culture.* Philadelphia: Temple University Press, 1989.

———. *Voice Over: The Making of Black Radio.* Philadelphia: Temple University Press, 1999.

Bertrand, Michael T. *Race, Rock, and Elvis.* Urbana: University of Illinois Press, 2000.

Bloom, Jack M. *Class, Race and the Civil Rights Movement.* Bloomington: Indiana University Press, 1987.

"Bobby Bland." *The Tennessean,* Aug. 3, 1978, 42

Booth, Stanley. "A Hound Dog to the Manor Born." *Esquire,* Feb. 1968, 106–8, 48–52.

———. *Rhythm Oil: A Journey through the Music of the American South.* New York: Pantheon Books, 1991.

Bowman, Rob. *Soulsville, U.S.A.: The Story of Stax Records.* New York: Schirmer Books, 1997.

"Boyle Keeps Eyes on Nineteen Negroes." *Memphis Press-Scimitar,* Dec. 11, 1940, 1.

Burke, Bill. "Dewey Phillips Set for Shiloh Honor." *Memphis Press-Scimitar,* June 23, 1985, 5.

Burnett, Brown. "The Blues." *Memphis Commercial Appeal,* Dec. 9, 1984, H5.

Cantor, Louis. *Wheelin' on Beale.* New York: Pharos Press, 1992.

Capers, Gerald M., Jr. *The Biography of a River Town: Memphis, Its Heroic Age.* Chapel Hill: University of North Carolina Press, 1939.

Chadwick, Vernon, ed. *In Search of Elvis: Music, Race, Art, Relgion.* Boulder: Westview Press, 1997.

Chaffin, Tom. "DJ: First Soul Brother of the Airwaves." *Atlanta Journal/Atlanta Constitution,* Feb. 9, 1992, M1–M4.

Charters, Samuel. "Workin' on the Building: Roots and Influences." In *Nothing but the Blues: The Music and the Musicians,* edited by Lawrence Cohn et al., 20. New York: Abbeville Press, 1993.

Chilton, John. *Let the Good Times Roll: The Story of Louis Jordan and His Music.* Ann Arbor: University of Michigan Press, 1992.

Christgau, Robert. *Any Old Way You Choose It.* New York: Penguin, 1973.

Church, Annette E., and Roberta Church. *The Robert B. Churches of Memphis: A Father and Son Who Achieved in Spite of Race.* Ann Arbor: Edwards Bros., 1974.

Clayton, Rose, and Dick Heard, eds. *Elvis Up Close: In the Words of Those Who Knew Him Best.* New York: Turner Publishing, 1994.

Clements, Ida. "'Phillips Sent Me' Has Become Vital Part of City's Lexicon." *Memphis Commercial Appeal,* June 9, 1950, 12.

Cobb, James C. *The Most Southern Place on Earth: The Mississippi Delta and the Roots of Regional Identity.* New York: Oxford University Press, 1992.

Cohn, Lawrence et al., eds. *Nothing but the Blues: The Music and the Musicians.* New York: Abbeville Press, 1993.

Cohodas, Nadine. *Spinning Blues into Gold: The Legendary Chess Records.* New York: St. Martin's Press, 2000.

Coppock, Paul. *Memphis Memoirs.* Memphis: Memphis State University Press, 1980.

———. "Mid-South Memoirs." *Memphis Commercial Appeal,* Oct. 28, 1979, G7.

Daniel, Pete. *Lost Revolutions: The South in the 1950s.* Chapel Hill: University of North Carolina Press, 2000.

Davis, Francis. *History of the Blues.* New York: Hyperion, 1995.

"Dewey Phillips, Forty-two, Disk Jockey, Dies." *Memphis Press-Scimitar,* Sept. 30, 1968, 32.

"Dewey Phillips still Critical." *Memphis Press-Scimitar,* Sept. 5, 1950, 5.

Dewitt, Howard A. *Elvis, the Sun Years: The Story of Elvis Presley in the Fifties.* Ann Arbor: Popular Culture, 1993.

"Disc Jockey Phillips Badly Hurt Again." *Memphis Press-Scimitar,* March 10, 1952, 11.

Dickerson, James L. *Goin' Back to Memphis: A Century of Blues, Rock 'n' Roll and Glorious Soul.* New York: Cooper Square Press, 1996.

Dittmer, John. *Local People: the Struggle for Civil Rights in Mississippi.* Urbana: University of Illinois Press, 1994.

Dowdy, G. Wayne. "Censoring Popular Culture: Political and Social Control in Segregated Memphis." *West Tennessee Historical Society Papers* 55 (Dec. 2001): 98–117.

Egerton, John. *Speak Now against the Day: The Generation before the Civil Rights Movement in the South.* New York: Alfred A. Knopf, 1994.

Eliot, Marc. *Rockonomics: The Money behind the Music.* New York: Franklin Watts, 1989.

Ellis, Bill. "Music Kingmaker." *Memphis Commercial Appeal,* Aug. 14, 1999, F1, F4.

Ertegun, Ahmet. "Great Sound Is No Great Secret." *Billboard,* Jan. 13, 1958, 24, 39.

Escott, Colin, and Martin Hawkins. *Good Rockin' Tonight: Sun Records and the Birth of Rock 'n' Roll.* New York: St. Martin's Press, 1991.

———. *Sun Records: The Brief History of the Legendary Record Label.* New York: Quick Fox, 1975.

Evans, David. "Goin' Up the Country: Blues in Texas and the Deep South." In *Nothing but the Blues: The Music and the Musicians,* edited by Lawrence Cohn et al., 81. New York: Abbeville Press, 1993.

Fairclough, Adam. *Race and Democracy: The Civil Rights Struggle in Louisiana, 1915–1972.* Athens: University of Georgia Press, 1995.

Faragher, Scott, and Katherine Harrington. *Memphis in Vintage Postcards.* Charleston, S.C.: Arcadia Publishing, 2000.

Filene, Benjamin. *Romancing the Folk: Public Memory and American Roots Music.* Chapel Hill: University of North Carolina Press, 2000.

"First Soul Brother of the Airwaves." *Atlanta Journal/Atlanta Constitution,* Feb. 9, 1992, M1, M4.

Floyd, John. *Sun Records: An Oral History.* New York: Avon Books, 1998.

Fong-Torres, Ben, ed. *The* Rolling Stone *Interviews,* vol. 2. New York: Warner Books, 1973.

"Forgotten 15,000,000." *Sponsor,* Oct. 10, 1949, 25.

Fortas, Alan. *Elvis: From Memphis to Hollywood.* Ann Arbor: Popular Culture, 1992.

Fox, Jesse W. "Beale Street and the Blues." *West Tennessee Historical Society Papers* 13 (1959): 129.

Fox, Ted. *In the Groove: The People behind the Music,* 127. New York: St. Martin's Press, 1986.

Freed, Alan. "I Told You So." *Downbeat,* Sept. 19, 1956, 44.

Freeman, Mike. "Interview with Calvin Newborn." *Memphis Downtowner Magazine* 2 (Jan. 1993): 16.

———. "Interview with George Klein." *Memphis Downtowner Magazine* 7 (Dec. 1998): 18.

Gates, David. "Good Rockin'." *Newsweek,* Aug. 18, 1997, 54–55.

George, Nelson. *The Death of Rhythm and Blues.* New York: Plume, 1988.

Gillett, Charlie. *Making Tracks: Atlantic Records and the Growth of a Multi-Billion-Dollar Industry.* New York: E. P. Dutton, 1974.

———. *The Sound of the City: The Rise of Rock and Roll,* rev. and expanded ed. New York: Pantheon, 1983.

Goldman, Albert. *Elvis.* New York: McGraw Hill, 1981.

Gordon, Robert. *Can't Be Satisfied: The Life and Times of Muddy Waters.* Boston: Little, Brown, 2002.

———. *It Came from Memphis.* Boston: Faber and Faber, 1995.

"Growing Up with Elvis: The George Klein Interview." *Goldmine,* Aug. 7, 1992, 32.

Guralnick, Peter. *Last Train to Memphis: The Rise of Elvis Presley.* New York: Little Brown, 1994.

———. "Million Dollar Quartet." *New York Times Magazine,* March 25, 1979, 30.

———, and Ernst Jorgensen. *Elvis Day by Day.* New York: Ballantine Books, 1999.

Halberstam, David. *The Fifties.* New York: Villard Books, 1993.

Haspel, Randy. "Tell 'Em Philips Sencha: Dewey Phillips—the First Rock and Roll Deejay." *Memphis Magazine* 3 (June 1978): 134–42.

Hazen, Cindy, and Mike Freeman. *Memphis Elvis-Style.* New York: John F. Blair, 1997.

Heilbutt, Tony. *The Gospel Good News and Bad Times.* New York: E. P. Dutton, 1992.

Hoskyns, Barney. *Say It One Time for the Broken-Hearted.* Glasgow: Fontana, 1987.

Howard, Edwin. "The Front Row." *Memphis Press-Scimitar,* July 28, 1954, 23.

———. "Profit Sharing Announced by WHBQ." *Memphis Press-Scimitar,* March 19, 1951, 11.

Humphrey, Marke A. "Bright Lights, Big City: Urban Blues." In *Nothing but the Blues: The Music and the Musicians,* edited by Lawrence Cohn et al., 189. New York: Abbeville Press, 1993.

———. "Holy Blues: The Gospel Tradition." In *Nothing but the Blues: The Music and the Musicians,* edited by Lawrence Cohn et al., 112–13. New York: Abbeville Press, 1993.

"Hungry DJ's a Growing Headache." *Billboard,* Dec. 23, 1950, 1, 11, 42.

Hurley, Jack et al. *Pictures Tell the Story: Ernest C. Withers, Reflections in History.* Norfolk: Chrysler Museum of Art, 2000.

Hutchins, Fred L. "Beale Street as It Was." *West Tennessee Historical Society Papers* 26 (1972): 57.

Jackson, John A. *Big Beat Heat: Alan Freed and the Early Years of Rock and Roll.* New York: Macmillan, 1991.

Jalenak, James B. "Beale Street Politics: A Study of Negro Political Activity in Memphis, Tennessee." Undergraduate thesis, Yale University, Jan. 1961.

Johnson, Robert. "Those Reports True—Elvis and Dewey Had a Falling Out." *Memphis Press-Scimitar,* Aug. 28, 1957, 15, 30.

———. "TV News and Views" and "Good Evening." *Memphis Press-Scimitar,* Feb. 5, 1955; May 4, Aug. 22, Oct. 17, 1956; Aug. 21, Sept. 1, 1957; March 18, July 9, 1958; Aug. 7, 1959; March 7, 1961; Oct. 1, 1968; June 10, 1972.

———. "WHBQ Radio Will End Affiliation with ABC." *Memphis Press-Scimitar,* Sept. 30, 1957, 25.

Kaye, Elizabeth. "The Memphis Blues Again." *Rolling Stone,* Feb. 13, 1986, 75ff.

———. "The *Rolling Stone* Interview: Sam Phillips." *Rolling Stone,* Feb. 13, 1986, 53–59, 86–88.

Kennedy, Rick, and Randy McNutt. *Little Labels—Big Sound: Small Record Companies and the Rise of American Music.* Bloomington: Indiana University Press, 1999.

Kingsley, James. "Dewey Phillips Is Found Dead." *Memphis Commercial Appeal,* Sept. 29, 1968, 2:6.

Kirby, Edward "Prince Gabe." *From Africa to Beale Street.* New York: Lubin Press, 1993.

Koch, Stephen. "Jordan." In *Arkansas Biography: A Collection of Notable Lives,* edited by Nancy A. Williams, associate editor Jeannie M. Whayne, 156–57. Fayetteville: University of Arkansas Press, 2000.

Kramer, Gary. "Atlantic and R&B Trend Developed Side by Side." *Billboard,* 24, 38–39.

Lee, George W. *Beale Street: Where the Blues Began,* New York: Robert O. Ballou, 1934.

———. "Poetic Memories of Beale Street." *West Tennessee Historical Society Papers* 26 (1972): 68.

Lemann, Nicholas. *The Promised Land: The Great Black Migration and How It Changed America.* New York: Alfred A. Knopf, 1991.

Lewis, Virginia Emerson. "Fifty Years of Politics in Memphis, 1900–1950," Ph.D. diss., New York University, 1955.

Levine, Lawrence W. *Black Culture and Black Consciousness: Afro-American Folk Thought from Slavery to Freedom.* New York: Oxford University Press, 1977.

Lomax, Alan. *The Land Where the Blues Began.* New York: Pantheon, 1993.

Lornell, Kip. *Happy in the Service of the Lord: Afro-American Gospel Quartets in Memphis.* Urbana: University of Illinois Press, 1988.

Lott, Eric. *Love and Theft: Blackface Ministrelsy and the American Working Class.* New York: Oxford University Press, 1993.

Mabry, Donald. "The Rise and Fall of Ace Records: A Case Study in the Independent Record Business." *Business History Review* 64 (Autumn 1990): 411–50.

MacDonald, J. Fred. *Don't Touch That Dial! Radio Programming in American Life, 1920–1960.* Chicago: Nelson-Hall, 1979.

Magness, Perre. "Era of Film Censorship Lasted Twenty-six Years." *Memphis Commercial Appeal,* May 18, 1989, E2.

Malone, Bill C. *Country Music, U.S.A.: A Fifty-Year History.* Austin: University of Texas Press, 1968.

Marcus, Greil. *Mystery Train: Images of America in Rock 'n' Roll Music.* New York: E. P. Dutton, 1975.

Mattfeld, Julius. *Variety Music Cavalcade 1620–1969: A Chronology of Vocal and Instrumental Music Popular in the United States.* New York: Prentice-Hall, 1971.

McKee, Margaret, and Fred Chisenhall. *Beale Black and Blue: Life and Music on Black America's Main Street.* Baton Rouge: Louisiana State University Press, 1981.

Melton, Gloria Brown, "Blacks in Memphis, Tennessee, 1920–1955: A Historical Study." Ph.D. diss., Washington University, 1982.

Miller, William D. *Mr. Crump of Memphis.* Baton Rouge: Louisiana State University Press, 1964.

Mitchell, Henry. "New Dewey Phillips TV Show Opens Today on Channel 13." *Memphis Commercial Appeal,* Dec. 31, 1956, 10.

Moore, Scotty. *That's Alright, Elvis: The Untold Story of Elvis' First Guitarist and Manager, as told to James Dickerson.* New York: Schirmer Books, 1997.

Morrison, Craig. *Go Cat Go! Rockabilly Music and Its Makers.* Urbana: University of Illinois Press, 1996.

Morthland, John. "Elvis: The King Remembered: An Oral History." *Country Music* 10 (Jan.–Feb. 1980): 45.

Murrells, Joseph. *Million-Selling Records from the 1900s to the 1980s: An Illustrated Directory.* New York: Arco Publications, 1984.

Nager, Larry. "Dewey Took Giant Steps across Music Color Line." *Memphis Commercial Appeal,* Sept. 28, 1993, C1.

———. "Forty Years of Sun." *Memphis Commercial Appeal,* March 22, 1992, G1–2.

———. *Memphis Beat: The Lives and Times of America's Musical Crossroads.* New York: St. Martin's Press, 1998.

———. "The Unknown Record Man." *Memphis Flyer,* July 11–17, 1996, 24–25.

"Nat D. Williams: Tan Town Disc Jester." *Tan Magazine* (March 1955): 69.

Oakley, Giles. *The Devil's Music: A History of the Blues.* New York: Taplinger, 1977.

Osborne, Jerry. *Elvis: Word for Word,* 34–40. New York: Harmony Books, 1999.

Ownby, Ted. *American Dreams in Mississippi: Consumers, Poverty and Culture, 1830-1998,* 124–29. Chapel Hill: University of North Carolina Press, 1999.

Palmer, Robert. "Sam Phillips: The Sun King, a Revised History of the Roots of Rock and Roll." *Memphis Magazine* 3 (Dec. 1978): 36.

Petreycik, Rick. "Interview with Sam Phillips." *Oxford American,* no. 34 (July–Aug. 2000): 56–60.

"Pharmacist Accuses Dewey Phillips." *Memphis Press-Scimitar,* July 10, 1963, 29.

Pichaske, David. *A Generation in Motion: Popular Music and Culture in the Sixties.* New York: Schirmer Books, 1979, 37.

Porteous, Clark. "Three Memphians Die in Mid-South Traffic." *Memphis Press-Scimitar,* Sept. 4, 1950, 1–2.

Porterfield, Nolan. *Last Cavalier: The Life and Times of John A. Lomax.* Urbana: University of Illinois Press, 1996.

Raichelson, Richard. *Beale Street Talks: A Walking Tour down the Home of the Blues.* Memphis: Arcadia, 1994.

Raiteri, Charles. Liner notes for *Dewey Phillips: Red Hot and Blue Classic Radio Transcriptions.* Produced by Charles Raiteri and Colin Escott (Zu-Zazz Z2012).

Reagon, Bernice Johnson, ed. "William Herbert Brewster Sr." In *We'll Understand*

It Better By and By: Pioneering African American Gospel Composers. Washington: Smithsonian Institution Press, 1992

Redd, Lawrence N. *Rock Is Rhythm and Blues: The Impact of Mass Media.* East Lansing: Michigan State University Press, 1974.

Ringel, Judy. "A Star Is Born: Elvis, 1955–1956." *Memphis Magazine* 26 (April 2001): 75.

"Rites Tomorrow for Disc Jockey." *Memphis Commercial Appeal,* Sept. 30, 1968, 30.

Roediger, David R. *The Wages of Whiteness: Race and the Making of the American Working Class,* 2d ed. New York: Verso Press, 1991.

Salem, James M. *The Late Great Johnny Ace and the Transition from R&B to Rock 'n' Roll.* Urbana: University of Illinois Press, 1999.

Segrave, Kerry. *Payola in the Music Industry: A History, 1880–1991.* Jefferson, N.C.: McFarland, 1994.

Selby, Shawn. "They Knocked the Rock: Congress and the Payola Hearings." M.A. thesis, Ohio University, 2002.

Shaw, Arnold. *Honkers and Shouters: The Golden Years of Rhythm and Blues.* New York: Macmillan, 1978.

Shaw, Norm. "Sam Phillips Interview." *Bluespeak,* Aug. 1996, 6.

Shelton, William E. "Lloyd T. Binford and Memphis Censorship." M.A. thesis, Memphis State University, 1970.

Sigafoos, Robert A. *Cotton Row to Beale Street: A Business History of Memphis.* Memphis: Memphis State University Press, 1979.

Silver, Louis. "Six Dead, Scores Hurt as Death Travels Mid-South Highways." *Memphis Commercial Appeal,* Sept. 4, 1950, 1, 3.

Smith, Wes. *The Pied Pipers of Rock 'n' Roll: Radio Deejays of the Fifties and Sixties.* Marietta, Ga.: Longstreet Press, 1989.

Spottswood, Richard. "Country Girls, Classic Blues, and Vaudeville Voices: Women and the Blues." In *Nothing but the Blues: The Music and the Musicians,* edited by Lawrence Cohn et al., 88–99. New York: Abbeville Press, 1993.

Stanley, David, with Frank Coffey. *The Elvis Encyclopedia.* Santa Monica: General Publishing Group, 1994.

Stokes, Melvyn. *Race and Class in the American South since 1890.* Oxford: Berg, 1994.

Street, John. *Rebel Rock: The Politics of Popular Music.* New York: Basil Blackwell, 1986.

"Thirty Years of Payola: The Inside Story." *Pulse Magazine,* April 11, 1988, 1–29.

Toll, Robert C. *Blacking Up: The Minstrel Show in Nineteenth-Century America.* New York: Oxford University Press, 1974.

Tosches, Nick. *Country: The Biggest Music In America.* New York: Stein and Day, 1977.

———. "Rockabilly!" In *The Illustrated History of Country Music,* edited by Patrick Carr, 217–37. New York: Dolphin, 1980.

Tucker, David. *Lieutenant Lee of Beale Street.* Nashville: Vanderbilt University Press, 1971.

———. *Memphis since Crump: Bossism, Blacks and Civic Reformers.* Knoxville: University of Tennessee Press, 1980.

Tucker, Stephen. "Rethinking Elvis and the Rockabilly Moment." In *In Search of Elvis: Music, Race, Art, Religion,* edited by Vernon Chadwick, 19–28. Boulder: Westview Press, 1997.

TV Guide, Sept. 22–28, 1956, 19. Dorothy Phillips Collection.

Van Wyngarden, Bruce. "Redefining the Memphis Sound." In *The Making of Modern Memphis, 1976–1996,* edited by John Branston (special publication of *Memphis Magazine,* 1996), pt. 3, 43.

Vincent, Ted. *Keep Cool: The Black Activists Who Built the Jazz Age.* London: Pluto, 1995.

Ward, Brian. *Just My Soul Responding: Rhythm and Blues, Black Consciousness, and Race Relations.* Berkeley: University of California Press, 1998.

West, Red, Sonny West, and Dave Hebler, as told to Steve Dunleavy. *Elvis, What Happened?* New York: Ballantine Books, 1977.

Wexler, Jerry. "R. and B. Jockeys Ride Payola." *Billboard,* Jan. 13, 1951, 1, 13, 40.

———, and David Ritz. *Rhythm and the Blues: A Life in American Music.* New York: Alfred A. Knopf, 1993.

Whisenhunt, Elton. "Weary Engineers Move WHBQ Overnight." *Memphis Press-Scimitar,* Jan. 10, 1953, 7.

Whitmer, Peter. *The Inner Elvis: A Psychological Biography of Elvis Aaron Presley,* 94. New York: Hyperion, 1996.

Williams, Gilbert A. "William T. 'Hoss' Allen." In *Legendary Pioneers of Black Radio,* 30. Westport: Praeger Publishers, 1998.

Williams, Nat D. "Down on Beale." *Pittsburgh Courier,* Jan. 21, 1950, 21.

Withers, Ernest C. *The Memphis Blues Again: Six Decades of Memphis Music Photographs.* Selected and with text by Daniel Wolff. New York: Viking Studio, Penguin Group, 2001.

Wolff, Daniel J. "To Make a Shining Light." In *Pictures Tell the Story: Ernest C. Withers, Reflections in History,* edited by Jack Hurley et al., 110–30. Norfolk: Chrysler Museum of Art, 2000.

Zimmerman, Peter Coats. *Tennessee Music: Its People and Places.* San Francisco: Miller Freeman, 1998.

Audio and Visual Sources

All Day and All Night. Documentary film video, 1990, produced by Judy Peiser and directed by Robert Gordon and Louis Guida. Memphis: Center for Southern Folklore, 1990.

Daddy-O-Dewey: A Natural Star. Documentary film video, 1997, produced and directed by Charles Raiteri. Personal collection.

Dewey Phillips: Red Hot and Blue Classic Radio Transcriptions (Zu-Zazz Z2012), LP (vinyl) produced and directed by Charles Raiteri and Colin Escott.

Red Hot and Blue: Dewey Phillips Live Radio Broadcasts from 1952–1964 (1995), compact disc produced and directed by Richard James Hite. Inside Sounds/ Memphis Archives, 1995.

Rock 'n' Roll Invaders: The AM-Radio Deejays. Documentary film video written, produced, and directed by Paul Eichgrom. Toronto: Dramarama Productions in association with Bravo Network, CHUM Television, and CFCF-TV, 1996.

"Sam Phillips: The Man Who Invented Rock 'n' Roll." *A&E Biography,* June 18, 2000. Produced by Morgan Neville and Peter Guralnick.

Sun Days with Elvis. Magnum Music Group (MAG 002), 1996.

Government Documents

Code of Ordinances City of Memphis, Tennessee, Adopted May 2, 1967. Tallahassee: Published by the Board of Commissioners, 1967.

Klewer, Edwin B. *The Memphis Digest 1931,* 2 vols., 3 pts. Memphis: S. C. Toof, 1931.

Memphis City Court. Judges' Trial Docket, Criminal, Dewey Phillips Docket no. E38297, 477–78, July 10, 1963.

Phillips, Dewey Mills. Record of Arrests: Nov. 25, 1959; March 3, June 26, 1960; Feb. 16, March 6, Oct. 13, 1961; Oct. 3, 1963. Bureau of Records and Identification, Shelby County Sheriff's Department, Jail Annex, Memphis, Tenn.

United States Census of Population, 1950, Census Tract Statistics, Memphis, Tennessee, Selected Population and Housing Characteristics, vol. 3, ch. 30, 7. Prepared under the supervision of Howard G. Brunsman. Washington: Government Printing Office, 1952.

U.S. Censuses of Population and Housing, 1960, Census Tracts, Memphis Tennessee, Standard Metropolitan Statistical Area. Prepared under the supervision of Howard G. Brunsman and Wayne F. Daugherty. Washington: U.S. Dept. of Commerce, Bureau of the Census, 1961.

U.S. Congress, House Committee on Interstate and Foreign Commerce. *Communications Act Amendments: Hearings before a Subcommittee of the Comittee on Interstate and Foreign Commerce, House of Representatives, 86th Cong., 2d Sess, on Conditional Grants, Pregrant Procedure, Local Notice, Local Hearings, Payoffs, Suspension of Licenses, and Deceptive Practices in Broadcasting,* pt. 1: Feb. 8, 9, 10, 15, 17, 18, 19, March 4, 1960; pt. 2: Jan. 27, 28, 29, May 2, 3, Aug. 30, 31, 1960. Washington: Government Printing Office, 1960.

———. *Responsibilities of Broadcasting Licensees and Station Personnel: Hearings before a Subcommittee of the Committee on Interstate and Foreign Commerce, House of Representatives, 86th Cong., 2d Sess. on Payola and other Deceptive Practices in the Broadcast Field,* Jan. 27, 28, 29, May 2, 3, Aug. 30, 31, 1960, pt. 2, 900. Washington: Government Printing Office, 1960.

Index

Ace, Johnny, 122; on Amateur Night, 53; poker and Dewey, 51

Ackerman, Paul: on payola, 125–26

Acuff, Roy, 138, 139

Adams, Nick, 162

Adamsville, Tenn., 160, 184; as burial site, 31; Dewey's youth in, 30–33

African Americans: as artists, 36, 62, 142; Beale Street and, 46–47; broadening demographics of, 117; Dewey and, 54–55, 87–88, 115; as percentage of Memphis population, 46, 240n6; purchasing power of, 38–39; rhythm and blues and, 36; rural background of, 138; on Sun label, 137–38. *See also* blacks

Alamo, Tenn., 181

Alburty, Robert: black programming and, 59–60

Allen, Bill "Hoss," 65, 82; quoted, 81

Allen, Steve, 15

Amateur Night at the Palace, 52–53; and Midnight Rambles, 60; Nat D. Williams and, 147

American Bandstand, 156, 177, 188

American Federation of Musicians (AFM), 107

American Graffiti, 2, 81

Anderson, Queen C., 83–85

Armstrong, Louis, 97, 225

Arnold, Eddy, 136, 138, 142–43

"Arthur": and Home of the Blues, 91

Atkins, Chet: on Elvis, 80

Atlantic Records, 98, 123–24

automobile accidents: Dewey and, 179–86, 193–94; report of, 185, 259n22

Axton, Estelle, 209

Axton, Packy, 209

Baker, LaVern, 89, 94, 122, 140

"Ballad of Bridey Murphy," 120–21

Baptist Hospital (Memphis), 87

Barba, Marjorie (Dewey's sister), on Dewey and drugs, 197; on Dewey and Elvis, 145; on Dewey's death, 217; on Dot leaving Dewey, 208; on Odesssa Phillips, 32

Barlow, William: criticism of Dewey, 226; racial ventriloquy and, 78, 245n14

Barrasso, Anselmo, 52

Basie, Count, 56, 97

Battle of Hurtgen Forest (World War II), 35

Beale Black and Blue, 146

Beale Street, 3, 38, 87; and all-white audience, 94; as avenue, 240n3; black and white separation on, 51, 90, 241n21; businesses on, 50; as capital of black America, 45–46; and Dewey, 45–63, 87–89; early history of, 46; and Elvis, 144–47, 154; geographic boundaries, 45–46; and Home of the Blues Record Shop, 89–92; and

Index

Louis Cantor, who grew up in Memphis, went to Humes High School with Elvis Presley. He also listened to Dewey Phillips on WHBQ regularly and was a friend of Elvis's best friend in high school, George Klein. While an undergraduate at Memphis State University, now the University of Memphis, Cantor worked as a control board operater and newscaster in WDIA in Memphis. A professor-emeritus of history at Indiana University, he is now an adjunct professor of history at the University of Memphis.

Music in American Life

Good Friends and Bad Enemies: Robert Winslow Gordon and the Study of
American Folksong *Debora Kodish*
Fiddlin' Georgia Crazy: Fiddlin' John Carson, His Real World, and the World
of His Songs *Gene Wiggins*
America's Music: From the Pilgrims to the Present (rev. 3d ed.) *Gilbert Chase*
Secular Music in Colonial Annapolis: The Tuesday Club, 1745–56
John Barry Talley
Bibliographical Handbook of American Music *D. W. Krummel*
Goin' to Kansas City *Nathan W. Pearson, Jr.*
"Susanna," "Jeanie," and "The Old Folks at Home": The Songs of Stephen C.
Foster from His Time to Ours (2d ed.) *William W. Austin*
Songprints: The Musical Experience of Five Shoshone Women *Judith Vander*
"Happy in the Service of the Lord": Afro-American Gospel Quartets
in Memphis *Kip Lornell*
Paul Hindemith in the United States *Luther Noss*
"My Song Is My Weapon": People's Songs, American Communism, and the
Politics of Culture, 1930–50 *Robbie Lieberman*
Chosen Voices: The Story of the American Cantorate *Mark Slobin*
Theodore Thomas: America's Conductor and Builder of Orchestras,
1835–1905 *Ezra Schabas*
"The Whorehouse Bells Were Ringing" and Other Songs Cowboys Sing
Guy Logsdon
Crazeology: The Autobiography of a Chicago Jazzman *Bud Freeman,
as Told to Robert Wolf*
Discoursing Sweet Music: Brass Bands and Community Life in Turn-of-the-
Century Pennsylvania *Kenneth Kreitner*
Mormonism and Music: A History *Michael Hicks*
Voices of the Jazz Age: Profiles of Eight Vintage Jazzmen *Chip Deffaa*
Pickin' on Peachtree: A History of Country Music in Atlanta, Georgia
Wayne W. Daniel
Bitter Music: Collected Journals, Essays, Introductions, and Librettos
Harry Partch; edited by Thomas McGeary
Ethnic Music on Records: A Discography of Ethnic Recordings Produced in the
United States, 1893 to 1942 *Richard K. Spottswood*
Downhome Blues Lyrics: An Anthology from the Post-World War II Era
Jeff Todd Titon
Ellington: The Early Years *Mark Tucker*
Chicago Soul *Robert Pruter*
That Half-Barbaric Twang: The Banjo in American Popular Culture
Karen Linn
Hot Man: The Life of Art Hodes *Art Hodes and Chadwick Hansen*
The Erotic Muse: American Bawdy Songs (2d ed.) *Ed Cray*
Barrio Rhythm: Mexican American Music in Los Angeles *Steven Loza*

...ois Press
... of the
...an University Presses.

...ress

...6903
...iu

The Late Great Johnny Ace and the Transition from R&B to Rock 'n' Roll
    James M. Salem
Tito Puente and the Making of Latin Music   Steven Loza
Juilliard: A History   Andrea Olmstead
Understanding Charles Seeger, Pioneer in American Musicology   Edited by
    Bell Yung and Helen Rees
Mountains of Music: West Virginia Traditional Music from Goldenseal
    Edited by John Lilly
Alice Tully: An Intimate Portrait   Albert Fuller
A Blues Life   Henry Townsend, as told to Bill Greensmith
Long Steel Rail: The Railroad in American Folksong (2d ed.)   Norm Cohen
The Golden Age of Gospel   Text by Horace Clarence Boyer; photography by
    Lloyd Yearwood
Aaron Copland: The Life and Work of an Uncommon Man   Howard Pollack
Louis Moreau Gottschalk   S. Frederick Starr
Race, Rock, and Elvis   Michael T. Bertrand
Theremin: Ether Music and Espionage   Albert Glinsky
Poetry and Violence: The Ballad Tradition of Mexico's Costa Chica
    John H. McDowell
The Bill Monroe Reader   Edited by Tom Ewing
Music in Lubavitcher Life   Ellen Koskoff
Zarzuela: Spanish Operetta, American Stage   Janet L. Sturman
Bluegrass Odyssey: A Documentary in Pictures and Words, 1966–86
    Carl Fleischhauer and Neil V. Rosenberg
That Old-Time Rock & Roll: A Chronicle of an Era, 1954–63   Richard Aquila
Labor's Troubadour   Joe Glazer
American Opera   Elise K. Kirk
Don't Get above Your Raisin': Country Music and the Southern
    Working Class   Bill C. Malone
John Alden Carpenter: A Chicago Composer   Howard Pollack
Heartbeat of the People: Music and Dance of the Northern Pow-wow
    Tara Browner
My Lord, What a Morning: An Autobiography   Marian Anderson
Marian Anderson: A Singer's Journey   Allan Keiler
Charles Ives Remembered: An Oral History   Vivian Perlis
Henry Cowell, Bohemian   Michael Hicks
Rap Music and Street Consciousness   Cheryl L. Keyes
Louis Prima   Garry Boulard
Marian McPartland's Jazz World: All in Good Time   Marian McPartland
Robert Johnson: Lost and Found   Barry Lee Pearson and Bill McCulloch
Bound for America: Three British Composers   Nicholas Temperley
Lost Sounds: Blacks and the Birth of the Recording Industry, 1890–1919
    Tim Brooks

The Creation of Jazz: Music, Race, and Culture in Urban America
  Burton W. Peretti
Charles Martin Loeffler: A Life Apart in Music *Ellen Knight*
Club Date Musicians: Playing the New York Party Circuit *Bruce A. MacLeod*
Opera on the Road: Traveling Opera Troupes in the United States, 1825–60
  Katherine K. Preston
The Stonemans: An Appalachian Family and the Music That Shaped
  Their Lives *Ivan M. Tribe*
Transforming Tradition: Folk Music Revivals Examined *Edited by*
  Neil V. Rosenberg
The Crooked Stovepipe: Athapaskan Fiddle Music and Square Dancing in
  Northeast Alaska and Northwest Canada *Craig Mishler*
Traveling the High Way Home: Ralph Stanley and the World of Traditional
  Bluegrass Music *John Wright*
Carl Ruggles: Composer, Painter, and Storyteller *Marilyn Ziffrin*
Never without a Song: The Years and Songs of Jennie Devlin, 1865–1952
  Katharine D. Newman
The Hank Snow Story *Hank Snow, with Jack Ownbey and Bob Burris*
Milton Brown and the Founding of Western Swing *Cary Ginell, with special*
  assistance from Roy Lee Brown
Santiago de Murcia's "Códice Saldívar No. 4": A Treasury of Secular Guitar
  Music from Baroque Mexico *Craig H. Russell*
The Sound of the Dove: Singing in Appalachian Primitive Baptist Churches
  Beverly Bush Patterson
Heartland Excursions: Ethnomusicological Reflections on Schools of Music
  Bruno Nettl
Doowop: The Chicago Scene *Robert Pruter*
Blue Rhythms: Six Lives in Rhythm and Blues *Chip Deffaa*
Shoshone Ghost Dance Religion: Poetry Songs and Great Basin Context
Judith Vander
Go Cat Go! Rockabilly Music and Its Makers *Craig Morrison*
'Twas Only an Irishman's Dream: The Image of Ireland and the Irish in
  American Popular Song Lyrics, 1800–1920 *William H. A. Williams*
Democracy at the Opera: Music, Theater, and Culture in New York City,
  1815–60 *Karen Ahlquist*
Fred Waring and the Pennsylvanians *Virginia Waring*
Woody, Cisco, and Me: Seamen Three in the Merchant Marine *Jim Longhi*
Behind the Burnt Cork Mask: Early Blackface Minstrelsy and Antebellum
  American Popular Culture *William J. Mahar*
Going to Cincinnati: A History of the Blues in the Queen City *Steven C. Tracy*
Pistol Packin' Mama: Aunt Molly Jackson and the Politics of Folksong
  Shelly Romalis
Sixties Rock: Garage, Psychedelic, and Other Satisfactions *Michael Hicks*

The University of Illinois Press
is a founding member of the
Association of American University Presses.

_____

University of Illinois Press
1325 South Oak Street
Champaign, IL 61820-6903
www.press.uillinois.edu